# World Economic and Financial Surveys

# WORLD ECONOMIC OUTLOOK
## April 2011

## Tensions from the Two-Speed Recovery
### Unemployment, Commodities, and Capital Flows

**International Monetary Fund**

©2011 International Monetary Fund

Production: IMF Multimedia Services Division
Cover and Design: Luisa Menjivar and Jorge Salazar
Composition: Maryland Composition


Cataloging-in-Publication Data

**World economic outlook (International Monetary Fund)**
    World economic outlook : a survey by the staff of the International Monetary Fund. —
Washington, DC : International Monetary Fund, 1980–
    v. ; 28 cm. — (1981–1984: Occasional paper / International Monetary Fund, 0251-6365).
— (1986– : World economic and financial surveys, 0256-6877)

Semiannual. Some issues also have thematic titles.
Has occasional updates, 1984–

    1. Economic development — Periodicals. 2. Economic forecasting — Periodicals.
3. Economic policy — Periodicals. 4. International economic relations — Periodicals.
I. International Monetary Fund. II. Series: Occasional paper (International Monetary Fund).
III. Series: World economic and financial surveys.

HC10.80

ISBN 978-1-61635-059-8


Please send orders to:
International Monetary Fund, Publication Services
P.O. Box 92780, Washington, D.C. 20090, U.S.A.
Tel.: (202) 623-7430 Fax: (202) 623-7201
E-mail: publications@imf.org
www.imfbookstore.org

Mixed Sources
Product group from well-managed
forests, controlled sources and
recycled wood or fiber
www.fsc.org  Cert no. SW-COC-002142
© 1996 Forest Stewardship Council
FSC

# CONTENTS

## Tables

**Online Tables**

## Figures

# ASSUMPTIONS AND CONVENTIONS

A number of assumptions have been adopted for the projections presented in the *World Economic Outlook.* It has been assumed that real effective exchange rates remained constant at their average levels during February 8–March 8, 2011, except for the currencies participating in the European exchange rate mechanism II (ERM II), which are assumed to have remained constant in nominal terms relative to the euro; that established policies of national authorities will be maintained (for specific assumptions about fiscal and monetary policies for selected economies, see Box A1); that the average price of oil will be $107.16 a barrel in 2011 and $108.00 a barrel in 2012 and will remain unchanged in real terms over the medium term; that the six-month London interbank offered rate (LIBOR) on U.S. dollar deposits will average 0.6 percent in 2011 and 0.9 percent in 2012; that the three-month euro deposit rate will average 1.7 percent in 2011 and 2.6 percent in 2012; and that the six-month Japanese yen deposit rate will yield on average 0.6 percent in 2011 and 0.3 percent in 2012. These are, of course, working hypotheses rather than forecasts, and the uncertainties surrounding them add to the margin of error that would in any event be involved in the projections. The estimates and projections are based on statistical information available through late March 2011.

The following conventions are used throughout the *World Economic Outlook:*

. . .  to indicate that data are not available or not applicable;

—  between years or months (for example, 2010–11 or January–June) to indicate the years or months covered, including the beginning and ending years or months;

/  between years or months (for example, 2010/11) to indicate a fiscal or financial year.

"Billion" means a thousand million; "trillion" means a thousand billion.

"Basis points" refer to hundredths of 1 percentage point (for example, 25 basis points are equivalent to ¼ of 1 percentage point).

WEO aggregated data excludes Libya for projection years due to the uncertain political situation.

Except for GDP growth and inflation, projections for Côte d'Ivoire are not shown due to the uncertain political situation.

In figures and tables, shaded areas indicate IMF staff projections.

If no source is listed on tables and figures, data are drawn from the WEO database.

When countries are not listed alphabetically, they are ordered on the basis of economic size.

Minor discrepancies between sums of constituent figures and totals shown reflect rounding.

As used in this report, the terms "country" and "economy" do not in all cases refer to a territorial entity that is a state as understood by international law and practice. As used here, the term also covers some territorial entities that are not states but for which statistical data are maintained on a separate and independent basis.

Composite data are provided for various groups of countries organized according to economic characteristics or region. Unless otherwise noted, country group composites represent calculations based on 90 percent or more of the weighted group data.

The country group composites for fiscal data are calculated as the sum of the U.S dollar values for the relevant individual countries. This differs from the calculations in the October 2010 and earlier issues of the *World Economic Outlook,* for which the composites were weighted by GDP valued at purchasing power parities (PPPs) as a share of total world GDP.

The boundaries, colors, denominations, and any other information shown on the maps do not imply, on the part of the International Monetary Fund, any judgment on the legal status of any territory or any endorsement or acceptance of such boundaries.

This version of the *World Economic Outlook* is available in full on the IMF's website, www.imf.org. Accompanying it on the website is a larger compilation of data from the WEO database than is included in the report itself, including files containing the series most frequently requested by readers. These files may be downloaded for use in a variety of software packages.

Inquiries about the content of the *World Economic Outlook* and the WEO database should be sent by mail, forum, or fax (telephone inquiries cannot be accepted) to

World Economic Studies Division
Research Department
International Monetary Fund
700 19th Street, N.W.
Washington, D.C. 20431, U.S.A.
Forum address: www.imf.org/weoforum   Fax: (202) 623-6343

# PREFACE

The analysis and projections contained in the *World Economic Outlook* are integral elements of the IMF's surveillance of economic developments and policies in its member countries, of developments in international financial markets, and of the global economic system. The survey of prospects and policies is the product of a comprehensive interdepartmental review of world economic developments, which draws primarily on information the IMF staff gathers through its consultations with member countries. These consultations are carried out in particular by the IMF's area departments—namely, the African Department, Asia and Pacific Department, European Department, Middle East and Central Asia Department, and Western Hemisphere Department—together with the Strategy, Policy, and Review Department; the Monetary and Capital Markets Department; and the Fiscal Affairs Department.

The analysis in this report was coordinated in the Research Department under the general direction of Olivier Blanchard, Economic Counsellor and Director of Research. The project was directed by Jörg Decressin, Senior Advisor, Research Department, and Petya Koeva Brooks, Division Chief, Research Department. The primary contributors to this report are Abdul Abiad, John Bluedorn, Rupa Duttagupta, Jaime Guajardo, Thomas Helbling, Joong Shik Kang, Michael Kumhof, Dirk Muir, Andrea Pescatori, Shaun Roache, John Simon, and Petia Topalova. Other contributors include Joshua Felman, Benjamin Hunt, Florence Jaumotte, Mika Kortelainen, Daniel Leigh, Troy Matheson, Stephen Snudden, Marco Terrones, and Robert Tetlow. Kevin Clinton provided comments and suggestions. Toh Kuan, Gavin Asdorian, Shan Chen, Angela Espiritu, Murad Omoev, Andy Salazar, Min Kyu Song, Ercument Tulun, Jessie Yang, Nese Erbil, David Reichsfeld, and Marina Rousset provided research assistance. Saurabh Gupta, Mahnaz Hemmati, Laurent Meister, Emory Oakes, and Steve Zhang managed the database and the computer systems. Tita Gunio, Shanti Karunaratne, and Cristina Tumale were responsible for word processing. Linda Griffin Kean of the External Relations Department edited the manuscript and coordinated the production of the publication. Additional technical support was provided by external consultants Vladimir Bougay, Anastasia Francis, Aleksandr Gerasimov, Wendy Mak, Shamiso Mapondera, Nhu Nguyen, and Pavel Pimenov.

The analysis has benefited from comments and suggestions by staff from other IMF departments, as well as by Executive Directors following their discussion of the report on March 28, 2011. However, both projections and policy considerations are those of the IMF staff and should not be attributed to Executive Directors or to their national authorities.

The world economic recovery continues, more or less as predicted. Indeed, our growth forecasts are nearly unchanged since the January 2011 *WEO Update* and can be summarized in three numbers: We expect the world economy to grow at about 4½ percent a year in both 2011 and 2012, but with advanced economies growing at only 2½ percent while emerging and developing economies grow at a much higher 6½ percent.

Earlier fears of a double-dip recession—which we did not share—have not materialized. The main worry was that in advanced economies, after an initial recovery driven by the inventory cycle and fiscal stimulus, growth would fizzle. The inventory cycle is now largely over and fiscal stimulus has turned to fiscal consolidation, but private demand has, for the most part, taken the baton.

Fears have turned to commodity prices. Commodity prices have increased more than expected, reflecting a combination of strong demand growth and supply shocks. Although these increases conjure up the specter of 1970s-style stagflation, they appear unlikely to derail the recovery. In advanced economies, the decreasing share of oil, the disappearance of wage indexation, and the anchoring of inflation expectations all combine to suggest there will be only small effects on growth and core inflation. The challenge will be stronger however in emerging and developing economies, where the consumption share of food and fuel is larger and the credibility of monetary policy is often weaker. Inflation may well be higher for some time but, as our forecasts suggest, we do not expect a major adverse effect on growth. However, risks to the recovery from additional disruptions to oil supply are a concern.

The recovery, however, remains unbalanced.

In most advanced economies, output is still far below potential. Unemployment is high, and low growth implies that it will remain so for many years to come. The source of low growth can be traced to both precrisis excesses and crisis wounds: In many countries, especially the United States, the housing market is still depressed, leading to anemic housing investment. The crisis itself has led to a dramatic deterioration in fiscal positions, forcing a shift to fiscal consolidation while not eliminating market worries about fiscal sustainability. And in many countries banks are struggling to achieve higher capital ratios in the face of increasing nonperforming loans.

The problems of the European Union periphery, stemming from the combined interactions of low growth, fiscal woes, and financial pressures, are particularly acute. Reestablishing fiscal and financial sustainability in the face of low or negative growth and high interest rates is a substantial challenge. And, while extreme, the problems of the EU periphery point to a more general problem: an underlying low rate of growth of potential output. Adjustment is very hard when growth is very low.

The policy advice to advanced economies remains largely the same as in the October 2010 *World Economic Outlook,* and so far has been only partly heeded: increased clarity on banks' balance sheet exposures and ready recapitalization plans if needed; smart fiscal consolidation that is neither too fast, which could kill growth, nor too slow, which would kill credibility; the redesign of financial regulation and supervision; and, especially in Europe, an increased focus on reforms to increase potential growth.

In emerging market economies, by contrast, the crisis left no lasting wounds. Their initial fiscal and financial positions were typically stronger, and the adverse effects of the crisis were more muted. High underlying growth and low interest rates are making fiscal adjustment much easier. Exports have largely recovered, and whatever shortfall in external demand they experienced has typically been made up through increases in domestic demand. Capital outflows have turned into capital inflows, due to both better growth prospects and higher interest rates than in the advanced economies.

The challenge for most emerging market economies is thus quite different from that of the advanced economies—namely, how to avoid overheating in the face of closing output gaps and higher capital flows. Their response should be twofold: first, to rely on a combination of fiscal consolidation and higher interest rates to maintain output at potential and, second, to use macroprudential tools—including, where needed, capital controls—to avoid increases in systemic risk stemming from inflows. Countries are often tempted to resist the exchange rate appreciation that is likely to come with higher interest rates and higher inflows. But appreciation increases real income, is part of the desirable adjustment, and should not be resisted.

Overall, the macro policy agenda for the world economy remains the same but, with the passage of time, more urgent. For the recovery to be sustained, advanced economies must achieve fiscal consolidation. To do this and to maintain growth, they need to rely more on external demand. Symmetrically, emerging market economies must rely less on external demand and more on domestic demand. Appreciation of emerging market economies' currencies relative to those of advanced economies is an important key to this global adjustment. The need for careful design at the national level and coordination at the global level may be as important today as at the peak of the crisis two years ago.

Olivier Blanchard
*Economic Counsellor*

# EXECUTIVE SUMMARY

The recovery is gaining strength, but unemployment remains high in advanced economies, and new macroeconomic risks are building in emerging market economies. In advanced economies, the hand-off from public to private demand is advancing, reducing concerns that diminishing fiscal policy support might cause a "double-dip" recession. Financial conditions continue to improve, although they remain unusually fragile. In many emerging market economies, demand is robust and over-heating is a growing policy concern. Developing economies, particularly in sub-Saharan Africa, have also resumed fast and sustainable growth. Rising food and commodity prices pose a threat to poor households, adding to social and economic tensions, notably in the Middle East and North Africa. Oil price increases since January 2011 and information on supply, including on spare capacity, suggest that the disruptions so far would have only mild effects on economic activity. An earthquake in Japan has exacted a terrible human toll. Its macroeconomic impact is projected to be limited, although uncertainty remains elevated. Overall, with the recovery stronger on the one hand but oil supply growth lower on the other, projections for global real GDP growth in 2011–12 are little changed from the January 2011 *WEO Update*. But downside risks have risen.

World real GDP growth is forecast to be about 4½ percent in 2011 and 2012, down modestly from 5 percent in 2010. Real GDP in advanced economies and emerging and developing economies is expected to expand by about 2½ percent and 6½ percent, respectively. Downside risks continue to outweigh upside risks. In advanced economies, weak sovereign balance sheets and still-moribund real estate markets continue to present major concerns, especially in certain euro area economies; financial risks are also to the downside as a result of the high funding requirements of banks and sovereigns. New downside risks are building on account of commodity prices, nota-

bly for oil, and, relatedly, geopolitical uncertainty, as well as overheating and booming asset markets in emerging market economies. However, there is also the potential for upside surprises to growth in the short term, owing to strong corporate balance sheets in advanced economies and buoyant demand in emerging and developing economies.

Many old policy challenges remain unaddressed even as new ones come to the fore. In advanced economies, strengthening the recovery will require keeping monetary policy accommodative as long as wage pressures are subdued, inflation expectations are well anchored, and bank credit is sluggish. At the same time, fiscal positions need to be placed on sustainable medium-term paths by implementing fiscal consolidation plans and entitlement reforms supported by stronger fiscal rules and institutions. This need is particularly urgent in the United States to stem the risk of globally destabilizing changes in bond markets. The U.S. policy plans for 2011 have actually switched back from consolidation to expansion. Efforts should be made to reduce the projected deficit for fiscal year 2011. Measures to trim discretionary spending are a move in this direction. However, to make a sizable dent in the projected medium-term deficits, broader measures such as Social Security and tax reforms will be essential. In Japan, the immediate fiscal priority is to support reconstruction. Once reconstruction efforts are under way and the size of the damage is better understood, attention should turn to linking reconstruction spending to a clear fiscal strategy for bringing down the public debt ratio over the medium term. In the euro area, despite significant progress, markets remain apprehensive about the prospects of countries under market pressure. For them what is needed at the euro area level is sufficient, low-cost, and flexible funding to support strong fiscal adjustment, bank restructuring, and reforms to promote competitiveness and growth. More generally, greater trust needs to be reestablished in euro area banks through ambitious stress tests and restructuring and recapitalization programs. Moreover, reform of the global financial system remains very much a work in progress.

The challenge for many emerging and some developing economies is to ensure that present boom-like conditions do not develop into overheating over the coming year. Inflation pressure is likely to build further as growing production comes up against capacity constraints, with large food and energy price increases, which weigh heavily in consumption baskets, motivating demands for higher wages. Real interest rates are still low and fiscal policies appreciably more accommodative than before the crisis. Appropriate action differs across economies, depending on their cyclical and external conditions. However, a tightening of macroeconomic policies is needed in many emerging market economies.

- For external surplus economies, many of which manage their currencies and do not face fiscal problems, removal of monetary accommodation and appreciation of the exchange rate are necessary to maintain internal balance—reining in inflation pressure and excessive credit growth—and assist in global demand rebalancing.
- Many external deficit economies need to tighten fiscal and monetary policies, possibly tolerating some overshooting of the exchange rate in the short term.
- For some surplus and deficit economies, rapid credit and asset price growth warn of a threat to financial stability. Policymakers in these economies will need to act soon to safeguard stability and build more resilient financial systems.
- Many emerging and developing economies will need to provide well-targeted support for poor households that struggle with high food prices.

Capital flows to emerging market economies resumed remarkably quickly after the crisis. However, as policy rates in advanced economies rise from their unusually low levels, volatile flows may again exit the emerging market economies. Depending on country-specific circumstances, and assuming appropriate macroeconomic and prudential policies are in place, measures designed to curb capital inflows can play a role in dampening the impact of their excessive volatility on the real economy. However, such measures are not a substitute for macroeconomic tightening.

Greater progress in advancing global demand rebalancing is essential to put the recovery on a stronger footing over the medium term. This will require action by many countries, notably fiscal adjustment in key external deficit economies and greater exchange rate flexibility and structural reforms that eliminate distortions that boost savings in key surplus economies.

There is broad agreement on the contours of the policy responses sketched here. However, with the peak of the crisis now past, the imperative for action and willingness to cooperate among policymakers is diminishing. It would be a mistake for advanced economies to delay fiscal adjustment in the face of a difficult political economy at home. Additionally, while the removal of distortions that boost saving in key external surplus economies would support growth and help achieve fiscal consolidation in key advanced economies, insufficient progress on one front should not serve as an excuse for inaction on the other front. It would also be a mistake for emerging market economies to delay exchange rate adjustment in the face of rising inflation pressure. Many emerging market economies cannot afford to delay additional policy tightening until the advanced economies undertake such tightening themselves. The task facing policymakers is to convince their national constituencies that these policy responses are in their best economic interests, regardless of the actions others are taking.

## The Recovery Has Solidified, but Unemployment Remains High

The global recovery is continuing broadly as anticipated in the October 2010 and January 2011 *World Economic Outlook* (WEO) projections (Figure 1.1; Table 1.1). World growth decelerated to about 3¾ percent during the second half of 2010, from about 5¼ percent during the first half. This slowdown reflects a normal inventory cycle. As fears of a global depression receded in 2009, businesses at first slowed their rate of destocking, and then, as confidence continued to improve, began to rebuild depleted inventories. This fostered a sharp rebound in industrial production and trade, which lasted through the first half of 2010. As this phase progressed, inventory rebuilding and, as a consequence, industrial production and trade moved into lower gear in the second half of last year. In the meantime, however, reduced excess capacity, accommodative policies, and further improvements in confidence and financial conditions encouraged investment and sharply reduced the rate of job destruction. Consumption also regained strength. Consequently, the recovery has become more self-sustaining, risks of a double-dip recession in advanced economies have receded, and global activity seems set to accelerate again.

Nonetheless, the pace of activity remains geographically uneven, with employment lagging.

- In major advanced economies, economic growth is modest, especially considering the depth of the recession, reaching just 3 percent in 2010. In the United States and the euro area, the economy is following a path as weak as that following the recessions of the early 1990s, despite a much deeper fall (Figure 1.1, middle panel).
- In contrast, many emerging and developing economies have seen robust growth, reaching more than 7 percent in 2010, and have low unemployment rates, although unemployment tends to disproportionately affect young people. In a growing number of these economies, there is

evidence of tightening capacity constraints, and many face large food price increases, which present other social challenges.

- Overall, growth is insufficiently strong to make a major dent in high unemployment rates (Figure 1.1, top panel). Some 205 million people are still looking for jobs, which is up by about 30 million worldwide since 2007, according to the International Labor Organization. The increase in unemployment has been very severe in advanced economies; in emerging and developing economies, high youth unemployment is a particular concern, as noted above.

The recovery is broadly moving at two speeds, with large output gaps in advanced economies and closing or closed gaps in emerging and developing economies, but there are appreciable differences among each set of countries (Chapter 2). Economies that are running behind the global recovery typically suffered large financial shocks during the crisis, often related to housing booms and high external indebtedness. Among the advanced economies, those in Asia have experienced a strong rebound (Figure 1.1, bottom left panel). The recovery of euro area economies that suffered housing busts or face financial market pressures has been weaker than in Germany and some other euro area economies. Among emerging and developing economies, those in Asia are in the lead, followed by those in sub-Saharan Africa, whereas those in eastern Europe are only just beginning to enjoy significant growth.

## Financial Conditions Are Improving

Reinforcing and reflecting generally positive outcomes, strong profits have spurred equity price gains and lowered bond prices, and volatility has decreased (Figure 1.2, top and bottom panels). Stock prices in emerging Asia, Latin America, and the United States have approached precrisis peaks (Figures 1.2 and 1.3, top panels). Financial stocks in the euro area, however, have been sluggish, reflecting contin-

## Table 1.1. Overview of the *World Economic Outlook* Projections

*(Percent change unless noted otherwise)*

| | | | Year over Year | | | | Q4 over Q4 | | |
| --- | --- | --- | --- | --- | --- | --- | --- | --- | --- |
| | | | Projections | | Difference from January 2011 WEO Projections | | Estimates | Projections | |
| | 2009 | 2010 | 2011 | 2012 | 2011 | 2012 | 2010 | 2011 | 2012 |
| **World Output[1]** | **−0.5** | **5.0** | **4.4** | **4.5** | **0.0** | **0.0** | **4.7** | **4.5** | **4.4** |
| **Advanced Economies** | **−3.4** | **3.0** | **2.4** | **2.6** | **−0.1** | **0.1** | **2.7** | **2.6** | **2.5** |
| United States | −2.6 | 2.8 | 2.8 | 2.9 | −0.2 | 0.2 | 2.7 | 3.0 | 2.7 |
| Euro Area[2] | −4.1 | 1.7 | 1.6 | 1.8 | 0.1 | 0.1 | 2.0 | 1.5 | 2.1 |
| Germany | −4.7 | 3.5 | 2.5 | 2.1 | 0.3 | 0.1 | 4.0 | 1.9 | 2.5 |
| France | −2.5 | 1.5 | 1.6 | 1.8 | 0.0 | 0.0 | 1.5 | 1.7 | 2.0 |
| Italy | −5.2 | 1.3 | 1.1 | 1.3 | 0.1 | 0.0 | 1.5 | 1.3 | 1.2 |
| Spain | −3.7 | −0.1 | 0.8 | 1.6 | 0.2 | 0.1 | 0.6 | 1.1 | 1.9 |
| Japan | −6.3 | 3.9 | 1.4 | 2.1 | −0.2 | 0.3 | 2.5 | 2.5 | 1.3 |
| United Kingdom | −4.9 | 1.3 | 1.7 | 2.3 | −0.3 | 0.0 | 1.5 | 2.2 | 2.4 |
| Canada | −2.5 | 3.1 | 2.8 | 2.6 | 0.5 | −0.1 | 3.2 | 2.8 | 2.5 |
| Other Advanced Economies[3] | −1.2 | 5.7 | 3.9 | 3.8 | 0.1 | 0.1 | 4.8 | 4.3 | 3.7 |
| Newly Industrialized Asian Economies | −0.8 | 8.4 | 4.9 | 4.5 | 0.2 | 0.2 | 6.1 | 5.9 | 3.8 |
| **Emerging and Developing Economies[4]** | **2.7** | **7.3** | **6.5** | **6.5** | **0.0** | **0.0** | **7.4** | **6.9** | **6.9** |
| Central and Eastern Europe | −3.6 | 4.2 | 3.7 | 4.0 | 0.1 | 0.0 | 3.7 | 3.7 | 4.0 |
| Commonwealth of Independent States | −6.4 | 4.6 | 5.0 | 4.7 | 0.3 | 0.1 | 4.7 | 4.5 | 3.7 |
| Russia | −7.8 | 4.0 | 4.8 | 4.5 | 0.3 | 0.1 | 4.7 | 4.3 | 3.5 |
| Excluding Russia | −3.1 | 6.0 | 5.5 | 5.1 | 0.4 | −0.1 | . . . | . . . | . . . |
| Developing Asia | 7.2 | 9.5 | 8.4 | 8.4 | 0.0 | 0.0 | 9.2 | 8.4 | 8.5 |
| China | 9.2 | 10.3 | 9.6 | 9.5 | 0.0 | 0.0 | 9.8 | 9.4 | 9.5 |
| India | 6.8 | 10.4 | 8.2 | 7.8 | −0.2 | −0.2 | 9.7 | 7.7 | 8.0 |
| ASEAN-5[5] | 1.7 | 6.9 | 5.4 | 5.7 | −0.1 | 0.0 | 6.1 | 5.4 | 5.6 |
| Latin America and the Caribbean | −1.7 | 6.1 | 4.7 | 4.2 | 0.4 | 0.1 | 5.2 | 5.0 | 4.6 |
| Brazil | −0.6 | 7.5 | 4.5 | 4.1 | 0.0 | 0.0 | 5.0 | 5.0 | 4.0 |
| Mexico | −6.1 | 5.5 | 4.6 | 4.0 | 0.4 | −0.8 | 4.4 | 4.4 | 3.7 |
| Middle East and North Africa | 1.8 | 3.8 | 4.1 | 4.2 | −0.5 | −0.5 | . . . | . . . | . . . |
| Sub-Saharan Africa | 2.8 | 5.0 | 5.5 | 5.9 | 0.0 | 0.1 | . . . | . . . | . . . |
| *Memorandum* | | | | | | | | | |
| European Union | −4.1 | 1.8 | 1.8 | 2.1 | 0.1 | 0.1 | 2.1 | 1.8 | 2.4 |
| World Growth Based on Market Exchange Rates | −2.1 | 3.9 | 3.5 | 3.7 | 0.0 | 0.1 | . . . | . . . | . . . |
| **World Trade Volume (goods and services)** | **−10.9** | **12.4** | **7.4** | **6.9** | **0.3** | **0.1** | . . . | . . . | . . . |
| Imports | | | | | | | | | |
| Advanced Economies | −12.6 | 11.2 | 5.8 | 5.5 | 0.3 | 0.3 | . . . | . . . | . . . |
| Emerging and Developing Economies | −8.3 | 13.5 | 10.2 | 9.4 | 0.9 | 0.2 | . . . | . . . | . . . |
| Exports | | | | | | | | | |
| Advanced Economies | −12.2 | 12.0 | 6.8 | 5.9 | 0.6 | 0.1 | . . . | . . . | . . . |
| Emerging and Developing Economies | −7.5 | 14.5 | 8.8 | 8.7 | −0.4 | −0.1 | . . . | . . . | . . . |
| **Commodity Prices (U.S. dollars)** | | | | | | | | | |
| Oil[6] | −36.3 | 27.9 | 35.6 | 0.8 | 22.2 | 0.5 | . . . | . . . | . . . |
| Nonfuel (average based on world commodity export weights) | −15.8 | 26.3 | 25.1 | −4.3 | 14.1 | 1.3 | . . . | . . . | . . . |
| **Consumer Prices** | | | | | | | | | |
| Advanced Economies | 0.1 | 1.6 | 2.2 | 1.7 | 0.6 | 0.1 | 1.6 | 2.2 | 1.5 |
| Emerging and Developing Economies[4] | 5.2 | 6.2 | 6.9 | 5.3 | 0.9 | 0.5 | 6.3 | 5.9 | 4.2 |
| **London Interbank Offered Rate (percent)[7]** | | | | | | | | | |
| On U.S. Dollar Deposits | 1.1 | 0.5 | 0.6 | 0.9 | −0.1 | 0.0 | . . . | . . . | . . . |
| On Euro Deposits | 1.2 | 0.8 | 1.7 | 2.6 | 0.5 | 0.9 | . . . | . . . | . . . |
| On Japanese Yen Deposits | 0.7 | 0.4 | 0.6 | 0.3 | 0.0 | 0.1 | . . . | . . . | . . . |

Note: Real effective exchange rates are assumed to remain constant at the levels prevailing during February 8–March 8, 2011. When economies are not listed alphabetically, they are ordered on the basis of economic size. The aggregated quarterly data are seasonally adjusted.

[1]The quarterly estimates and projections account for 90 percent of the world purchasing-power-parity weights.

[2]Excludes Estonia.

[3]Excludes the United States, Euro Area, and Japan but includes Estonia.

[4]The quarterly estimates and projections account for approximately 79 percent of the emerging and developing economies.

[5]Indonesia, Malaysia, Philippines, Thailand, and Vietnam.

[6]Simple average of prices of U.K. Brent, Dubai, and West Texas Intermediate crude oil. The average price of oil in U.S. dollars a barrel was $79.03 in 2010; the assumed price based on futures markets is $107.16 in 2011 and $108.00 in 2012.

[7]Six-month rate for the United States and Japan. Three-month rate for the Euro Area.

ued vulnerability to peripheral euro area economies (Figure 1.2, middle panel). Government bond and bank credit default swap spreads in peripheral euro area economies remain high, pointing to significant vulnerabilities (Figure 1.4, middle panel). Stocks in Japan are lagging because of the appreciation of the yen and the impact of the recent earthquake. Credit growth remains very subdued in the advanced economies. Bank lending conditions in the major advanced economies, including those of the euro area, are slowly easing after a prolonged period of incremental tightening (Figure 1.4, top panel); for small and medium-size firms, they are easing or tightening only modestly. In the meantime, credit growth has again reached high levels in many emerging market economies, particularly in Asia and Latin America (Figure 1.3, bottom panel).

Global capital flows rebounded sharply following the collapse during the crisis, but they are still below precrisis averages in many economies (Figure 1.5, middle and bottom panels; Chapter 4). Accordingly, stock markets and credit in emerging market economies have rebounded unusually fast from deep falls (Box 1.1). Strong growth prospects and relatively high yields are attracting flows into emerging markets. Sluggish activity and damaged financial systems continue to depress flows between advanced economies. These forces raise policy challenges that are discussed in more detail later in this chapter as well as in the April 2011 *Global Financial Stability Report*.

- Capital flows to some larger emerging market economies—for example, Brazil, China, India, Indonesia, Mexico, Peru, Poland, and Turkey—are all within the range of or above precrisis levels. The recovery has been led so far by portfolio and bank flows, with a falling share of foreign direct investment inflows. These developments mark a departure from earlier experience and may raise the risk of future instability, including capital outflows. However, during fall 2010 the capital-flow-driven rally in emerging market assets slowed again. Other regions, such as east and west Africa, have yet to see much of a rebound in capital inflows.

- Flows between advanced economies have been hit hard by the financial disintermediation wrought by the crisis (Figure 1.5, middle panel).

## Figure 1.1.  Global Indicators

*(Annual percent change unless noted otherwise)*

Global activity has evolved broadly in line with the October 2010 WEO forecast. Growth is low in advanced economies and unemployment is high. In the United States and the euro area, the recoveries are tracking those of the 1990s, despite much deeper falls in output during the Great Recession. Emerging and developing economies that have not been hit hard by the crisis are already in expansionary territory.

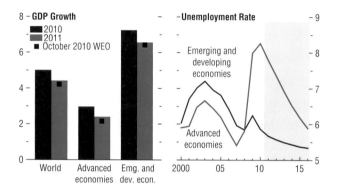

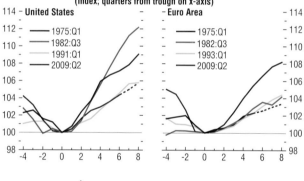

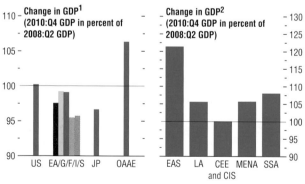

Source: IMF staff estimates.
[1]US: United States; EA/G/F/I/S: euro area/Germany/France/Italy/Spain; JP: Japan; OAAE: other advanced Asian economies.
[2]EAS: emerging Asia; LA: Latin America; CEE and CIS: central and eastern Europe and Commonwealth of Independent States; MENA: Middle East and North Africa; SSA: sub-Saharan Africa. Due to data limitations, annual data are used for MENA and SSA.

## Figure 1.2. Recent Financial Market Developments

Equity prices have moved close to precrisis peaks in the United States but are lagging in Europe and Japan, reflecting, respectively, concerns about the financial sector and exports. Volatility has receded. Corporate spreads have returned to a low level. Long-term government bond yields have moved up in response to stronger activity but remain below levels reached in early 2010.

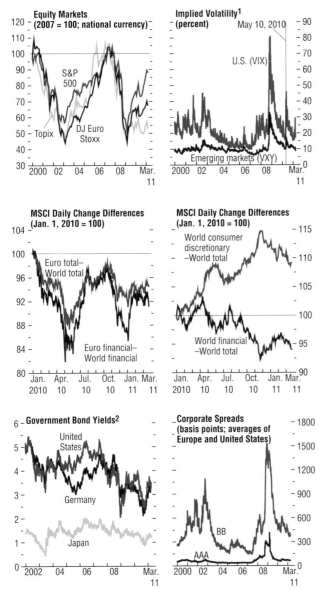

Sources: Bloomberg Financial Markets; and IMF staff calculations.
[1]VIX = Chicago Board Options Exchange Market Volatility Index; VXY = JPMorgan Emerging Market Volatility Index.
[2]Ten-year government bonds.

Capital flows from the United States have returned to precrisis levels but have been redirected to emerging market economies and away from advanced economies. Capital flows from the euro area, especially via banks, are still well below precrisis levels. Reduced flows to other advanced economies account for most of this reduction, although flows to emerging market economies are also weak.

Changes in financial conditions are unlikely to give significant additional support to output growth over the near term. Given the state of the "real" recovery, risk aversion and volatility are already low in the major financial markets, as evidenced by the vigorous recovery of equity markets and a narrowing of credit risk spreads. Although bank lending conditions in advanced economies are still far from normal, further progress is likely to be slow. Securitization markets remain in disrepair. Banks will need time to switch toward more stable deposits and long-term wholesale funding. Supervision and regulation are being tightened for good reason. In addition, conditions are likely to remain volatile because of continued uncertainty about how the crisis in the euro area will be resolved. Indices of broad financial conditions compiled by the IMF staff confirm this qualitative reading. They suggest that conditions are easing slowly and to a similar degree in the United States, the euro area, and Japan; simple forecasts point to further, very gradual easing (Figure 1.4, bottom panel; Appendix 1.1).

Robust capital flows to key emerging market economies may well continue, although questions about macroeconomic policies and geopolitical uncertainty could slow flows over the near term. The growth differential between these economies and advanced economies is not forecast to diminish significantly. Together with emerging economies' demonstrated resilience during the financial crisis, this supports further structural reallocation of portfolios toward these economies. However, uncertainty about the extent and possibility of policy rate hikes in the face of rising inflation may already be acting as a brake on such flows, as is heightened geopolitical uncertainty. A strengthening recovery in the United States, rising yields (Chapter 4), and renewed uncertainty in the euro area could also temper such flows in the future.

## Commodity Prices Are Resurgent

Commodity prices have quickly returned to high levels, owing to structural as well as cyclical and special factors, and market pressures remain elevated. The key structural change is rapid growth in emerging and developing economies, which has lifted and changed the pattern of commodity consumption. At the same time, supply responses have been slow, with production running into sharply higher marginal costs. The key cyclical factor was stronger-than-expected growth in demand for commodities during the second half of 2010, which drove up oil prices for 2011 to about $90 a barrel by early January 2011, up from the $83 a barrel expected in April 2010. Special factors include the Organization of Petroleum Exporting Countries' (OPEC's) lower-than-expected output response when prices rose above $70–$80, a price range previously declared to be "fair," which increased market concern about supply. Another special factor has been unrest in the Middle East and North Africa since January 2011. For food, the main special factor was weather-related supply shocks.

Stronger-than-anticipated global demand for commodities has reduced inventories and caused a strong, sustained, and broad-based increase in prices (Appendix 1.2). The overall IMF commodity price index rose by 32 percent from the middle of 2010 to February 2011—recuperating about three-quarters of the 55 percent decline after the cyclical peak in July 2008 through early 2009. Food prices are within reach of their 2008 peaks. Fortunately, good harvests in sub-Saharan Africa have offered a measure of protection to some of the world's poor. However, social unrest in the Middle East and North Africa could place further upward pressure on food prices if the governments of large grain importers inside and outside the region step up their purchases to ensure sufficient supply in these subsidized domestic food markets.

Commodity supplies are expected to respond to higher prices in 2011. There is spare capacity in the energy sector, which could make up for production losses on account of civil war in Libya, and an

## Figure 1.3. Emerging Market Conditions

Equity prices in Asia and Latin America are close to precrisis peaks. In addition, credit spreads have returned to low levels, capital flows have picked up remarkably quickly, and private sector credit growth is reaching high levels again in many emerging market economies.

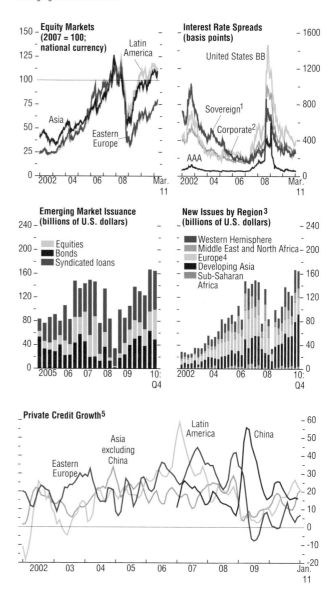

Sources: Bloomberg Financial Markets; Capital Data; IMF, *International Financial Statistics;* and IMF staff calculations.
[1]JPMorgan EMBI Global Index spread.
[2]JPMorgan CEMBI Broad Index spread.
[3]Total of equity, syndicated loans, and international bond issues.
[4]Central and eastern Europe and Commonwealth of Independent States.
[5]Annualized percent change of three-month moving average over previous three-month moving average.

## Figure 1.4. Developments in Mature Credit Markets

Bank lending conditions either are no longer tightening significantly or are easing again, but credit growth rates remain very low. The main concerns with respect to global financial stability stem from very high funding requirements of banks and sovereigns, especially in peripheral countries of the euro area. Further gradual easing of credit conditions can be expected.

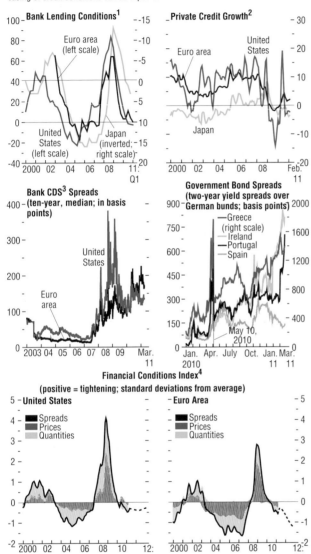

Sources: Bank of America/Merrill Lynch; Bank of Japan; Bloomberg Financial Markets; European Central Bank; Federal Reserve; Haver Analytics; Thomson Datastream; and IMF staff calculations.

[1]Percent of respondents describing lending standards as tightening "considerably" or "somewhat" minus those indicating standards as easing "considerably" or "somewhat" over the previous three months. Survey of changes to credit standards for loans or lines of credit to firms for the euro area; average of surveys on changes in credit standards for commercial/industrial and commercial real estate lending for the United States; diffusion index of "accommodative" minus "severe," Tankan survey of lending attitudes of financial institutions, for Japan.

[2]Annualized percent change of three-month moving average over previous three-month moving average.

[3]CDS = credit default swap.

[4]Historical data are monthly, and forecasts (dashed lines) are quarterly.

anticipated return to more normal weather conditions should result in increased agricultural output. At the same time, demand growth should moderate somewhat, reflecting usual cyclical patterns. These developments are forecast to allow for more balanced growth in both supply and demand. Nonetheless, the outlook for oil markets remains quite uncertain, as perceptions of geopolitical supply risks can be volatile.

- Crude oil supply is responding sluggishly to the ongoing pickup in demand, largely reflecting the policy stance of OPEC. Constraints on non-OPEC capacity and disruption of production in Libya mean that the call on other OPEC suppliers will increase in 2011.[1] Current OPEC spare capacity levels, estimated at about 4½ percent of global demand, are sufficient to make up for losses of supply from Libya and to meet the expected increase in demand. If the supply response materializes, it should restrain further upward price pressure. Current WEO projections are based on futures market prices during March 2011, which saw oil prices stabilizing at about $108 a barrel, some 35 percent above 2010 levels, or some 20 percent above levels assumed for 2011 in the January 2011 *WEO Update*.

- Global food output should recover quickly from recent supply shocks, with increased global acreage and more normal weather conditions pointing to favorable harvest prospects in 2011. Low inventories will take time to rebuild, and so prices are likely to remain more volatile than usual. Governments will need to ensure that the poor have sufficient access to food while food prices stay high.

Regarding medium-term prospects for key commodities, genuine resource scarcity concerns are now widespread (Chapter 3). A gradual, significant downshift in oil supply trend growth is quite possible but might present only a limited drag on annual global growth of less than ¼ percent in the medium term. This relatively small effect reflects the small share of oil in overall economic production and consumption and the scope to adjust production and consumption to rising prices over the long term. However, given low (and falling) short-term

[1]The "call on OPEC" is the difference between global demand and supply from sources other than OPEC crude oil production, including OPEC natural gas liquids (NGL) production.

supply and demand elasticities, such a trend could also bring abrupt price changes that could have very damaging short-term effects on economic activity.

## The Recovery Is Expected to Solidify

Given the improvement in financial markets, buoyant activity in many emerging and developing economies, and growing confidence in advanced economies, economic prospects for 2011–12 are good, notwithstanding new volatility caused by fears about disruptions to oil supply. As in the January *WEO Update,* activity is projected to pick up from the recent dip, with global growth reaching about 4½ percent during 2011–12 (see Table 1.1; Figure 1.6, top panel). Real GDP is expected to expand by about 2½ percent in advanced economies and by 6½ percent in emerging and developing economies. This entails a modest slowdown relative to the growth rates reached in 2010.

Leading indicators already show evidence of a pickup in growth following the inventory-led slowdown. After stagnating during much of the fall, industrial production has begun to regain speed, reflected in the return of manufacturing purchasing managers indices (PMIs) to more expansionary levels (Figure 1.7, top panel). Service sector PMIs suggest that the recovery is now broadening to this large part of the global economy. Retail sales are going strong in emerging market economies and have bounced back in advanced economies, led by the United States (Figure 1.7, middle panel). At the same time, the impact of recent oil price hikes is expected to be relatively limited.[2] A much wider reading of coincident indicators, summarized in the IMF's Growth Tracker, confirms a return of momentum (Figure 1.8, top panel).

---

[2]Oil factor shares would imply output losses of a bit more than ½ percentage point, assuming the price increases during February and March are permanent. There are, however, important mitigating factors that would noticeably lower the effect on global growth. Fuel subsidies in many emerging and developing economies insulate end-users from increases in world oil prices at least temporarily. The terms-of-trade gains of oil exporters will lead to higher imports from oil importers as will higher government spending on social programs in some Middle Eastern economies. Finally, with the supply disruption expected to ease somewhat throughout the year, end-users could well accommodate higher oil expenditures in part by drawing on savings.

### Figure 1.5. Current and Forward-Looking Trade Indicators[1]

*(Annualized percent change of three-month moving average over previous three-month moving average unless noted otherwise)*

World trade and industrial production slowed during 2010:H2, reflecting a global inventory cycle. Imports of emerging and developing economies are back to precrisis trends, but those in advanced economies continue to lag. Capital flows from advanced to emerging economies have picked up. However, according to some measures they slowed down during fall 2010. Flows between advanced economies remain in the doldrums.

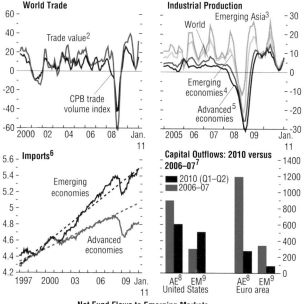

Sources: Bureau of Economic Analysis; U.S. Treasury; EPFR Global; European Central Bank; Haver Analytics; Netherlands Bureau for Economic Policy Analysis for CPB trade volume index; and IMF staff calculations.
[1]Not all economies are included in the regional aggregations. For some economies, monthly data are interpolated from quarterly series.
[2]In SDR terms.
[3]China, India, Indonesia, Malaysia, Philippines, and Thailand.
[4]Argentina, Brazil, Bulgaria, Chile, China, Colombia, Hungary, India, Indonesia, Latvia, Lithuania, Malaysia, Mexico, Pakistan, Peru, Philippines, Poland, Romania, Russia, South Africa, Thailand, Turkey, Ukraine, and Venezuela.
[5]Australia, Canada, Czech Republic, Denmark, euro area, Hong Kong SAR, Israel, Japan, Korea, New Zealand, Norway, Singapore, Sweden, Switzerland, Taiwan Province of China, United Kingdom, and United States.
[6]Actual (solid line) versus 1997–2006 log linear trend (dashed line).
[7]Billions of U.S. dollars for the United States and euros for euro area, annualized.
[8]AE = advanced economies.
[9]EM = emerging market economies.
[10]EMEA = Europe, Middle East, and Africa.

## Figure 1.6. Global Outlook

*(Real GDP; quarterly percent change from one year earlier unless noted otherwise)*

Global growth is forecast to reaccelerate. However, the recovery will remain two-speed in nature, with emerging and developing economies posting strong growth but not advanced economies. Activity is forecast to moderate somewhat in emerging Asia and Latin America, following strong rebounds, as capacity constraints begin to bind.

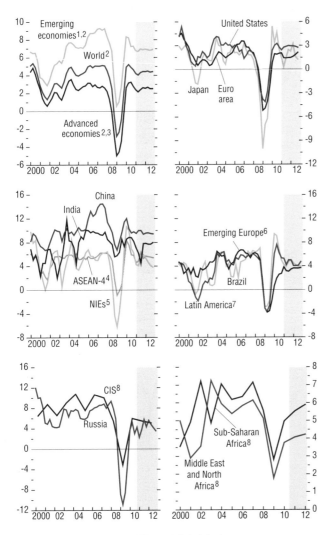

Sources: Haver Analytics; and World Economic Outlook database.
[1]Comprises China, India, Russia, South Africa, Turkey, and economies listed in footnotes 4, 6, and 7.
[2]Includes only economies that report quarterly data.
[3]Australia, Canada, Czech Republic, Denmark, euro area, Hong Kong SAR, Israel, Japan, Korea, New Zealand, Norway, Singapore, Sweden, Switzerland, Taiwan Province of China, United Kingdom, and United States.
[4]Indonesia, Malaysia, Philippines, and Thailand.
[5]Newly industrialized Asian economies (NIEs) comprise Hong Kong SAR, Korea, Singapore, and Taiwan Province of China.
[6]Bulgaria, Hungary, Latvia, Lithuania, and Poland.
[7]Argentina, Brazil, Chile, Colombia, Mexico, Peru, and Venezuela.
[8]Annual percent change from one year earlier. For MENA, aggregated data excludes Libya for the forecast years due to the uncertain political situation.

Various forces are interacting to propel the recovery:

- In advanced economies, investment is recovering with the rebound of industrial production because capital stocks are down and little excess capacity remains (Figures 1.7 and 1.8, bottom panels). The rebound in production is benefiting from low interest rates, easing financing conditions, and generally healthy corporate balance sheets and profitability. At the same time, consumption is being spurred by reduced job layoffs, the gradual recovery of employment, and previously postponed purchases of durable goods.[3] Household saving rates are not projected to rise much over the next couple years (Figure 1.9, middle panel). Deleveraging is thus expected to continue at its present pace, except in a few economies in the euro area that are still struggling with the crisis (Figure 1.9, lower panel).

- In much of Latin America and Asia and in low-income countries in sub-Saharan Africa, recovery has brought output back to precrisis peaks, and many economies have already moved into expansion territory (Figure 1.6, middle and bottom panels). Activity in these economies is being boosted by accommodative macroeconomic policies, rising exports and commodity prices, and—in several—capital inflows. Growth in sub-Saharan Africa is also projected to stay high, reflecting sustained strength in domestic demand and rising global demand for commodities (Figure 1.6, bottom panel). Economic prospects across the Middle East are quite diverse and still fairly uncertain at the time of writing. In eastern European and Commonwealth of Independent States (CIS) economies that were heavily affected by the crisis, activity is also rebounding.

Inflation pressure is forecast to broaden, mainly in emerging and developing economies. At the global level, headline inflation picked up to 4 percent in February, exceeding 2 percent in advanced economies and exceeding 6 percent in emerg-

---

[3]Postponement of such purchases led in 2009 to an unusually large drop in industrial production relative to GDP (see Figure 1.8, bottom panel).

ing and developing economies (Figure 1.10, top panel). This reflects mainly the behavior of food and energy prices and the fact that these components have a higher weight in the consumer price index (CPI) in lower-income countries. Thus, core inflation is running well below headline inflation, although it has been rising quickly in emerging and developing economies, from 2¼ percent in March 2010 to 3¾ percent in February 2011. Looking ahead, core inflation is projected to rise further as excess capacity is slowly worked off. Headline inflation will still moderate if commodity prices broadly stabilize as expected.

- In advanced economies, headline inflation is projected to return below 2 percent in 2011, settling at about 1½ percent during the course of 2012 as food and energy price hikes abate and wages accelerate only gradually amid weak labor markets (see Table 1.1).

- In emerging and developing economies, inflation pressure is broadening (Figure 1.10, top and bottom panels). Assuming broadly stable food and energy prices, the WEO forecast sees headline inflation at close to 7 percent in 2011 and receding to below 5 percent in 2012 (see Table 1.1).

The forecast assumes that macroeconomic policies remain generally supportive. For the major advanced economies, financial markets foresee only limited tightening of monetary policies over the coming year (Figure 1.11, top panel). Fiscal policy tightening is projected to be modest in 2011, following some loosening in 2010 (Figure 1.12, middle panel). Markets also expect only limited removal of monetary accommodation in emerging and developing economies (Figure 1.11, bottom panel). Concerns that the global recovery might be set back by fiscal tightening in advanced economies appear less pertinent. First, the withdrawal of fiscal stimulus projected for 2011 now appears limited, reaching only ¼ percent of GDP. Second, it seems there is a handoff from public to private demand as the driver of growth, even in advanced economies. This is evidenced, for example, by continued recovery in the euro area, notwithstanding a broadly neutral fiscal stance during 2010.

### Figure 1.7. Current and Forward-Looking Growth Indicators[1]

*(Annualized percent change of three-month moving average over previous three-month moving average unless noted otherwise)*

Forward-looking indicators have remained expansionary, pointing to higher growth in 2011:H1. Consumption has gradually strengthened in advanced economies. Although investment has recently been less dynamic in these economies, it should pick up again as production reaccelerates. Indicators point to continued robust activity in many emerging and developing economies.

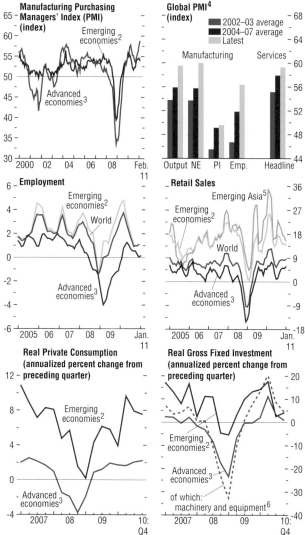

Sources: Haver Analytics; NTC Economics; and IMF staff calculations.
[1]Not all economies are included in the regional aggregations. For some economies, monthly data are interpolated from quarterly series.
[2]Argentina, Brazil, Bulgaria, Chile, China, Colombia, Hungary, India, Indonesia, Latvia, Lithuania, Malaysia, Mexico, Pakistan, Peru, Philippines, Poland, Romania, Russia, South Africa, Thailand, Turkey, Ukraine, and Venezuela.
[3]Australia, Canada, Czech Republic, euro area, Hong Kong SAR, Israel, Japan, Korea, New Zealand, Norway, Singapore, Sweden, Switzerland, Taiwan Province of China, United Kingdom, and United States.
[4]NE: new orders; PI: purchased inventory; Emp.: employment.
[5]China, India, Indonesia, Malaysia, Philippines, and Thailand.
[6]Purchasing-power-parity weighted averages of metal products and machinery for the euro area, plants and equipment for Japan, plants and machinery for the United Kingdom, and equipment and software for the United States.

### Figure 1.8. Prospects for Near-Term Activity

A reading of a large number of indicators for many countries—summarized in this Growth Tracker—suggests that activity is reaccelerating in many countries. In advanced economies, industrial production remains fairly low, considering the state of demand as captured by GDP. This is because consumption of durables has been postponed, as has investment. Some further catch-up is likely over the coming year.

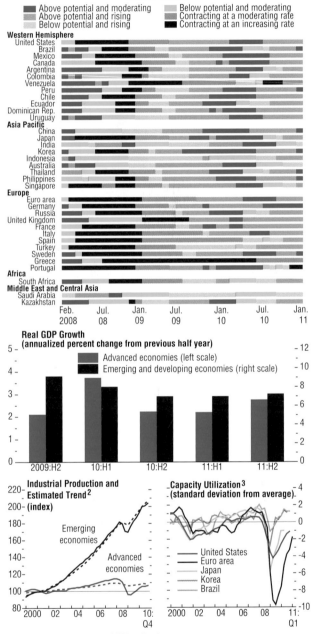

Sources: Haver Analytics; and IMF staff estimates.
[1]The Growth Tracker is described in Matheson (2011). Within regions, countries are listed by economic size.
[2]Trend (dashed lines) is estimated using a cointegrating relationship of industrial production with advanced or emerging economy GDP, respectively.
[3]Data are standardized using averages and standard deviations taken from the 10 years before the crisis.

## Risks Are Smaller but Remain to the Downside

The degree of uncertainty about the outlook for 2011 has declined since the October 2010 *World Economic Outlook*. However, downside risks have increased relative to the January 2011 *WEO Update,* mainly because of geopolitical uncertainty.

The fall in uncertainty relative to 2010 is confirmed by the distribution of analysts' forecasts for the yield curve and inflation as well as data on options prices for the Standard & Poor's (S&P) 500 index and oil, which are summarized in the IMF's fan chart (Figure 1.13, top panel). In particular, the dispersion of analysts' forecasts for real GDP growth is substantially smaller than it was in 2010 and is now close to the historical baseline (Figure 1.13, bottom panel). The fan chart suggests that markets continue to see a greater potential for upside rather than downside surprises for growth from equity prices (Figure 1.13, middle panel).[4] Interestingly, although forecasters generally see appreciably higher inflation, they now see more scope for inflation surprises on the downside rather than the upside, which has opposite implications for surprises with respect to real GDP growth. However, this result is essentially driven by forecasts for the United States, Japan, and China.

The key downside risk to growth relates to the potential for oil prices to surprise further on the upside because of supply disruptions. To explore these risks in more detail, the IMF staff developed a downside scenario under which greater-than-expected temporary supply disruptions push oil prices up to an average of $150 per barrel for 2011, after which they recede to the average levels currently expected for 2012. In advanced economies, the level of real GDP in 2012 would then be ¾ percent lower than in current WEO projections; in emerging and developing economies, the effects would vary widely, from an output loss of close to ¾ percent in Asia and sub-Saharan Africa, to ½ percent in Latin America, to output gains in the Middle East and North Africa as well as the Commonwealth of Independent States. Global output losses would

[4]For details on the construction of the fan chart, see Elekdag and Kannan (2009).

be much larger in the event of a permanent shock to oil supply.

According to the April 2011 *Global Financial Stability Report*, financial risks have declined since October 2010. Improvements in macroeconomic performance and strong prospects for emerging market assets are supporting overall financial stability. Accommodative macroeconomic conditions are helping to ease balance sheet risks and are spurring an increase in risk appetite. However, significant fiscal and financial vulnerabilities still lurk behind recent benign market developments, especially in the euro area. More generally, downside risks stem from high leverage and limited improvements in credit quality in advanced economies and gradually building credit risks in some major emerging market economies. These are the key downside risks for global economic and financial stability:

• *Weak sovereign balance sheets in advanced economies:* Risks relate to the major funding requirements of sovereigns and the potential for high volatility in interest rates and risk premiums. Currently, these are focused on vulnerable euro area economies (see below). However, risks also flow from fiscal policy in the United States, given large funding requirements and heavy reliance on external sources.[5] As discussed in previous issues of the *World Economic Outlook*, there is little risk of a large, broad-based increase in government bond rates in the short term, but there is a chance of sudden changes, especially in risk premiums, that could threaten global financial stability.[6]

---

[5]See Box 1.4 in the October 2010 *World Economic Outlook*.

[6]This is because the recovery in advanced economies is forecast to be subdued; savings in surplus emerging market economies are projected to rise relative to investments; and there are few plausible alternative outlets in emerging market economies to the large volume of debt instruments issued by advanced economies (see Chapter 1 of the October 2010 *World Economic Outlook*). Looking further ahead, Dobbs and Spence (2011) argue that the global economy will soon have to cope with too little capital, not too much, as rapid urbanization in emerging and developing economies boosts demand for infrastructure, while demand rebalancing in China and demographic change in advanced economies lower the supply of savings. However, whether or not real interest rates rise depends on many factors that are very hard to predict, such as prospects for investment in aging societies, retirement ages, the relationship between aging and health, financial developments in emerging and developing economies, international migration, technological change, and policy responses, to mention just a few.

**Figure 1.9. Balance Sheets and Saving Rates**
*(Percent)*

Deleveraging is ongoing in many advanced economies, mainly in the household sector. However, saving rates are not expected to rise much over the coming two years, suggesting a gradual rise in consumption as employment picks up. Conditions remain vulnerable in peripheral countries of the euro area.

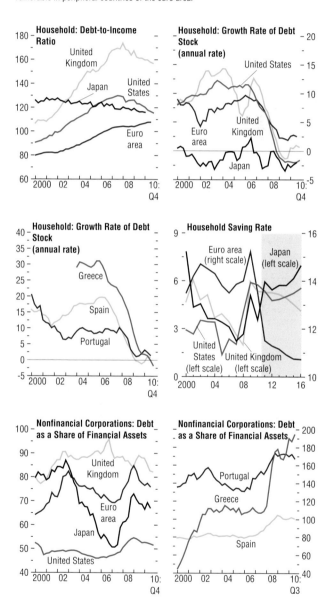

Sources: Haver Analytics; and IMF staff estimates.

## Figure 1.10. Global Inflation

*(Twelve-month change in the consumer price index unless noted otherwise)*

Inflation is rising everywhere. However, core inflation and wages remain subdued in advanced economies, held back by high unemployment. In many emerging and developing economies, inflation pressures are broadening amid accommodative macroeconomic policies and increasingly binding capacity constraints.

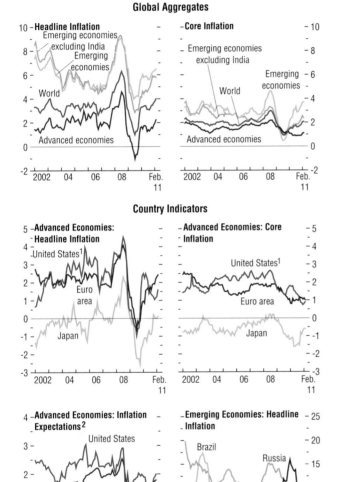

Sources: Consensus Economics; Haver Analytics; and IMF staff calculations.
[1] Personal consumption expenditure deflator.
[2] One-year-ahead *Consensus Forecasts*. The December values are the average of the surrounding November and January values.
[3] Consumer price index for industrial workers.

- *Imbalances in real estate markets:* Real estate markets are moribund in a number of advanced economies. Downside risk from a shadow inventory of homes at risk of foreclosure in the United States is still significant—this is discussed in more depth in the April 2011 *Global Financial Stability Report*. In the meantime, new risks are building because of booming real estate markets in emerging market economies.

- *Overheating in emerging market economies:* Growth in these economies could surprise on the upside in the short term because of relatively loose macroeconomic policies (see below), but medium-term risks are to the downside. These risks are explored in Box 1.2, which presents an alternative scenario to the WEO projections that is based on tighter cyclical conditions in emerging market economies than assumed in the WEO projections. Under this scenario, higher interest rates, weaker future income growth, and the impact of fiscal adjustment correct excesses that have built up during the boom phase but at the price of a global economic bust, including a large drop in commodity prices. Global imbalances between advanced economies and emerging Asia would widen again under such a scenario, while imbalances involving commodity exporters would diminish.

The most tangible downside risk still arises from tension in the euro area periphery, which may spread to the core European economies. Despite increasing clarity, markets remain apprehensive about the sufficiency of funding available under the European Financial Stability Facility and European Financial Stability Mechanism and the functioning of the permanent European Stability Mechanism. The hollowing out of the traditional investor base for government bonds in the most vulnerable euro area sovereigns continued as new rules for bondholder bail-ins were announced at the same time that markets question the sustainability of public debt levels in some economies. Risks are exacerbated by continuing weakness among financial institutions in much of Europe, a lack of transparency about their exposures, and weak sovereign balance sheets. Although the periphery accounts for only a small portion of the euro area's overall output and trade, substantial financial linkages with core countries, as well as financial spillovers through higher risk aversion and lower equity prices, could generate a significant slowdown in demand. A pessimistic scenario created for the January 2011 *WEO Update* suggests that if these risks materialize, they could lower euro area output by 3 percentage points and global output by 1 percentage point relative to the baseline forecast.

At the same time, there are some upside risks:

- *Consumption in advanced economies:* Demand for consumer durables may continue to recover faster than expected in advanced economies, as household saving rates stabilize and fears of job losses recede. This would be both good and bad news: activity would be stronger, but where household balance sheets are still weak, vulnerabilities would persist and global imbalances would widen again—that is, the sustainability of the recovery would not improve.

- *Recovering investment:* Investment in machinery and equipment may rebound more vigorously, owing to strong corporate profits and balance sheets. This has already taken place to some extent in the United States, although the investment-to-GDP ratio remains well below precrisis readings.

- *Short-term demand buoyancy in emerging and developing economies:* Upside surprises in advanced economies would add to demand pressures in emerging and developing economies while boosting energy prices. In the short term, growth in emerging market economies could also surprise on the upside for domestic reasons. However, over the medium term, the aforementioned downside risk of overheating predominates.

## Differences in the Pace of Activity Present Short-Term Policy Challenges

The conjunctural setting—sobering for advanced economies and positive for emerging and developing economies—is creating new tensions, especially in key emerging and developing economies. Rising commodity prices and diminishing excess capacity are pushing up inflation in these economies. Key emerging market economies are also experiencing a credit boom. At the same time, authorities are often reluctant to tighten macroeconomic policies because

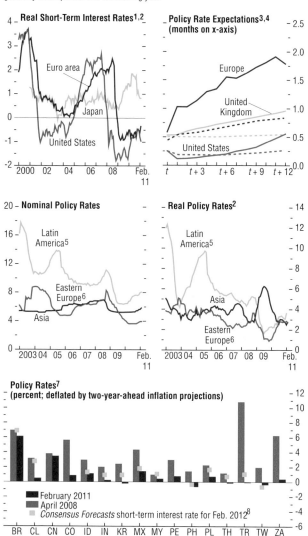

**Figure 1.11. Measures of Monetary Policy and Liquidity in Selected Advanced and Emerging Economies**
*(Percent, unless noted otherwise)*

Short-term real interest rates are appropriately low in many advanced economies and not expected to rise much over the coming year. However, interest rates appear low in many emerging market economies as well. Significant policy rate hikes are generally not expected over the coming year.

Sources: Bloomberg Financial Markets; Consensus Economics; Eurostat; Haver Analytics; and IMF staff calculations.
[1]Three-month treasury bill.
[2]Relative to core inflation.
[3]Expectations are based on the federal funds rate for the United States, the sterling overnight interbank average rate for the United Kingdom, and the euro interbank offered forward rates for Europe; updated April 4, 2011.
[4]Dashed lines are from the October 2010 WEO.
[5]Argentina, Brazil, Chile, Colombia, Mexico, and Peru.
[6]Bulgaria, Hungary, Latvia, Lithuania, and Poland.
[7]BR: Brazil; CL: Chile; CN: China; CO: Colombia; ID: Indonesia; IN: India; KR: Korea; MX: Mexico; MY: Malaysia; PE: Peru; PH: Philippines; PL: Poland; TH: Thailand; TR: Turkey; TW: Taiwan Province of China; ZA: South Africa.
[8]As of February 2011; overnight interbank rate for Turkey.

## Figure 1.12. General Government Fiscal Balances and Public Debt

*(Percent of GDP unless noted otherwise)*

Fiscal deficits and public debt are very high in many advanced economies. Although policy became much less stimulatory in 2010, real GDP growth picked up, suggesting a handoff from public to private demand. For 2011, fiscal consolidation is expected to be modest in advanced economies. As a result, the adjustment required to achieve prudent debt levels by 2030 remains very large. Fiscal adjustment will be larger in economies with high external surpluses than in economies with high deficits, which is consistent with widening global imbalances.

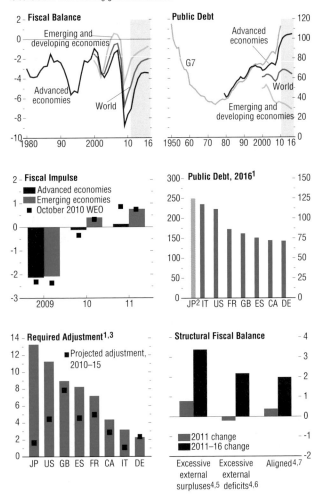

Sources: IMF, *Fiscal Monitor;* and IMF staff calculations.

[1]CA: Canada, DE: Germany, ES: Spain, FR: France, GB: United Kingdom, IT: Italy, JP: Japan, US: United States.

[2]Left scale for Japan.

[3]Cyclically adjusted primary balance adjustment needed to bring the debt ratio to 60 percent by 2030. For Japan, the scenario assumes a reduction in net debt to 80 percent of GDP; this corresponds to a gross debt target of about 200 percent of GDP.

[4]Based on the IMF staff's Consultative Group on Exchange Rate Issues (CGER). CGER economies include Argentina, Australia, Brazil, Canada, Chile, China, Colombia, Czech Republic, euro area, Hungary, India, Indonesia, Israel, Japan, Korea, Malaysia, Mexico, Pakistan, Poland, Russia, South Africa, Sweden, Switzerland, Thailand, Turkey, United Kingdom, and United States. For a detailed discussion of the methodology for the calculation of exchange rates' over- or undervaluation, see Lee and others (2008).

[5]These economies account for 18.5 percent of global GDP.

[6]These economies account for 27.4 percent of global GDP.

[7]These economies account for 39.2 percent of global GDP.

they fear that growth in advanced economies could disappoint, higher domestic interest rates could lead to exchange rate overshooting or unmanageable capital flows, and lower public spending could add to pain inflicted by rising food prices. In response, a number of emerging market economies are resorting to prudential tightening, and some have adopted capital controls to mitigate potential costs related to overheating. However, insufficient macroeconomic policy tightening raises the risk of a hard landing.

The rise in commodity prices is easier to manage for advanced economies. The three main challenges facing many of these economies are to preserve or regain fiscal credibility, repair and reform the financial sector, and reduce high unemployment.

Despite these differences, the policy challenges facing both advanced and emerging and developing economies are tightly linked. Advanced economies' policy responses, such as easy monetary policy, have spillover effects on emerging and developing economies. Conversely, the policies adopted by emerging and developing economies, such as exchange rate policies and capital controls, are affecting not only the advanced economies but also other emerging and developing economies. However, spillovers do not in themselves indicate that there are fundamental macroeconomic policy conflicts of interest between countries. In general, stronger and more far-sighted policies would deliver not only better national outcomes but also better global outcomes than projected here.

## Advanced Economies Need to Repair Public and Financial Balance Sheets

In many advanced economies, output gaps are still large and are projected to close only gradually over the medium term, and unemployment rates remain stubbornly high. In the United States and the euro area, respectively, unemployment rates are close to 9 percent and 10 percent, and output gaps for 2010 are estimated at somewhat less than 5 percent and 3 percent of potential GDP. Among major advanced economies, the United States and Spain suffered by far the largest increases in unemployment relative to precrisis levels; others saw increases of about 2½ percentage points or less. Quick reductions in these rates appear unlikely because output gaps are projected to close only gradually as fiscal policy is tightened and financial sector repair occurs over time. Furthermore, employment-intensive activities take a long time to recover after banking or housing crises.[7]

### Monetary Policy Can Remain Accommodative in Most Economies

Many advanced economy central banks can accommodate hikes in food and energy prices mainly because the weight of food and energy in the consumer basket is relatively small, people have learned from experience that such hikes do not set off a cycle of inflation, and excess capacity will exert downward pressure on wages. Moreover, in major economies bank credit is still very sluggish. The Federal Reserve and Bank of Japan are forecast to keep their interest rates very low during 2011, in view of the subdued wage claims and large output gaps (see Figure 1.11, top panel). The European Central Bank (ECB) is expected to raise rates as it sees growing upside risks to price stability, but it has prolonged unconventional support in recognition of still-high financial risks. Economic conditions and underlying price pressures are somewhat stronger in other advanced economies, and these central banks have already raised rates (for example, Australia, Canada, Israel, Korea, Norway, Sweden). Most of their policy rates remain accommodative, in a 1 to 3 percent range, and they will have to do more as unemployment rates fall and food and energy prices put pressure on wages. In this set of economies, markets generally expect hikes on the order of ½ to 1½ percentage points over the coming year.[8]

However, even advanced economy central banks with well-established inflation-targeting regimes may struggle to protect their credibility when hit with a succession of one-time price shocks or trend increases in the prices of specific items in consumer baskets. The Bank of England, for example, has seen

---

[7]See Chapter 3 of the April 2010 *World Economic Outlook* and Dowling, Estevão, and Tsounta (2010).

[8]Another problem faced by some of these economies after the crisis has been accelerating real estate prices in the face of low interest rates—as in a number of emerging market economies the authorities are resorting to macroprudential measures to slow down these price rises (for example, Canada, Hong Kong SAR).

---

### Figure 1.13. Risks to the Global Outlook

Risks to global growth have receded, as evidenced by the falling dispersion of analysts' forecasts. Nonetheless, they remain mainly to the downside. For 2012, this reflects mainly concerns about high oil prices.

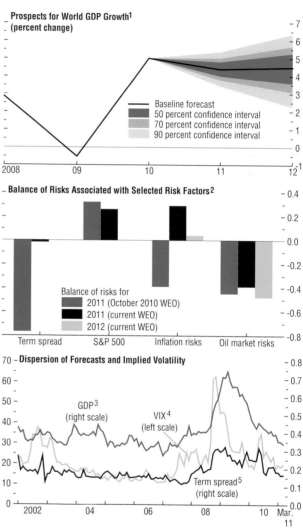

Sources: Bloomberg Financial Markets; Chicago Board Options Exchange; Consensus Economics; and IMF staff estimates.

[1]The fan chart shows the uncertainty around the WEO central forecast with 50, 70, and 90 percent probability intervals. As shown, the 70 percent confidence interval includes the 50 percent interval, and the 90 percent confidence interval includes the 50 and 70 percent intervals. See Appendix 1.2 in the April 2009 WEO for details.

[2]Bars depict the coefficient of skewness expressed in units of the underlying variables. The values for inflation risks and oil market risks are entered with the opposite sign, since they represent downside risks to growth. The balance of risk for 2012 is not available for the S&P 500 index and the term spread.

[3]The series measures the dispersion of GDP forecasts for the G7 economies (Canada, France, Germany, Italy, Japan, United Kingdom, United States), Brazil, China, India, and Mexico.

[4]VIX: Chicago Board Options Exchange Market Volatility Index.

[5]The series measures the dispersion of term spreads implicit in interest rate forecasts for Germany, Japan, the United Kingdom, and the United States.

inflation running above its 2 percent midpoint target for much of the period since 2005, reflecting food and energy price increases, value-added tax hikes, and depreciation of the currency. CPI inflation is now about 4½ percent, although wage inflation seems well contained. Households' inflation expectations are creeping up, but other measures of inflation expectations have changed little over the past year. This experience suggests that central bankers will need to communicate very clearly how they intend to respond to one-time or relative price shocks. The objective should be to accommodate foreign price inflation as long as it does not pose significant threats to domestic price inflation.

There is no need to actively unwind unconventional measures, at least not in the near term, as fears that they will stoke inflation pressure are misplaced. As discussed in previous issues of the *World Economic Outlook*, to the extent that these measures inject liquidity, this can be reabsorbed. Unconventional measures fall into two categories:

• Quantitative easing—that is, purchases of government bonds to lower long-term interest rates: In the United States and the United Kingdom, new programs for purchases appear unnecessary, given current prospects for activity and developments in inflation expectations. For Japan, the jury is still out: core inflation is recovering gradually but still running close to zero, and deflation therefore appears far from vanquished.

• Qualitative easing—that is, measures to support the functioning of specific markets or ensure availability of sufficient liquidity: Many of these measures have already unwound naturally. In some economies and some markets, notably the euro area, they need to be maintained until there is a lasting improvement in liquidity. However, the authorities must ensure that these measures do not postpone fundamental bank restructuring.

Available evidence suggests that as long as monetary policy successfully stabilizes output in advanced economies, spillovers to emerging and developing economies will not be detrimental (Box 1.3). By contrast, concerns about detrimental spillovers from insufficiently ambitious fiscal adjustment in advanced economies are quite relevant, given the effects on global interest rates,

investment, and potential output. In short, as long as advanced economies implement policies that foster their own sustained recovery, emerging and developing economies will benefit. To the extent that policies in advanced economies disappoint, spillovers from fiscal (and financial) policy shortcomings are likely to be much worse than from monetary shortcomings.

## Much Stronger Efforts Are Needed to Maintain or Rebuild Fiscal Credibility

Preserving or regaining fiscal credibility in the face of high public deficits and debt presents a major challenge for many advanced economies. Most of these economies are planning to tighten fiscal policy significantly in 2011, but the pace of fiscal consolidation in 2011 will be far below earlier estimates—the October 2010 *World Economic Outlook* foresaw a reduction in structural deficits of almost 1 percent of GDP, whereas current WEO projections are for a reduction of only ¼ percent of GDP (Figure 1.12, middle panel). This reflects mainly a major change in the policy stance of the United States, where the structural deficit is now projected to widen by 0.6 percent of GDP rather than contract by 0.9 percent of GDP in 2011. Its economy appears sufficiently strong to withstand modest consolidation. Furthermore, the short-term impact of the stimulus deployed in the United States on jobs and growth is likely to be low relative to its cost. Recent measures to trim discretionary spending will reduce the federal deficit for fiscal year 2011 below the projection recently released in the president's draft fiscal year 2012 budget. However, more sizable reductions in medium-term deficits are needed and will require broader reforms, including to Social Security and taxation. In Japan, structural fiscal tightening will also be more gradual than expected in the October 2010 WEO projections, due to a new stimulus program and support for reconstruction after the earthquake. Once reconstruction efforts are under way and the size of the damage is better understood, attention should turn to linking reconstruction spending to a clear fiscal strategy for bringing down the public debt ratio over the medium term.

Elsewhere, fiscal policy is projected to be appropriately contractionary. In the euro area, structural deficits are projected to fall by about 1 percent of GDP; in the United Kingdom, cutbacks are larger, reaching 1¾ percent of GDP. This is in line with previous budgetary plans.

Some economies under extreme pressure from markets have embarked on ambitious medium-term reforms. Many other advanced economies have defined adjustment strategies in broad terms and have begun to implement them. However, with the exception of those that are front-loading their adjustment and those with strong fiscal frameworks (for example, Canada, Germany, United Kingdom), these economies have generally not explained the measures underlying their adjustment plans in enough detail.[9] In this regard, only limited progress has been made over the past six months, which is not to deny the continuation of discussion and debate. Hence, projections for structural fiscal balances over the medium term are largely unchanged for the major advanced economies relative to those of the October 2010 *World Economic Outlook*. Most advanced G20 economies are still projected to meet their target of halving deficits by 2013 relative to 2010.[10] The United States remains committed to achieving this target. Because of the loosening of fiscal policy for 2011, meeting it now requires about 5 percent of GDP cumulative structural adjustment for the federal government during fiscal years 2012–13, which may be difficult to achieve.[11] Furthermore, under IMF staff estimates, the U.S. gross-debt-to-GDP ratio is not projected to stabilize over the forecast horizon and would exceed 110 percent by 2016, compared with less than 90 percent in the euro area and almost 250 percent in Japan (see Figure 1.12, middle panel).

Among the major euro area countries, all are committed to reducing deficits to below 3 percent of GDP by 2013. However, based on currently announced plans and WEO growth projections, only Germany is forecast to achieve this objective—leav-

ing France, Spain, and—to a much lesser extent— Italy to identify new measures.

Little progress has been made in many economies in specifying measures to redress remaining medium-term imbalances, and so advanced economies will still have to enact very large fiscal adjustments in order to reduce their general government gross-debt-to-GDP ratio to a level of 60 percent by 2030 (Figure 1.12, bottom panel).[12] According to a scenario developed in the IMF's April 2011 *Fiscal Monitor*, the required adjustments amount to more than 10 percent of GDP for Japan and the United States; 5 to 10 percent of GDP for France, Spain, and the United Kingdom; and 3 to 4 percent of GDP for Canada, Germany, and Italy. Among the smaller, vulnerable economies, the required adjustments lie between about 6 percent of GDP for Portugal and more than 10 percent of GDP for Greece and Ireland. These countries have, in fact, recently enacted stringent measures in the face of increased market pressures (see the November 2010 *Fiscal Monitor*).

The absence of well-specified medium-term plans in several economies raises increasingly serious concerns, particularly about the United States. As activity continues to pick up, large sovereign funding requirements will put upward pressure on interest rates, slowing the recovery of the private sector and lowering potential output. This could cause abrupt increases in interest rates in the United States (from especially low levels) that could destabilize global bond markets, with particularly deleterious effects on emerging market economies (Chapter 4). Gradual increases would slow investment and potential growth in advanced as well as emerging and developing economies. While the immediate concern in Japan should be to support reconstruction, measures that support a reduction of its high public debt ratio over the medium term need to be specified to maintain the strong confidence of its investor base.

More generally, as the share of retirees begins to grow more rapidly over the coming decade, fundamental reform of entitlement programs, which is indispensable to attaining sustainable public

---

[9]For a detailed assessment of medium-term fiscal plans of 25 economies, see Bornhorst and others (2010).

[10]In its fiscal strategy of June 2010, Japan committed to halving the government primary deficit in percent of GDP by fiscal year 2015 and achieving a primary surplus by fiscal year 2020 at the latest.

[11]For the general government, the reduction in the structural deficit would amount to about 4 percent of GDP in calendar years 2012–13.

[12]Similar results are described in the October 2010 *World Economic Outlook*. For Japan, the scenario assumes a reduction in net debt to 80 percent of GDP; this corresponds to a gross debt target of about 200 percent of GDP.

finances, may become even harder to achieve. An increasingly fractionalized political sphere in a number of advanced economies, including Japan and the United States, poses additional fiscal risks, as is well known from the political economy literature on fiscal policy.[13]

### Financial Sector Repair Must Be Accelerated

The main short-term challenges relate to instability within the euro area. Policymakers should take advantage of the moderately improved conditions to make real progress in addressing them. At the euro area level, what is needed is sufficient, low-cost, and flexible funding for countries that are facing market pressures and need external help to support adjustment. In addition, major reforms to euro area economic governance are necessary to help prevent the recurrence of such turmoil in the future. Significant progress was made on both fronts during March 2011 but important issues remain to be addressed. In the meantime, the ECB should continue to ensure orderly conditions in funding markets and help prevent excessive volatility in sovereign debt markets. The priorities for countries under pressure are fiscal adjustment and entitlement and structural reform. Also important is a new round of strong, broad, and transparent stress tests, backed by credible restructuring and recapitalization programs, to strengthen confidence in euro area banking systems. This is essential to break the negative feedback loop between sovereign and banking sector instability and to rebuild competitiveness.

There has been major progress over the past year in addressing euro area challenges (Chapter 2). Notwithstanding improving conditions and confidence, even after all these and further efforts are deployed, there is likely to be continued uncertainty while markets monitor the implementation of the new measures and refine their views on public and external debt sustainability. In short, there are no

quick solutions, but strong measures are necessary to nurture adjustment and anchor expectations and thereby lower the probability of panic scenarios.

In the meantime, financial repair and reform need to move forward on a variety of other fronts. The challenges are discussed in depth in the April 2011 *Global Financial Stability Report*. In the United States, programs are needed to facilitate principal write-downs of distressed first mortgages and second liens to clear out a large shadow inventory of nonperforming mortgages, including for households facing negative equity in their homes, and avoid unnecessary foreclosures. This would pave the way for further repair and reform of mortgage credit and securitization markets. More generally, in the United States and elsewhere, the postcrisis supervisory and regulatory architecture is still very much a work in progress. The shadow banking system and institutions that are too large, or too complex, to fail pose problems that have not yet been fully addressed. Furthermore, stronger supervision and resolution frameworks are needed for cross-border financial institutions; this will require significantly enhanced international cooperation, including in day-to-day supervision.

### Emerging Market Economies Need to Guard against Overheating and Credit Booms

In many emerging and developing economies, output is already above precrisis trends, suggesting that recovery is complete and expansion under way. Output of all emerging and developing economies stands about 2½ percent above precrisis (1997–2006) trends (Figure 1.14, bottom panel). In many of the major emerging market economies outside central and eastern Europe and the CIS, unemployment rates are below precrisis levels. Headline inflation is now exceeding 6 percent, up from 5¾ percent in January 2010—excluding India, the increase in inflation rate amounts to 1¼ percentage points.[14] Over the same period, core inflation increased from about 2 percent to 3¾ percent,

---

[13]Roubini and Sachs (1989), Roubini and others (1989), Alesina and Drazen (1991), and Poterba (1994) present empirical evidence suggesting that economic shocks prompt action but that more fragmented governments have typically postponed fiscal adjustments. For a general discussion of the role of political economy in distorting fiscal policy, see Alesina and Perotti (1995).

[14]In India, the CPI for industrial workers suggests that inflation fell from about 16 percent in January 2010 to less than 10 percent in December 2010, helped by less food price inflation on account of postdrought recovery in agricultural output. Nonethe-

suggesting that inflation pressure is broadening. In a number of the larger economies, headline inflation is running close to or above central bank targets (Figure 1.15, left panel). Furthermore, some economies are experiencing a credit boom.

- Output of developing Asia and Latin America stands, respectively, about 7 percent and 2 percent above 1997–2006 trends. Some major economies show clear evidence of appreciable positive gaps. In Argentina and Indonesia, output is about 13 to 15 percent above precrisis trends; in Brazil and India, it is about 7 percent higher. WEO projections assume that potential growth rates in these economies have recently been higher than 1997–2006 averages: accordingly, they place estimates of output gaps for these countries generally in the zero to 1½ percent positive range. In China, output is also appreciably above precrisis trends, although much larger investment in productive capacity than in the other economies has limited constraints on production. In many of these economies, both headline and core inflation either are rising from low levels or are fairly high already.

- Output in sub-Saharan Africa and the Middle East and North Africa has broadly returned to precrisis trends. Some of these economies are already experiencing higher inflation; pressures will build, not least owing to accelerating activity in commodity exporters.

- In Mexico, Russia, and Turkey, output is appreciably below precrisis trends. WEO projections suggest that much of the output lost relative to 1997–2006 trends has been lost permanently and therefore point to much smaller negative or closing output gaps; for Turkey, they even point to a positive output gap.

At the same time, a number of major emerging market economies and a few advanced economies with close links to them feature very buoyant credit and asset price growth (Figure 1.16, top panel). This set of economies accounts for about one-quarter of global GDP in purchasing-power-parity terms or about half of emerging and developing economy output. The issue is whether they are experiencing

less, inflation has remained stubbornly high and well above the central bank's stated objective.

## Figure 1.14. Emerging Tensions

Commodity prices have risen fast, and capacity constraints are appearing in a growing number of emerging market economies. Terms of trade of emerging and developing economies have improved again, fueling domestic demand in commodity exporters. The high share of food and fuel in consumer baskets in these countries means their economies are particularly sensitive to food and fuel price shocks.

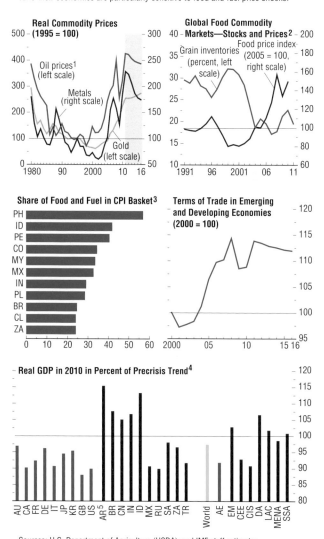

Sources: U.S. Department of Agriculture (USDA); and IMF staff estimates.
[1]Simple average of spot prices of U.K. Brent, Dubai Fateh, and West Texas Intermediate crude oil.
[2]Global end-year inventories as a percent of consumption, with USDA projections for 2011.
[3]CL: Chile; CO: Colombia; MY: Malaysia; PE: Peru; PH: Philippines; PL: Poland.
[4]Precrisis trend obtained by extrapolating 1996–2006 real GDP growth. AR: Argentina; AE: advanced economies; AU: Australia; BR: Brazil; CA: Canada; CEE: central and eastern Europe; CIS: Commonwealth of Independent States; CN: China; DA: developing Asia; DE: Germany; EM: emerging economies; FR: France; GB: United Kingdom; ID: Indonesia; IN: India; IT: Italy; JP: Japan; KR: Korea;  LAC: Latin America and the Caribbean; MENA: Middle East and North Africa;  MX: Mexico; RU: Russia; SA: Saudi Arabia; SSA: sub-Saharan Africa; TR: Turkey; US: United States; ZA: South Africa.
[5]Private analysts are of the view that real GDP growth was significantly lower than the official estimates in 2008 and 2009, although the discrepancy between private and official estimates of real GDP growth has narrowed in 2010. This may affect the estimates of output relative to trend.

## Figure 1.15. Overheating Indicators and Capital Inflows

Among G20 economies, a growing number of emerging market economies and a few advanced economies either are close to or are already overheating. Macroeconomic policies in these economies are still accommodative. Capital inflows have also rebounded, exceeding precrisis averages in a number of emerging market economies. With limited recourse to capital controls, these economies have relied widely on prudential measures.

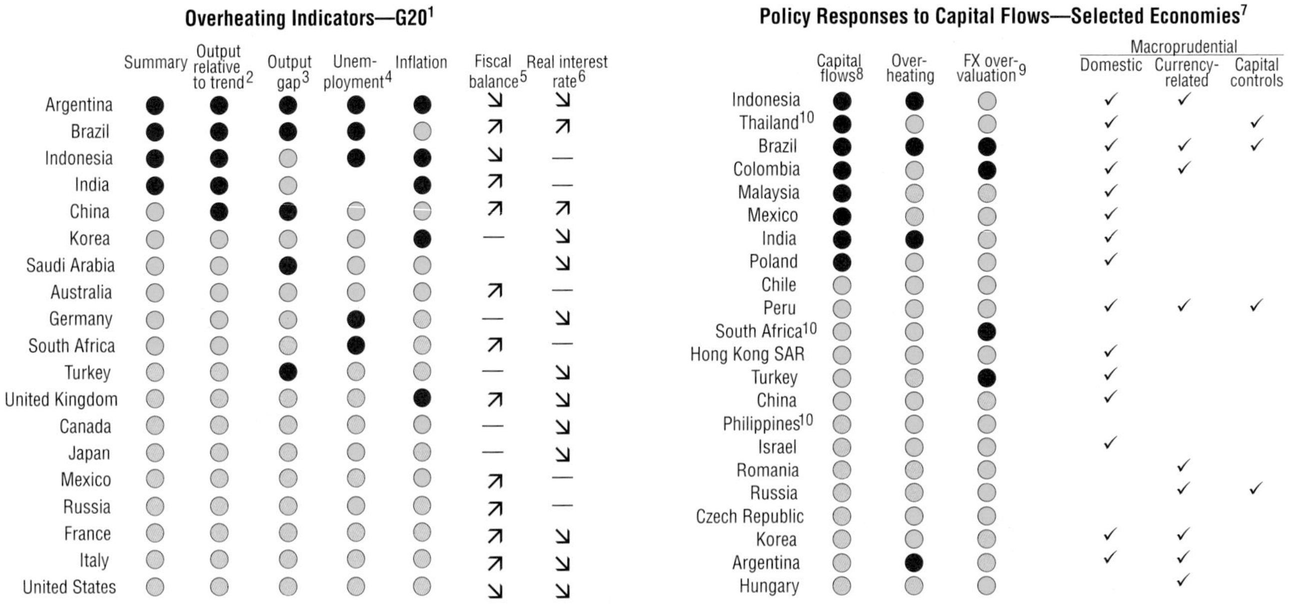

**Overheating Indicators—G20[1]**

| | Summary | Output relative to trend[2] | Output gap[3] | Unem- ployment[4] | Inflation | Fiscal balance[5] | Real interest rate[6] |
|---|---|---|---|---|---|---|---|
| Argentina | ● | ● | ● | ● | ● | ↘ | ↘ |
| Brazil | ● | ● | ● | ● | ◐ | ↗ | ↗ |
| Indonesia | ● | ● | ◐ | ● | ● | ↘ | — |
| India | ● | ● | ◐ | | ● | ↗ | — |
| China | ◔ | ● | ● | ◔ | ◔ | ↗ | ↗ |
| Korea | ◔ | ◔ | ◔ | ◔ | ● | — | ↘ |
| Saudi Arabia | ◔ | ◔ | ● | ◔ | ◔ | | ↘ |
| Australia | ◔ | ◔ | ◔ | ◔ | ◔ | ↗ | — |
| Germany | ◔ | ◔ | ● | ◔ | ◔ | — | ↘ |
| South Africa | ◔ | ◔ | ◔ | ● | ◔ | ↗ | — |
| Turkey | ◔ | ◔ | ● | ◔ | ◔ | — | ↘ |
| United Kingdom | ◔ | ◔ | ◔ | ◔ | ● | ↗ | ↘ |
| Canada | ◔ | ◔ | ◔ | ◔ | ◔ | — | ↘ |
| Japan | ◔ | ◔ | ◔ | ◔ | ◔ | — | ↘ |
| Mexico | ◔ | ◔ | ◔ | ◔ | ◔ | ↗ | — |
| Russia | ◔ | ◔ | ◔ | ◔ | ◔ | ↗ | — |
| France | ◔ | ◔ | ◔ | ◔ | ◔ | ↗ | ↘ |
| Italy | ◔ | ◔ | ◔ | ◔ | ◔ | ↗ | ↘ |
| United States | ◔ | ◔ | ◔ | ◔ | ◔ | ↘ | ↘ |

**Policy Responses to Capital Flows—Selected Economies[7]**

| | Capital flows[8] | Over- heating | FX over- valuation[9] | Macroprudential Domestic | Macroprudential Currency- related | Macroprudential Capital controls |
|---|---|---|---|---|---|---|
| Indonesia | ● | ◔ | ◔ | ✓ | ✓ | |
| Thailand[10] | ● | ◔ | ◔ | ✓ | | ✓ |
| Brazil | ● | ● | ● | ✓ | ✓ | ✓ |
| Colombia | ● | ◔ | ● | ✓ | ✓ | |
| Malaysia | ● | ◔ | ◔ | ✓ | | |
| Mexico | ● | ◔ | ◔ | ✓ | | |
| India | ● | ● | ◔ | ✓ | | |
| Poland | ● | ◔ | ◔ | ✓ | | |
| Chile | ◔ | ◔ | ◔ | | | |
| Peru | ◔ | ◔ | ◔ | ✓ | ✓ | ✓ |
| South Africa[10] | ◔ | ◔ | ● | | | |
| Hong Kong SAR | ◔ | ◔ | ◔ | ✓ | | |
| Turkey | ◔ | ◔ | ● | ✓ | | |
| China | ◔ | ◔ | ◔ | ✓ | | |
| Philippines[10] | ◔ | ◔ | ◔ | ✓ | | |
| Israel | ◔ | ◔ | ◔ | | | |
| Romania | ◔ | ◔ | ◔ | | ✓ | |
| Russia | ◔ | ◔ | ◔ | | ✓ | ✓ |
| Czech Republic | ◔ | ◔ | ◔ | | | |
| Korea | ◔ | ◔ | ◔ | ✓ | ✓ | |
| Argentina | ◔ | ● | ◔ | ✓ | ✓ | |
| Hungary | ◔ | ◔ | ◔ | | | ✓ |

Sources: Haver Analytics; and IMF staff calculations.

[1]For each indicator, except inflation, economies are assigned "traffic lights" based on where they stand relative to other G20 economies. For inflation, economies with an inflation-targeting regime are assigned a red light if inflation is above the upper bound of their target and a yellow light if inflation is in the upper half of the target range; for nontargeters, a red light denotes historically high inflation, and a yellow light denotes rising inflation (above historically moderate levels). Individual indicators vary for idiosyncratic reasons (e.g., South Africa has a red light for unemployment because the rate is currently lower than precrisis levels, even though unemployment is still above 20 percent). For this reason, a summary column is included, which shows the average across individual indicators; economies are ranked according to this average.

[2]Output above the precrisis trend is indicated by a red light. Output less than 95 percent of the trend is indicated by a green light.

[3]An output gap above zero is indicated by a red light. A gap below 2 percent is indicated by a green light.

[4]The unemployment indicator is based on a comparison of current unemployment levels to average precrisis levels during 2002–07.

[5]Arrows in the fiscal balance column represent the forecast change in the structural balance as a percent of GDP over the period 2010–11. An increase of more than 0.5 percent of GDP is indicated by an up arrow; a decrease of more than 0.5 percent of GDP is indicated by a down arrow.

[6]Real policy interest rates below zero are identified by a down arrow; real interest rates above 3 percent are identified by an up arrow.

[7]For the purposes of this figure, policy responses are divided into three categories: (1) domestically focused macroprudential measures are those affecting the domestic activities of banks, such as loan-to-valuation ratio limits; (2) currency-related measures aim to limit institutions' and residents' exposure to currency fluctuations; and (3) capital controls are measures that distinguish between residents and nonresidents.

[8]Gross capital flows over the past year compared with the average during 2000–07. Current flows above 150 percent of the average are assigned a red light; a yellow light denotes flows above 100 percent. Economies are ranked based on this ratio.

[9]Economies with exchange rates higher than warranted by medium-term fundamentals are assigned a red light. Economies with lower-than-warranted exchange rates are assigned a green light. FX = foreign exchange.

[10]Has relaxed capital outflow restrictions.

the kind of credit boom that inevitably ends with a bust. Evidence is not reassuring in this regard.

• Credit and asset price behavior is disconcerting in China and Hong Kong SAR, showing boom-like dimensions (Figure 1.16, middle and bottom panels).[15] In both economies, the authorities have

adopted various macroprudential measures to rein in excesses and stand ready to do more. In the case of China, the authorities have managed credit, increased reserve requirements, and raised interest rates several times. Nonetheless, in both economies credit growth remains high compared with the run-ups to previous credit booms and busts, and there

[15]To identify a "credit boom," real credit and credit-to-GDP ratios are detrended with the help of a Hodrick-Prescott filter, in line with the methods adopted by Mendoza and Terrones (2008) and Gourinchas, Valdés, and Landerretche (2001). A credit boom

exists when the cyclical component of credit exceeds the average historical cyclical component by 1.75 times the standard deviations of the credit variable.

are mounting concerns about the potential for steep corrections in property prices and their implications.

- Brazil, Colombia, India, Indonesia, and Turkey have experienced a noticeable pickup in real credit growth, generally close to or well into a 10 to 20 percent range (more in the case of Turkey). Over the past five years, credit almost doubled in real per capita terms in these economies. Such expansions are close to those experienced before previous credit booms and busts (see Figure 1.16, middle and bottom panels).[16] Other telltale signs of an emerging credit boom include accelerating inflation and rapid increases in the prices of property. In India, credit growth has just begun to increase again, after a boom through much of 2007 was followed by a sharp slowdown during 2008–09. Nonetheless, from a five-year perspective, per capita real credit growth has been very buoyant, with much flowing into real estate and large infrastructure projects. Similar considerations apply to Peru, where credit is also generated outside the banking system.[17]

- Conditions are less buoyant in Malaysia and Singapore. Real credit growth in these economies has exceeded 10 percent on only a few occasions over the past five years. Both raw and cyclically adjusted credit indicators suggest that conditions do not match those seen just ahead of previous busts. However, their real exchange rates have appreciated significantly and asset markets have boomed.

## Macroeconomic and Prudential Policies Need to Tighten

There is a risk that these boom-like conditions may intensify over the coming year. Inflation pressure is likely to build further in response to growing capacity constraints, with large food and energy price increases—which weigh heavily in consumption baskets—motivating demands for higher wages.

[16]The increase in credit has been ongoing for some time. Because the detrending methods cited previously remove much of this increase, these countries do not meet the necessary criteria under a strict definition of a credit boom.

[17]In Nigeria, a number of banks were found to be insolvent or undercapitalized in 2009, following a credit boom in the preceding years.

**Figure 1.16. Emerging Market Economies with Strong Credit Expansion[1]**

A number of major emerging market economies (EMEs) and a few advanced economies with close links to these economies feature very buoyant credit and asset price growth. The EMEs with such conditions account for about one-quarter of global GDP in purchasing-power-parity terms, or about half of EME output. Furthermore, these economies have been experiencing relatively strong credit growth for a number of years, raising concerns about the quality of this credit.

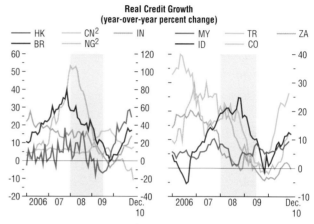

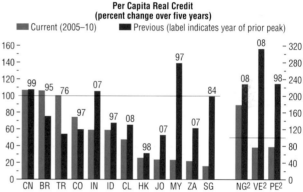

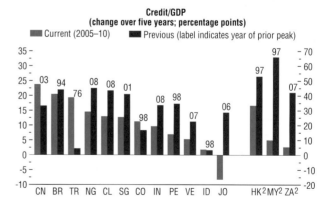

Sources: IMF, *International Financial Statistics;* and IMF staff calculations.
[1]BR: Brazil; CL: Chile; CN: China; CO: Colombia; HK: Hong Kong SAR; ID: Indonesia; IN: India; JO: Jordan; MY: Malaysia; NG: Nigeria; PE: Peru; SG: Singapore; TR: Turkey; VE: Venezuela; ZA: South Africa.
[2]Right scale.

Real interest rates are still low. Fiscal policies are still much more accommodative than before the crisis, and public expenditures may rise on account of greater outlays for food subsidies. Households are becoming increasingly leveraged, with rapid consumer credit growth adding to rapid mortgage credit growth. And demand for exports is likely to pick up as durables consumption and investment in advanced economies recover further.

### Food and energy prices pose significant risks of second-round effects

The risk that food and energy price increases will start an inflationary spiral is much greater in emerging and developing economies than in advanced economies. Households typically spend large shares of their incomes on food and energy (Figure 1.14, middle panel). In addition, excess capacity has generally been eroded or is eroding fast, and monetary authorities are, to varying degrees, still building their credibility. Food price shocks have had an especially severe impact on the poor, exerting political pressure for wage hikes and a more accommodative fiscal policy stance—this should be met with well-targeted social support programs. Furthermore, oil prices may well continue to surprise on the upside.

### Policy interest rates appear too low

In many emerging market economies, monetary conditions appear very accommodative (Figure 1.11, middle panel). A number of these economies have already hiked policy rates (for example, Brazil, China, India, Indonesia, Malaysia, Peru, Poland, Russia, Thailand, Uruguay), increased cash reserve requirements (for example, China, India, Indonesia, Russia, Turkey), or restrained credit growth (for example, China). However, real interest rates remain far below precrisis levels in many of these economies, and the extent of expected tightening seems limited relative to what is needed (Figure 1.11, bottom panel).

### Fiscal policy seems too accommodative, given the strength of activity

Although rising commodity and asset prices have given government revenues an unexpected boost, current projections are for a limited decline in budget deficits of emerging and developing economies, by about 1½ percentage points of GDP in 2011 (Figure 1.12, top panel) and ½ percentage point in 2012. The deficit would still reach about 1 percent of GDP in 2012, even though output growth is expected to be above precrisis trend. During 2006–08, in contrast, budgets in these economies were in surplus. Although robust output growth is expected to lower the debt-to-GDP ratio, a number of emerging market economies with high public debt should take advantage of strong activity and terms-of-trade-related revenues to rebuild fiscal room for policy maneuvering.

### Policies need to tighten to varying degrees

Many emerging market economies will need to tighten policies to lower the risk of a hard landing. Requirements differ according to cyclical and external positions, and Chapter 2 presents more detailed assessments for the various regions. In most economies, further removal of monetary accommodation appears indispensable, as does prudential tightening to rein in rapid growth in real estate and some other sectors. Economies with high public debt should take advantage of strong cyclical conditions to improve their public balance sheets (for example, Brazil, India). Furthermore, in most economies, some appreciation of the exchange rate is called for because of either cyclically large current account surpluses (for example, China), terms-of-trade improvements, or greater resilience to shocks. In short, policies required to achieve internal and external balance go in broadly the same direction.

A number of emerging market economies have seen a historically sharp turnaround in capital flows following the crisis. Once U.S. policy tightening begins, flows could slow abruptly. This is an additional reason for emerging market economies to ensure that their domestic policies are suitably countercyclical and that banking regulation and supervision are well targeted. Provided appropriate macroeconomic and prudential policies are in place, capital controls can be helpful in limiting damage caused by volatile capital flows. In fact, when inflows bypass regulated financial institutions and lead to vulnerability on nonfinancial entities' balance sheets (for example, in the case of direct borrowing from abroad), capital controls may be the only instrument available to the authorities in the short term. However, the effectiveness of capital controls beyond the short term remains in question, and their benefits should be weighed against likely costs, including multilateral disruptions. As Chapter 4 argues, over the medium term, deeper and better supervised and regulated financial and product markets are critical for containing vulnerabilities related to volatile capital flows.

In economies where real exchange rate overshooting relative to medium-term fundamentals exceeds what can be justified by their cyclically more advanced positions posing serious concerns, and where further accumulation of reserves seems undesirable, measures to curb capital inflows can complement macroeconomic and prudential policies. However, policymakers need to bear in mind that such measures are not substitutes for general macroeconomic tightening. A reading of what emerging market economies have done recently suggests that recourse to capital controls has been limited; where they have been adopted, fiscal policy has often been tightened, but sometimes not by enough to control growing pressure on real interest rates and capacity constraints (see Figure 1.15).

## Global Demand Rebalancing Is Not Progressing

Previous issues of the *World Economic Outlook* underscored the importance of global demand rebalancing for sustained, healthy recovery, with an increase in net exports in deficit economies and a decrease in net exports in surplus economies, notably in emerging Asia. The two interact in strong ways, as increased net exports in advanced economies offset the loss of demand implied by fiscal consolidation. Capital flows are spurring the reallocation of global demand toward emerging market economies. However, a disproportionate burden of demand rebalancing since the beginning of the crisis has been borne by economies that do not have large current account surpluses but attract flows because of the openness

### Figure 1.17.  Global Imbalances

Global imbalances are projected to widen again over the medium term because domestic demand growth in economies with large surpluses is not expected to be higher than before the crisis. Demand growth in deficit economies is not expected to be much lower, as significant fiscal adjustment has yet to be specified. Reserve accumulation in economies with excessive current account surpluses has dwarfed private capital inflows, motivated primarily by concerns about competitiveness. Exchange rates of emerging economies with deficits have appreciated disproportionately. The IMF staff's assessment of the valuation of real exchange rates has remained broadly unchanged relative to October 2010, with the U.S. dollar strong and Asian currencies (other than the yen) undervalued relative to medium-term fundamentals.

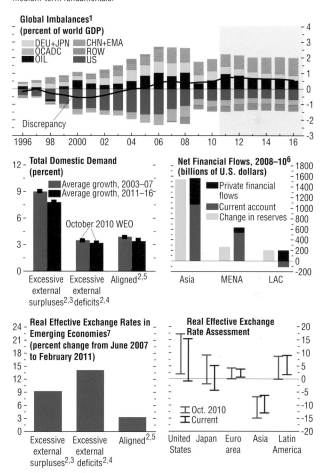

Sources: Federal Reserve; and IMF staff estimates.
[1]CHN+EMA: China, Hong Kong SAR, Indonesia, Korea, Malaysia, Philippines, Singapore, Taiwan Province of China, and Thailand; DEU+JPN: Germany and Japan; OCADC: Bulgaria, Croatia, Czech Republic, Estonia, Greece, Hungary, Ireland, Latvia, Lithuania, Poland, Portugal, Romania, Slovak Republic, Slovenia, Spain, Turkey, and United Kingdom; OIL: oil exporters; ROW: rest of the world; US: United States.
[2]Based on the IMF staff's Consultative Group on Exchange Rate Issues (CGER). CGER countries include Argentina, Australia, Brazil, Canada, Chile, China, Colombia, Czech Republic, euro area, Hungary, India, Indonesia, Israel, Japan, Korea, Malaysia, Mexico, Pakistan, Poland, Russia, South Africa, Sweden, Switzerland, Thailand, Turkey, United Kingdom, and United States. For a detailed discussion of the methodology for the calculation of exchange rates' over- or undervaluation, see Lee and others (2008).
[3]These economies account for 18.5 percent of global GDP.
[4]These economies account for 27.4 percent of global GDP.
[5]These economies account for 39.2 percent of global GDP.
[6]Asia: developing Asia; MENA: Middle East and North Africa; LAC: Latin America and the Caribbean.
[7]Emerging CGER economies only.

### Figure 1.18.  External Developments

*(Index, 2000 = 100; three-month moving average unless noted otherwise)*

After depreciating significantly, the euro has regained some strength lately, while the U.S. dollar weakened modestly. The yen has continued to appreciate while the renminbi has moved broadly sideways in real effective terms. Currencies of most other emerging economies have tended to appreciate. International reserves are now higher than before the crisis in all emerging and developing economy regions.

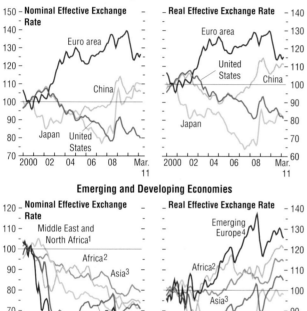

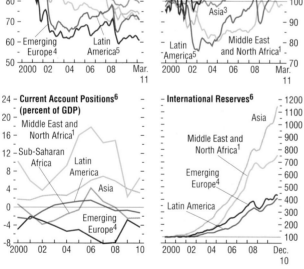

Sources: IMF, *International Financial Statistics;* and IMF staff calculations.

[1]Bahrain, Djibouti, Egypt, Islamic Republic of Iran, Jordan, Kuwait, Lebanon, Libya, Oman, Qatar, Saudi Arabia, Sudan, Syrian Arab Republic, United Arab Emirates, and Republic of Yemen.

[2]Botswana, Burkina Faso, Cameroon, Chad, Republic of Congo, Côte d'Ivoire, Equatorial Guinea, Ethiopia, Gabon, Ghana, Guinea, Kenya, Madagascar, Mali, Mauritius, Mozambique, Namibia, Niger, Nigeria, Rwanda, Senegal, South Africa, Tanzania, Uganda, and Zambia.

[3]Asia excluding China.

[4]Bulgaria, Croatia, Hungary, Latvia, Lithuania, Poland, Romania, and Turkey.

[5]Argentina, Brazil, Chile, Colombia, Mexico, Peru, and Venezuela.

[6]Regional groupings follow WEO classifications.

and depth of their capital markets (Figure 1.17, bottom panel).

Current account balances of key surplus economies—for example, China, Japan, and oil exporters—have receded, as have those of deficit economies—for example, the United States, Spain, and eastern Europe (Figure 1.17, top panel). However, this has taken place mainly via declining demand growth in deficit economies rather than stronger demand growth in surplus economies.[18] It reflects both structural factors (for example, lowered expectations about future incomes in deficit economies; the appreciation of the yen) and cyclical factors (for example, the depressed state of demand for investment goods and consumer durables in deficit economies and lower prices for commodity-exporting surplus economies). Although temporary fiscal stimulus in China and other surplus economies has helped, sustained, positive rebalancing—accelerated domestic demand in surplus economies relative to precrisis trends—has played only a modest role (Figure 1.17, middle panel). Since publication of the October 2010 *World Economic Outlook*, external surplus economies have made little additional progress in rebalancing demand.

There has been significant realignment of real effective exchange rates among advanced economies relative to precrisis levels but only limited realignment in emerging market economies with large surpluses (Figure 1.18). This has created tensions. Emerging market economies with flexible exchange rates, open capital accounts, and relatively deep markets have seen large capital inflows that have pushed up their exchange rates, in some cases into overvaluation territory (for example, Latin America). Others with managed exchange rates (for example, most of emerging Asia) are reluctant to allow revaluation as long as systemic surplus economies are not moving decisively.

- Among advanced economies, the appreciation of the yen and the depreciation of sterling by more than 20 percent in real effective terms are most noteworthy. Official intervention recently helped stabilize the yen at about pre-earthquake levels,

[18]History suggests that levels of imports of countries hit by crises tend to stay below precrisis trends for a long time (see Chapter 4 of the October 2010 *World Economic Outlook*).

following an abrupt and unwarranted apprecia-tion. The euro has depreciated by roughly 10 per-cent. All three currencies are now broadly in line with medium-term fundamentals. The U.S. dollar is about 5 percent below its 2007 level yet still remains somewhat high relative to its fundamen-tals (Figure 1.17, bottom panel).

- Among emerging market surplus currencies, the renminbi and the currencies of other Asian sur-plus economies (for example, Malaysia, Singapore, Thailand) have appreciated by 5 to 10 percent. Nonetheless, Asian currencies are weak relative to medium-term fundamentals (Figure 1.17, bottom panel). The currency of China still appears sub-stantially weaker than warranted by medium-term fundamentals; the Korean won, which depreci-ated by some 25 percent during the crisis, is also weaker than warranted.

- A few emerging market economies are bearing a disproportionate share of global demand rebalanc-ing. This may reflect their more flexible exchange rates and more open capital accounts than their peers in Asia. Latin American currencies have typically appreciated in real effective terms, as have the currencies of other emerging market economies (see Figure 1.18, middle and bottom panels)—this has raised competitiveness concerns, for example, in Brazil, Colombia, South Africa, and Turkey.

Accumulation of official foreign exchange reserves in the major surplus economies presents an important obstacle to global demand rebalancing. During 2008–10, surplus economies in Asia—mostly China—used inflows on current and private capital accounts to accumulate reserves (see Figure 1.17, middle panel). Although these economies understandably want to have an adequate buffer against the volatility of capital flows, a key motiva-tion for the acquisition of foreign exchange reserves seems to be to prevent nominal exchange rate appreciation and preserve competitiveness. In some economies, this is delaying required internal adjust-ments, contributing to excessively rapid credit growth and asset price booms; in others, steriliza-tion presents a growing budgetary burden, without having much effect on the fundamental drivers of capital flows.

A pessimistic reading of developments in global imbalances and their role in further recovery is confirmed by the latest developments and WEO projections. Global current account imbalances are projected to remain wide (Figure 1.17, top panel). Specifically, projections foresee no domestic demand acceleration relative to precrisis trends in Asian economies with excessive current account surpluses. Savings-investment projections tell a similar story (Table A16 in the Statistical Appendix). Consistent with a soft landing, saving rates in developing Asia are projected to rise by about 1¼ percentage points of GDP through 2016, while investment rates move broadly sideways—similar to projections in the October 2010 *World Economic Outlook*. As a share of global GDP, savings in developing Asia would rise noticeably, exceeding precrisis levels sometime around 2013. Moreover, as discussed in Box 1.2, if conditions in Asia are already more overheated than is captured in the WEO projections, global imbal-ances could again widen appreciably unless exchange rates are allowed to appreciate.

Emerging market surplus economies remain hesi-tant about allowing their exchange rates to appreci-ate. Some point to the experience of Japan following the Plaza Agreement as cause for concern about such a strategy. However, a reading of this experience and that of others suggests that rebalancing away from foreign demand need not come at the expense of strong growth.[19] The conditions facing Japan were in many ways unique, and the bad post-Plaza outcome was due largely to a credit bubble that developed after exceptional policy stimulus was combined with financial sector deregulation. When the bubble burst, exposing underlying vulnerabilities, political economy constraints meant that restructuring pro-gressed too slowly (Box 1.4). The Japanese experi-ence thus underlines the importance of prompt corrective policy actions in emerging market as well as advanced economies.

In sum, global demand rebalancing remains a major concern for the sustainability of the recovery over the medium term. Activity in the United States may firm up during 2011. Little real exchange rate appreciation may be boosting activity in China,

---

[19]See Chapter 4 of the April 2010 *World Economic Outlook*.

## Figure 1.19. Unemployment[1]

Unemployment remains above precrisis levels in many economies, including the United States. Globally, unemployment is expected to average about 6 percent this year, with rates ranging from 4 percent in east Asia to 10 percent in the Middle East. Unemployment rates are projected to be lower in regions where growth was higher last year. Youth unemployment remains high, at 25 percent in the Middle East and between 15 and 20 percent elsewhere. Employment-to-population ratios are low in many regions suggesting that many people are being forced into the informal sector.

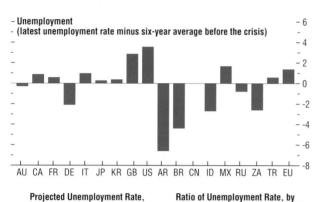

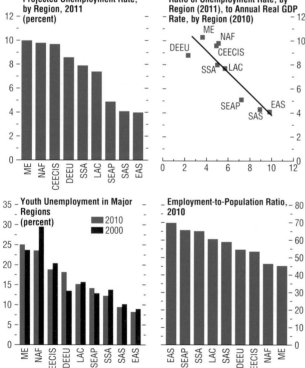

Sources: Haver Analytics; International Labor Organization; and IMF staff estimates.
[1]AR: Argentina; AU: Australia; BR: Brazil; CA: Canada; CEECIS: central and southeastern Europe (non-EU) and Commonwealth of Independent States; CN: China; DE: Germany; DEEU: developed economies and European Union; EAS: east Asia; EU: euro area; FR: France; GB: United Kingdom; ID: Indonesia; IT: Italy; JP: Japan; KR: Korea; LAC: Latin America and the Caribbean; ME: Middle East; MX: Mexico; NAF: north Africa; RU: Russia; SAS: south Asia; SEAP: southeast Asia and the Pacific; SSA: sub-Saharan Africa; TR: Turkey; US: United States; ZA: South Africa.

while fundamental reforms to boost consumption are being put in place. But unless fiscal adjustment soon starts in earnest in the United States, the exchange rate of the renminbi becomes more market-determined, currencies of other emerging surplus economies appreciate, and various European and emerging economies implement ambitious structural reforms, little progress will be made with respect to global demand rebalancing, and the recovery will stand on increasingly hollow legs over the medium term.[20]

## Unemployment Needs to Be Reduced

Unemployment poses grave economic and social challenges, which are being amplified in emerging and developing economies by high food prices (Figure 1.19). The young face particular difficulties. Historically, for Organization for Economic Cooperation and Development countries the unemployment rate for young people ages 15 to 24 has been about two and a half times the rate for other groups. Though youth unemployment typically increases sharply during recessions, the increase this time was greater than in the past: in a set of eight countries for which long time-series of youth unemployment are available, the increase averaged 6½ percentage points during the Great Recession, compared with 4 percentage points in previous recessions.

The three lines of defense against unemployment are supportive macroeconomic policies, financial sector repair, and specific labor market measures. Monetary policy is expected to stay easy in advanced economies. However, there is an urgent need to accelerate bank restructuring and recapitalization to relaunch credit to small and medium-size firms, which account for the bulk of employment. Temporary employment subsidies targeted at these firms could help restart hiring. Such programs may subsidize the hiring of many workers who would have found jobs anyway or cause replacement of those currently employed with the targeted group of unemployed.[21] However, to the extent that subsidies flow to small and medium-size firms, they may at

[20]For a full-fledged scenario to illustrate the benefits of joint policy action along these lines, see Group of Twenty (2010).
[21]See Chapter 3 of the April 2010 *World Economic Outlook*.

least help alleviate the effects of still-tight bank lending conditions. Where unemployment has increased for structural reasons or where it was high even before the crisis, broader labor and product market reforms are essential to create more jobs.

The high and increasing burden of unemployment on young people poses risks to social cohesion.[22] Youth unemployment tends to be high in economies with labor markets that offer strong job protection to experienced workers, feature high minimum wages, and offer insufficient apprenticeship programs and vocational training. In many emerging and developing economies, strong job protection in the formal sector pushes employment, especially of the young, into the informal sector. The right policy response is to find a middle ground—through appropriate product and labor market regulation—between the protected/formal and unprotected/informal segments of the labor market. Spain, for example, has initiated reforms in this direction. Lowering the fixed costs of employment supports hiring in times of high uncertainty. In addition, strong apprenticeship programs are needed for those who cannot attend university.

## Policies Are Not Yet Sufficiently Proactive

Many old policy challenges remain unaddressed, while new ones come to the fore. Old challenges that continue to loom large include repairing and reforming financial sectors; specifying medium-term fiscal adjustment plans and entitlement reform in advanced economies; and implementing exchange rate and structural policies that foster global demand rebalancing in emerging market economies with large external surpluses. The main new challenges relate to disruptions to the supply of commodities and growing macroeconomic and financial risks in key emerging market economies. In the meantime, unemployment is very high in many advanced and a number of

emerging market economies. Addressing the various macroeconomic and financial policy challenges is essential for stronger output and employment growth.

Advanced economies urgently need to make more progress in addressing medium-term problems. High on the priority list are financial repair and reforms and medium-term fiscal adjustment. Financial sector measures hold the key to more rapid macroeconomic policy normalization, which would help guard against the buildup of new imbalances, including in emerging market economies. In general, more certainty about policy prospects could help support the recovery of investment and employment while anchoring financial markets.

Many emerging and developing economies appear to have enjoyed a large improvement in output-inflation performance over the past decade, akin to what has been termed the "Great Moderation" in advanced economies. The challenge for emerging and some developing economies is to ensure that this "real" moderation is not harmed by rising food and commodity prices and growing financial excesses. With changes in monetary or fiscal stances affecting the economy only with appreciable lags, the time for policymakers to act is now, lest another boom-bust cycle develop. Appropriate action differs across economies, depending on their cyclical and external conditions. However, a tightening of macroeconomic policies is needed in many economies. In emerging economies with large external surpluses, exchange rate appreciation is necessary to maintain internal balance—reining in inflation pressure and excessive credit growth—and assist in global demand rebalancing. Prudential tools and capital controls can play a useful complementary role but should not serve as substitutes for macroeconomic tightening. Social policies need to offer the poor sufficient protection from high food prices.

Greater progress in advancing global demand rebalancing is essential to put the recovery on a stronger footing over the medium term. This will require actions by many, notably fiscal adjustment in key external deficit economies and greater exchange rate flexibility and structural reforms that eliminate distortions that boost saving in key surplus economies.

The broad contours of the macroeconomic policy response sketched here were very well received at the G20 meeting in Seoul in November 2010. However,

---

[22]Surveys conducted in the United States from 1972 to 2006 found that individuals who have lived through a recession during the formative years between 18 and 25 tend to believe less in personal effort, perceive stronger inequalities, and have less confidence in public institutions (see Giuliano and Spilimbergo, 2009). There is also evidence that the adverse effects on lifetime earnings are most pronounced for those who are unemployed when they are 18 to 25 years old (see Kahn, 2010).

with the peak of the crisis behind policymakers, the imperative for action and willingness to cooperate are diminishing. It would be a mistake for advanced economies to delay fiscal adjustment until emerging market surplus economies remove distortions that are holding back global demand rebalancing. While the removal of distortions that boost saving in key emerging external surplus economies would help support growth and achieve fiscal consolidation in key advanced economies, insufficient progress on this front should not serve as an excuse for fiscal inaction. Furthermore, many emerging market economies cannot afford to wait until advanced economies tighten their policies before proceeding to enact substantial tightening themselves. The task facing policymakers is to convince their national constituencies that these policies are in their best economic interests, regardless of what others are doing.

Policymakers will need to ensure that adjustment and structural reform do not hollow out support for globalization. On the one hand, it is reassuring that economies eschewed protectionism during the Great Recession. On the other hand, it is disconcerting that support for open markets seems to be waning, as evidenced, for example, by disappointing progress in the Doha Round. Open trade has been a strong engine of growth. If the design of expenditure and taxation policies and structural reforms does not foster popular support for globalization, there is a risk that activity in advanced and emerging as well as developing economies will settle on a much lower growth path than during the decade preceding the crisis. Policymakers will thus need to pay greater attention than ever to the impact of adjustment on income distribution.

## Appendix 1.1. Financial Conditions Indices

*The author of this appendix is Troy Matheson.*

Financial Conditions Indices (FCIs) have recently been developed for the United States and the euro area for use in assessing current financial conditions and how they may evolve over the medium term.[23] This appendix discusses the methodology and indicators used to develop the FCIs, provides a brief

description of how the FCIs are forecast, and assesses historical FCI-based output gap forecasts.

FCIs can be broadly considered as a weighted average of various indicators of financial conditions. They are standardized to have a zero mean and a standard deviation of 1—positive values represent a tightening of financial conditions and negative values represent an easing. One useful feature of the FCIs is that they can be decomposed into contributions from each of the indicators that went into their construction. Figure 1.20 shows FCIs for the United States and the euro area, along with total contributions from three types of indicators: spreads (interest rates, interest spreads, yield curves), prices (exchange rates, prices), and quantities (money, credit, bank lending surveys).

### Estimating FCIs

The FCIs are estimated using a dynamic factor model (DFM).[24] The DFM assumes that each standardized indicator of financial conditions, $y_t$, can be decomposed into a common component, $\chi_t$, and an idiosyncratic component, $\varepsilon_t$. The common component captures the bulk of the covariation between $y_t$ and the other indicators in the data set, whereas the idiosyncratic component is assumed mainly to affect only $y_t$:

$$y_t = \chi_t + \varepsilon_t, \text{ where } \varepsilon_t \sim N(0, \psi), \quad \text{(A.1.1.1)}$$

where $\chi_t = \lambda F_t$. The common component is thus simply a scaled common factor, $F_t$, which is estimated using the entire set of financial indicators. The FCI is defined to be this common factor.

The dynamics of the FCI are captured by an autoregressive process:

$$F_t = \Sigma_{i=1}^{p} \beta_i F_{t-i} + \nu_t, \text{ where } \nu_t \sim N(0, 1), \quad \text{(A.1.1.2)}$$

where the $\beta_i$s are coefficients and $p$ is the lag length of the process. The lag length, $p$, is selected using the Swartz-Bayesian information criteria (SBIC).

---

[23]Swiston (2008) developed an FCI for the United States using a different methodology from the one used here.

[24]See Giannone, Reichlin, and Small (2008); Matheson (2010, 2011); and Liu, Romeu, and Matheson (forthcoming). The detailed assumptions underlying the model and its estimation with the Kalman filter can be found in Giannone, Reichlin, and Sala (2005).

A key advantage of this framework is that FCIs can be estimated when values for some indicators are missing due to publication lags, which allows all available information to be used in a timely fashion.

### Data Description

For each country, selecting data from a broad set of financial indicators is a crucial step. Most series are measured at a monthly frequency, with the remainder measured at daily or quarterly frequencies. Before estimation, all series are converted to monthly frequency, transformed to be free of long-term trends (nonstationarity), if necessary, and standardized.[25] The sample period for the FCIs used here begins in 1994. Indicators that are not available for the entire period, such as survey data for the euro area, are backdated using the DFM. In practice, the FCIs are forecast to the end of the quarter for which the most recent financial indicators are available.

The indicators used in each country's FCI and information about how the indicators are classified and transformed are available online (www.imf.org/weoforum). The online tables also include estimated factor loadings, $\chi$, which reflect the weight of each indicator. Each loading can take a positive or negative value, depending on whether a high or low value of the indicator in question implies a tightening or an easing in financial conditions. The Senior Loan Officer Survey (SLOS) data (for which a positive number indicates a tightening of financial conditions) generally have high positive factor loadings. Some of the indicators in the "spreads" category also have high factor loadings, such as the BAA/10-year government bond spread in the United States and the high-yield corporate/10-year government bond spread in the euro area. Negative loadings generally predominate in the "prices" categories, reflecting a tendency for prices to rise when financial conditions ease.

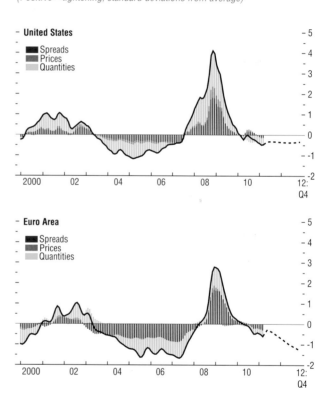

**Figure 1.20.  Financial Conditions Indices[1]**
*(Positive = tightening; standard deviations from average)*

Sources: Haver Analytics; and IMF staff calculations.
[1]Historical data are monthly, and forecasts (dashed lines) are quarterly.

---

[25]The quarterly series are interpolated, whereas the daily series are converted to monthly averages. Quarterly log differences are taken of the nonstationary indicators. The remaining indicators are not transformed.

## Forecasting Financial Conditions

To forecast the FCIs, we adopt the following baseline closed economy quarterly vector-autoregressive model (VAR):

$$\begin{bmatrix} Y_t \\ \pi_t \\ r_t \end{bmatrix} = \Sigma_{i=1}^{k} \begin{bmatrix} A_{Y,Y,i} & A_{Y,\pi,i} & A_{Y,r,i} \\ A_{\pi,Y,i} & A_{\pi,\pi,i} & A_{\pi,r,i} \\ A_{r,Y,i} & A_{r,\pi,i} & A_{r,r,i} \end{bmatrix} \begin{bmatrix} Y_{t-i} \\ \pi_{t-i} \\ r_{t-i} \end{bmatrix} + \begin{bmatrix} \mu_{Y,t} \\ \mu_{\pi,t} \\ \mu_{r,t} \end{bmatrix}, \tag{A.1.1.3}$$

where $Y_t$ is the output gap, $\pi_t$ is headline inflation, and $r_t$ is a short-term real interest rate ($A$s are coefficients, $\mu$s are residuals, and the lag length of the process is $k$).[26]

For each country, the FCI is added to this baseline VAR, and FCI forecasts are made conditional on the projected paths for the other variables. Specifically, given forecasts for the output gap, inflation, and real interest rates,[27] the augmented VAR is essentially used to "back out" the implied FCI forecast.

## Forecasting Performance

An out-of-sample forecast evaluation exercise is conducted for the period from the first quarter of 2004 to the present to gauge the reliability of the FCI forecasts. The FCI is estimated once every quarter using all data that would have been available at the beginning of the third month of each quarter.[28] All variables are forecast using the VAR (with no conditioning information). Using the latest available estimates of the output gap as the target for the forecasts, root mean squared errors (RMSEs) are computed for forecasts two and four quarters ahead of the real GDP data that would have been available at the time.

For comparison purposes, RMSEs are also computed for a variety of other forecasts: an autoregres-

sive forecast (AR); a forecast from the baseline VAR, without the FCI; and forecasts from the baseline VAR augmented with each of the underlying indicators separately.[29] The RMSEs for each model relative to those of the AR are displayed in the right panels of the tables; a number less than 1 indicates that the forecast is more accurate than the AR forecast.

For both the United States and the euro area, the forecasting performance of the VAR augmented with the FCI is good relative to the other models. The FCI forecast outperforms the AR and all other VAR forecasts for the United States. For the euro area, the FCI forecast is at least as accurate as almost all other models, with the VAR augmented with an indicator from the SLOS the only exception.

## Appendix 1.2. Commodity Market Developments and Prospects

*The authors of this appendix are Thomas Helbling, Shaun Roache, and Joong Shik Kang. Nese Erbil, Marina Rousset, and David Reichsfeld provided research assistance.*

### Overview of Recent Developments and Prospects

Prices of all major commodities have risen strongly since mid-2010, rather than broadly stabilizing as expected at the time of the October 2010 *World Economic Outlook*. The overall IMF commodity price index rose by 32 percent between June 2010 and February 2011. The price index has now recovered more than half the decline from the cyclical peak in July 2008 and remains high in real terms. Food price gains were particularly prominent in the second half of 2010, while oil supply risks have taken center stage with the unrest in the Middle East and North Africa (MENA) since late January 2011.

The spread of unrest to oil exporters in the MENA region has raised oil supply risks and led to some small oil supply disruptions, as output losses in Libya have largely been offset by higher production in Saudi Arabia and other producers in the Persian

---

[26]Inflation and the real interest rate are de-meaned prior to estimation.

[27]These are taken from a much larger, more sophisticated model—the Global Projection Model, GPM (Carabenciov and others, forthcoming).

[28]Due to a lack of available data, the data vintages that would have existed in real time are not used. Instead, the most recent vintage of data is used to simulate the data available each time a forecast is made. Real-time output gaps and short-term real interest rates are simply truncated from the most recent GPM estimates.

[29]In each quarter, all VARs and ARs are reestimated, and all lag lengths are reselected using the SBIC.

Gulf. In response to this shock, oil prices rose from about $95 a barrel in late January to $110 in early March, partly reflecting increases in desired inventories for precautionary reasons.

Beyond this so far mild oil supply shock, however, much of the unexpected commodity price strength since mid-2010 has reflected easing fears of a double dip due to financial stress in the euro area and cyclical momentum, given steady upward revisions to global economic growth last year (Figure 1.21, top panels). Commodity-intensive emerging economies, including China, remain important contributors to demand growth, but consumption, particularly of energy, has also recovered rapidly in advanced economies. In some cases, demand growth has been stronger than expected, given past relationships between economic growth and commodity consumption, which highlight the uncertainty caused by structural changes in commodity markets due to fast, commodity-intensive growth in emerging market economies. The supply response to stronger-than-anticipated demand has as usual been limited, as reflected in low short-term supply price elasticities. As a result, market equilibrium was achieved with unexpectedly large draws on inventories for many commodities. Tightening in physical commodity markets is evident in the flattening of futures curves and, in some cases including oil and copper, a shift into backwardation (Figure 1.21, middle panels).

Weather-related supply shocks were important in food markets in the second half of 2010. Specifically, adverse weather conditions during 2010 led to harvest shortfalls in wheat (Russia, Ukraine), rice, rubber, cotton, and local vegetables (south and southeast Asia), corn (United States), and sugar (India). One of the strongest La Niña weather events in 50 years contributed to some of these conditions, particularly in Asia. Demand remained robust, partly reflecting a sharp rebound in biofuel production. The price responses to supply setbacks were exacerbated by trade restrictions (for example, grain export bans in Russia and grain export quotas in Ukraine in 2010). All of these developments delayed restocking and kept inventories for some important crops very low.

Monetary policy developments and improving financial conditions also contributed to higher commodity

**Figure 1.21. Commodity Prices**

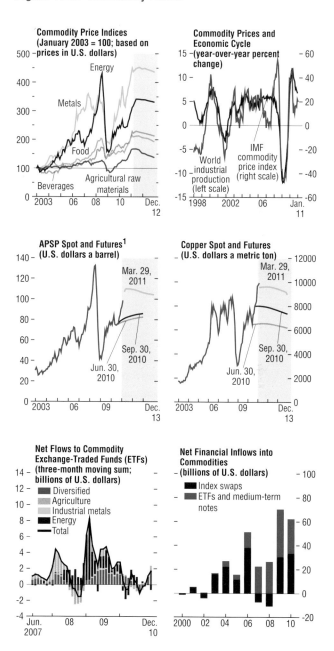

Sources: Bloomberg Financial Markets; and IMF staff estimates.
[1]APSP (average petroleum spot price) denotes an equally weighted average of three crude spot prices: West Texas Intermediate, Dated Brent, and Dubai Fateh.

prices, in part by keeping inventory financing costs lower for longer than expected earlier in 2010. In addition, renewed U.S. dollar depreciation has also played a role.

The financialization of commodity markets continued apace, with commodity assets under financial management reaching a new high of about $376 billion at the end of 2010.[30] Net flows into both exchange-traded products and commodity index swaps were substantial and similar to levels seen in 2009, indicating strong interest among both retail and institutional investors (Figure 1.21, bottom panels). The effects of these flows remain the subject of debate but, in theory, the price impact of commodity financial investment is ambiguous. On one hand, well-informed, rational investors should add liquidity to the commodity derivatives markets and thereby lower price volatility. Their presence should also facilitate price discovery and keep prices more closely aligned with underlying demand-supply fundamentals. On the other hand, ill-informed investors could follow their emotions or rigid investment rules rather than fundamentals, which would add to price volatility. Mirroring the ambiguities on the theoretical side, there is no solid empirical evidence to support the claim that commodity financial investment has been a major factor in recent price cycles or in commodity price formation more generally.

## Outlook

Macroeconomic prospects remain supportive for commodity prices. WEO growth projections suggest that emerging market economies, including China, will continue leading the expansion. Demand growth is expected to slow somewhat, however, partly because economic growth in some major emerging market economies is projected to moderate. In addition, commodity consumption may realign with activity levels rather than growing faster than activity as in 2010. The supply response to higher demand is widely expected to pick up, and futures prices reflect expectations that spare capacity will be tapped in some sectors at current high prices (oil) and that weather conditions will return to normal (food). Overall, the commodity price projections are thus predicated on

[30]According to estimates by Barclays Capital.

some easing in demand-supply balances and for a moderation of upward price pressures.

Commodity price risks remain tilted to the upside, however, with the possibility of supply shortfalls still being the main concern. Oil price risks are a particular concern, given the combination of somewhat weaker but still strong global growth, reduced downside risks to global growth from other sources, and increased geopolitical oil supply hazards. So far, the market response to the supply disruptions in Libya has been modest in historical comparison, given the magnitude of lost supply. Offsetting production increases by other members of Organization of Petroleum Exporting Countries (OPEC) have provided an element of stability, but perceptions of oil supply risks could still become more volatile, especially in an environment of robust growth. Food price risks remain elevated because of low inventory buffers.

Beyond the next 12 months, the capacity for supply to keep pace with the level of demand consistent with WEO growth projections has become more uncertain for a broad range of resources, including crude oil as highlighted in Chapter 3. Over the medium term, real commodity prices will likely need to stay high, or even rise further, to ensure additional supplies of higher-cost resources.

## Energy Market Developments and Prospects

Oil prices have surged to about $110 a barrel, as precautionary demand and risk premiums have increased in response to the oil supply shock triggered by events in the MENA region. Before the onset of the unrest in the region, oil prices had already moved decisively above the $70–$80 range that had anchored price fluctuations through much of 2010. Short-term oil price volatility (as measured by implied volatility on three- and six-month oil futures call options) has remained low, notwithstanding increased oil supply risks, close to the average levels registered before the global financial crisis.

The run-up in oil prices preceding the onset of the oil supply shock reflected a number of factors. Annual growth in oil demand in 2010 was 3.4 percent, the highest rate since 2004 and roughly twice the rate expected at the beginning of the year (Table 1.2; Figure 1.22, top-right panel). Part of

## Table 1.2. Global Oil Demand and Production by Region
*(Millions of barrels a day)*

| | 2009 | 2010 | 2011 Proj. | 2010 H1 | 2010 H2 | Year-over-Year Percent Change 2004–06 Avg. | 2007 | 2008 | 2009 | 2010 | 2011 Proj. | 2010 H1 | 2010 H2 |
|---|---|---|---|---|---|---|---|---|---|---|---|---|---|
| **Demand** | | | | | | | | | | | | | |
| Advanced Economies | 44.9 | 45.7 | 45.6 | 45.2 | 46.2 | 0.5 | −0.4 | −3.5 | −4.0 | 1.8 | −0.2 | 0.6 | 2.9 |
| Of Which: | | | | | | | | | | | | | |
| United States | 19.1 | 19.5 | 19.6 | 19.3 | 19.7 | 1.1 | −0.1 | −5.9 | −3.7 | 2.4 | 0.3 | 1.6 | 3.2 |
| Euro Area | 10.5 | 10.5 | 10.3 | 10.3 | 10.6 | 0.1 | −1.5 | −0.6 | −6.0 | −0.3 | −1.1 | −2.8 | 2.2 |
| Japan | 4.4 | 4.4 | 4.3 | 4.4 | 4.4 | −1.4 | −3.1 | −4.9 | −8.8 | 1.3 | −2.8 | 0.7 | 1.9 |
| Newly Industrialized Asian Economies | 4.6 | 4.9 | 4.9 | 4.8 | 4.9 | 1.5 | 4.5 | −1.5 | 3.5 | 5.5 | 1.4 | 5.8 | 5.2 |
| Emerging and Developing Economies | 40.1 | 42.2 | 43.8 | 41.6 | 42.8 | 4.4 | 4.3 | 3.1 | 1.9 | 5.2 | 3.6 | 5.4 | 5.0 |
| Of Which: | | | | | | | | | | | | | |
| Commonwealth of Independent States | 4.0 | 4.3 | 4.4 | 4.2 | 4.4 | 1.2 | 2.5 | 2.7 | −5.4 | 7.1 | 2.5 | 6.3 | 7.8 |
| Developing Asia | 23.6 | 24.9 | 25.9 | 24.8 | 24.9 | 4.9 | 5.2 | 1.7 | 5.6 | 5.5 | 4.2 | 6.1 | 4.8 |
| China | 8.4 | 9.4 | 10.0 | 9.1 | 9.6 | 9.4 | 4.6 | 2.3 | 8.0 | 12.0 | 6.5 | 14.5 | 9.9 |
| India | 3.3 | 3.3 | 3.4 | 3.4 | 3.3 | 3.9 | 6.5 | 4.0 | 5.7 | 2.3 | 3.2 | 2.6 | 2.0 |
| Middle East and North Africa | 8.7 | 9.0 | 9.3 | 8.8 | 9.1 | 5.3 | 3.6 | 5.4 | 3.2 | 3.2 | 3.0 | 3.7 | 2.8 |
| Western Hemisphere | 5.6 | 5.9 | 6.1 | 5.8 | 6.0 | 4.4 | 5.7 | 5.4 | 0.1 | 5.0 | 3.3 | 4.8 | 5.1 |
| World | 85.0 | 87.9 | 89.4 | 86.8 | 89.0 | 2.1 | 1.6 | −0.6 | −1.3 | 3.4 | 3.5 | 2.9 | 3.9 |
| **Production** | | | | | | | | | | | | | |
| OPEC (current composition)[1,2] | 33.5 | 34.5 | 35.7 | 34.2 | 34.8 | 4.4 | −1.0 | 2.9 | −6.0 | 4.7 | 3.5 | 2.9 | 3.1 |
| Of Which: | | | | | | | | | | | | | |
| Saudi Arabia | 9.5 | 9.8 | . . . | 9.6 | 9.9 | 2.4 | −4.7 | 4.2 | −9.1 | 3.1 | . . . | 1.7 | 4.6 |
| Nigeria | 2.1 | 2.4 | . . . | 2.3 | 2.5 | 2.3 | −4.7 | −8.2 | −0.4 | 16.1 | . . . | 16.3 | 16.0 |
| Venezuela | 2.4 | 2.4 | . . . | 2.4 | 2.4 | 3.2 | −7.8 | −2.0 | −7.8 | 3.1 | . . . | 4.7 | 1.5 |
| Iraq | 2.5 | 2.4 | . . . | 2.4 | 2.4 | 15.5 | 9.9 | 14.3 | 2.5 | −2.2 | . . . | −1.1 | −3.3 |
| Non-OPEC[2] | 51.7 | 52.8 | 53.6 | 52.6 | 53.1 | 0.8 | 0.8 | −0.2 | 1.8 | 2.2 | 1.5 | 2.6 | 1.8 |
| Of Which: | | | | | | | | | | | | | |
| North America | 13.6 | 14.1 | 14.2 | 14.0 | 14.3 | −1.2 | −0.5 | −3.8 | 2.2 | 3.7 | 0.3 | 3.6 | 3.7 |
| North Sea | 4.2 | 3.8 | 3.7 | 4.0 | 3.6 | −6.8 | −5.0 | −5.0 | −4.3 | −8.8 | −2.0 | −7.4 | −10.4 |
| Russia | 10.2 | 10.5 | 10.5 | 10.4 | 10.5 | 4.8 | 2.4 | −0.7 | 2.0 | 2.4 | 0.6 | 3.0 | 1.7 |
| Other Former Soviet Union[3] | 3.1 | 3.1 | 3.2 | 3.1 | 3.1 | 9.0 | 11.5 | 3.2 | 9.2 | 1.1 | 2.7 | 2.2 | 0.0 |
| Other Non-OPEC | 20.6 | 21.4 | 22.0 | 21.1 | 21.6 | 1.7 | 1.1 | 3.2 | 1.8 | 3.6 | 3.2 | 4.0 | 3.2 |
| World | 85.2 | 87.4 | 89.4 | 86.8 | 87.9 | 2.2 | 0.1 | 1.0 | −1.4 | 3.2 | 1.6 | 2.7 | 2.3 |
| **Net Demand[4]** | **−0.2** | **0.6** | **0.0** | **−0.1** | **1.2** | **−0.4** | **1.3** | **−0.3** | **−0.2** | **0.7** | **. . .** | **−0.1** | **1.3** |

Sources: International Energy Agency, Oil Market Report, March 2011; and IMF staff calculations.

[1]OPEC = Organization of Petroleum Exporting Countries. Includes Angola (subject to quotas since January 2007) and Ecuador, which rejoined OPEC in November 2007 after suspending its membership from December 1992 to October 2007.

[2]Totals refer to a total of crude oil, condensates, natural gas liquids, and oil from nonconventional sources.

[3]Other Former Soviet Union includes Azerbaijan, Belarus, Georgia, Kazakhstan, Kyrgyz Republic, Tajikistan, Turkmenistan, Ukraine, and Uzbekistan.

[4]Difference between demand and production. In the percent change columns, the figures are percent of world demand.

the stronger-than-expected oil demand growth is explained by faster actual global economic growth in 2010, on the order of 1 to 1½ percent compared with forecasts in late 2009 and early 2010. Another part of the oil demand surprise reflects oil-specific factors, including energy policy shifts in China that reduced the supply of electricity to some sectors and led to increased diesel demand. Upward surprises in oil demand were also recorded in major advanced economies, notably the United States,

where fuel demand was stronger than expected, and in Japan, where oil-generated power substituted for maintenance-related losses in nuclear power for part of the year (Figure 1.22, top-left panel).

Oil supply responded to the unexpected increase in oil demand, but not to the full extent possible. Global oil production is estimated to have increased by 3.2 percent in 2010. Higher-than-expected non-OPEC production contributed about half of the surprise increase in supply (Figure 1.22, upper-middle-right

**Figure 1.22. World Energy Market Developments**

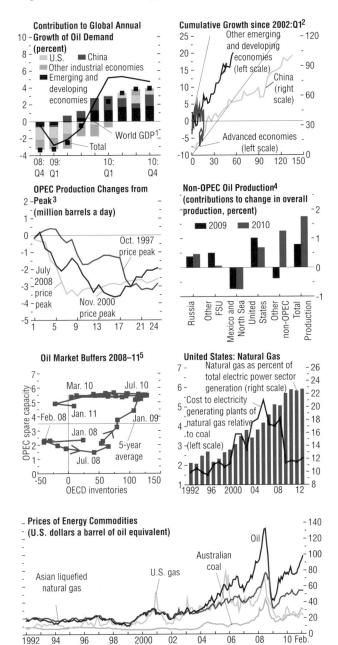

Sources: IMF Primary Commodity Price System; International Energy Agency, *Oil Market Report*, March 2011; and IMF staff calculations.

[1]Annual change, in percent.

[2]Data through 2010:Q4 for advanced economies and China; through 2010:Q3 for emerging economies. GDP growth on x-axis, and oil demand growth on y-axis.

[3]Organization of Petroleum Exporting Countries (OPEC) membership as of the first month of each episode. Months from oil price peak on x-axis.

[4]North Sea: Norway and United Kingdom. Other FSU: other former Soviet Union.

[5]Organization for Economic Cooperation and Development (OECD) stocks, deviations from five-year average (million barrels) on x-axis, OPEC effective spare capacity (million barrels a day) on y-axis.

panel). Declines in the North Sea were more than offset by higher production elsewhere, notably in Brazil, China, Russia, and the United States, reflecting incentives for investment and field decline management embodied in rising oil prices and, in the case of Russia, changes to the tax regime to cover high production and development costs. OPEC crude oil production, which is subject to production quotas, rose by 1.8 percent, contributing one-quarter to the increase in global supply (Figure 1.22, upper-middle-left panel). OPEC production of natural gas liquids (NGLs, including ethane, propane, butane, and natural gasoline) rose by more than 10 percent, contributing another quarter of global supply growth.

With supply growth lagging, market clearing required an unexpectedly strong draw on inventories from the second half of 2010, and inventory-to-use ratios are now approaching average levels over past cycles (Figure 1.22, lower-middle-left panel). Similarly, oil futures curves flattened rather than sloping upward as in the earlier stages of the global recovery, indicating an end to cyclical weakness in oil market conditions. More recently, futures curves have moved into backwardation, indicating a further tightening in physical markets that is anticipated to ease somewhat through 2011.

Near-term oil market prospects depend importantly on prospects for greater stability in some oil exporters in the MENA region and the interaction between the strength of the global expansion, oil demand dynamics, and the supply response. Current WEO projections point to moderating global economic growth over the next 12 months, suggesting a slowing of oil demand growth momentum. This should be reinforced by a partial unwinding of the overshoot in oil demand that typically accompanies the early stages of recovery in global activity (see Chapter 3).

On the supply side, modest capacity growth is expected in non-OPEC countries in 2011, reflecting in part the oil investment bottlenecks of 2006–08. As a result, the call on OPEC will increase markedly in 2011 under the WEO baseline projections.[31]

[31]The "call on OPEC" is the difference between global demand and supply from sources other than OPEC crude oil production, including OPEC NGL production. In Table 1.2, the figure for OPEC production in 2011 reflects the call on OPEC and OPEC NGL production.

OPEC production decisions will thus play a key role in determining oil market outcomes. OPEC members have already begun to tap their spare capacity to offset losses from supply disruptions in other MENA region producers. This commitment has helped keep oil supply risks in check. However, ensuring oil market stability with continued robust global growth will likely require increases in OPEC crude oil production above and beyond those necessitated by supply disruptions in the MENA region. The acceleration in OPEC crude oil production in December 2010 and January 2011—when oil prices were closing in on the $100 a barrel threshold—suggests that OPEC members remain concerned about accelerated price increases. Nevertheless, the absence of an elastic production response when prices moved beyond the $70–$80 range has led to some uncertainty in markets about OPEC producers' implicit price targets.

The magnitude of the actual oil supply shock has, in historical comparison, been moderate to date. However, MENA oil supply risks will probably only gradually unwind through 2011. The oil supply risks and continued robust global activity—notwithstanding some slowing—means that upside risks to oil prices will remain high. Oil derivative markets have indeed started to price in higher risks of price spikes over the next few years. Against this backdrop, oil market risks have become an important concern for global economic stability, as discussed previously in the chapter. In contrast, the oil market risks from the replacement of nuclear by thermal power in Japan because of the damage to nuclear plants after the Tohoku earthquake should be minor. The replacement will eventually lead to higher fossil fuel imports in Japan, but the impact on global oil demand should remain limited, on the order of 0.1 to 0.3 percent. Past experience and incentives from current energy prices suggest that more than half of the increased fossil fuel needs will be met through increased imports of liquefied natural gas and, to a lesser extent, coal.

In the medium term, even assuming that supply disruptions in the MENA region are short-lived, oil prices are expected to remain high, reflecting the tension between continued robust oil demand growth and the downward shift in the trend growth

rate of global oil production. The tensions are expected to remain moderate in the WEO baseline. As discussed in greater detail in Chapter 3, they could intensify however, and on balance risks to prices remain on the upside given downside risk to supply, reflecting above- and below-ground constraints on oil investment and, as highlighted by events in the MENA region, geopolitical risks.

Price differences across fossil fuels remain large, and the shift in market share away from crude oil is likely to continue (Figure 1.22, bottom panel). Natural gas prices in the North American market have remained low compared with those of crude oil, reflecting the additional supply from shale gas extraction. The market share for natural gas will thus continue to increase in the United States, as end-user demand responds further to price incentives (Figure 1.22, lower-middle-right panel). Natural gas could also play a more prominent role in the energy mix elsewhere, given that large shale gas deposits have also been identified in other regions.[32] Similarly, coal is relatively cheaper than crude oil, and coal consumption growth has exceeded that of other fossil fuels over the past decade, highlighting the importance of coal in meeting rapidly growing world demand for primary energy.

## Metal Market Developments and Prospects

Metal prices rallied strongly in the second half of 2010 and early 2011, with the IMF base metal price index increasing by 40 percent (Figure 1.23, top-left panel).[33] As for commodities more generally, the sharp price increases were driven largely by the stronger-than-expected recovery both in emerging market and in advanced economies, although supply disruptions also played a role. Reflecting the influence of common macroeconomic factors and increases in risk appetite across financial markets, the comovement between metal prices and global equity prices remained strong throughout 2010.

Global consumption of all base metals except tin is estimated to have reached a new high in 2010

---

[32]Box 3.2 analyzes prospects for moving the U.S. shale gas "revolution" to the global stage.

[33]Copper and tin prices reached record highs.

**Figure 1.23. Developments in Base Metal Markets**

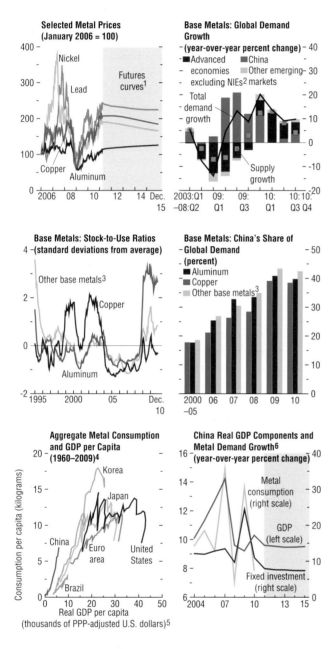

Sources: Bloomberg Financial Markets; London Metal Exchange; Thomson Datastream; World Bureau of Metal Statistics; and IMF staff estimates.
[1]Prices as of March 30, 2011.
[2]NIEs = newly industrialized Asian economies, which include Hong Kong SAR, Korea, Singapore, and Taiwan Province of China.
[3]Weighted average of lead, nickel, tin, and zinc.
[4]Aggregate of aluminum, copper, lead, nickel, tin, and zinc.
[5]PPP = purchasing power parity.
[6]GDP and components in real terms, metal consumption in volume terms.

(Figure 1.23, top-right panel).[34] Supply responded to rising prices but only sluggishly, reflecting in part the impact of stricter environmental standards (for example, power-related aluminum production cuts in China) and labor disputes (for example, strikes in Chile's copper mines). As a result, inventory buffers have been declining, normalizing to historical averages. The stock-to-use ratio for copper is already below its historical average (Figure 1.23, middle-left panel). The impact on overall inventory movements of newly introduced exchange-traded funds (ETFs) backed by physical holdings of base metals has so far been limited, reflecting features of these investment vehicles that are less attractive than futures-backed alternatives under current market conditions.[35] As of end-February, the share of London metal exchange stocks accounted for by these products varied between 0.1 to 2.3 percent.

Turning to the outlook, the analysis in Box 1.5 of the October 2010 *World Economic Outlook* suggests that base metal markets are in a phase of increased scarcity, as reflected in the rise of the trend component in prices over the past decade or so. Increased scarcity in base metals is due in part to increasing metal demand from emerging market economies, particularly China. During 2003–07, China contributed two-thirds of the increase in world consumption of aluminum and copper and almost all the increase in world consumption of lead, tin, and zinc (Table 1.3). Since 2008, China's contribution has exceeded even net world consumption growth for all metals, with consumption of copper, lead, and nickel increasing by more than 50 percent. Reflecting this strong growth, China's share in global base metal consumption has doubled to about 40 percent during the past 10 years (Figure 1.23, middle-right panel).

---

[34]Base metal demand grew by more than 8 percent (year over year) during the second half of 2010, whereas global economic growth was less than 5 percent (year over year) during the same period.

[35]Physically backed ETFs for copper, nickel, and tin were introduced in December 2010. Because these metals are trading in backwardation, a capital loss is expected from holding inventories in addition to the high physical carrying costs of inventories. In contrast, the time spread works in favor of futures-backed alternatives, which can benefit from a positive roll yield.

**Table 1.3. Consumption of Base Metals**
*(Annual percent change unless noted otherwise)*

| | Growth in Consumption of | | | | | | | China's Industrial Production |
| --- | --- | --- | --- | --- | --- | --- | --- | --- |
| | Aluminum | Copper | Lead | Nickel | Tin | Zinc | World GDP | |
| **1995–2002 World** | **3.2** | **3.4** | **3.1** | **2.2** | **1.5** | **3.7** | **3.4** | **10.9** |
| *Of Which:* | | | | | | | | |
| China (percent) | 46.1 | 57.5 | 54.5 | 29.4 | 14.9 | 39.6 | 6.8 | . . . |
| Other Emerging Markets[1] (percent) | 13.5 | 19.3 | 29.2 | −8.9 | 14.5 | 11.2 | . . . | . . . |
| **2003–07 World** | **8.0** | **3.8** | **4.7** | **3.0** | **6.0** | **3.8** | **4.7** | **16.6** |
| *Of Which:* | | | | | | | | |
| China (percent) | 67.6 | 67.4 | 94.2 | 130.3 | 95.7 | 99.3 | 9.4 | . . . |
| Other Emerging Markets[1] (percent) | 7.7 | 19.7 | −0.7 | −5.6 | 0.6 | 11.2 | . . . | . . . |
| **2008–10 World** | **1.9** | **2.1** | **3.6** | **3.6** | **1.7** | **2.9** | **2.4** | **13.1** |
| *Of Which:* | | | | | | | | |
| China (percent) | 159.5 | 226.3 | 175.5 | 153.0 | 104.3 | 166.7 | 12.3 | . . . |
| Other Emerging Markets[1] (percent) | 5.2 | −12.8 | −9.3 | −7.7 | 41.0 | −0.3 | . . . | . . . |

Sources: World Bureau of Metal Statistics, *World Metal Statistics Yearbook* (various issues).
[1]Brazil, India, Mexico, and Russia.

China's metal consumption is currently higher than that of other countries at a similar stage of development, likely reflecting the exponential growth in its manufacturing sector over the past two decades (Figure 1.23, bottom-left panel). However, China's metal consumption growth is expected to moderate during 2011 and subsequent years, given recent efforts to restrain bank lending and infrastructure investment and the potential for a gradual rebalancing of the economy away from metal-intensive sources of growth (Figure 1.23, bottom-right panel). The moderation in base metal consumption growth in China is expected to be partly offset by increased demand from advanced economies, where base metal consumption still is some 15 percent below precrisis levels despite ongoing recovery. The global demand impact of temporarily higher metal demand due to the reconstruction in Japan after the Tohoku earthquake, however, is likely to be minor.

Production and capacity growth, though responding to high prices, is not expected to rise in lockstep with demand, especially for copper, due to slow development of mining capacity and rising energy costs. Risks to the price outlook remain to the upside, as inventory buffers for most metals have been declining. Demand growth in China is expected to moderate, but there is potential for upside surprises given continued large-scale infra-

structure construction and public housing projects in the pipeline.[36]

## Food Market Developments and Prospects

The IMF Food Price Index reached a new high during early 2011 after rising by about 41 percent since mid-2010. Price increases have been broad-based and led by an 82 percent surge in grain prices, but some major grains, including rice, are still significantly below their 2008 highs (Figure 1.24, top-left panel). Other food groups with higher income elasticity are pushing past previous highs, however, including oilseeds, meat, sugar, and seafood (Figure 1.24, top-right panel). No single factor explains the resurgence in food prices, but the catalyst was a series of weather-related supply shocks, including drought and wildfires in Kazakhstan, Russia, and Ukraine (wheat); a hot and wet summer in the United States (corn); and the more widespread effects of a particularly strong La Niña weather pattern around the Pacific rim (rice, sugar, local vegetables). Together these shocks contributed to a 2.7 percent downward revision to global grain production for 2010–11 (Figure 1.24, upper-middle-left panel).[37]

---

[36]Described in China's new five-year plan, which went into effect in January 2011.

[37]Refers to the projections by U.S. Department of Agriculture for the international marketing year 2010/11 for corn (maize), rice, and wheat.

## Figure 1.24. Developments in Markets for Major Food Crops

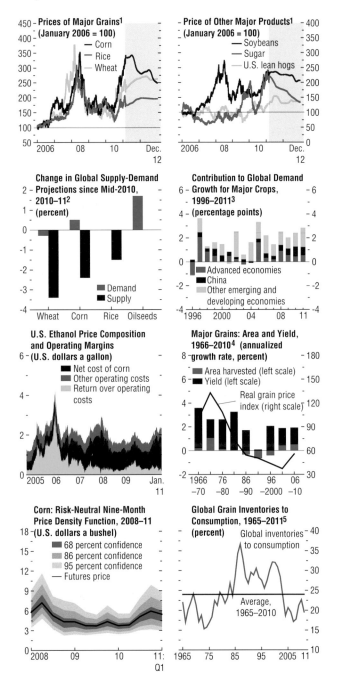

Sources: Bloomberg Financial Markets; Chicago Mercantile Exchange; Iowa State University Center for Agriculture and Rural Development; UN Food and Agriculture Organization; U.S. Department of Agriculture (USDA); and IMF staff calculations.
[1]Futures prices for March 2011 through December 2012.
[2]USDA projection for the international year 2010/11.
[3]Includes grains and oilseeds. Demand for 2011 is projected by the USDA.
[4]Area-weighted yield for nine grains and prices.
[5]End-year inventories as a percent of consumption, with USDA projections for 2011.

While supply has disappointed, demand for major food crops has remained robust, largely reflecting growth in emerging market economies. During the most recent global recession, demand growth was unusually strong and has now picked up to about 2.5 percent (Figure 1.24, upper-middle-right panel). Emerging market economies, including China, account for 70 to 80 percent of demand growth during the past three years. One notable recent development has been the increasing presence of China as an importer in global grain markets, especially corn, after many years of self-sufficiency. Consumption of oilseeds, including soybeans, has been particularly strong, reflecting their higher income elasticity, and China remains the world's largest oilseed importer by a large margin.

Demand for biofuel feedstock has also rebounded more rapidly than expected as the U.S. corn ethanol sector recovered from the widespread bankruptcies of 2008–09. Ethanol operating margins remain thin, but the sector has retained considerable policy support, which serves to buttress ethanol prices (Figure 1.24, lower-middle-left panel). Higher prices of alternative feedstock, particularly sugar, have also supported demand for corn-based ethanol. About 40 percent of the U.S. corn harvest—equivalent to 14 percent of total global corn consumption—was used as ethanol feedstock in 2010, a 5 percentage point increase over the previous year.

All these factors contributed to tighter physical markets that delayed the rebuilding of inventories depleted during the nine years preceding the first global food price surge in 2008. For some food crops, especially corn, stocks remain very low, which has exacerbated price volatility.

The outlook for food prices over the near term and beyond will depend largely on supply developments. History suggests that more normal weather conditions over the next 12 months should allow harvests to recover most of the losses incurred during 2010.[38] For example, during years in which global wheat output declined by more than 5 percent, the subsequent year recorded an increase of 7 percent, significantly above trend growth. Over the medium term, supply should continue to rise in response to higher prices. Yield

[38]The best-fitting univariate time-series models of annual global production also indicate that supply shocks are typically reversed quickly.

growth has slowed somewhat in recent years, possibly due to reduced state funding of agricultural research and development in advanced economies.[39] Offsetting slower yield growth, acreage under cultivation has begun to increase, after two decades of stagnation, but the pace of expansion may remain gradual, in part reflecting the relative scarcity of productive well-irrigated land in regions with a well-established distribution infrastructure (Figure 1.24, lower-middle-right panel).

Improving supply should ease tightness somewhat and allow prices to retreat modestly from their recent highs through 2011, but risks to the price outlook remain decisively to the upside. This view is reflected by market pricing, with futures curves relatively flat or backwardated, indicating that tightness should ease, whereas options suggest that risks have become more skewed to the upside (Figure 1.24, bottom-left panel, for corn). The most immediate risk is that the final phases of the current La Niña weather pattern will continue to threaten yields in the Southern Hemisphere. Other risks include persistently higher energy prices or the imposition of international trade restrictions in response to supply shocks. Most important, global food inventories remain low, particularly for grains (Figure 1.24, bottom-right panel). The process of rebuilding stocks will take time, and until these buffers return to more normal levels, food prices will remain highly sensitive to shocks that tighten physical markets.

## Recent Commodity Market Developments: Implications for the Global Economy

The challenges posed by high and rising commodity prices are most immediate for emerging and developing economies for two main reasons. First, the share of food in the typical consumption basket is larger in these economies than in advanced economies. As a result, the pass-through of food prices in international markets to headline inflation tends to be higher in these economies. Second, there is greater potential that changes in commodity prices will affect their terms of trade and trade balances, given relatively larger shares of commodities in both imports and exports.

[39]Discussed in Appendix 1.1 of the April 2010 *World Economic Outlook*.

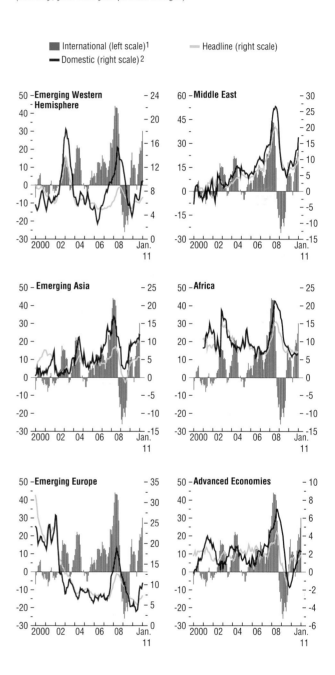

**Figure 1.25. Changes in International and Domestic Food Prices and Headline Inflation**

*(Monthly; year-over-year percent changes)*

Sources: Haver Analytics; IMF Primary Commodity Price System; and IMF staff calculations.
[1] IMF commodity food and beverage price index in U.S. dollars.
[2] Food and beverage inflation.

The upturn in headline inflation across many emerging and developing economies has coincided with a pickup in commodity prices since mid-2010 (Figure 1.25). In particular, higher food prices have contributed significantly to higher inflation. This reflects the pass-through of world food prices, but also—in some significant cases, including China and India—higher prices in local food markets, such as for fresh fruit and vegetables. Headline and fuel inflation have risen most in the Middle East, a region that is a large net food importer, followed by emerging Asia, a region hit hard by bad weather in the second half of 2010 and output gaps that are either closing or already positive. In contrast, food prices and headline inflation are little changed in sub-Saharan Africa, where many economies are less integrated into global food markets and have enjoyed relatively bountiful local harvests over the past 12 months. The prices of some important staple crops, including corn (maize), have thus remained relatively stable in much of the region, indicating that international food prices are only one factor in determining local food inflation.

Further pass-through of recent commodity price increases to headline inflation seems likely across the global economy. Food prices remain the most important source of risk due to tight market conditions, which should ease only gradually, and their higher pass-through to domestic prices in emerging and developing economies. Some of the factors behind rising commodity prices are temporary, and first-round effects on headline inflation should generally be accommodated, but country-specific circumstances may require a monetary policy response. The cost-push from large commodity price increases is more likely to result in second-round effects, including rising long-term inflation expectations, in economies where the weight of food and energy in the consumer price index is relatively large and monetary policy credibility not yet solidly established—primarily in some emerging and developing economies (see Chapter 1).[40]

Recent commodity price developments have also had a broad impact on the terms of trade and trade balances. The estimated direct (first-round) effects of

the expected price increases under the IMF's updated baseline projections for commodity prices are substantial. The latest baseline anticipates increases in prices for crude oil, food, and metals of about 31, 26, and 24 percent, respectively, in 2011, compared with the October 2010 WEO baseline. Overall, the terms-of-trade gains from higher commodity prices are expected to improve the trade balances of emerging and developing economies by about 1¼ percent of GDP in 2011. However, variation across regions and economies is wide, as shown in Figure 1.26. Large terms-of-trade gains from high oil export prices should more than offset losses from high food import prices in the Middle East; economies in emerging Asia and emerging Europe are generally expected to experience declines in their trade balances, reflecting their high dependence on commodity imports. Within Africa, economies without any major commodity resources to export, especially oil and metals, would suffer most from high food prices. However, many net food importers benefit from the natural hedge provided by their exports of metals, oil, and other commodities. Most advanced economies are expected to experience a modest deterioration in their terms of trade.

To assess the effects of further significant increases in commodity prices, the same exercise was conducted using price levels consistent with a plausible shock derived from prevailing market expectations embedded in commodity futures options. These derivative prices can provide an indication of the probability distribution of prices over various time horizons.[41] In a scenario that compares the effects of higher food prices relative to the current baseline, food prices are assumed to be on average about 58 percent higher in 2011 than the previous year. A scenario involving broad increases in commodity prices was also considered in which, in addition to higher food prices, all energy prices are assumed to be 53 percent higher than the previous year, and base metal prices are assumed to increase by 40 percent. A summary of these assumptions and the comparison with the current baseline are provided in Table 1.4.

The impact of higher food prices varies by region (Table 1.5). The overall effect on Africa is marginal,

---

[40]As noted in Chapter 3 of the October 2008 *World Economic Outlook,* emerging and developing economies are more likely than advanced economies to lack monetary policy credibility and solidly anchored inflation expectations.

[41]Specifically, the upper standard deviation bound of the risk-neutral density function for the commodity price was selected as the upside scenario.

**Figure 1.26.  First-Round Impact of Commodity Price Changes on the Trade Balances of Selected Emerging and Developing Economies**[1]

*(2011 April WEO forecast over 2010 October WEO forecast; 2011 trade balance in percent of 2009 GDP)*

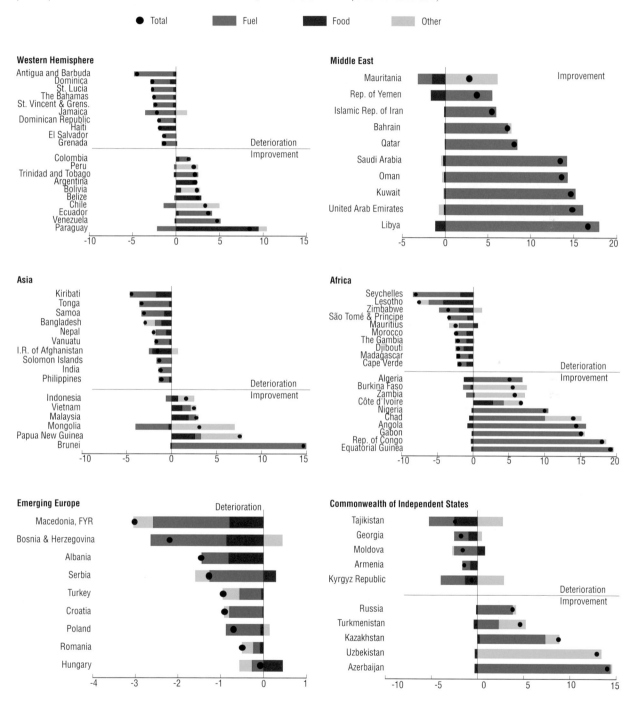

Source: IMF staff calculations.
[1]Country export and import weights by commodities were derived from trade data for 2005–08. Economies are ranked by the overall change in the trade balance, with the largest 10 improvements and deteriorations shown in each figure, subject to data availability.

**Table 1.4. Annual Price Changes for Key Commodities**
*(Percent)*

|  | Food | | Oil | | Metals | | Energy | |
|---|---|---|---|---|---|---|---|---|
|  | 2011 | 2012 | 2011 | 2012 | 2011 | 2012 | 2011 | 2012 |
| Baseline | 24.1 | −4.7 | 35.6 | 0.8 | 26.5 | −0.8 | 31.9 | 0.1 |
| Food Price Shock | 57.5 | 7.3 | . . . | . . . | . . . | . . . | . . . | . . . |
| Overall Price Shock | 57.5 | 7.3 | 53.4 | 18.2 | 39.8 | 12.1 | 53.4 | 18.2 |

Source: IMF staff calculations.

but this masks large terms-of-trade losses for net food importers, about 0.5 percent of GDP in 2011, relative to the baseline. The Middle East would also experience large trade balance deterioration, by more than 0.4 percent of GDP in 2011. In contrast, the dominance of food exporters in Latin America would lead to a significant improvement of about 0.4 percent in the trade position.

The effects of broadly higher commodity prices improve the external position of emerging economies, although regional variations are important. In particular, large improvements for the Middle East, the former Soviet Union, Latin America, and Africa are partially offset by deterioration in emerging Asia and emerging Europe (Table 1.5).

Higher prices of food, fuel, and other commodities also have important distributional effects. The urban poor, especially in emerging and developing economies, are more likely to suffer from high prices than other income groups. For the rural poor, much will depend on land ownership, because farmers benefit from higher prices. Recent commodity price developments are likely to be another setback to the poverty reduction achieved in the early to mid-2000s. Hence, another policy priority will be to mitigate the effects of higher prices of food and other commodities on the poor through targeted and cost-effective social safety nets.[42]

[42] See Chapter 3 of the October 2008 *World Economic Outlook* and Coady and others (2010) on social safety net policies and high commodity prices.

**Table 1.5. Trade Balance Impact of Higher Prices[1]**
*(Changes from baseline in percent of 2009 GDP)*

|  | Higher Food Prices | | Higher Overall Prices | |
|---|---|---|---|---|
|  | 2011 | 2012 | 2011 | 2012 |
| **Advanced Economies** | **0.0** | **0.0** | **−0.4** | **−0.3** |
| United States | 0.0 | 0.0 | −0.3 | −0.3 |
| Japan | −0.1 | −0.1 | −0.8 | −0.6 |
| Euro Area | −0.1 | 0.0 | −0.7 | −0.5 |
| **Emerging and Developing Economies** | **0.1** | **0.0** | **0.8** | **0.7** |
| Africa | −0.1 | −0.1 | 2.5 | 2.0 |
| *Of Which:* Net Food Importers | −0.5 | −0.3 | 3.8 | 3.3 |
| Asia and Pacific | 0.1 | 0.0 | −0.5 | −0.5 |
| *Of Which:* Net Food Importers | −0.1 | −0.1 | −0.6 | −0.6 |
| Commonwealth of Independent States | −0.2 | −0.1 | 2.7 | 2.4 |
| *Of Which:* Net Food Importers | −0.3 | −0.1 | 3.1 | 2.6 |
| Europe | −0.1 | 0.0 | −0.8 | −0.5 |
| *Of Which:* Net Food Importers | −0.1 | 0.0 | −0.7 | −0.5 |
| Middle East | −0.4 | −0.2 | 5.6 | 5.2 |
| *Of Which:* Net Food Importers | −0.4 | −0.2 | 5.6 | 5.2 |
| Western Hemisphere | 0.4 | 0.2 | 1.0 | 0.7 |
| *Of Which:* Net Food Importers | −0.2 | −0.1 | 0.9 | 0.9 |

Source: IMF staff calculations.

[1]Country export and import weights by commodities were derived from trade data for 2005–08.

## Box 1.1. House Price Busts in Advanced Economies: Repercussions for Global Financial Markets

Financial booms and busts in the advanced economies can have profound effects on global financial markets and global economic activity. Most recently, a bust that started in a small segment of the U.S. housing market interacted with financial imbalances and vulnerabilities elsewhere, turning into the deepest global recession since the Great Depression. But house price busts are nothing new. This raises the questions of how and why this time was different from previous cycles and what we can learn from this episode.

This box addresses these questions by building on recent research by Claessens, Kose, and Terrones (2011 and forthcoming). The main findings are that recent house price busts in advanced economies had more severe implications for global financial markets because of (1) how widespread house price busts were this time around compared with earlier episodes and (2) the unusual synchronization and buoyancy of advanced and emerging market financial conditions in the run-up to the crisis. Global factors that drive financial cycles seem to have become stronger while country-specific factors have receded, including in house price cycles.

### How Did This Cycle Differ from Previous Cycles?

House price busts in advanced economies generally last 18 quarters and are associated with a 30 percent house price drop (Figure 1.1.1).[1] In emerging markets, busts last for 15 quarters and are associated with a 40 percent house price drop. A key difference from previous cycles is that the recent house price busts in the advanced economies were shorter and shallower, yet more violent—the average price decline per quarter was steeper than in the past.[2] Although some busts are ongoing, the

The main author of this box is Marco E. Terrones.
[1]House price busts are defined as more intense forms of house price contractions. To be considered a bust, real house prices need to fall (from peak to trough) by more than 15 percent. House price busts are typically associated with sharp contractions in economic activity. Moreover, they are longer lasting and (by design) more severe than other downturns.

[2]Twenty-eight house price bust episodes were observed in the advanced economies during 1970:Q1–2007:Q4. The advanced economies that have experienced at least one such bust include Austria, Canada, Denmark, Finland, France, Ireland, Italy, Japan, Netherlands, New Zealand, Norway,

**Figure 1.1.1. Financial Disruptions**

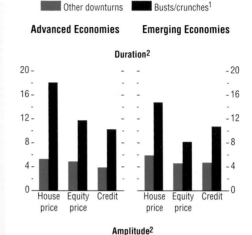

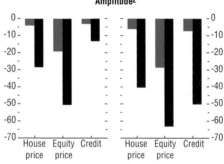

Source: IMF staff estimates.
[1]Busts refer to the bottom quartile of house and equity price drops, respectively. Crunches refer to the bottom quartile of credit contractions.
[2]Duration is the number of quarters between peak and trough. Amplitude is the decline during the downturn. Duration corresponds to sample means, whereas amplitude corresponds to sample medians. Disruptions refers to the bottom quartile of the downturn of each financial variable.

duration of completed house price busts was only 40 percent of the historical average, and the drop in house prices was only 60 percent of the norm.[3]

Spain, Sweden, Switzerland, and United Kingdom. House price series are mostly from the Organization for Economic Cooperation and Development and correspond to various measures of indices of house or land prices, depending on the source country.
[3]Among ongoing house price busts, depth and duration are similarly less than what was typically observed in previous busts at comparable stages.

**Box 1.1** *(continued)*

### Figure 1.1.2. Effect of Advanced Economy House Price Busts

*(Percent change from one year earlier;t = 0 denotes peak; quarters on the x-axis)*

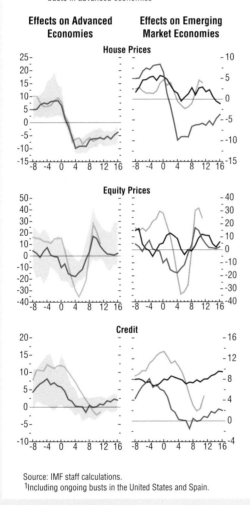

Source: IMF staff calculations.
[1]Including ongoing busts in the United States and Spain.

Financial markets in advanced and emerging market economies also experienced sharper swings in this cycle compared with previous cycles. Figure 1.1.2 plots median growth rates for house prices, equity prices, and real credit for advanced economies that experienced a house price bust and, in the panels on the right, for all emerging market economies at about the time of these busts. Overlaid on this figure are data on current house price busts (left panels) and financial effects in emerging markets (right panels). Note that during house price busts in advanced economies, house prices decline for an extended period, typically about four years. In contrast, house price growth rates in emerging market economies slow down somewhat during the first year of the event and then accelerate slightly.

Figure 1.1.2 also shows that recent house price busts were accompanied by a sharp drop in equity prices and a slowdown in credit. Credit and housing markets in many advanced economies remain weak: households are highly leveraged and banks are restructuring their balance sheets. Unlike in the past, however, the drop and recovery in equity prices have been rapid and steep. Also in contrast with past experience, the effects of the recent price busts in emerging markets have been more severe:

- House and equity prices in emerging market economies have been more responsive to financial developments in advanced economies; however, they have recovered rapidly. In some economies, house and equity prices are already reaching very high levels, which in some cases exceed precrisis levels.

- The rate of credit expansion in emerging markets slowed significantly in the aftermath of the house price busts. In part, this is because a number of emerging market economies experienced a credit boom in the run-up to the financial turmoil.[4] Credit growth in most emerging markets has started to accelerate recently, and in one group of economies credit is very buoyant once again.

---

[4]Following Mendoza and Terrones (2008), credit booms are defined as excessive real credit expansions above trend. Some of the economies that experienced a boom during 2007–08 include India, South Africa, and Venezuela. Hong Kong SAR is currently experiencing a credit boom, and China is near boom territory. (There is also evidence that several eastern European economies and Nigeria, which are not included in the sample of emerging market economies, also experienced a credit boom.)

**Box 1.1** *(continued)*

*Why Did This Cycle Differ from Previous Cycles?*

Two main factors contributed to the difference between this cycle and previous cycles. First, in this cycle, an unusually large number of countries experienced either a house price contraction or bust at the same time. Data through the third quarter of 2010 indicate that virtually all 21 advanced economies experienced a price contraction[5] and that five economies have experienced (Denmark, New Zealand, United Kingdom) or are experiencing (Spain, United States) a house price bust. The closest historical episode to the current one was observed in the early 1990s. A key difference from the past, however, is that this is the first time the United States, which accounts for the lion's share of global financial transactions, has experienced a house price bust.

Second, the degree of financial market synchronization across countries was higher this time. The cross-country synchronization for a financial variable can be measured with a concordance index, which shows the fraction of time the variable is in the same cyclical phase in two economies. The historical analysis examines the nature and interaction of financial cycles for 21 advanced economies and 23 emerging market economies using quarterly data over 1960–2007. The results are set out in Table 1.1.1.

As shown, house prices, equity prices, and credit are in the same cyclical phase at least half the time.

[5]A few of these house price contractions, including in Canada, Greece, and Japan, are ongoing and are short of being categorized as price busts.

[6]These results are not driven by the experience in emerging Europe, which is highly financially integrated with western Europe, because these economies are not included in the sample due to a lack of data.

In the run-up to the global financial crisis (that is, 2003–07), however, financial cycles were more synchronized across economies, particularly in credit and equity markets.[6] This could reflect a variety of factors, including the growing importance of global factors in determining financial fluctuations, the growing role of large international financial institutions, and increased international financial integration.

These are some additional key findings:

- Equity markets in advanced and emerging market economies are highly synchronized, but housing markets are less so. These findings are consistent with the notion that equity markets are more closely integrated internationally and housing markets are less integrated but not independent of each other. The latter reflects the fact that, even though housing is the quintessential nontradable asset, the key determinants of house prices (such as income and interest rates) do tend to move together internationally.

- Credit markets are strongly synchronized across advanced economies and between advanced and emerging market economies. However, they are less synchronized between emerging market economies. This may reflect the strong cross-border linkages of banks in advanced economies and their important role in emerging market economies. In addition, credit shocks originating in large advanced economies, such as the United States, have a significant effect on credit conditions in emerging markets. In the run-up to the financial crisis, credit markets across advanced and emerging market economies were particularly synchronized, reflecting in part

**Table 1.1.1. Cross-Country Financial Market Synchronization**

|  | Advanced Economies | Emerging Market Economies | Advanced and Emerging Market Economies |
|---|---|---|---|
| House Prices | 0.59 | 0.49 | 0.50 |
| 2003–07 | 0.74 | 0.49 | 0.60 |
| Equity Prices | 0.71 | 0.62 | 0.61 |
| 2003–07 | 0.90 | 0.80 | 0.81 |
| Credit | 0.74 | 0.48 | 0.65 |
| 2003–07 | 0.92 | 0.83 | 0.87 |

Source: IMF staff estimates.

Note: The reported statistics correspond to the median of the country averages.

**Box 1.1** *(continued)*

accommodative monetary conditions, including low interest rates in advanced economies.

*Implications for Policy*

In the past, macroeconomic and prudential policies were based primarily on domestic consider-ations. The much greater synchronization of finan-cial and housing markets evident in this cycle means that surveillance and domestic policies need to take much greater account of international developments than in the past. It may not be sufficient to ensure that loans made to residents by domestic financial institutions are prudently managed and that the domestic housing market is sound. In the future, policymakers may need to be aware of developments in geographically distant financial markets and take action to protect their financial institutions from risks emanating from these markets.

More immediately, financial markets in emerg-ing market economies have rapidly recovered from the adverse impact of the recent house price busts in advanced economies. Fueled by accommodative macroeconomic policies and strong capital inflows, house and equity prices in these economies are buoyant and, in some cases, have already surpassed precrisis levels. The authorities need to carefully monitor these developments, consider tightening macroeconomic policy, and strengthen macropru-dential regulation.

In contrast, credit and housing markets in advanced economies are still weak, which is typical following house price busts. Action to accelerate mending of household balance sheets and bank restructuring would help end the ongoing house price downturns and busts and improve credit conditions.

## Box 1.2. *World Economic Outlook* Downside Scenarios

The scenarios presented here use the IMF's Global Integrated Monetary and Fiscal Model (GIMF) to consider the possible implications for the world outlook if potential output in some regions of the world is overestimated in the baseline forecast. Although there is general consensus that potential output is now lower than projected before the recent financial crisis, there is a risk that the downward revisions were not large enough. The scenarios consider plausible misperceptions of the current level of potential output and its growth over the WEO forecast horizon in the United States, emerging Asia, and some other emerging economies. The results illustrate how these misperceptions could lead to notably higher inflation in the near term and sharply lower growth and increasing external imbalances once policymakers and markets recognize the error.

Two alternative scenarios are considered. In the first, the implications of the policy errors associated with the overestimation of potential output are simply greater macroeconomic volatility as the economies affected converge to the true level of potential output. In the second, the policy errors are more costly. The initial acceleration in inflation becomes more entrenched in expectations, and a more prolonged period of below-potential growth is required to re-anchor inflation expectations.

Estimating sustainable economic output from historical data is difficult in the best of times. However, it is even more challenging when the most recent data contain a boom-bust episode like the one the global economy just endured. Estimates of the current level of potential output for many economies may not have fully accounted for the extent of capital destruction wrought by the financial crisis or its impact on structural unemployment. Projected potential output growth rates may be overly optimistic, assuming that too much of the growth momentum over the past decade reflected underlying fundamentals rather than being symptomatic of the financial excesses that eventually led to the crisis.

In these scenarios it is assumed that the baseline forecast overestimates the level of potential output in 2015 by roughly 6 percent in China, 4 percent

in emerging Asia excluding China, 3 percent in the United States, and 2.5 percent in the remaining countries.[1] Estimates of potential output in the euro area and Japan are assumed to be broadly correct. Where applicable, both the initial starting points and the rates of growth over the WEO forecast horizon contain errors. It is assumed that starting point errors at end-2010 are approximately 1.5 percent in the United States and the remaining countries and 2 percent in China and emerging Asia excluding China. The remaining errors arise from overestimating potential output growth for each year of the forecast horizon. This implies errors in the annual growth rate of potential output of roughly ¾ percentage point in China, ½ percentage point in other emerging Asian economies, and ¼ percentage point in the United States and the remaining countries. It is assumed that no one recognizes the error until 2013.[2]

In the first scenario, once policymakers recognize the error, monetary policy must be tightened sharply to return inflation to target. Markets also respond and drive lending rates up by an additional amount that is roughly proportional to the magnitude of the misperception about supply capacity. Essentially, the realization that monetary conditions have been excessively loose for an extended period raises concerns about underlying asset quality. Consequently, the scenario incorporates temporary but persistent increases in private market interest rates of an additional 150 basis points in China, 100 basis points in the United States and emerging Asia excluding China, and 50 basis points in the euro area and the remaining countries (Figure 1.2.1).

In the first two years, real GDP grows according to the baseline forecast. However, given the misperception of supply capacity, demand pressures emerge in many regions of the world, and inflation

The main author of this box is Benjamin Hunt. Mika Kortelainen and Stephen Snudden contributed.

[1]The block of remaining countries includes all the world economies except the United States, the euro area, Japan, China, and emerging Asia.

[2]An alternative approach would be to have policymakers learn gradually about their misperceptions regarding the level of potential output and start to tighten policy prior to 2013. If this were the case, then real GDP would turn out to be below the baseline prior to 2013, and the subsequent macroeconomic volatility would be reduced.

## Box 1.2 *(continued)*

**Figure 1.2.1. WEO Downside Scenario 1: Implications of Overestimating Potential Output**
*(Percentage point difference from baseline)*

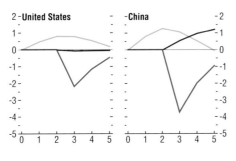
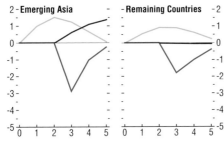
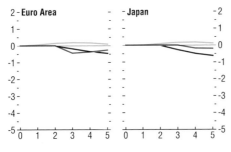

Source: Global Integrated Monetary and Fiscal Model simulations.

rises above the baseline forecast. It rises most sharply in China and other emerging Asian economies, but it also rises in the United States and the remaining countries. Although not explicit in the analysis, it is likely that the demand and inflation pressures would be most acute in the emerging market economies contained within the block of remaining countries, notably those heavily dependent on commodity

exports. Even though rising inflation would signal the potential output error to the Federal Reserve, slow recovery in the labor market coupled with an overly optimistic view of the level for structural unemployment could prevent a timely adjustment in monetary conditions. Competitiveness concerns in other regions of the world could lead to conditions remaining too loose there also, despite high inflation.

Policymakers and markets do not recognize the true level of potential output and its future path until 2013. This leads to tightening in monetary policy rates and additional increases in private market interest rates. Higher interest rates, recognition of weaker future income growth, and the consequent fiscal adjustment would all contribute to a sharp slowdown in private consumption and investment growth. Real GDP growth declines in 2013 by almost 4 percent in China, 3 percent in other emerging Asian economies, and roughly 2 percent in the United States and the remaining countries. The declines in growth are much milder in the euro area and Japan. Growth remains notably below the WEO baseline in 2014, but returns close to the baseline by 2015. The sharp slowdown in growth is sufficient to return inflation close to the baseline by 2015.

Under this scenario, global imbalances would widen further. Economies that already have high surpluses (China and other emerging Asian economies) experience an improvement in their current account balances because aggregate demand adjustment is largest in those regions. As consumption and investment demand slow rapidly, import growth falls sharply, leading to a rising trade balance. In the United States and the remaining countries, current accounts are largely unchanged as weaker import growth broadly matches the pace of slowing export growth. For the euro area and Japan, with no required adjustment in domestic demand, weaker trading partner growth translates to slower export growth, and their current accounts deteriorate.

In the second scenario, the initial burst in inflation becomes more entrenched in expectations, which is conceivable in a global environment where high and rising commodity prices are likely to be fueling

## Box 1.2 *(continued)*

headline rates well above recent historical experience. In addition to more persistent high inflation, it is assumed that market concerns over asset quality following the boom are more acute. Consequently, once policymakers recognize the error and tighten policy rates, markets drive lending rates up further than in the first scenario. Market interest rates rise above policy rates by an additional 300 basis points in China, 200 basis points in the United States and emerging Asia excluding China, and 100 basis points in the euro area and remaining countries (Figure 1.2.2).

Again the scenario assumes that in the first two years GDP growth rates match those in the baseline, but with potential output lower than expected, excess demand pressures drive inflation above the paths in the baseline. Once monetary policymakers and markets recognize the error in 2013, the larger response in interest rates leads to a sharper slowdown in growth. The slowdown is most dramatic in China, where GDP growth falls by roughly 5 percentage points, followed by emerging Asia, where growth declines by almost 4 percentage points. Growth falls by close to 3 percentage points in the United States and by just over 2 percentage points in the remaining countries. The greater persistence in inflation means that interest rates must remain higher for longer to keep GDP growth rates considerably below baseline in 2014 and 2015. Despite substantial excess supply opening up in these economies, inflation has not returned to target by the end of the WEO forecast horizon, implying that growth would need to be maintained below its potential rate beyond 2015. Not surprisingly, with real activity more adversely affected by the misperception of the level of potential output in this scenario, global imbalances widen even further.

For policymakers, these scenarios illustrate how plausible errors in estimating potential output can lead to considerable volatility in growth and inflation and a widening of global imbalances if the error is only slowly recognized. Further, should high inflation become entrenched in expectations, significant permanent losses in real GDP would be required to reestablish low and stable inflation. Policymakers should look carefully to core inflation outcomes to inform their estimates about underlying potential output and structural unemployment

**Figure 1.2.2. WEO Downside Scenario 2: Implications of Overestimating Potential Output with Sticky Inflation**
*(Percentage point difference from baseline)*

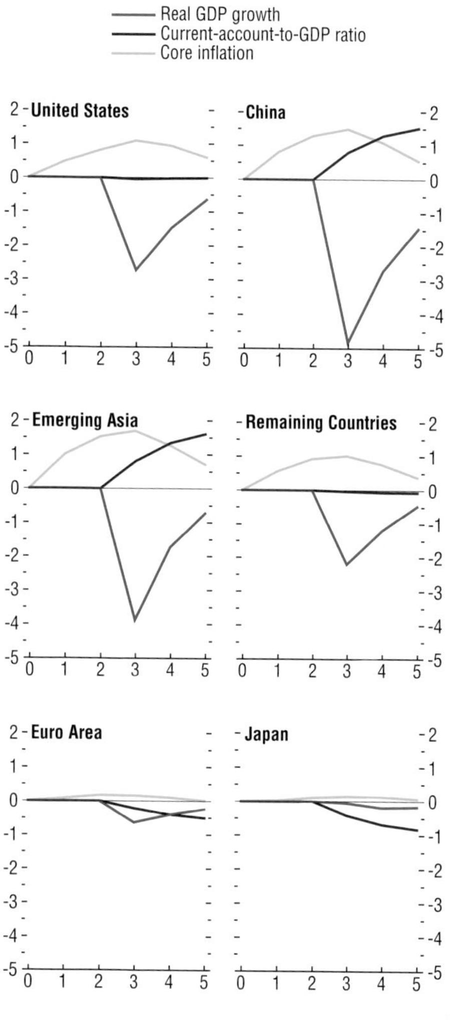

Source: Global Integrated Monetary and Fiscal Model simulations.

and should be prepared to revise those estimates regularly. For emerging economies already exhibiting signs of overheating, competitiveness concerns should be of secondary importance. Containing inflation pressures early could substantially reduce future economic volatility.

## Box 1.3. International Spillovers and Macroeconomic Policymaking

The duration and severity of the Great Recession induced a variety of unconventional policy responses in a number of countries. This is especially true in the United States, where an alphabet soup of liquidity support programs has been complemented by two rounds of so-called quantitative easing. The latest round, dubbed "QE2" by some, has been met with opprobrium in some circles, in part because the Federal Reserve's aggressive attempts to return employment to normal levels are seen as damaging to the interests of smaller economies, particularly those that do not consider themselves to have substantial excess supply. Out of this experience have come renewed calls for international policy coordination. This box takes a selective look at this issue, focusing on monetary policy coordination but with a few words on fiscal policy at the end.

To presage the results, policy coordination can deliver outcomes that are superior to those of policies that are driven only by national interests. However, it turns out that the case for systematic coordination of monetary policy is not as strong as one might think, although the range of models in which this question has been analyzed is still quite limited. More research is clearly warranted. By contrast, the case for coordination is easier to make for fiscal policy.

Popular discussion suggests that the argument in favor of policy coordination—in particular for large economies or collections of small ones—is irrefutable. After all, in times of widespread deficiency in domestic demand, all economies have an incentive to "export their way out of recession," even if the arithmetic of trade accounts makes that an impossible feat. The economic literature, however, is not nearly so clear-cut. In the context of monetary policy, Obstfeld and Rogoff (1995) laid down a marker by showing in a simple two-country model that policies that are "self-oriented" are difficult to beat. Subsequent contributions to the literature have mitigated this result, but arguably not in a way that undermines the case for self-oriented monetary policy, at least as a reasonable

The author of this box is Robert Tetlow.

approximation of the optimal policy.[1] If the theory is ambiguous, quantitative assessments are even more so, if only because there have been so few.

To illustrate, consider the policy choices available to the monetary authority of a small economy operating in a world that is dominated by a much larger economy. In order to encompass the rigidities and imperfections in exchange rate pass-through emphasized by the literature to date in making a case for coordination, we use a version of the IMF's Global Economic Model (GEM) used in Laxton and Pesenti (2003).[2] Both economies are assumed to implement monetary policy by means of a Taylor-type rule, the most general form of which is

$$R = \alpha_R R_{t-1} + (1 - \alpha_R)(rr^* + \bar{\pi}_t) + \alpha_y y_t$$
$$+ \alpha_\pi(\bar{\pi}_t - \pi^*) + \alpha_e(\Delta e_t - \Delta e^*),$$

where $R$ is the nominal policy rate; $\bar{\pi}$ is (four-quarter) inflation; $\Delta e$ is the change in the (log of the) real exchange rate; and $rr^*$ is the equilibrium real interest rate. For this exercise, $rr^*$ and the target rate of inflation, $\pi^*$, are taken as constants and normalized to zero; some implications of this assumption are discussed below.

Assume that the large economy does not consider the effects of its policy decisions on the small economy—which is natural given the relative sizes of the two economies. One way to characterize the critique of recent U.S. monetary policy is to consider policy rules for the large economy that place a large coefficient on its output gap, sacrificing other objectives in order to rapidly return economic activity to equilibrium levels following shocks. With this

[1]The case for the coordination of monetary policy usually hinges on rigidities that slow down the pass-through of foreign shocks into domestic aggregate price levels. Incomplete or delayed exchange rate pass-through hinders the adjustment of the real wage to its equilibrium level, inducing fluctuations in employment that would otherwise not occur. An incomplete sampling of references might include Betts and Devereux (2000), Pappa (2004), and Corsetti and Pesenti (2005).

[2]GEM is a linearized microfounded, two-country model with tradable and nontradable goods, monopolistic competition in labor and some goods markets, sticky prices, and incomplete pass-through stemming both from the presence of intermediate goods and from adjustment costs. See Laxton and Pesenti (2003) for details.

## Box 1.3 *(continued)*

in mind, the exercise below encompasses this and other policy stances by allowing the coefficient on the large economy output gap, $\alpha_y$, to vary from zero to 3.[3] The small economy takes the large economy's policy rule as given and then chooses the coefficient on the exchange rate term in the small-economy policy rule, holding other coefficients constant to minimize the following loss function:[4]

$$L = \Sigma_{i=0}^{\infty} \, y_{t+i}^2 + (\bar{\pi}_{t+i} - \pi^*)^2 + \tfrac{1}{2} \, (\Delta R_{t+i})^2.$$

If the large economy's policy choice is harmful to the small economy's performance, and if controlling the exchange rate is helpful for offsetting the large economy's policy choices, $\alpha_e$ for the small economy will differ substantially from zero, and the effect on the small economy's economic performance, as measured by its loss function, will be large.[5]

The results of this exercise are summarized in Figure 1.3.1. The coefficient on the large economy's output gap is indexed on the horizontal axis. Focusing first on the blue line, there are several observations of note. First, the downward slope of the line shows that as the large economy places increasing importance on combating output fluctuations, the small economy's exchange rate coefficient *falls;* only when the large economy pays almost no (direct) attention to output is there a reason for the small

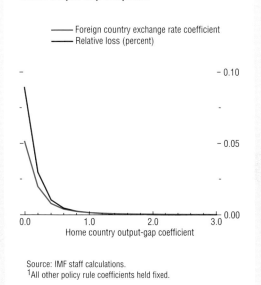

Figure 1.3.1. Optimized Exchange Rate Coefficient and Relative Loss as a Function of Home Output Gap Response[1]

—— Foreign country exchange rate coefficient
—— Relative loss (percent)

Source: IMF staff calculations.
[1]All other policy rule coefficients held fixed.

economy to respond to the exchange rate, at least through standard monetary policy channels. Second, the quantitative implications for monetary policy with respect to the exchange rate are not very large: at no time does the feedback coefficient rise above 0.1.[6] These results suggest that large and small economies' objectives are largely complementary: when the large economy acts to stabilize real activity within its own borders, it reduces what would otherwise be negative demand spillovers to the rest of the world. The fact that the coefficient on the exchange rate in the small economy's policy rule is never very large is a reminder that stabilizing inflation, as the economy does in all cases here, goes a considerable way toward stabilizing output, regardless of the feedback coefficient on the gap.

[3]For a model of this class, $\alpha_y = 3$ is a very large coefficient. For the home economy, the baseline parameters for the policy rule are $\alpha_R = 1$, $\alpha_\pi = 0.7$, $\alpha_y = varying$, and $\alpha_e \equiv 0$. Results are similar for different parameterizations of the home economy rule and, in particular, for $\alpha_e \neq 0$. For the foreign country, $\alpha_R = 0.97$, $\alpha_\pi = 0.7$, $\alpha_y = 0.4$, and $\alpha_e = optimized$. The foreign country's coefficients are very close to the optimal coefficients, conditional on no feedback on the exchange rate.

[4]Formally, the optimization is done numerically by minimizing the loss function, subject to the (linear) model; the form of the policy rule; the home economy model, including its policy rule; and the variance-covariance matrix of stochastic shocks. This is the same loss function that is used in Laxton and Pesenti (2003).

[5]The experiment conducted here is a restricted version of one where all four parameters of both economies' policy rules are optimized economy by economy, defining what is known as a Nash strategy in Taylor rules, or jointly using a weighted average of the two economies' loss functions, defining a cooperative strategy in Taylor rules. This broader exercise proved to be numerically problematic for a model as large and complex as the GEM; however, the experiments that were feasible suggested that the same conclusions as described in the text would be forthcoming.

[6]Although this exercise was carried out for particular rules for both economies, the basic conclusions are the same for reasonable specifications. However, the results will differ if the parameterization of the policy rule for the foreign economy is well away from optimal, when the exchange rate term is omitted. Under such circumstances the optimized exchange rate term will crudely proxy for the inappropriate feedback terms on output or inflation.

## Box 1.3 (continued)

Now consider the red line. The line shows the incremental cost, in percent (right scale), of omitting the exchange rate term altogether. Given how small the feedback coefficients are on the exchange rate term, it is probably not surprising that the loss from eschewing feedback on the exchange rate is very small, never larger than 0.1 percent. The upshot, in this context at least, is the conclusion of Obstfeld and Rogoff (2002): two economies practicing inward-looking policies will produce policy outcomes that are quite good, even if they are not quite optimal. It is important to note that it is not that spillovers from the large economy to the small economy are inconsequential. Rather, a properly designed monetary policy, focused narrowly on key macroeconomic objectives, insulates the small economy well. It does this by aligning private agents' expectations with policymakers' goals; the former becomes an instrument, of sorts, of the latter.[7]

There are, of course, some caveats. First, the results depend on the monetary authorities knowing not only their own economy's model but that of the other economy as well.[8] Second, the optimization exercise was carried out for a computed variance-covariance matrix of shocks, but if the shocks during a particular episode turn out to be atypical, the prescribed policy response might be inappropriate. This is true particularly if the shocks in question alter the dynamic structure of the economy.[9] Third, these results are conditional on

the model and all its features, including linearity and rational expectations. These can be important. The linear analysis carried out here, for example, ignores the effective lower bound on nominal interest rates, a binding constraint on some authorities at the moment. And the extant literature has considered only a limited range of distortions that might provide a case for cooperation. Undoubtedly, there is a need for further research on these and other issues. Nevertheless, the results shown here—which are consistent with the economic literature—do suggest that the case for coordination of monetary policy is limited, at least under normal circumstances and with conventional models.

We have seen that the case for monetary policy coordination is not as obvious as might be expected. Does this finding generalize to fiscal policy? It was noted above that the analysis here was conducted taking the equilibrium real interest rate, $rr^*$, as a constant. This is a reasonable assumption for economies with a record of stable monetary policy. Under such circumstances, the conduct of monetary policy is a relatively simple exercise in stabilizing the economy around a given steady state. The situation for fiscal policy can be quite different. Although it is beyond the scope of this box to demonstrate, fiscal policy can affect the equilibrium real interest rate, the sustainable level of output, and the neutral level of the policy instrument, sometimes in ways that are difficult to measure. Fiscal policy, therefore, involves balancing gains or losses in the short term against permanent but deferred losses or gains in the long term as the economy approaches its new steady state. So if an economy's monetary policy is already broadly reasonable, the stakes when it comes to adjusting fiscal policy are generally higher. Moreover, fiscal policy in large economies, or collections of small ones, can affect the world real interest rate and hence the steady state of other economies. It seems reasonable to conclude, therefore, that the case for coordination of macroeconomic stabilization policies is stronger for fiscal policy than for monetary policy.

---

[7]Specifically not included in the class of policy regimes covered here is an exchange rate target, de facto or de jure. Under an exchange rate target, the foreign economy inherits whichever monetary policy the home economy adopts. Box 1.1 of the April 2010 *World Economic Outlook* explores exchange rate targeting regimes during the recent crisis.

[8]How serious this misspecification will be depends on the circumstances. It is worth noting that the apparent misspecification of the variance-covariance matrix of shocks is often a symptom of a more generalized misspecification of the underlying model. Frankel and Rockett (1988) provide a quantitative assessment of what can go wrong in policy coordination when decision makers' models are misspecified.

[9]For example, shocks that are larger and more persistent than normal could elicit macroeconomic outcomes that cause private agents to doubt the monetary or fiscal policy regime. Coordinated policies could be used to ensure the reestablish-

ment of rational expectations equilibrium. For an example along these lines, see Eusepi and Preston (2008).

## Box 1.4. Did the Plaza Accord Cause Japan's Lost Decades?

The rebalancing debate has sparked renewed interest in Japan's experience since the 1980s. Some argue that this is a cautionary tale, exemplifying the dangers of reorienting economies through currency appreciation (*People's Daily*, 2010). They claim that the appreciation of the yen after the Plaza Accord forced the authorities to introduce an offsetting macroeconomic stimulus, which then led to an extraordinary asset price boom followed by an extraordinarily painful bust. Japan was one of the world's fastest-growing economies for three decades but has averaged only 1.1 percent real GDP growth since 1990, while prices have steadily declined. Consequently, the size of Japan's economy today is about the same as in the early 1990s. The sequence of events is clear and striking. But there are reasons to doubt that it was truly inevitable, whether the Plaza Accord was really the direct cause of Japan's "Lost Decades."

### What Happened?

The events began in September 1985, when delegates from the G5 countries met at the Plaza Hotel in New York, declared the U.S. dollar overvalued, and announced a plan to correct the situation.[1] The essence of the plan was that the main current account surplus countries (Japan and Germany) would boost domestic demand and appreciate their currencies. In effect, this agreement marked a major change in policy regime: the Federal Reserve was signaling that after a long and successful fight against inflation, it was now prepared to ease policies, allow the dollar to decline, and focus more on growth. This signal was backed by coordinated currency market intervention and a steady reduction in U.S. short-term rates. Accordingly, it triggered an exceptionally large appreciation of the yen, amounting to 46 percent against the dollar and 30 percent in real effective terms by the end of 1986. (The deutsche mark appreciated similarly.)

As a result, Japan's export and GDP growth essentially halted in the first half of 1986. With the

economy in recession and the exchange rate appreciating rapidly, the authorities were under considerable pressure to respond. They did so by introducing a sizable macroeconomic stimulus. Policy interest rates were reduced by about 3 percentage points, a stance that was sustained until 1989. A large fiscal package was introduced in 1987, even though a vigorous recovery had already started in the second half of 1986. By 1987, Japan's output was booming, but so were credit growth and asset prices, with stock and urban land prices tripling from 1985 to 1989. Then, in January 1990, the stock price bubble burst. Share prices lost a third of their value within a year, and two decades of dismal economic performance followed (Figure 1.4.1). Today, nominal stock and land prices are back at their early 1980s levels, one-quarter to one-third of their previous peaks.

The critical question is whether this sequence was inevitable. In other words, did the appreciation force Japan to introduce a powerful stimulus to sustain growth, which then triggered a bubble, which caused the Lost Decades when it collapsed? Let's consider each step in turn.

### Was Such a Large Stimulus Needed?

Studies suggest that, in fact, the monetary policy easing may have been excessive. Estimates by Jinushi, Kuroki, and Miyao (2000) and Leigh (2010), among others, suggest that the policy rate was up to 4 percentage points too low during 1986–88 relative to an implicit Taylor rule based on the output and inflation outlook. Why, then, did the central bank sustain such a policy? A key reason is that current inflation remained reasonably well behaved, which led some economists to argue that soaring growth rates did not represent a cyclical boom but rather a "new era" of higher potential growth. This growth was particularly gratifying because it was led by domestic demand, a key commitment under Plaza.

But IMF reports at the time suggest another factor was also at work. The authorities worried that higher interest rates would further strengthen the yen and feared that appreciation would eventually have serious effects on the economy. In the end, external demand did indeed diminish. But it did

---

The main authors of this box are Joshua Felman and Daniel Leigh.

[1] The G5 comprises France, Germany, Japan, the United Kingdom, and the United States.

## Box 1.4 *(continued)*

not collapse. Real exports continued to grow in the five years after Plaza, by an average of 2½ percent a year (half the rate of the previous five years), while the current account surplus diminished by a moderate 2 percentage points of GDP. (Similarly, Germany's currency appreciation failed to derail its export or GDP expansion, even with a smaller monetary response.) Put another way, excessive stimulus was adopted in part because there was excessive concern about the impact of appreciation.

### Did the Stimulus Cause the Bubble?

Although the monetary easing was certainly large, it is far from clear that it alone was responsible for the asset price bubble. Chapter 3 of the October 2009 *World Economic Outlook* and Posen (2003) have examined the link between monetary policy and asset price booms in advanced economies over the past 25 years. They conclude that policy easing is neither necessary nor sufficient to generate asset price booms and busts. In Japan's case, two other elements seem to have played a large role. As Hoshi and Kashyap (2000) explain, financial deregulation in the 1970s and early 1980s allowed large firms to access capital markets instead of depending on bank financing, leading banks to lend instead to real estate developers and households seeking mortgages. As a result, bank credit to these two sectors grew by about 150 percent during 1985–90, roughly twice as fast as the 77 percent increase in overall bank credit to the private sector. Finally, because the dangers of real estate bubbles were not well understood in those years, the Japanese government did not deploy countervailing regulatory and fiscal policies until 1990.

### Did the Bubble's Collapse Cause the Lost Decades?

The aftermath of the bubble proved extraordinarily painful for Japan. But the collapse of a bubble does not inevitably have such powerful and long-lasting effects. What was special about Japan's case? A key factor was the buildup of considerable leverage in the financial system, similar to what occurred in the United States before 2008. Tier 1 capital of Japanese banks in the 1980s was very low, much lower than elsewhere, as global standards (the Basel

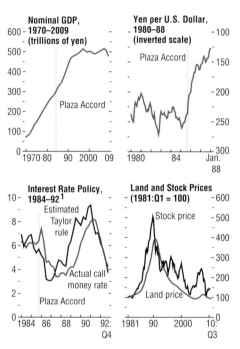

**Figure 1.4.1. Japan: Selected Macroeconomic Indicators**

Sources: Bank of Japan; Cabinet Office (Japan); Haver Analytics; and IMF staff estimates.
[1]For details on the estimation of the Taylor rule, see Leigh (2010).

I accord) had not yet gone into effect. Moreover, much of the collateral for loans was in the form of real estate, whereas under the *keiretsu* system a significant portion of bank assets consisted of shares in other firms from the same group. So, when real estate and share prices collapsed, the banking system was badly damaged.

This underlying vulnerability was exacerbated by a slow policy response. The authorities delayed forcing banks to recognize the losses on their balance sheets and allowed them to continue lending to firms that had themselves become insolvent, a process Caballero, Hoshi, and Kashyap (2008) call "zombie lending." This process continued into the early 2000s, stifling productivity growth and prolonging Japan's slump. Why did the authorities not force faster restructuring? Possibly because restructuring

**Box 1.4** *(continued)*

**Figure 1.4.2.  Japan and China: Balance Sheets and Export Content**

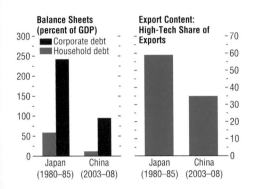

Sources: Haver Analytics; and IMF staff estimates.

would have required additional bank capital, which they were not in a position to provide in light of the strong political backlash after an initial injection of public capital in 1995. Consequently, the authorities exercised forbearance instead.

The postbubble slump may also have been exacerbated by the macroeconomic policy response and adverse external shocks. Some argue that premature monetary tightening and the lack of a clear commitment to raising inflation led to unduly high real interest rates (Ito and Mishkin, 2006; Leigh, 2010). In addition, the tightening of fiscal policy in 1997 may have undercut the nascent 1995–96 recovery (Posen, 2003; Corbett and Ito, 2010). Finally, adverse external shocks played a role, including the 1997–98 Asian financial crisis.

In sum, Japan's experience shows that currency appreciation does not, in fact, inevitably lead to "lost decades." The appreciation did not inevitably require such a large macroeconomic stimulus. The stimulus did not inevitably lead to the bubble. Nor did the bubble's collapse inevitably lead to the Lost Decades. Instead, it was the particular combination of circumstances and choices that led to that result.

*Lessons for Rebalancing Today*

Calibrating a policy response to exceptionally large appreciations and movements in asset prices remains an extraordinarily difficult task. But some pointers can be gleaned from Japan's experience. The keys are to

- avoid an excessive macroeconomic response to currency appreciations;
- use prudential policies to prevent vulnerabilities from building up, especially in the form of leverage;
- address banking problems quickly if they do materialize; and
- provide significant macroeconomic support when banking systems and economies come under stress.

An even broader lesson is that bubbles can prove dangerous. Accordingly, Japan has introduced a two-perspective framework for monetary policy, with one pillar focusing on price stability and the other looking out for financial imbalances such as asset price bubbles.

But even as Japan's experience offers lessons to countries considering rebalancing today, the direct parallels are limited. Most notably, circumstances in China today differ from those in Japan in the 1980s in ways that should help it avoid Japan's disappointing outcomes (Figure 1.4.2). First, the leverage of households, corporations, and the government in China is lower now than it was in Japan before the bubble (N'Diaye, 2010), and the risk of excessive borrowing may thus be smaller. Second, as Chapter 4 of the April 2010 *World Economic Outlook* and Igan, Fabrizio, and Mody (2007) find, climbing the quality ladder helps offset the impact on growth of currency appreciation, and China has more room to climb the export quality ladder than Japan did. (At the same time, the impact on labor-intensive industries may be greater.) Third, Japan had a floating exchange rate regime in the 1980s, but China has a managed exchange rate supported by vast foreign currency reserves and strong restrictions on capital inflows. This difference in currency regimes should help China avoid the sharp appreciation observed in Japan. Most important, China should be able to reap the benefits of learning from Japan's experience.

## References

Alesina, Alberto, and Allan Drazen, 1991, "Why Are Stabilizations Delayed?" *American Economic Review,* Vol. 81, No. 5, pp. 1170–88.

Alesina, Alberto, and Roberto Perotti, 1995, "Fiscal Expansions and Fiscal Adjustments in OECD Countries," *Economic Policy*, Vol. 10, No. 21, pp. 205–48.

Betts, Caroline, and Michael B. Devereux, 2000, "International Monetary Policy Coordination and Competitive Depreciation: A Reevaluation," *Journal of Money, Credit and Banking*, Vol. 32, No. 4, part 1, pp. 722–45.

Bornhorst, Fabian, Nina Budina, Giovanni Callegari, Asmaa ElGanainy, Raquel Gomez Sirera, Andrea Lemgruber, Andrea Schaechter, and Joong Beom Shin, 2010, "A Status Update on Fiscal Exit Strategies," IMF Working Paper 10/272 (Washington: International Monetary Fund).

Brooks, Robin, and Alberto Ramos, 2010, "Inflation Generalization in Emerging Markets," *Goldman Sachs Global Markets Daily* (December 23).

Caballero, Ricardo J., Takeo Hoshi, and Anil K. Kashyap, 2008, "Zombie Lending and Depressed Restructuring in Japan," *American Economic Review,* Vol. 98, No. 5, pp. 1943–77.

Carabenciov, Ioan, Charles Freedman, Roberto Garcia-Saltos, Douglas Laxton, Ondrej Kamenik, and Petar Manchev, forthcoming, "GPM6—The Global Projection Model with Six Regions," IMF Working Paper (Washington: International Monetary Fund).

Claessens, Stijn, M. Ayhan Kose, and Marco E. Terrones, forthcoming, "How Do Business and Financial Cycles Interact?" IMF Working Paper (Washington: International Monetary Fund).

———, 2011, "Financial Cycles: What? How? When?" in *NBER International Seminar in Macroeconomics 2010*, ed. by Richard Clarida and Francesco Giavazzi (Cambridge, Massachusetts: National Bureau of Economic Research).

Coady, David, Robert Gillingham, Rolando Ossowski, John M. Piotrowski, Shamsuddin Tareq, and Justin Tyson, 2010, "Petroleum Product Subsidies: Costly, Inequitable, and Rising," IMF Staff Position Note 10/05 (Washington: International Monetary Fund).

Corbett, Jenny, and Takatoshi Ito, 2010, "What Should the US and China Learn from the Past US-Japan Conflict?" *VoxEU* (April 30). www.voxeu.org/index.php?q=node/4856.

Corsetti, Giancarlo, and Paolo Pesenti, 2005, "International Dimensions of Optimal Monetary Policy," *Journal of Monetary Economics,* Vol. 52, No. 2, pp. 281–305.

Dobbs, Richard, and Michael Spence, 2011, "The Era of Cheap Capital Draws to a Close," *McKinsey Quarterly* (February).

Dowling, Thomas, Marcello M. Estevão, and Evridiki Tsounta, 2010, "The Great Recession and Structural Unemployment," *United States: Selected Issues Paper*, IMF Country Report No. 10/248 (Washington: International Monetary Fund).

Elekdag, Selim, and Prakash Kannan, 2009, "Incorporating Market Information into the Construction of the Fan Chart," IMF Working Paper 09/178 (Washington: International Monetary Fund).

Estevão, Marcello M., and Tiago Severo, 2010. "Financial Shocks and TFP Growth," IMF Working Paper 10/23 (Washington: International Monetary Fund).

Eusepi, Stefano, and Bruce Preston, 2008, "Stabilizing Expectations under Monetary and Fiscal Policy Coordination," NBER Working Paper No. 14391 (Cambridge, Massachusetts: National Bureau of Economic Research).

Frankel, Jeffrey A., and Katharine E. Rockett, 1988, "International Macroeconomic Policy Coordination When Policy-Makers Do Not Agree on the Model," *American Economic Review*, Vol. 78, No. 3, pp. 318–40.

Giannone, Domenico, Lucrezia Reichlin, and Luca Sala, 2005, "Monetary Policy in Real Time," in *NBER Macroeconomics Annual 2004,* ed. by Mark Gertler and Kenneth Rogoff (Cambridge, Massachusetts: MIT Press), pp. 161–200.

Giannone, Domenico, Lucrezia Reichlin, and David Small, 2008, "Nowcasting: The Real-Time Informational Content of Macroeconomic Data," *Journal of Monetary Economics*, Vol. 55, No. 4, pp. 665–76.

Giuliano, Paola, Prachi Mishra, and Antonio Spilimbergo, 2009, "Democracy and Reforms," IZA Discussion Paper No. 4032 (Bonn: Institute for the Study of Labor).

Gourinchas, Pierre Olivier, Rodrigo Valdés, and Oscar Landerretche, 2001, "Lending Booms: Latin America and the World," *Economia,* Vol. 1, No. 2 (Spring), pp. 41–63.

Group of Twenty, 2010, "G20 Mutual Assessment Process— Alternative Policy Scenarios," report prepared by staff of the International Monetary Fund for the G20 Mutual Assessment Process, G-20 Toronto Summit, Toronto, Canada, June 26–27 (Washington: International Monetary Fund). www.imf.org/external/np/g20/pdf/062710a.pdf.

Hoshi, Takeo, and Anil Kashyap, 2000, "The Japanese Banking Crisis: Where Did It Come From and How Will It End?" *NBER Macroeconomics Annual* 1999, ed. by Ben S. Bernanke and Julio J. Rotemberg (Cambridge, Massachusetts: National Bureau of Economic Research), pp. 129–212.

Igan, Deniz, Stefania Fabrizio, and Ashoka Mody, 2007, "The Dynamics of Product Quality and International Competitiveness," IMF Working Paper 07/97 (Washington: International Monetary Fund).

Ito, Takatoshi, and Frederic S. Mishkin, 2006, "Two Decades of Japanese Monetary Policy and the Deflation Problem," in *Monetary Policy under Very Low Inflation in the Pacific Rim*, ed. by Takatoshi Ito and Andrew K. Rose, NBER East Asia Seminar on Economics, Vol. 15 (Chicago: University of Chicago Press), pp. 131–201.

Jinushi, Toshiki, Yoshihiro Kuroki, and Ryuzo Miyao, 2000, "Monetary Policy in Japan since the Late 1980s: Delayed Policy Actions and Some Explanations," in *Japan's Financial Crisis and Its Parallels to U.S. Experience,* ed. by Ryoichi Mikitani and Adam S. Posen (Washington: Institute for International Economics).

Kahn, Lisa, 2010, "The Long-Term Labor Market Consequences of Graduating from College in a Bad Economy," *Labor Economics,* Vol. 17, No. 2, pp. 303–16.

Laxton, Douglas, and Paolo Pesenti, 2003, "Monetary Rules for Small, Open, Emerging Economies," *Journal of Monetary Economics,* Vol. 50 (July), pp. 1109–46.

Leigh, Daniel, 2010, "Monetary Policy and the Lost Decade: Lessons from Japan," *Journal of Money, Credit and Banking*, Vol. 42, No. 5, pp. 833–57.

Liu, Philip, Rafael Romeu, and Troy D. Matheson, forthcoming, "Real-Time Forecasts of Economic Activity for Latin American Countries," IMF Working Paper (Washington: International Monetary Fund).

Matheson, Troy D., 2010, "An Analysis of the Informational Content of New Zealand Data Releases: The Importance of Business Opinion Surveys," *Economic Modelling,* Vol. 27, No. 1, pp. 304–14.

———, 2011, "New Indicators for Tracking Growth in Real Time," IMF Working Paper 11/43 (Washington: International Monetary Fund).

Mendoza, Enrique, and Marco E. Terrones, 2008, "An Anatomy of Credit Booms: Evidence from Macro Aggregates and Micro Data," NBER Working Paper No. 14049 (Cambridge, Massachusetts: National Bureau of Economic Research).

N'Diaye, Papa M'B. P., 2010, "Transforming China: Insights from the Japanese Experience of the 1980s," IMF Working Paper 10/284 (Washington: International Monetary Fund).

Obstfeld, Maurice, and Kenneth Rogoff, 1995, "Exchange Rate Dynamics Redux," *Journal of Political Economy*, Vol. 103, No. 3, pp. 624–60.

———, 2002, "Global Implications of Self-Oriented National Monetary Rules," *Quarterly Journal of Economics*, Vol. 117, No. 2, pp. 503–36.

Ostry, Jonathan D., Atish R. Ghosh, Karl Habermeier, Marcos Chamon, Mahvash S. Qureshi, and Dennis B. S. Reinhardt, 2010, "Capital Inflows: The Role of Controls," IMF Staff Position Note 10/04 (Washington: International Monetary Fund).

Ostry, Jonathan D., Atish R. Ghosh, Karl Habermeier, Luc Laeven, Marcos Chamon, Mahvash S. Qureshi, and Annamaria Kokenyne, 2011, "Managing Capital Inflows: What Tools to Use?" IMF Staff Discussion Note 11/06 (Washington: International Monetary Fund).

Pappa, Evi, 2004, "Do the ECB and the Fed Really Need to Cooperate? Optimal Monetary Policy in a Two-Country World," *Journal of Monetary Economics*, Vol. 51, No. 4, pp. 753–79.

*People's Daily*, 2010, "No Repeat of Japan's Mistake: Official" (September 20). http://english.people.com.cn/90001/90778/90859/7145687.html.

Posen, Adam, 2003, "It Takes More Than a Bubble to Become Japan," in *Asset Prices and Monetary Policy,* ed. by Anthony Richards and Tim Robinson (Sydney: Reserve Bank of Australia).

Poterba, James M., 1994, "State Responses to Fiscal Crises: The Effects of Budgetary Institutions and Politics," *Journal of Political Economy,* Vol. 102, No. 4, pp. 799–821.

Roubini, Nouriel, and Jeffrey Sachs, 1989, "Political and Economic Determinants of Budget Deficits in the Industrial Democracies," *European Economic Review,* Vol. 33 (May), pp. 903–34.

———, Seppo Honkapohja, and Daniel Cohen, 1989, "Government Spending and Budget Deficits in the Industrial Countries," *Economic Policy,* Vol. 4, No. 8, pp. 100–32.

Swiston, Andrew, 2008, "A U.S. Financial Conditions Index: Putting Credit Where Credit Is Due," IMF Working Paper 08/161 (Washington: International Monetary Fund).

*The global economy is now two years into its recovery. From the outset, it was expected to be a multispeed recovery—the April 2009* World Economic Outlook *projected that the economies that would be growing the fastest by 2011 were those that had avoided large precrisis imbalances, had seen the smallest output collapses during the crisis, and had the most room for policy maneuvering after the crisis. Two years later, that picture is broadly unchanged, but the contours of the recovery are clearer (Figure 2.1). Some advanced economies have significant output gaps and elevated unemployment rates; many low-income countries are growing at rapid but sustainable rates; and there are signs of overheating in a number of emerging market economies.*

The uneven nature of this recovery can be seen in the output gaps across regions (Figure 2.2). Emerging Asia and much of Latin America are now operating close to potential, and there are economies in these regions where credit is reaccelerating and signs of overheating are emerging. Meanwhile, the economies at the center of the recent crisis, the United States and Europe, have substantial excess capacity. These divergences have important implications for the outlook, risks, and policy priorities in each region. Therefore, this chapter highlights the extent to which regions differ in their cyclical positions.

Similarly, there are large disparities in some economies' external positions. Past issues of the *World Economic Outlook* have stressed the need for external rebalancing in some regions—most notably the United States and emerging Asia—to reduce global vulnerabilities. This chapter revisits this topic to highlight, where relevant, the extent to which regions diverge in their external (current account balance) positions.

The chapter begins by assessing the outlook and key policy challenges in the regions where large output

**Figure 2.1. Global Average Projected Real GDP Growth during 2011–12**
*(Percent)*

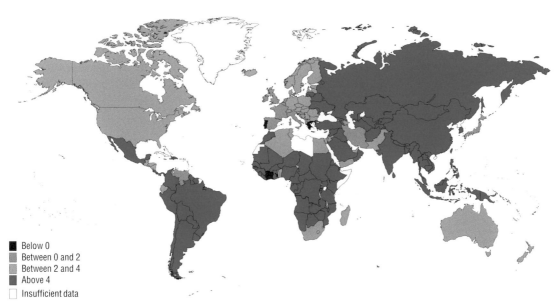

- ■ Below 0
- ■ Between 0 and 2
- ■ Between 2 and 4
- ■ Above 4
- □ Insufficient data

Source: IMF staff estimates.
Note: Projections are not provided for Libya due to the uncertain political situation.

**Figure 2.2.  Output Gaps[1]**

*(Percent of potential GDP)*

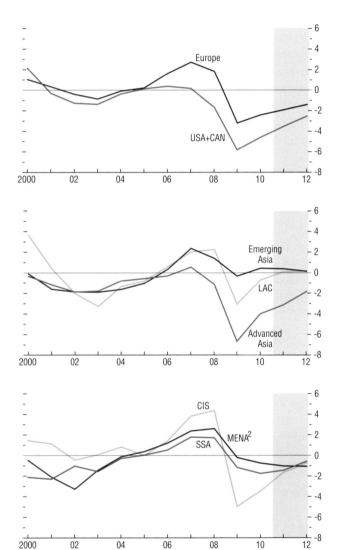

Source: IMF staff estimates.
[1]Advanced Asia: Australia, Japan, and New Zealand; CIS: Commonwealth of Independent States, Georgia, and Mongolia; LAC: Latin America and the Caribbean; MENA: Middle East and North Africa; SSA: sub-Saharan Africa; USA+CAN: United States and Canada. Regional aggregates are computed on the basis of purchasing-power-parity weights.
[2]Excludes Libya for the projection years due to the uncertain political situation.

gaps persist—the United States and Canada, Europe, and the Commonwealth of Independent States (CIS). It then examines regions where output gaps are closing or have already closed—Asia, Latin America and the Caribbean (LAC), sub-Saharan Africa (SSA), and the Middle East and North Africa (MENA).

## Recovery Proceeds in the United States

*The U.S. economy continues to recover, with easing financial conditions supporting private final demand in the face of higher commodity prices (Figures 2.3 and 2.4). Job creation has recently accelerated, but the pace of improvement in the labor market remains disappointing considering the size of the job losses during the decline. A further rebalancing from domestic to external demand would add to growth and help to close the large U.S. output gap.*

Following a burst of strong growth driven by inventory restocking in late 2009 and early 2010, economic growth slowed but then strengthened again in the second half of 2010. This strengthening was supported by private final demand, and by the fourth quarter consumer spending was rising at its fastest pace in five years. Although overall credit growth remains weak and household deleveraging continues, financial conditions have generally improved—corporate borrowing rates remain very low, and tight bank lending conditions are now starting to ease not just for large firms but for small and medium-size firms. Reflecting the pickup in economic activity and supported by unconventional monetary easing, equity markets have recovered about two-thirds of the capitalization lost during the crisis. This has helped rebuild consumer confidence, which is still being held down by labor and housing headwinds.

Recovery in the labor market remains lackluster. After shedding more than 8½ million jobs in 2008 and 2009, the labor market has added just under 1½ million jobs since the trough, barely sufficient to keep up with the growth of the working-age population. The employment-population ratio is thus largely unchanged since the start of the recovery. About a third of the decline in the unemployment rate since October 2009—to 8.8 percent in March—is attributable to a decline in labor force participation, which now stands at its lowest level in a quarter century.

**Figure 2.3.  United States and Canada: Average Projected Real GDP Growth during 2011–12**
*(Percent)*

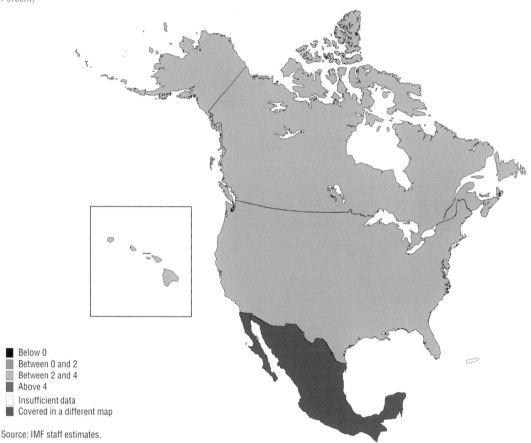

- ■ Below 0
- ▨ Between 0 and 2
- ▨ Between 2 and 4
- ▨ Above 4
- □ Insufficient data
- ■ Covered in a different map

Source: IMF staff estimates.

Long-term unemployment and broader measures of underemployment—including the share of workers involuntarily working part-time or only marginally attached to the labor force—remain well above historic highs. The crisis may also have increased structural unemployment in the United States, because severe sectoral and regional shocks created mismatches between labor skill supply and demand. IMF staff research shows that, historically, the negative effect of skill mismatches on unemployment rates is exacerbated by depressed housing markets, a key aspect of the recent crisis.[1]

The U.S. economy is projected to grow by 2¾ percent and 3 percent in 2011 and 2012, respectively, with gradually firming private final demand offsetting the waning support from federal fiscal policy (Table

[1]See Dowling, Estevão, and Tsounta (2010); and Estevão and Tsounta (2011).

2.1). The fiscal package approved in mid-December implies slightly more than a ½ percentage point addition to growth this year, although recent proposals to curb federal spending would reduce the overall impulse from federal fiscal policy. The drag on 2011 growth from oil price increases largely offsets the boost from the Federal Reserve's unconventional policies and from stronger net exports. Unemployment is projected to remain high, declining only moderately to about 7¾ percent in 2012.

The risks to the outlook remain tilted to the downside. The external environment continues to pose tail risks. Renewed financial turmoil in the euro area could substantially tighten financial conditions and weaken global demand. And a spike in oil and commodity prices, possibly due to continuing tensions in the Middle East and North Africa, could dampen confidence and weaken consumer spending. On the domestic front, house prices could decline by more

## Figure 2.4. United States: Gaining Traction

The recovery is starting to take hold, as private consumption continues to accelerate, albeit slowly. And growth in 2011 will get a boost from the December fiscal package. Quantitative easing has helped fend off deflation pressure arising from a still-large output gap. But vulnerabilities remain: the labor and real estate markets remain weak, and fiscal vulnerabilities need to be addressed.

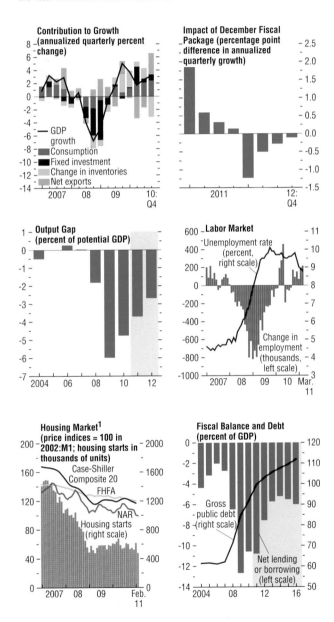

Sources: Haver Analytics; and IMF staff estimates.
[1]FHFA: Federal Housing Finance Agency. NAR: National Association of Realtors.

than expected, given the large shadow inventory of distressed properties, with adverse effects on household and financial balance sheets. There are, however, a number of upside risks to the outlook. Healthy corporate balance sheets could support stronger hiring and capital investment if business confidence improves. And private consumption, particularly of durables, may surprise on the upside given pent-up demand.

Given the substantial slack in the economy—the output gap is estimated to remain above 3 percent this year—inflation is expected to stay subdued, with price increases of 2¼ percent this year and 1½ percent next year. While food and, especially, energy prices have risen, their share in the consumer basket is small, and second-round effects are likely to be minor because the economy is operating well below potential.

The sluggish pace of the economic recovery calls for supportive macroeconomic policies, but fiscal room is becoming increasingly limited. In this context, the right policy mix for the United States is one of continued monetary accommodation alongside moves to put fiscal balances on a sounder footing. A credible strategy to stabilize public debt in the medium term, and a down payment on fiscal consolidation in 2011, are urgently needed.

With output still significantly below potential, inflation persistently low, and the unemployment rate stubbornly high, continued monetary accommodation is warranted. Although the Federal Reserve's second round of quantitative easing is expected to have only a modest effect on growth, it seems to have reduced perceptions of deflation risks; in the weeks following the news in August that the new round of quantitative easing was imminent, inflation expectations rose and long-term yields fell to new lows. Long-term yields have since increased as signs of a strengthening recovery emerged and traders scaled back their expectations of the extent of future asset purchases by the Federal Reserve.

Although some targeted fiscal measures are justifiable at this point given the weak state of labor and housing markets, the recent stimulus package delivers only a small growth dividend for its considerable budgetary cost. Also, the fiscal deficit is now projected to reach 10¾ percent this year—the largest

**Table 2.1. Selected Advanced Economies: Real GDP, Consumer Prices, Current Account Balance, and Unemployment**
*(Annual percent change unless noted otherwise)*

| | Real GDP | | | Consumer Prices[1] | | | Current Account Balance[2] | | | Unemployment[3] | | |
|---|---|---|---|---|---|---|---|---|---|---|---|---|
| | | Projections | | | Projections | | | Projections | | | Projections | |
| | 2010 | 2011 | 2012 | 2010 | 2011 | 2012 | 2010 | 2011 | 2012 | 2010 | 2011 | 2012 |
| **Advanced Economies** | **3.0** | **2.4** | **2.6** | **1.6** | **2.2** | **1.7** | **−0.2** | **−0.3** | **−0.2** | **8.3** | **7.8** | **7.4** |
| United States | 2.8 | 2.8 | 2.9 | 1.6 | 2.2 | 1.6 | −3.2 | −3.2 | −2.8 | 9.6 | 8.5 | 7.8 |
| Euro Area[4,5,6] | 1.7 | 1.6 | 1.8 | 1.6 | 2.3 | 1.7 | −0.6 | 0.0 | 0.0 | 10.0 | 9.9 | 9.6 |
| Japan | 3.9 | 1.4 | 2.1 | −0.7 | 0.2 | 0.2 | 3.6 | 2.3 | 2.3 | 5.1 | 4.9 | 4.7 |
| United Kingdom[4] | 1.3 | 1.7 | 2.3 | 3.3 | 4.2 | 2.0 | −2.5 | −2.4 | −1.9 | 7.8 | 7.8 | 7.7 |
| Canada | 3.1 | 2.8 | 2.6 | 1.8 | 2.2 | 1.9 | −3.1 | −2.8 | −2.6 | 8.0 | 7.6 | 7.3 |
| Other Advanced Economies[7] | 5.7 | 3.9 | 3.8 | 2.3 | 3.1 | 2.6 | 5.1 | 5.5 | 4.8 | 5.0 | 4.5 | 4.4 |
| *Memorandum* | | | | | | | | | | | | |
| Newly Industrialized Asian Economies | 8.4 | 4.9 | 4.5 | 2.3 | 3.8 | 2.9 | 7.1 | 6.3 | 6.0 | 4.1 | 3.6 | 3.6 |

[1]Movements in consumer prices are shown as annual averages. December–December changes can be found in Table A6 in the Statistical Appendix.
[2]Percent of GDP.
[3]Percent. National definitions of unemployment may differ.
[4]Based on Eurostat's harmonized index of consumer prices.
[5]Current account position corrected for reporting discrepancies in intra-area transactions.
[6]Excludes Estonia.
[7]Excludes the United States, Euro Area, and Japan but includes Estonia.

among the advanced economies—and gross debt of the general government will likely exceed 110 percent of GDP by 2016.[2] Indeed, the United States stands out as the only large advanced economy where the cyclically adjusted fiscal deficit is expected to increase in 2011 compared with 2010 despite the ongoing economic recovery.[3] The United States remains committed to meeting the G20 target of halving the deficit between 2010 and 2013, but the high deficit this year may make this difficult.

This unsustainable fiscal outlook calls for a down payment on fiscal consolidation this year. The proposals recently put forward by the National Commission on Fiscal Responsibility and Reform and other analysts contain many useful ideas and provide comprehensive blueprints on which policymakers can build. These proposed measures include reforms to entitlement programs, caps on discretionary spending, revenue-raising tax reforms, and strengthening of fiscal institutions. Meanwhile, the president's

draft budget implies a very large near-term fiscal withdrawal—a reduction of some 5 percentage points of GDP in the federal structural primary deficit over fiscal years 2012 and 2013 on the basis of IMF staff macroeconomic and policy assumptions—which will be challenging to implement, especially in an environment of weak growth and elevated unemployment. Such an adjustment would be larger than any two-year adjustment since 1960 (the first year for which data on structural balances are available), which strengthens the case for smoothing the fiscal adjustment beginning in 2011 within a credible medium-term framework.

Although the current account deficit is not expected to widen substantially in the coming years, deficits will persist—the medium-term current account deficit is projected to remain close to last year's level, in part because of insufficient fiscal adjustment. Should much-needed fiscal consolidation take place in the coming years, this will help bring down external deficits. A more robust recovery will then require a larger contribution to growth from net exports to offset a smaller contribution from domestic demand.

Despite the restoration of financial stability, fragilities in the housing sector continue to weigh down banks' balance sheets, and there remain difficult challenges in implementing financial sector reforms.

[2]The fiscal projections reflect IMF staff views on the economic outlook (which are generally more pessimistic than the authorities') and assessments of likely policies. Given the ongoing debate in Congress, the IMF staff assumes more front-loaded (and deeper) discretionary spending cuts than proposed in the president's draft budget and delayed action on revenue-raising measures.
[3]The April 2011 *Fiscal Monitor* discusses the U.S. fiscal policy stance in greater detail.

The recent overhaul of financial system regulation and supervision has been encouraging, but implementation will be the key test. Critical priorities will be to implement a systemic approach to oversight, with stronger regulation (especially for systemically important institutions), greater transparency and accountability in securities and derivatives markets, and close monitoring of the shadow banking sector. The U.S. authorities have presented Congress with a set of proposals to reform housing finance markets, as mandated by the Dodd-Frank Act. The recommendations include winding down government-sponsored entities (Fannie Mae and Freddie Mac) and crafting more focused housing policies, including more explicit and targeted government support. The eventual reform will need to strike the right balance between delivering an appropriate level of explicit government intervention and discouraging another cycle of overinvestment.

Economic developments in Canada last year mirrored those in the United States, with the pace of economic activity moderating in midyear. The deceleration reflected not only the drag on Canadian exports from weak U.S. activity and strong import growth from investment spending amid an appreciating currency, but also a cooling of some domestic activity, as housing activity softened from unsustainably high levels, consumer spending temporarily moderated, and the effect of the fiscal stimulus faded. Canada's GDP is projected to expand by 2¾ percent this year, with domestic demand in general and private investment in particular, in line with strong commodity prices, being the primary drivers of growth; the strong loonie is expected to continue to be a drag on growth. Risks to the growth outlook are tilted to the downside, with the main domestic risk being deterioration of housing markets and household balance sheets. Key external risks are lower-than-expected activity in the United States and renewed sovereign strains in Europe.

Canada's macroeconomic policies rightly remain accommodative as output remains about 2 percent below potential. Given the downside risks to the growth outlook, muted inflation pressures, and the forthcoming withdrawal of stimulus, a wait-and-see attitude seems appropriate regarding further increases in the policy rate. On the fiscal front, recent moves to smooth the up-front fiscal adjustment are welcome, and the authorities have a sound and credible plan to return to budget surpluses beginning in fiscal year 2015. Over the longer term, challenges from population aging and health care inflation require further plans to cement fiscal sustainability. On the financial front, Canada's supervisory and regulatory approach has been sound, and it has helped prevent the excesses that hurt other advanced economies during the recent crisis. However, continued vigilance is needed to maintain financial stability, particularly in light of high concentration in the financial system, substantial exposure to U.S. risks, and historically high household debt levels.

## A Gradual and Uneven Recovery Is under Way in Europe

*In Europe, the recovery is proceeding modestly (Figure 2.5). Overall, real activity in the region remains below its potential level and unemployment is still high. There is, however, substantial variation across economies. The degree of economic slack is larger in the periphery of the euro area than in the core, whereas the largest emerging market economies in the region are already operating at or above capacity.*

The recovery in Europe has been gaining traction, despite renewed financial turbulence in peripheral countries of the euro area during the last quarter of 2010. Concerns about banking sector losses and fiscal sustainability led to widening sovereign spreads in these countries, in some cases reaching highs not seen since the launch of the Economic and Monetary Union. But the situation was contained by strong policy responses at both the national and the EU level—that is, measures to improve fiscal balances and push forward with structural reforms in the affected countries, extraordinary liquidity support, securities purchases by the European Central Bank (ECB), and funding from the European Financial Stabilization Mechanism (EFSM) and the European Financial Stability Facility (EFSF) to support the joint EU/IMF program for Ireland. Consequently, the damage to economic activity was limited to the affected economies and did not spread to the rest of Europe, where growth has become more broad-based and self-sustained (Figure 2.6).

**Figure 2.5.  Europe: Average Projected Real GDP Growth during 2011–12**
*(Percent)*

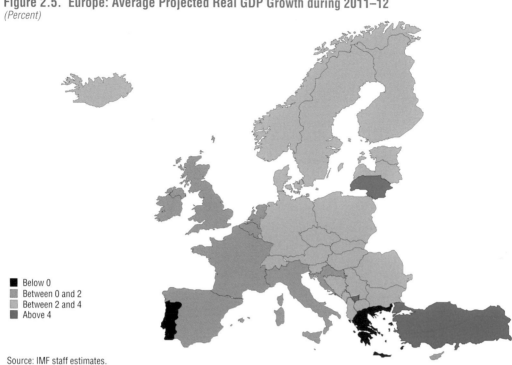

Below 0
Between 0 and 2
Between 2 and 4
Above 4

Source: IMF staff estimates.

The outlook is for a continued gradual and uneven expansion (Table 2.2). Advanced Europe's real GDP is projected to grow at 1¾ percent in 2011 and 2 percent in 2012. Emerging Europe's growth is expected to be 3¾ percent in 2011 and 4 percent in 2012. Economic prospects across the region are likewise divergent, largely reflecting differences in the state of public and private sector balance sheets and the stance of macroeconomic policies.

- In Germany, growth is expected to moderate from 3½ percent last year to 2½ percent this year, mainly due to the withdrawal of fiscal support and the slowdown in external demand growth. In France, growth is projected to be modest, at 1½ percent this year, as consumption growth is subdued by the retrenchment of fiscal stimulus and export growth is weakened by slowing external demand. In Italy, the recovery is expected to remain weak, as long-standing competitiveness problems constrain export growth and the planned fiscal consolidation weighs on private demand. Growth is projected to be much lower in the periphery of the euro area because these economies

are suffering a sharp and protracted contraction in public and private balance sheets—which is needed to resolve fiscal and competitiveness imbalances—and also face more severe structural unemployment problems (Box 2.1).

- In advanced economies outside the euro area, recovery prospects are similarly differentiated. For instance, growth in the United Kingdom is projected at 1¾ percent in 2011 as necessary front-loaded fiscal consolidation dampens domestic demand. But in Sweden, real activity is expected to expand by 3¾ percent this year amid rapidly improving financial conditions and nascent signs of overheating in the real estate sector.

- In emerging Europe, the rapid recovery is projected to continue in Turkey, where robust private demand and buoyant credit growth are lifting economic activity above its potential level amid still-accommodative macroeconomic policies. In Poland, growth is expected to remain solid at about 3¾ percent this year as corporate profitability rises, the absorption of EU funds continues, and bank lending resumes. The recovery is projected to remain more subdued

## Figure 2.6. Europe: A Gradual and Uneven Recovery Continues[1]

The recovery is proceeding at a moderate pace. Real activity in the region remains below its potential level, and inflation pressure is broadly contained. But there are substantial differences across economies. Growth has generally become more broad-based and self-sustained in both advanced and emerging Europe. In the euro area periphery, however, continued financial turbulence is dampening the outlook for these economies.

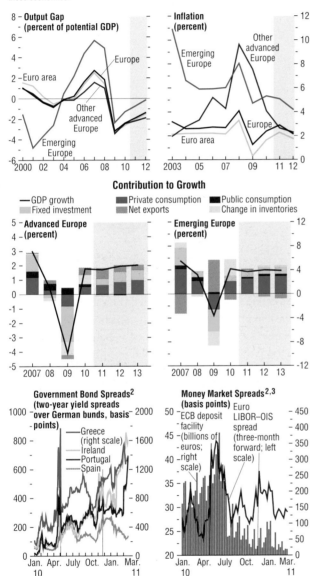

Sources: Bloomberg Financial Markets; and IMF staff estimates.
[1]Euro Area: Austria, Belgium, Cyprus, Finland, France, Germany, Greece, Ireland, Italy, Luxembourg, Malta, Netherlands, Slovak Republic, Slovenia, and Spain. Emerging Europe: Albania, Bosnia and Herzegovina, Bulgaria, Croatia, Hungary, Kosovo, Latvia, Lithuania, Former Yugoslav Republic of Macedonia, Montenegro, Poland, Romania, Serbia, and Turkey. Other advanced Europe comprises Czech Republic, Denmark, Estonia, Iceland, Norway, Portugal, Sweden, Switzerland, and United Kingdom. Aggregates are computed on the basis of purchasing-power-parity weights.
[2]Vertical lines on each panel correspond to May 10 and November 30, 2010.
[3]ECB: European Central Bank; LIBOR: London interbank offered rate; OIS: overnight index swap.

in some of the economies that experienced unsustainable domestic booms (Romania).

Downside risks to the outlook continue to prevail. In the near term, continued strains in more vulnerable euro area sovereigns and banks pose a significant threat to financial stability and growth, as discussed in Chapter 1 of the April 2011 *Global Financial Stability Report.* This is mainly due to continuing weakness among financial institutions in many of the region's advanced economies and a lack of transparency about their exposures. Financial institutions and sovereigns are closely linked, with spillovers occurring in both directions. Substantial cross-border linkages, as well as financial spillovers through higher risk aversion and lower equity prices, could generate a slowdown in growth and demand that would hinder the regional and global recoveries. Another downside risk to growth stems from higher-than-expected commodity prices. In the medium term, the main risk remains that deep-rooted fiscal and competitiveness imbalances in peripheral economies and incomplete action to address banking sector vulnerabilities in many euro area economies could lead to a long period of slow growth.

Comprehensive, rapid, and decisive policy actions are required to address these downside risks. Important steps have already been taken at both the national and the EU level. But further bold steps are needed to secure fiscal sustainability, resolve banking sector problems, reform EU policy frameworks, and rekindle growth.

Securing public debt sustainability remains a priority for most European economies. Current fiscal consolidation plans are broadly appropriate and rightfully differentiated in the near term. In 2011, the largest economies in the region (France, Germany, Spain, United Kingdom) will implement differing measures (in size and composition) to reduce their deficits. Sovereigns that have come under market pressure (Greece, Ireland, Portugal) will continue with sizable front-loaded consolidation. Nonetheless, in many European countries, more needs to be done to underpin medium-term adjustment plans with concrete and sustained policies. In addition, current plans for medium-term fiscal adjustment still need to be strengthened in the face of looming increases in pension and health spending.[4] Some economies have taken steps toward entitlement spending reforms (for

[4]See Bornhorst and others (2010) for details.

## Table 2.2. Selected European Economies: Real GDP, Consumer Prices, Current Account Balance, and Unemployment
(Annual percent change unless noted otherwise)

| | Real GDP | | | Consumer Prices[1] | | | Current Account Balance[2] | | | Unemployment[3] | | |
|---|---|---|---|---|---|---|---|---|---|---|---|---|
| | | Projections | | | Projections | | | Projections | | | Projections | |
| | 2010 | 2011 | 2012 | 2010 | 2011 | 2012 | 2010 | 2011 | 2012 | 2010 | 2011 | 2012 |
| **Europe** | **2.1** | **2.0** | **2.2** | **2.4** | **2.9** | **2.2** | **0.3** | **0.2** | **0.2** | . . . | . . . | . . . |
| **Advanced Europe[4]** | **1.7** | **1.7** | **1.9** | **1.9** | **2.5** | **1.8** | **0.8** | **0.8** | **0.9** | **9.3** | **9.2** | **8.9** |
| Euro Area[5,6,7] | 1.7 | 1.6 | 1.8 | 1.6 | 2.3 | 1.7 | −0.6 | 0.0 | 0.0 | 10.0 | 9.9 | 9.6 |
| Germany | 3.5 | 2.5 | 2.1 | 1.2 | 2.2 | 1.5 | 5.3 | 5.1 | 4.6 | 6.9 | 6.6 | 6.5 |
| France | 1.5 | 1.6 | 1.8 | 1.7 | 2.1 | 1.7 | −2.1 | −2.8 | −2.7 | 9.7 | 9.5 | 9.1 |
| Italy | 1.3 | 1.1 | 1.3 | 1.6 | 2.0 | 2.1 | −3.5 | −3.4 | −3.0 | 8.5 | 8.6 | 8.3 |
| Spain | −0.1 | 0.8 | 1.6 | 2.0 | 2.6 | 1.5 | −4.5 | −4.8 | −4.5 | 20.1 | 19.4 | 18.2 |
| Netherlands | 1.7 | 1.5 | 1.5 | 0.9 | 2.3 | 2.2 | 7.1 | 7.9 | 8.2 | 4.5 | 4.4 | 4.4 |
| Belgium | 2.0 | 1.7 | 1.9 | 2.3 | 2.9 | 2.3 | 1.2 | 1.0 | 1.2 | 8.4 | 8.4 | 8.2 |
| Austria | 2.0 | 2.4 | 2.3 | 1.7 | 2.5 | 2.0 | 3.2 | 3.1 | 3.1 | 4.4 | 4.3 | 4.3 |
| Greece | −4.5 | −3.0 | 1.1 | 4.7 | 2.5 | 0.5 | −10.4 | −8.2 | −7.1 | 12.5 | 14.8 | 15.0 |
| Portugal | 1.4 | −1.5 | −0.5 | 1.4 | 2.4 | 1.4 | −9.9 | −8.7 | −8.5 | 11.0 | 11.9 | 12.4 |
| Finland | 3.1 | 3.1 | 2.5 | 1.7 | 3.0 | 2.1 | 3.1 | 2.8 | 2.6 | 8.4 | 8.0 | 7.8 |
| Ireland | −1.0 | 0.5 | 1.9 | −1.6 | 0.5 | 0.5 | −0.7 | 0.2 | 0.6 | 13.6 | 14.5 | 13.3 |
| Slovak Republic | 4.0 | 3.8 | 4.2 | 0.7 | 3.4 | 2.7 | −3.4 | −2.8 | −2.7 | 14.4 | 13.3 | 12.1 |
| Slovenia | 1.2 | 2.0 | 2.4 | 1.8 | 2.2 | 3.1 | −1.2 | −2.0 | −2.1 | 7.2 | 7.5 | 7.2 |
| Luxembourg | 3.4 | 3.0 | 3.1 | 2.3 | 3.5 | 1.7 | 7.7 | 8.5 | 8.7 | 6.1 | 5.9 | 5.8 |
| Estonia | 3.1 | 3.3 | 3.7 | 2.9 | 4.7 | 2.1 | 3.6 | 3.3 | 3.1 | 16.9 | 14.8 | 12.8 |
| Cyprus | 1.0 | 1.7 | 2.2 | 2.6 | 3.9 | 2.8 | −7.0 | −8.9 | −8.7 | 6.8 | 6.5 | 6.3 |
| Malta | 3.6 | 2.5 | 2.2 | 2.0 | 3.0 | 2.6 | −0.6 | −1.1 | −2.3 | 6.5 | 6.5 | 6.4 |
| United Kingdom[6] | 1.3 | 1.7 | 2.3 | 3.3 | 4.2 | 2.0 | −2.5 | −2.4 | −1.9 | 7.8 | 7.8 | 7.7 |
| Sweden | 5.5 | 3.8 | 3.5 | 1.9 | 2.0 | 2.0 | 6.5 | 6.1 | 5.8 | 8.4 | 7.4 | 6.6 |
| Switzerland | 2.6 | 2.4 | 1.8 | 0.7 | 0.9 | 1.0 | 14.2 | 13.2 | 12.8 | 3.6 | 3.4 | 3.3 |
| Czech Republic | 2.3 | 1.7 | 2.9 | 1.5 | 2.0 | 2.0 | −2.4 | −1.8 | −1.2 | 7.3 | 7.1 | 6.9 |
| Norway | 0.4 | 2.9 | 2.5 | 2.4 | 1.8 | 2.2 | 12.9 | 16.3 | 16.0 | 3.6 | 3.6 | 3.5 |
| Denmark | 2.1 | 2.0 | 2.0 | 2.3 | 2.0 | 2.0 | 5.0 | 4.8 | 4.8 | 4.2 | 4.5 | 4.4 |
| Iceland | −3.5 | 2.3 | 2.9 | 5.4 | 2.6 | 2.6 | −8.0 | 1.1 | 2.1 | 8.1 | 7.5 | 6.5 |
| **Emerging Europe[8]** | **4.2** | **3.7** | **4.0** | **5.3** | **5.1** | **4.2** | **−4.3** | **−5.4** | **−5.7** | . . . | . . . | . . . |
| Turkey | 8.2 | 4.6 | 4.5 | 8.6 | 5.7 | 6.0 | −6.5 | −8.0 | −8.2 | 11.9 | 11.4 | 11.0 |
| Poland | 3.8e | 3.8 | 3.6 | 2.6 | 4.1 | 2.9 | −3.3 | −3.9 | −4.2 | 9.0 | 9.0 | 8.7 |
| Romania | −1.3 | 1.5 | 4.4 | 6.1 | 6.1 | 3.4 | −4.2 | −5.0 | −5.2 | 7.6 | 6.6 | 5.8 |
| Hungary | 1.2 | 2.8 | 2.8 | 4.9 | 4.1 | 3.5 | 1.6 | 1.5 | 0.9 | 11.2 | 11.5 | 10.9 |
| Bulgaria | 0.2 | 3.0 | 3.5 | 3.0 | 4.8 | 3.7 | −0.8 | −1.5 | −2.0 | 10.3 | 8.0 | 6.7 |
| Serbia | 1.8 | 3.0 | 5.0 | 6.2 | 9.9 | 4.1 | −7.1 | −7.4 | −6.6 | 19.4 | 19.6 | 19.8 |
| Croatia | −1.4 | 1.3 | 1.8 | 1.0 | 3.5 | 2.4 | −1.9 | −3.6 | −3.6 | 12.3 | 12.8 | 12.3 |
| Lithuania | 1.3 | 4.6 | 3.8 | 1.2 | 3.1 | 2.9 | 1.8 | −0.9 | −2.9 | 17.8 | 16.0 | 14.0 |
| Latvia | −0.3 | 3.3 | 4.0 | −1.2 | 3.0 | 1.7 | 3.6 | 2.6 | 1.5 | 19.0 | 17.2 | 15.5 |

[1]Movements in consumer prices are shown as annual averages. December–December changes can be found in Tables A6 and A7 in the Statistical Appendix.
[2]Percent of GDP.
[3]Percent. National definitions of unemployment may differ.
[4]Includes Estonia.
[5]Current account position corrected for reporting discrepancies in intra-area transactions.
[6]Based on Eurostat's harmonized index of consumer prices.
[7]Excludes Estonia.
[8]Includes Albania, Bosnia and Herzegovina, Kosovo, former Yugoslav Republic of Macedonia, Montenegro, and Serbia.

example, France, Greece, Ireland, Italy, Spain), but more should be done in this area.

Remaining fragilities in Europe's financial system urgently need to be resolved. As discussed in Chapter 1 of the April 2011 *Global Financial Stability Report,* progress in strengthening capital positions and reducing leverage has been uneven in Europe.

Specifically, in the euro area, asset quality is uncertain, and banks face a wall of maturing debt and therefore remain vulnerable to funding pressures in wholesale markets. The desire to reduce the dependence on wholesale funding has sparked a deposit war in several economies, squeezing bank revenues. Overall, some euro area banks face significant capital shortfalls. To help address such weaknesses, it is critical to reduce uncertainty about asset quality, increase the capital buffers of viable banks, and identify and resolve weak banks. In this respect, some economies (for example, Spain) have made more progress than others. New stress tests that are more realistic, thorough, and transparent will increase clarity. But they will be effective only if embedded in coordinated national strategies to deal with vulnerable institutions—an approach policymakers committed to at the March EU summit. Meanwhile, excess capacity in banking systems needs to be removed by resolving the weak tail of banks. Without these reforms, financial systems in Europe will remain vulnerable, credit growth could come under further pressure, and the economic recovery could be undermined.

In most European economies, monetary policy can stay accommodative for as long as inflation pressures remain subdued. In advanced Europe, core inflation is projected to remain low because inflation expectations are well anchored and excess capacity is still large in most economies. Also, the impact of recent increases in commodity prices should prove temporary. This argues for low policy rates for now to support the recovery and help offset the dampening short-term effects of fiscal consolidation on domestic demand. Still, central banks will have to keep a watchful eye on wage developments and inflation expectations for potential second-round effects, especially in countries that are most advanced in their recoveries. In the euro area, remaining financial fragilities could hold back growth, justifying a slower pace of normalization. Moreover, the ECB's extraordinary measures will need to be removed only gradually as systemic uncertainty recedes. In emerging Europe, inflation prospects are more mixed, which reflects mainly different degrees of economic slack and variable pass-through of commodity prices into overall inflation. In some fast-growing emerging economies, policy rates may need to be normalized sooner to prevent overheating.

A key challenge ahead is to reform euro area and EU policy frameworks to help restore confidence and secure Europe's future stability and growth. The crisis revealed deep-rooted problems, with significant cross-border dimensions, in existing fiscal, structural, and financial stability policies. To address these problems, comprehensive solutions are needed.

The immediate priority is to reassure markets that sufficient resources are available from the euro-wide safety net to deal with downside risks. European leaders committed at the March EU summit to substantially increase the effective lending capacity of the EFSF. While this should bolster market confidence, the mechanism by which this is secured should be clarified as soon as possible, and a decision on adjusting the interest rate charged on EFSF loans is urgently needed to help support fiscal sustainability. Beyond 2013, the proposed permanent European Stability Mechanism provides a robust and orderly framework to assist euro area members, with strict conditionality to support discipline. Some additional flexibility on these instruments would be helpful to deal more directly with the interdependence of national banking systems and sovereign risks.

Beyond crisis-management measures, the crisis has highlighted the need to improve EU policy coordination on fiscal and structural issues. Shared responsibility for fiscal burdens needs to come with shared responsibility for fiscal policies. To this end, policymakers agreed in March to strengthen fiscal frameworks, through a stronger Stability and Growth Pact, minimum standards to be set for national frameworks, and enhanced coordination with the European Semester. Improved surveillance over structural bottlenecks, competitiveness, and imbalances is also needed to help address macroeconomic imbalances. In that respect, the recently agreed Euro Plus Pact and the forthcoming Excessive Imbalances Procedure are welcome coordination tools, but specific reforms will need to be identified and implemented without further delay. Furthermore, the surveillance process should be made more binding by introducing sanctions and ensuring that the delay between diagnosis and policy action is kept short.

Another lesson from the crisis is the need for an integrated, pan-European approach to supervision, regulation, and crisis management and resolution. Financial sector problems in specific countries can spread quickly across the region, and supervisory and regulatory gaps can have major spillovers. Hence, more joint responsibility and accountability for Europe's financial stability are urgently needed. This can be achieved through integrated crisis management and resolution as well as integrated supervision, which should help establish some consensus on burden sharing. Some steps in this direction are being taken with the creation of the European Systemic Risk Board and the establishment of the European Supervisory Authorities. But the success of these new institutions will depend on adequate resources, good information gathering and sharing, and focused coordination of their activities. More important, overall progress toward an integrated European financial stability framework has been disappointingly slow, especially considering its importance for achieving an efficient and stable market for financial services that spreads risks among countries and fosters economic growth in Europe.

In many ways, the European Union and the euro area are at a crossroads. Popular support for the euro remains strong, considering the tensions created by sharing sovereign risk. But unless economies make a quantum leap toward a more integrated approach to fiscal policy and assume joint responsibility for financial stability, support for burden sharing may be much lower in future crises. If taken, however, these steps can deliver the major benefits that derive from

risk sharing via a truly integrated and better supervised and regulated financial market.

## A Moderate Recovery Continues in the Commonwealth of Independent States

*The recovery in the CIS is proceeding at a steady pace (Figure 2.7). Having suffered a collapse during the crisis, real activity in the region remains substantially below its potential level, despite notable differences across economies.*

Several factors are supporting the recovery. Higher commodity prices are boosting production and employment in the region's commodity-exporting economies. Also, the rebound in real activity in Russia is benefiting other CIS economies through trade, remittances, and investment. In addition, there continues to be a gradual normalization of trade and capital flows to the region. Nevertheless, heavy dependence on external financing and lingering banking sector vulnerabilities are holding back growth in several CIS economies.

**Figure 2.7.  Commonwealth of Independent States: Average Projected Real GDP Growth during 2011–12**
*(Percent)*

■ Below 0
■ Between 0 and 2
■ Between 2 and 4
■ Above 4
□ Insufficient data
■ Covered in a different map

Source: IMF staff estimates.
Note: Includes Georgia and Mongolia.

## Figure 2.8. Commonwealth of Independent States: A Moderate Recovery is under Way

The recovery is continuing at a steady pace. Having suffered a collapse during the crisis, real activity in the CIS region remains substantially below its potential level, despite notable differences across economies. Inflation is on the rise, led by higher prices for food, which makes up a large share of the consumption basket in the region.

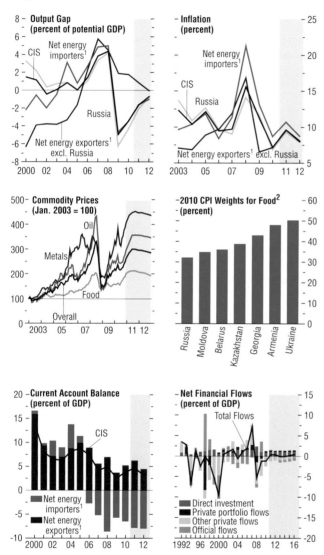

Sources: Haver Analytics; IMF, Primary Commodity Price System; and IMF staff estimates.

[1]Net energy exporters: Azerbaijan, Kazakhstan, Russia, Turkmenistan, and Uzbekistan. Net energy importers: Armenia, Belarus, Georgia, Kyrgyz Republic, Moldova, Mongolia, Tajikistan, and Ukraine. Aggregates for the external economy are sums of individual country data. Aggregates for all others are computed on the basis of purchasing-power-parity weights.

[2]Data for Belarus are for 2008; CPI = consumer price index.

Against this backdrop, real activity in the CIS is projected to expand by 5 percent in 2011 and 4¾ percent in 2012, coming closer to its potential level only gradually. Within the region, however, growth prospects differ substantially (Figure 2.8; Table 2.3):

- In Russia, growth is projected to pick up modestly to 4¾ percent in 2011 and 4½ percent in 2012, only gradually reducing the output gap. Private sector demand is likely to remain subdued as non-performing loans in the banking system constrain credit and consumption growth.

- Among other energy exporters, economies whose financial sectors have fewer external linkages are expected to continue to perform best. In particular, Turkmenistan is expected to benefit from high gas prices and be among the top performers in the region, growing by 9 percent in 2011. In Uzbekistan, growth is also projected to remain high, at 7 percent in 2011, supported by strong domestic demand, public investment, and commodity exports (including gold and cotton).

- For energy importers as a group, growth is projected at 5¼ percent in 2011 and 5 percent in 2012 as some of these economies (for example, Armenia, Moldova) benefit from the rebound in remittances from Russia and others from the return of financial stability (for example, Ukraine).

Despite the considerable degree of economic slack, inflation is on the rise across the region, led by higher food prices. Unfavorable weather conditions in 2010 reduced grain yields and contributed to price spikes. Food comprises a large share of the region's consumer price inflation basket (30 to 50 percent; see Figure 2.8), and so rising food prices are expected to substantially increase headline inflation. Given the limited credibility of monetary policy frameworks in the region, this will likely feed into more generalized wage and core inflation pressures.

Risks to the outlook in the region are broadly balanced. For most CIS economies, growth prospects remain highly dependent on the speed of recovery in Russia, which could surprise in either direction. Higher commodity prices represent an upside risk to growth in commodity-exporting economies in the region; increased global risk aversion or lower external demand from advanced economies present downside risks to growth.

## Table 2.3. Commonwealth of Independent States: Real GDP, Consumer Prices, Current Account Balance, and Unemployment

*(Annual percent change unless noted otherwise)*

| | Real GDP | | | Consumer Prices[1] | | | Current Account Balance[2] | | | Unemployment[3] | | |
|---|---|---|---|---|---|---|---|---|---|---|---|---|
| | | Projections | | | Projections | | | Projections | | | Projections | |
| | 2010 | 2011 | 2012 | 2010 | 2011 | 2012 | 2010 | 2011 | 2012 | 2010 | 2011 | 2012 |
| **Commonwealth of Independent States (CIS)[4]** | **4.6** | **5.0** | **4.7** | **7.2** | **9.6** | **8.1** | **3.8** | **4.7** | **3.2** | ... | ... | ... |
| Russia | 4.0 | 4.8 | 4.5 | 6.9 | 9.3 | 8.0 | 4.9 | 5.6 | 3.9 | 7.5 | 7.3 | 7.1 |
| Ukraine | 4.2 | 4.5 | 4.9 | 9.4 | 9.2 | 8.3 | −1.9 | −3.6 | −3.8 | 8.1 | 7.8 | 7.2 |
| Kazakhstan | 7.0 | 5.9 | 5.6 | 7.4 | 9.1 | 6.4 | 2.5 | 5.8 | 4.2 | 5.8 | 5.7 | 5.6 |
| Belarus | 7.6 | 6.8 | 4.8 | 7.7 | 12.9 | 9.7 | −15.5 | −15.7 | −15.2 | 0.7 | 0.7 | 0.7 |
| Azerbaijan | 5.0 | 2.8 | 2.5 | 5.7 | 10.3 | 7.5 | 27.7 | 28.4 | 24.2 | 6.0 | 6.0 | 6.0 |
| Turkmenistan | 9.2 | 9.0 | 6.4 | 4.4 | 6.1 | 7.3 | −11.4 | −4.7 | −3.9 | ... | ... | ... |
| Mongolia | 6.1 | 9.8 | 7.1 | 10.2 | 16.4 | 16.0 | −15.2 | −13.3 | −14.0 | 3.3 | 3.0 | 3.0 |
| **Low-Income CIS** | **6.0** | **5.0** | **4.8** | **7.4** | **11.4** | **9.2** | **11.0** | **13.1** | **10.3** | ... | ... | ... |
| Uzbekistan | 8.5 | 7.0 | 7.0 | 9.4 | 11.6 | 12.3 | 6.7 | 10.0 | 6.7 | 0.2 | 0.2 | 0.2 |
| Georgia | 6.4 | 5.5 | 4.8 | 7.1 | 12.6 | 7.9 | −9.8 | −13.0 | −12.0 | 16.8 | 16.7 | 16.5 |
| Armenia | 2.6 | 4.6 | 4.3 | 8.2 | 9.3 | 5.5 | −13.7 | −12.4 | −11.3 | 7.0 | 7.0 | 7.0 |
| Tajikistan | 6.5 | 5.8 | 5.0 | 6.5 | 13.9 | 9.7 | 2.2 | −4.1 | −7.2 | ... | ... | ... |
| Kyrgyz Republic | −1.4 | 5.0 | 6.0 | 7.8 | 18.8 | 9.3 | −7.4 | −6.7 | −7.8 | 5.8 | 5.6 | 5.5 |
| Moldova | 6.9 | 4.5 | 4.8 | 7.4 | 7.5 | 6.3 | −10.9 | −11.1 | −11.2 | 7.4 | 6.5 | 6.0 |
| *Memorandum* | | | | | | | | | | | | |
| Net Energy Exporters[5] | 4.4 | 5.0 | 4.6 | 6.9 | 9.4 | 8.0 | 5.3 | 6.3 | 4.5 | ... | ... | ... |
| Net Energy Importers[6] | 5.1 | 5.3 | 4.9 | 8.7 | 10.7 | 8.7 | −6.5 | −7.9 | −8.0 | ... | ... | ... |

[1]Movements in consumer prices are shown as annual averages. December–December changes can be found in Table A7 in the Statistical Appendix.
[2]Percent of GDP.
[3]Percent. National definitions of unemployment may differ.
[4]Georgia and Mongolia, which are not members of the Commonwealth of Independent States, are included in this group for reasons of geography and similarities in economic structure.
[5]Net Energy Exporters comprise Azerbaijan, Kazakhstan, Russia, Turkmenistan, and Uzbekistan.
[6]Net Energy Importers comprise Armenia, Belarus, Georgia, Kyrgyz Republic, Moldova, Mongolia, Tajikistan, and Ukraine.

The key policy challenge in the region is to exit from crisis-related macroeconomic and financial policies in a way that provides sufficient support to the incomplete recovery but does not jeopardize price stability.

- On the financial front, the main policy task is to address lingering vulnerabilities. The considerable banking risks in Russia, for instance, call for strengthening capital adequacy requirements, enhancing supervisory powers, and implementing legislation on consolidated supervision and connected lending. In several economies (Kazakhstan, Kyrgyz Republic, Tajikistan), the top priority is comprehensive and transparent strategies to address nonperforming loans in the banking sector.
- Because most economies in the region operate under pegged or heavily managed exchange rate regimes, there is only limited scope for monetary policy to respond to shocks. In this context, the increased exchange rate flexibility in Russia is welcome because

it reduces the scope for conflict between the exchange rate and inflation and deters speculative capital flows. Given steady increases in nonfood prices and unfavorable inflation prospects, an increase in policy interest rates would help prevent a wage-price spiral.

- On the fiscal front, the specific policy challenges vary across the region. In Russia, following the large fiscal stimulus (about 9 percent of GDP) implemented during the crisis, the main task is to deliver a more ambitious, credible, and growth-friendly plan for medium-term consolidation. In Kazakhstan, where fiscal policy continues to support the recovery, the efficiency of public spending should be ensured. In a number of economies (for example, Armenia, Georgia, Kyrgyz Republic) where the share of food in the consumption basket is high, poor households will bear the brunt of any price increases. Hence, there is a need to better target government support for low-income households.

## Rapid Growth Continues in Asia

*Broad-based recovery is continuing in most Asian economies, supported by strong export performance, buoyant private domestic demand, and in some cases rapid credit growth. Even though growth has moderated from cyclical highs to more sustainable rates, Asia continues to outpace other regions (Figure 2.9; Table 2.4). With the notable exception of Japan, output gaps in much of the region have closed or are quickly closing, inflation is on the rise, and overheating is becoming a concern. At the same time, limited progress has been made on external rebalancing in emerging Asia.*

Signs of overheating are starting to materialize in a number of economies. Continued high growth has meant that some economies in the region are now operating at or above potential (Figure 2.10). Credit growth is accelerating in some economies (Hong Kong SAR, India, Indonesia), and it remains high in China. Most of the increase in headline inflation in recent months has been due to a spike in food prices, but core inflation has also been increasing in a number of economies, most notably India. Furthermore, real estate prices have been rising at double-digit rates in a number of economies. Concerns that inflation pressures may induce

authorities to tighten the policy stance more rapidly than previously planned may have contributed to recent declines in equity and bond markets.

Against this backdrop, Asia is projected to continue expanding rapidly this year and next. Export growth is expected to moderate from last year's very rapid pace but will remain robust as gains in market share and increased intraregional trade partially offset the weakness in final demand from advanced economies. Capital flows to Asia are likely to continue, driven by both cyclical and structural factors. Autonomous private consumption growth should remain strong, supported by still-rich asset valuations and improved labor market conditions.

- After growing by 10¼ percent in 2010, China's growth is expected to remain robust at 9½ percent this year and next, with the drivers of growth shifting increasingly from public to private demand. Consumption will be buttressed by rapid credit growth, supportive labor market conditions, and continued policy efforts to raise household disposable income.
- Growth in India is expected to moderate but remain above trend, with GDP growth projected at 8¼ percent in 2011 and 7¾ percent in 2012.

**Figure 2.9. Asia: Average Projected Real GDP Growth during 2011–12**
*(Percent)*

Below 0
Between 0 and 2
Between 2 and 4
Above 4

Insufficient data

Source: IMF staff estimates.

## Table 2.4. Selected Asian Economies: Real GDP, Consumer Prices, Current Account Balance, and Unemployment

*(Annual percent change unless noted otherwise)*

| | Real GDP | | | Consumer Prices[1] | | | Current Account Balance[2] | | | Unemployment[3] | | |
|---|---|---|---|---|---|---|---|---|---|---|---|---|
| | | Projections | | | Projections | | | Projections | | | Projections | |
| | 2010 | 2011 | 2012 | 2010 | 2011 | 2012 | 2010 | 2011 | 2012 | 2010 | 2011 | 2012 |
| **Asia** | **8.2** | **6.7** | **6.8** | **4.3** | **4.7** | **3.4** | **3.3** | **3.1** | **3.1** | ... | ... | ... |
| **Advanced Asia** | **5.3** | **2.8** | **3.1** | **0.8** | **1.8** | **1.5** | **3.4** | **2.8** | **2.4** | **4.8** | **4.5** | **4.3** |
| Japan | 3.9 | 1.4 | 2.1 | −0.7 | 0.2 | 0.2 | 3.6 | 2.3 | 2.3 | 5.1 | 4.9 | 4.7 |
| Australia | 2.7 | 3.0 | 3.5 | 2.8 | 3.0 | 3.0 | −2.6 | −0.4 | −2.1 | 5.2 | 5.0 | 4.8 |
| New Zealand | 1.5 | 0.9 | 4.1 | 2.3 | 4.1 | 2.7 | −2.2 | −0.2 | −4.4 | 6.5 | 6.7 | 6.2 |
| **Newly Industrialized Asian Economies** | **8.4** | **4.9** | **4.5** | **2.3** | **3.8** | **2.9** | **7.1** | **6.3** | **6.0** | **4.1** | **3.6** | **3.6** |
| Korea | 6.1 | 4.5 | 4.2 | 3.0 | 4.5 | 3.0 | 2.8 | 1.1 | 1.0 | 3.7 | 3.3 | 3.3 |
| Taiwan Province of China | 10.8 | 5.4 | 5.2 | 1.0 | 2.0 | 2.0 | 9.4 | 11.6 | 10.9 | 5.2 | 4.6 | 4.5 |
| Hong Kong SAR | 6.8 | 5.4 | 4.2 | 2.4 | 5.8 | 4.4 | 6.6 | 5.2 | 5.5 | 4.3 | 3.6 | 3.8 |
| Singapore | 14.5 | 5.2 | 4.4 | 2.8 | 3.3 | 3.0 | 22.2 | 20.4 | 19.0 | 2.2 | 2.2 | 2.2 |
| **Developing Asia** | **9.5** | **8.4** | **8.4** | **6.0** | **6.0** | **4.2** | **3.3** | **3.3** | **3.6** | ... | ... | ... |
| China | 10.3 | 9.6 | 9.5 | 3.3 | 5.0 | 2.5 | 5.2 | 5.7 | 6.3 | 4.1 | 4.0 | 4.0 |
| India | 10.4 | 8.2 | 7.8 | 13.2 | 7.5 | 6.9 | −3.2 | −3.7 | −3.8 | ... | ... | ... |
| **ASEAN-5** | **6.9** | **5.4** | **5.7** | **4.4** | **6.1** | **4.7** | **3.5** | **2.7** | **2.2** | ... | ... | ... |
| Indonesia | 6.1 | 6.2 | 6.5 | 5.1 | 7.1 | 5.9 | 0.9 | 0.9 | 0.4 | 7.1 | 6.7 | 6.5 |
| Thailand | 7.8 | 4.0 | 4.5 | 3.3 | 4.0 | 3.4 | 4.6 | 2.7 | 1.9 | 1.0 | 1.2 | 1.2 |
| Malaysia | 7.2 | 5.5 | 5.2 | 1.7 | 2.8 | 2.5 | 11.8 | 11.4 | 10.8 | 3.3 | 3.2 | 3.1 |
| Philippines | 7.3 | 5.0 | 5.0 | 3.8 | 4.9 | 4.3 | 4.5 | 2.9 | 2.8 | 7.2 | 7.2 | 7.2 |
| Vietnam | 6.8 | 6.3 | 6.8 | 9.2 | 13.5 | 6.7 | −3.8 | −4.0 | −3.9 | 5.0 | 5.0 | 5.0 |
| **Other Developing Asia[4]** | **5.7** | **4.7** | **5.2** | **9.1** | **10.9** | **9.6** | **−0.6** | **−1.3** | **−1.8** | ... | ... | ... |
| *Memorandum* | | | | | | | | | | | | |
| Emerging Asia[5] | 9.4 | 7.9 | 7.9 | 5.5 | 5.7 | 4.0 | 3.9 | 3.8 | 4.0 | ... | ... | ... |

[1]Movements in consumer prices are shown as annual averages. December–December changes can be found in Tables A6 and A7 in the Statistical Appendix.

[2]Percent of GDP.

[3]Percent. National definitions of unemployment may differ.

[4]Other Developing Asia comprises Islamic Republic of Afghanistan, Bangladesh, Bhutan, Brunei Darussalam, Cambodia, Republic of Fiji, Kiribati, Lao People's Democratic Republic, Maldives, Myanmar, Nepal, Pakistan, Papua New Guinea, Samoa, Solomon Islands, Sri Lanka, Timor-Leste, Tonga, Tuvalu, and Vanuatu.

[5]Emerging Asia comprises all economies in Developing Asia and the Newly Industrialized Asian Economies.

Infrastructure will remain a key contributor to growth, and corporate investment is expected to accelerate as capacity constraints start to bind and funding conditions remain supportive.

- After very rapid growth last year, growth in the newly industrialized Asian economies (NIEs) is expected to moderate to a more sustainable 5 percent in 2011, roughly in line with potential. Although the deceleration reflects the end of the inventory cycle, exports and private consumption will remain important drivers of growth.

- The ASEAN-5 economies[5] are projected to expand by 5½ percent in 2011 and 5¾ percent in 2012. The ASEAN-5 will be led by Indonesia, where

[5]The Association of Southeast Asian Nations (ASEAN) includes Indonesia, Malaysia, Philippines, Thailand, and Vietnam.

strong consumption and a recovery in investment will raise growth to 6¼ percent this year and 6½ percent in 2012.

- Japan's growth of 4 percent in 2010 was one of the fastest among the advanced economies, driven by sizable fiscal stimulus and a rebound in exports. Looking forward, however, there are large uncertainties associated with the Tohuku earthquake. Official estimates of the damage to the capital stock are about 3 to 5 percent of GDP, roughly twice that of the 1995 Kobe earthquake. This figure, however, does not account for the effects of possible power shortages and ongoing risks associated with the crisis at the Fukushima Daiichi nuclear power plant. Assuming that the power shortages and the nuclear crisis are resolved within a few months, growth is projected to slow

## Figure 2.10. Asia: Still in the Lead[1]

Asia continues to outpace other regions, buoyed by resilient exports and strong domestic demand. In some emerging Asian economies, output gaps have closed, core inflation is on the rise, and credit growth is rapid. Persistently large current account surpluses still dominate capital inflows, but many countries continue to resist currency appreciation.

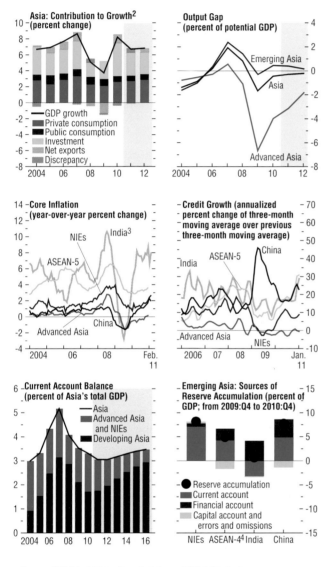

Sources: CEIC Asia database; Haver Analytics; and IMF staff estimates.
[1]Advanced Asia: Australia, Japan, and New Zealand; newly industrialized Asian economies (NIEs): Hong Kong SAR, Korea, Singapore, and Taiwan Province of China; developing Asia: rest of Asia; ASEAN-5: Indonesia, Malaysia, Philippines, Thailand, and Vietnam; emerging Asia: developing Asia and NIEs. Aggregates for the external economy are sums of individual country data. Aggregates for all others are computed on the basis of purchasing-power-parity weights.
[2]Excludes Bhutan, Brunei Darussalam, Fiji, Kiribati, Lao People's Democratic Republic, Samoa, Timor-Leste, Tonga, Tuvalu, and Vanuatu due to data limitations.
[3]Wholesale price index excluding food and energy.
[4]ASEAN-4: ASEAN-5 excluding Vietnam.

to 1½ percent in 2011 before recovering to 2 percent in 2012.[6]

• In Australia, flooding in key mining and agricultural regions is expected to subtract from growth in early 2011, but over the year this will be offset by stronger private investment in mining and stronger commodity exports; GDP is projected to grow by 3 percent this year and 3½ percent in 2012. Recent earthquakes will slow activity in New Zealand this year, with real GDP growth projected at 1 percent, but growth is expected to rise to 4 percent in 2012, led by reconstruction.

With continued rapid growth, output now close to potential levels, and monetary conditions remaining accommodative, inflation is expected to continue increasing this year across much of developing Asia. Inflation pressure is most evident in India, where despite some moderation, inflation has become more generalized and is projected to remain high—averaging 7½ percent this year. In other parts of developing Asia, inflation is lower but is on the rise. In China, price pressures that started in a narrow range of food products have broadened into other items, including housing, and inflation is projected to reach 5 percent this year. Similar patterns of accelerating and more generalized inflation are becoming evident in the region's other developing economies—for developing Asia as a whole, inflation is projected at 6 percent this year. In stark contrast, mild deflation continues in Japan, and inflation expectations there have not improved substantially.

Risks to the growth outlook come from both outside and inside the region. Despite a substantial increase in intraregional trade, two-thirds of the final demand for Asian exports still comes from outside the region, and renewed turbulence in the euro area would affect Asia primarily through trade linkages. An additional external risk is stronger-than-expected increases in oil and commodity prices. Turning to risks from within Asia, if accommodative policies fail to adjust sufficiently to nascent overheating pressures, near-term growth may surprise on the upside. But that could sow the seeds for a hard landing down the road. In particular, an abrupt slowdown of economic

[6]The April 2011 *Global Financial Stability Report* discusses the financial stability implications of the recent events in Japan.

activity in China, perhaps following a credit and property boom-bust cycle, would adversely affect the whole region. Such boom-bust dynamics are also a possibility in other emerging Asian economies, such as some of the NIEs (Hong Kong SAR, Singapore).

Although Asia's external surplus has narrowed substantially—from a peak of 5¼ percent of regional GDP in 2007 to about 3¼ percent of GDP in 2010—that narrowing is not expected to continue. As external demand recovers and fiscal stimulus is withdrawn, the region's external surpluses are projected to widen again in the coming years, with developing Asia in general and China in particular accounting for the bulk of the surplus, especially in the medium term (see Figure 2.10). In fact, there has been little progress toward rebalancing; the projected surpluses for the region are now larger than they were in the October 2010 *World Economic Outlook,* in both the near and medium term. Developing Asia's current account balances are substantially higher than fundamentals suggest, given the region's relatively low per capita income, higher expected growth rates, and relatively young population.

The primary challenge for Asian policymakers is to quickly normalize the stance of fiscal and monetary policies in the region and ensure that boom-like dynamics do not get out of hand. Monetary policy remains generally accommodative even as many economies have taken steps toward normalization. The further tightening currently expected by markets in some economies is not enough to prevent inflation from increasing. In addition to more rapid tightening of policy rates, greater exchange rate flexibility will be an important component of policy tightening. The primary response to the resurgence of foreign inflows to Asia has been the continued accumulation of reserves. Allowing the exchange rate to appreciate in response to inflows would be more conducive to normalizing the policy stance. In addition, strengthened supervision and prudential measures are needed to address concerns about deteriorating credit quality, which often accompanies credit and asset price booms. In China, for instance, there is rising concern that management of credit aggregates, used to exercise macroeconomic control, is being undermined by banks' financial innovation and off-balance-sheet activities.

Fiscal policy is projected to be less supportive of growth this year than last, but the pace of withdrawal is slow, given how rapidly the region has been growing. A more rapid exit would allow governments to build the fiscal room they need to cope with adverse shocks in the future. Countercyclical fiscal policy would also help cushion domestic demand against the effect of capital inflows. In Japan, the recent downgrade of sovereign debt has highlighted the importance of having a more credible fiscal adjustment plan. Once the extent of the earthquake's damage becomes clearer and reconstruction efforts are under way, the authorities will need a more credible fiscal strategy that brings down the public debt ratio over the medium term while addressing the need for additional reconstruction spending.

Managing capital inflows is another major policy challenge for Asia. For economies in the region that continue to run large current account surpluses but whose response to capital inflows has been continued reserve accumulation, the policy prescription is clear—greater exchange rate flexibility. Appreciation would not only help address challenges in liquidity management, but could reduce expectations of a large step appreciation, lessening speculative inflows. A stronger prudential framework would also help reduce the vulnerabilities that can arise from sizable and potentially volatile capital inflows.

Although renewed capital inflows have garnered the lion's share of attention in recent months, these flows are still dwarfed by the large current account surpluses in the region. In this area, too, the aforementioned need for greater exchange rate flexibility is critical. Appreciation would help stimulate domestic demand and help shift resources from the tradables to the nontradables sector, facilitating much-needed development of the services sector in some of the region's economies. But exchange rate policy must be complemented by structural reforms. Economies where private investment lags, such as among the ASEAN-5, will benefit from efforts to boost infrastructure and improve the business environment. And continued reforms to raise consumption in economies such as China—including efforts to expand pension and health care coverage and to develop the financial sector—will also be key ingredients of a comprehensive rebalancing package.[7]

---

[7]See, for example, Baldacci and others (2010).

**Figure 2.11. Latin America and the Caribbean: Average Projected Real GDP Growth during 2011–12**
*(Percent)*

■ Below 0
■ Between 0 and 2
■ Between 2 and 4
■ Above 4
□ Insufficient data

Source: IMF staff estimates.

## Latin America Faces Buoyant External Conditions

*The LAC region has weathered the global recession well and must now contend with the policy challenges of managing two strong tailwinds—high commodity prices and strong capital inflows. In a number of the larger countries, the baseline forecast is for moderation of the rapid rates of growth experienced in 2010 and a level of output more in line with potential, but overheating is a significant risk (Figure 2.11). In other, slower-growing countries that did not emerge as rapidly from the global recession, there are signs that output is moving closer to potential.*

Real activity expanded by about 6 percent last year, after contracting by 1¾ percent in 2009. Robust demand from China and rising commodity prices continue to underpin this strength (Figure 2.12). More recently, exports to other destinations have also bounced back. This has encouraged strong capital inflows and moderate current account deficits. Despite the support to current accounts from commodity prices, however, deficits are widening and are projected to continue widening on the back of robust domestic demand. The generally buoyant conditions are associated with rising inflation in South and Central America. On the other hand, Mexico is not facing overheating pressure at this time (see Figure 1.15).

Growth in the region is projected to average 4¾ percent in 2011 and 4¼ percent in 2012 (Table 2.5). The growth rate for 2011 is ⅔ percentage point higher than forecast in the October 2010 *World Economic Outlook* (see Figure 2.12). The main reason for this revision is greater confidence in the strength of the global recovery and improved prospects for commodity prices. As with any region, however, experiences vary.

- The outlook for commodity exporters is generally positive. In the group of financially integrated commodity exporters (FICE—Brazil, Chile, Colombia, Peru, Uruguay), growth is projected at 4¾ percent this year. There are signs, however, of potential overheating, and capital inflows have caused policy tension. For example, real credit growth in Brazil and Colombia is increasing by 10 to 20 percent a year according to the the most recent data (see Figure 2.12). Furthermore, per capita credit in Brazil roughly doubled over the past five years.

- Prospects for Mexico continue to be closely tied to those for the United States. In line with the modest improvement in the outlook for the U.S. economy, real activity in 2011 is now projected to expand by 4½ percent, about ¾ percentage point more than in the October forecast.

- In Central America, and Panama in particular, the recovery is strengthening on the back of external demand, and output gaps are almost closed. Support has also come from a recovery in remittance flows. These trends are expected to continue.

- The outlook for the Caribbean countries has improved in line with the global recovery. Growth in 2011 is now forecast to be 4¼ percent. Much of this, however, reflects the strong performance of the Dominican Republic and post-earthquake rebuilding in Haiti; excluding these countries, growth in the Caribbean is projected to be 2¼ percent. Nonetheless, the constraints on policy stemming from high public debt levels mean that the outlook for these countries remains closely tied to external developments.

There are risks to this forecast in both directions. In the near term, strong commodity export prices and capital flows present upside risks to growth. But these favorable conditions could also be triggers

**Figure 2.12.  Latin America and the Caribbean: Icarus or Daedalus?[1]**

The prospects for Latin America continue to improve, buoyed by China's demand for commodities and strong capital flows. These two forces, however, need to be carefully managed, lest they lead to overheating.

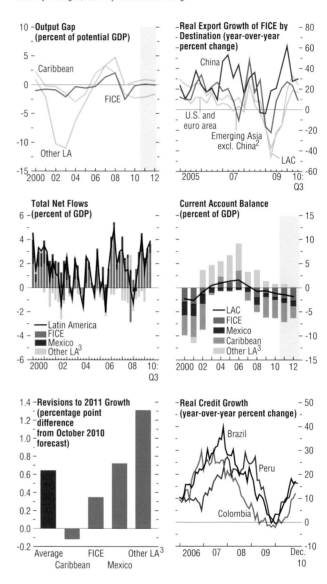

Sources: CEIC EMED database; Haver Analytics; IMF, *Balance of Payments Statistics;* IMF, *Direction of Trade Statistics;* national sources; and IMF staff estimates.
[1]Caribbean: Antigua and Barbuda, the Bahamas, Barbados, Belize, Dominica, Dominican Republic, Grenada, Guyana, Haiti, Jamaica, St. Kitts and Nevis, St. Lucia, St. Vincent and the Grenadines, Suriname, and Trinidad and Tobago; financially integrated commodity exporters (FICE): Brazil, Chile, Colombia, Peru, and Uruguay; Other Latin America (Other LA): Argentina, Bolivia, Costa Rica, Ecuador, El Salvador, Guatemala, Honduras, Nicaragua, Panama, Paraguay, and Venezuela; LAC: Caribbean, FICE, Other LA, and Mexico. Aggregates for the external economy are sums of individual country data. Aggregates for all others are computed on the basis of purchasing-power-parity weights.
[2]Emerging Asia comprises Hong Kong SAR, Indonesia, Korea, Malaysia, Philippines, Singapore, Taiwan Province of China, Thailand, and Vietnam.
[3]Other LA excludes Honduras, Nicaragua, and Panama due to data limitations.

## Table 2.5. Selected Western Hemisphere Economies: Real GDP, Consumer Prices, Current Account Balance, and Unemployment

*(Annual percent change unless noted otherwise)*

| | Real GDP | | | Consumer Prices[1] | | | Current Account Balance[2] | | | Unemployment[3] | | |
|---|---|---|---|---|---|---|---|---|---|---|---|---|
| | | Projections | | | Projections | | | Projections | | | Projections | |
| | 2010 | 2011 | 2012 | 2010 | 2011 | 2012 | 2010 | 2011 | 2012 | 2010 | 2011 | 2012 |
| **North America** | **3.1** | **2.9** | **3.0** | **1.9** | **2.3** | **1.8** | **−3.0** | **−3.1** | **−2.7** | ... | ... | ... |
| United States | 2.8 | 2.8 | 2.9 | 1.6 | 2.2 | 1.6 | −3.2 | −3.2 | −2.8 | 9.6 | 8.5 | 7.8 |
| Canada | 3.1 | 2.8 | 2.6 | 1.8 | 2.2 | 1.9 | −3.1 | −2.8 | −2.6 | 8.0 | 7.6 | 7.3 |
| Mexico | 5.5 | 4.6 | 4.0 | 4.2 | 3.6 | 3.1 | −0.5 | −0.9 | −1.1 | 5.4 | 4.5 | 3.9 |
| **South America** | **6.5** | **4.8** | **4.2** | **6.7** | **7.8** | **7.1** | **−1.1** | **−1.3** | **−1.8** | ... | ... | ... |
| Brazil | 7.5 | 4.5 | 4.1 | 5.0 | 6.3 | 4.8 | −2.3 | −2.6 | −3.0 | 6.7 | 6.7 | 6.7 |
| Argentina[4] | 9.2 | 6.0 | 4.6 | 10.5 | 10.2 | 11.5 | 0.9 | 0.1 | −0.5 | 7.7 | 9.0 | 8.5 |
| Colombia | 4.3 | 4.6 | 4.5 | 2.3 | 3.6 | 2.8 | −3.1 | −2.1 | −2.2 | 11.8 | 11.5 | 11.0 |
| Venezuela | −1.9 | 1.8 | 1.6 | 28.2 | 29.8 | 31.3 | 4.9 | 7.0 | 6.3 | 8.6 | 8.1 | 8.6 |
| Peru | 8.8 | 7.5 | 5.8 | 1.5 | 2.7 | 3.2 | −1.5 | −2.1 | −2.8 | 8.0 | 7.5 | 7.5 |
| Chile | 5.3 | 5.9 | 4.9 | 1.5 | 3.6 | 3.2 | 1.9 | 0.5 | −1.3 | 8.3 | 7.2 | 7.2 |
| Ecuador | 3.2 | 3.2 | 2.8 | 3.6 | 3.5 | 3.2 | −4.4 | −4.0 | −4.0 | 7.6 | 7.3 | 7.5 |
| Uruguay | 8.5 | 5.0 | 4.2 | 6.7 | 7.2 | 6.0 | 0.5 | −1.0 | −1.6 | 7.0 | 6.9 | 6.8 |
| Bolivia | 4.2 | 4.5 | 4.5 | 2.5 | 10.4 | 5.4 | 4.8 | 3.8 | 4.4 | ... | ... | ... |
| Paraguay | 15.3 | 5.6 | 4.5 | 4.7 | 9.6 | 9.0 | −3.2 | −4.1 | −3.7 | 6.1 | 5.9 | 5.5 |
| **Central America[5]** | **3.6** | **4.0** | **4.3** | **3.9** | **5.5** | **5.3** | **−5.1** | **−6.4** | **−6.6** | ... | ... | ... |
| **Caribbean[6]** | **3.4** | **4.2** | **4.5** | **7.1** | **7.2** | **5.9** | **−3.9** | **−4.0** | **−2.5** | ... | ... | ... |
| *Memorandum* | | | | | | | | | | | | |
| Latin America and the Caribbean[7] | 6.1 | 4.7 | 4.2 | 6.0 | 6.7 | 6.0 | −1.2 | −1.4 | −1.8 | ... | ... | ... |

[1]Movements in consumer prices are shown as annual averages. December–December changes can be found in Tables A6 and A7 in the Statistical Appendix.

[2]Percent of GDP.

[3]Percent. National definitions of unemployment may differ.

[4]Private analysts estimate that consumer price inflation has been considerably higher than the official estimates from 2007 onward. The Argentine authorities have announced that they are developing a national consumer price index (CPI) to replace the Greater Buenos Aires CPI currently in use. At the request of the authorities, the IMF is providing technical assistance in this effort. Private analysts are also of the view that real GDP growth was significantly lower than the official estimates in 2008 and 2009, although the discrepancy between private and official estimates of real GDP growth narrowed in 2010.

[5]Central America comprises Costa Rica, El Salvador, Guatemala, Honduras, Nicaragua, and Panama.

[6]The Caribbean comprises Antigua and Barbuda, The Bahamas, Barbados, Belize, Dominica, Dominican Republic, Grenada, Guyana, Haiti, Jamaica, St. Kitts and Nevis, St. Lucia, St. Vincent and the Grenadines, Suriname, and Trinidad and Tobago.

[7]Includes Mexico and economies from the Caribbean, Central America, and South America.

for demand and credit booms in a number of LAC economies. If unchecked, these could lead to an eventual bust. This pattern of near-term upside risk leading to medium-term downside risk is reinforced through the region's internal and external linkages. Because of Brazil's systemic importance to the region, many neighboring countries are currently benefiting from its strong growth. Conversely, an abrupt slowdown of economic activity in Brazil would adversely affect the region. A related risk is that a potential hard landing in China would bring a sharp drop in the prices of the region's commodity exports, dampening growth prospects. If a spike in oil prices were to dampen global growth, this could also be a trigger for a drop in the region's commodity exports. Finally, another bout of higher global risk aversion or unexpectedly rapid increases in U.S. interest rates could lead to a sharp reversal in capital flows, although the experience during the recent turmoil in the euro area periphery suggests that such disruptions are unlikely to be overwhelming.

Macroeconomic policies in the region should not fall behind the curve, given the risk of overheating. In countries where currencies are not under strong upward pressure on the back of strong capital flows and where monetary policy is still expansionary, policy rates should move faster toward more neutral levels. However, much of the focus should be on fiscal policies, particularly given the historical tendency throughout the region to adopt procyclical policies. In the FICE, this need stems from the pressure of strong capital flows, already-elevated exchange rates, and monetary policy rates that are higher than in other countries. In other countries, it is important to reduce debt burdens and regain room for fiscal mobility. Exchange rates should be allowed to continue to act as shock absorbers in the face of pressure stemming from economic conditions in the region that have improved more than those in more advanced economies, primarily because of terms-of-trade gains from high commodity export prices.

Macroprudential policies need to focus on maintaining and enhancing the resilience of these economies to potential problems from accelerating domestic credit and significant capital flows. This is most imperative in the FICE, but such policy improvements will also benefit other regional economies. As with macroeconomic policies, these need to be implemented in a forward-looking manner to stem potential credit growth excesses and sustained

capital inflows. While a number of countries in the region have been quite active on this front recently, introducing prudential measures (see Figure 1.15), more work remains to be done. Policies should ensure that capital flows are directed toward longer-term financing and that balance sheet exposures are actively and prudently managed.

## Growth Has Returned to Precrisis Rates in Many African Countries

*Sub-Saharan Africa has recovered well from the global financial crisis (Figure 2.13), and the region is now second only to developing Asia in its rate of expansion. Output gaps in many of the region's economies are starting to close, although South Africa is a notable exception.*

The region grew rapidly last year. Domestic demand growth remained robust, trade and commodity prices rebounded, and macroeconomic poli-

**Figure 2.13.  Sub-Saharan Africa: Average Projected Real GDP Growth during 2011–12**
*(Percent)*

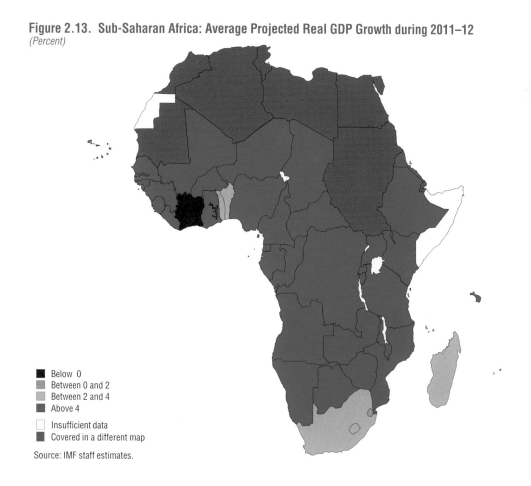

- Below 0
- Between 0 and 2
- Between 2 and 4
- Above 4

- Insufficient data
- Covered in a different map

Source: IMF staff estimates.

## Figure 2.14. Sub-Saharan Africa: Back to Precrisis Growth[1]

Growth in most economies, particularly the low-income countries, is back to precrisis rates. Recovery has been helped by strong domestic demand, stable financial flows, and terms-of-trade gains from strong commodity prices, which have also improved the region's external balance. As output gaps close, fiscal policy needs to stay countercyclical.

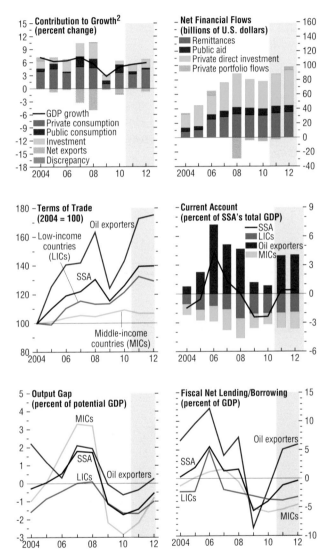

Source: IMF staff estimates.
[1]Aggregates for the external economy are sums of individual country data. Aggregates for terms of trade are weighted by the country's trade share in the group. Aggregates for all others are computed on the basis of purchasing-power-parity weights.
[2]Excludes Liberia and Zimbabwe due to data limitations.

cies continued to be accommodative (Figure 2.14). Terms-of-trade gains are supporting the region's external balances, and the gradual reorientation of exports toward faster-growing regions such as Asia has been sustained.

Against this backdrop, real activity in sub-Saharan Africa is projected to expand by 5½ percent this year and 6 percent next year. Within the region, however, prospects differ considerably.

- Growth in the region is being led by the low-income countries (LICs), which are projected to expand by 6 percent this year (Table 2.6). Ghana—which, following a substantial upward revision to its national accounts, is now the third-largest LIC in the region—is projected to grow by 13¾ percent this year, as oil production commences in the Jubilee oilfield and growth in the non-oil sector remains robust. The recovery in other LICs, such as Kenya and Ethiopia, is also expected to stay strong this year, supported by infrastructure investment and improving agricultural production.

- The expected strengthening of oil prices in 2011 will help sustain the recovery in the region's oil exporters. Following the sharp rebound in oil production last year in Nigeria, oil output is expected to stabilize this year, and the economy is set to expand by 7 percent. Most other oil-exporting economies are planning to use the buoyancy of global oil markets as an opportunity to return to fiscal surpluses and rebuild reserves, but fiscal policy remains procyclical in Nigeria due to the failure to adhere to the oil-price-based fiscal rule, which links spending to long-term average oil prices.

- In marked contrast to the robust growth in most of the region, recovery is expected to be relatively weak in South Africa, the region's largest economy. Despite an already sizable output gap, South Africa is expected to grow by only 3½ percent in 2011—a rate that is insufficient to reverse the substantial job losses of the past two years. The outlook primarily reflects the lack of strong domestic demand, as private investment is held back by excess capacity.

Risks to the region's growth outlook remain tilted to the downside. Despite the increasing importance of Asia, Europe remains a much larger trading

## Table 2.6. Selected Sub-Saharan African Economies: Real GDP, Consumer Prices, Current Account Balance, and Unemployment

*(Annual percent change unless noted otherwise)*

| | Real GDP | | | Consumer Prices[1] | | | Current Account Balance[2] | | | Unemployment[3] | | |
|---|---|---|---|---|---|---|---|---|---|---|---|---|
| | | Projections | | | Projections | | | Projections | | | Projections | |
| | 2010 | 2011 | 2012 | 2010 | 2011 | 2012 | 2010 | 2011 | 2012 | 2010 | 2011 | 2012 |
| **Sub-Saharan Africa** | **5.0** | **5.5** | **5.9** | **7.5** | **7.8** | **7.3** | **−2.4** | **0.4** | **0.4** | ... | ... | ... |
| **Oil Exporters** | **6.5** | **6.9** | **7.0** | **12.4** | **10.8** | **9.4** | **2.6** | **10.9** | **11.1** | ... | ... | ... |
| Nigeria | 8.4 | 6.9 | 6.6 | 13.7 | 11.1 | 9.5 | 6.4 | 14.6 | 13.3 | 4.5 | 4.5 | 4.5 |
| Angola | 1.6 | 7.8 | 10.5 | 14.5 | 14.6 | 12.4 | −1.8 | 6.2 | 9.5 | ... | ... | ... |
| Equatorial Guinea | −0.8 | 7.2 | 4.0 | 7.5 | 7.3 | 7.0 | −23.8 | −10.2 | −9.0 | ... | ... | ... |
| Gabon | 5.7 | 5.6 | 3.3 | 0.6 | 2.3 | 3.4 | 11.8 | 17.0 | 15.3 | ... | ... | ... |
| Republic of Congo | 9.1 | 7.8 | 4.7 | 5.0 | 5.9 | 5.2 | 2.7 | 12.5 | 16.0 | ... | ... | ... |
| Chad | 5.1 | 4.1 | 6.0 | 1.0 | 3.0 | 3.0 | −21.3 | −8.0 | −6.1 | ... | ... | ... |
| **Middle-Income** | **3.1** | **3.7** | **4.0** | **4.4** | **5.2** | **5.8** | **−3.1** | **−4.5** | **−5.1** | ... | ... | ... |
| South Africa | 2.8 | 3.5 | 3.8 | 4.3 | 4.9 | 5.8 | −2.8 | −4.4 | −5.1 | 24.8 | 24.4 | 23.7 |
| Botswana | 8.6 | 6.0 | 6.6 | 6.9 | 7.8 | 7.0 | −2.5 | −2.4 | −0.0 | ... | ... | ... |
| Mauritius | 4.0 | 4.1 | 4.2 | 2.9 | 7.4 | 4.6 | −9.5 | −11.6 | −9.6 | 7.5 | 7.8 | 7.9 |
| Namibia | 4.4 | 4.8 | 4.5 | 4.5 | 5.9 | 5.6 | −1.1 | −0.9 | −3.3 | ... | ... | ... |
| Swaziland | 2.0 | 0.5 | 1.5 | 4.5 | 7.9 | 6.1 | −20.6 | −16.0 | −12.9 | 25.0 | 25.0 | 25.0 |
| Cape Verde | 5.4 | 5.5 | 6.8 | 2.1 | 4.4 | 5.4 | −11.8 | −18.0 | −15.7 | ... | ... | ... |
| **Low-Income[4]** | **5.3** | **5.9** | **6.5** | **6.2** | **7.5** | **6.8** | **−7.0** | **−7.1** | **−6.7** | ... | ... | ... |
| Ethiopia | 8.0 | 8.5 | 8.0 | 2.8 | 12.9 | 11.2 | −4.3 | −8.1 | −8.1 | ... | ... | ... |
| Kenya | 5.0 | 5.7 | 6.5 | 3.9 | 7.2 | 5.0 | −7.9 | −9.3 | −7.9 | ... | ... | ... |
| Ghana | 5.7 | 13.7 | 7.3 | 10.7 | 8.7 | 8.7 | −7.2 | −6.8 | −5.2 | ... | ... | ... |
| Tanzania | 6.5 | 6.4 | 6.6 | 10.5 | 6.3 | 7.0 | −8.6 | −9.5 | −10.7 | ... | ... | ... |
| Cameroon | 3.0 | 3.5 | 4.5 | 1.3 | 3.0 | 2.5 | −3.9 | −3.1 | −3.0 | ... | ... | ... |
| Uganda | 5.2 | 6.0 | 6.5 | 9.4 | 6.1 | 11.0 | −9.9 | −10.6 | −9.2 | ... | ... | ... |
| Côte d'Ivoire[5] | 2.6 | −7.5 | 6.0 | 1.4 | 5.0 | 2.5 | 3.9 | ... | ... | ... | ... | ... |

[1]Movements in consumer prices are shown as annual averages. December–December changes can be found in Table A7 in the Statistical Appendix.

[2]Percent of GDP.

[3]Percent. National definitions of unemployment may differ.

[4]Includes Benin, Burkina Faso, Burundi, Central African Republic, Comoros, Democratic Republic of Congo, Eritrea, The Gambia, Ghana, Guinea, Guinea-Bissau, Lesotho, Liberia, Madagascar, Malawi, Mali, Mozambique, Niger, Rwanda, São Tomé and Príncipe, Senegal, Seychelles, Sierra Leone, Togo, Zambia, and Zimbabwe.

[5]Current account projections are not shown due to the uncertain political situation.

partner for the region's non-oil-exporting economies. A slowdown in Europe would particularly hurt the region's manufacturing exporters, such as South Africa. In addition, a sharper-than-expected pickup in fuel and food prices could adversely affect many of the region's oil-importing economies. This could have major social and fiscal costs in the LICs. Another risk factor is politics. In some economies, such as Côte d'Ivoire, political turmoil has already dampened growth prospects for 2011. But beyond that, with 2011 shaping up to be a busy year politically—with as many as 17 national elections scheduled—activity in some countries could be hindered by related political unrest.

Narrowing output gaps, alongside an incipient rekindling of inflation pressures by rising commodity prices, mean that policies to support demand are no longer appropriate except in a handful of economies.

The focus of fiscal policy should therefore turn to medium-term priorities, while monetary policy needs to be increasingly alert to the inflation outlook.

• The active use of countercyclical fiscal policy to support output during the crisis has left a legacy of wider fiscal deficits across the region. With growth in many economies now approaching potential, financing and medium-term debt sustainability considerations mostly point to the need to revisit medium-term trajectories for government spending and revenue. At the same time, fiscal buffers need to be rebuilt and fiscal room needs to be found for spending priorities such as health, education, and infrastructure. Such adjustments are already under way in, for example, South Africa. In Nigeria, however, where growth is much stronger, the fiscal stance has weakened and fiscal consolidation is overdue; anchoring fiscal policy through a strong oil-revenue-based rule would help maintain a countercyclical fiscal stance.

- Rising food prices are likely to affect the urban poor in particular, given the high share of food in their consumption baskets. In response, governments will need to consider targeted social safety nets—another reason to create greater room for fiscal policy maneuvering. At the same time, policymakers should remain alert to inflation pressure from rising commodity prices, especially with limited spare capacity in many economies. For South Africa and a number of middle-income countries where output remains well below potential, however, continued monetary accommodation will be appropriate.

Finally, a number of other policy areas require sustained attention. More intensive monitoring and sounder regulation of the financial sector are needed, as are continuing improvements to the business environment. Robust public financing mechanisms would also facilitate better planning and control of government spending, including infrastructure investment.

## The Recovery in the Middle East and North Africa Region Faces an Uncertain Environment

*The MENA region weathered the global crisis relatively well, and while the recovery is now proceeding, economic growth varies widely across the region. Spreading social unrest, rising sovereign risk premiums, and elevated commodity import prices will constrain growth prospects in several MENA economies. Although economic prospects across the MENA region are quite diverse, an ongoing regionwide repricing of risk is pushing up borrowing costs.*

Higher commodity prices and external demand are boosting production and exports in many economies in the region. In addition, government spending programs are continuing to foster recovery in many oil-exporting economies. At the same time,

**Figure 2.15. Middle East and North Africa: Average Projected Real GDP Growth during 2011–12**
(Percent)

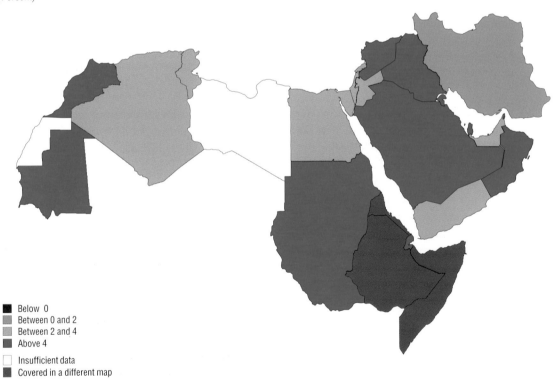

■ Below 0
▨ Between 0 and 2
▨ Between 2 and 4
■ Above 4

□ Insufficient data
■ Covered in a different map

Source: IMF staff estimates.
Note: Projections are not provided for Libya due to the uncertain political situation.

**Table 2.7. Selected Middle East and North African Economies: Real GDP, Consumer Prices, Current Account Balance, and Unemployment**

*(Annual percent change unless noted otherwise)*

| | Real GDP | | | Consumer Prices[1] | | | Current Account Balance[2] | | | Unemployment[3] | | |
|---|---|---|---|---|---|---|---|---|---|---|---|---|
| | | Projections | | | Projections | | | Projections | | | Projections | |
| | 2010 | 2011 | 2012 | 2010 | 2011 | 2012 | 2010 | 2011 | 2012 | 2010 | 2011 | 2012 |
| **Middle East and North Africa** | **3.8** | **4.1** | **4.2** | **6.9** | **10.0** | **7.3** | **6.5** | **12.7** | **11.2** | ... | ... | ... |
| **Oil Exporters[4]** | **3.5** | **4.9** | **4.1** | **6.7** | **10.6** | **7.1** | **9.2** | **16.9** | **15.0** | ... | ... | ... |
| Islamic Republic of Iran | 1.0 | −0.0 | 3.0 | 12.5 | 22.5 | 12.5 | 6.0 | 11.7 | 10.4 | ... | ... | ... |
| Saudi Arabia | 3.7 | 7.5 | 3.0 | 5.4 | 6.0 | 5.5 | 8.7 | 19.8 | 13.8 | 10.5 | ... | ... |
| Algeria | 3.3 | 3.6 | 3.2 | 4.3 | 5.0 | 4.3 | 9.4 | 17.8 | 17.4 | 10.0 | 9.8 | 9.5 |
| United Arab Emirates | 3.2 | 3.3 | 3.8 | 0.9 | 4.5 | 3.0 | 7.7 | 10.4 | 10.5 | ... | ... | ... |
| Qatar | 16.3 | 20.0 | 7.1 | −2.4 | 4.2 | 4.1 | 18.7 | 36.1 | 34.0 | ... | ... | ... |
| Kuwait | 2.0 | 5.3 | 5.1 | 4.1 | 6.1 | 2.7 | 31.8 | 39.4 | 39.4 | 1.6 | 1.6 | 1.6 |
| Iraq | 0.8 | 9.6 | 12.6 | 5.1 | 5.0 | 5.0 | −6.2 | −3.2 | −0.7 | ... | ... | ... |
| Sudan | 5.1 | 4.7 | 5.6 | 13.0 | 9.0 | 7.0 | −8.5 | −5.5 | −6.6 | 13.7 | 12.6 | 11.4 |
| **Oil Importers[5]** | **4.5** | **1.9** | **4.5** | **7.6** | **8.1** | **8.0** | **−3.8** | **−5.2** | **−4.5** | ... | ... | ... |
| Egypt | 5.1 | 1.0 | 4.0 | 11.7 | 11.5 | 12.0 | −2.0 | −2.7 | −2.3 | 9.2 | 9.2 | 9.1 |
| Morocco | 3.2 | 3.9 | 4.6 | 1.0 | 2.9 | 2.9 | −4.2 | −5.7 | −4.1 | 9.0 | 8.9 | 8.7 |
| Syrian Arab Republic | 3.2 | 3.0 | 5.1 | 4.4 | 6.0 | 5.0 | −4.4 | −4.6 | −4.8 | 8.4 | ... | ... |
| Tunisia | 3.7 | 1.3 | 5.6 | 4.4 | 4.0 | 3.3 | −4.8 | −7.8 | −5.8 | 13.0 | 14.7 | 14.4 |
| Lebanon | 7.5 | 2.5 | 5.0 | 4.5 | 6.5 | 3.0 | −10.2 | −12.9 | −12.8 | ... | ... | ... |
| Jordan | 3.1 | 3.3 | 3.9 | 5.0 | 6.1 | 5.6 | −5.4 | −8.5 | −8.7 | 12.5 | 12.5 | 12.5 |
| *Memorandum* | | | | | | | | | | | | |
| Israel | 4.6 | 3.8 | 3.8 | 2.7 | 3.0 | 2.5 | 3.1 | 3.3 | 3.1 | 6.7 | 5.5 | 5.0 |
| Maghreb[6] | 3.5 | 3.3 | 4.1 | 3.2 | 4.2 | 3.7 | 5.3 | 7.2 | 7.6 | ... | ... | ... |
| Mashreq[7] | 5.0 | 1.5 | 4.2 | 9.6 | 10.0 | 9.8 | −3.6 | −4.7 | −4.4 | ... | ... | ... |

[1]Movements in consumer prices are shown as annual averages. December–December changes can be found in Tables A6 and A7 in the Statistical Appendix.
[2]Percent of GDP.
[3]Percent. National definitions of unemployment may differ.
[4]Includes Bahrain, Libya, Oman, and Republic of Yemen. Excludes Libya for the projection years due to the uncertain political situation.
[5]Includes Djibouti and Mauritania.
[6]The Maghreb comprises Algeria, Libya, Mauritania, Morocco, and Tunisia. Excludes Libya for the projection years due to the uncertain political situation.
[7]The Mashreq comprises Egypt, Jordan, Lebanon, and Syrian Arab Republic.

political discontent, high unemployment, and rising food prices are causing social unrest in a number of countries, which is likely to dampen their short-term growth.

Taking into account these factors, GDP in the MENA region is projected to grow at 4 percent in 2011, edging up to about 4¼ percent in 2012. As in other regions, recovery prospects vary substantially across MENA economies (Figure 2.15; Table 2.7).

- In the group of oil exporters, growth is expected to pick up to 5 percent this year. The strongest performer is Qatar, where real activity is projected to expand by 20 percent in 2011, underpinned by continued expansion in natural gas production and large investment expenditures. In Saudi Arabia, GDP is expected to grow at about 7½ percent this year, supported by sizable government infrastructure investment. In the Islamic

Republic of Iran, growth in 2011 is expected to stall temporarily as subsidies for energy and other products are phased out—a much-needed reform that will yield benefits in the medium term. Disruption of oil production in Libya means that, given constraints on non-OPEC capacity, oil production from other OPEC suppliers will increase in 2011.

- In the group of oil importers, Egypt's GDP growth will fall significantly below the 5½ percent registered in the second half of 2010. This assumes a modest dampening effect on economic activity from the political turmoil: disruptions to tourism, capital flows, and financial markets are expected to be temporary. In Tunisia, growth is projected to slow to 1¼ percent in 2011, as the expected decline in tourism and foreign direct investment harms other sectors of the economy.

## Figure 2.16. Middle East and North Africa: The Recovery Continues in an Uncertain Environment[1]

Having weathered the global crisis relatively well, the recovery is now proceeding. The level of economic activity is still below but getting closer to potential. High unemployment, growing social unrest, and rising food prices are dampening growth prospects, especially in oil-importing economies. Current account surpluses in oil-exporting economies are expected to widen again as the recovery continues.

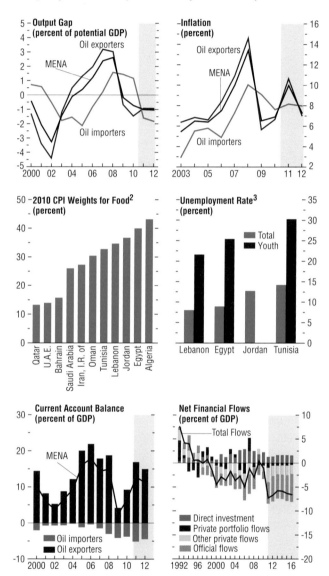

Sources: Haver Analytics; International Labor Organization; IMF, Primary Commodity Price System; national sources; and IMF staff estimates.

[1] Oil exporters: Algeria, Bahrain, Islamic Republic of Iran, Iraq, Kuwait, Libya, Oman, Qatar, Saudi Arabia, Sudan, United Arab Emirates (U.A.E.), and Republic of Yemen. Oil importers: Djibouti, Egypt, Jordan, Lebanon, Mauritania, Morocco, Syrian Arab Republic, and Tunisia. Aggregates for the external economy are sums of individual country data. Aggregates for all others are computed on the basis of purchasing-power-parity weights.

[2] Data for Algeria, Tunisia, and U.A.E. are for 2009. Data for Saudi Arabia are for 2008. Data for Lebanon are for 2007. CPI: consumer price index.

[3] Youth defined as persons ages 15 to 24 years. Data on youth unemployment rate are not available for Jordan.

As in other regions, inflation is on the rise in the MENA region, as higher commodity prices lift headline inflation (Figure 2.16). For the region as a whole, consumer price inflation is projected to increase to about 10 percent in 2011, led by the Islamic Republic of Iran, where fuel subsidies are being substantially reduced.

The key risks to this outlook are to the downside. Depending on its duration and intensity, the domestic effects of political and social turmoil could be larger than currently expected, particularly if sustained unrest spills over to additional countries in the region. Financial markets have not been immune, and credit default swap and bond spreads have already widened throughout the region. If persistent, such financial market developments could translate into higher funding costs for governments and firms. In addition, slower-than-expected recovery in advanced economies would adversely affect the region's export earnings, fiscal and external balances, and growth.

Turning to the external sector, current account surpluses in the MENA region are expected to widen again as the recovery proceeds, driven in part by elevated energy export prices. The overall regional current account surplus, which declined from 15 percent of GDP in 2008 to 2¼ percent of GDP in 2009, is now projected to rise to over 12 percent of GDP in 2011.

The key policy challenges across the region are daunting. For oil importers, the main priority is to raise growth and tackle chronically high unemployment, especially among young people. For oil exporters, the focus should be to strengthen or develop financial systems and promote economic diversification. Recent increases in public spending on non-energy-related sectors should be helpful in diversifying activity toward these sectors and rebalancing regional growth.

Fiscal policy has played a critical role in cushioning the impact of the global crisis on the region and in supporting its recovery. Government investment programs, especially in infrastructure, will continue to boost domestic demand in the near term in many oil-exporting economies. High debt levels, however, constrain the scope for fiscal maneuver in oil-importing economies. Nevertheless, to shield populations from surging commodity prices, many economies have recently increased food and fuel subsidies (Jordan, Kuwait, Tunisia), increased social transfers (Sudan, Syrian Arab Republic, Tunisia, Republic of Yemen), expanded civil service employment or salaries (Egypt, Jordan, Saudi Arabia, Sudan, Republic of Yemen), and introduced direct cash transfers (Bahrain, Kuwait).

In most MENA economies, chronically high unemployment, especially among young people and the educated, is a long-standing challenge that now must be tackled urgently. The fact that unemployment has remained high for so long suggests that the problem is largely structural—stemming from skill mismatches, labor market rigidities, and high reservation wages. A lasting solution to the region's unemployment problem will require a combination of permanently higher and inclusive economic growth and reforms to improve the responsiveness of labor markets.[8]

[8] See the IMF's October 2010 and May 2011 *Regional Economic Outlook* for the Middle East and Central Asia.

With regard to financial sector policy, the priorities should vary across economies. For the more financially developed economies of the Gulf Cooperation Council, the key task is to restore capital and liquidity buffers used up during the crisis and to improve regulatory and supervisory regimes in line with global efforts. This will help revive credit, which has been sluggish partly due to still-weak banking and corporate balance sheets following prominent corporate defaults (in Dubai, Kuwait, and Saudi Arabia, for example). For other economies in the region, the main challenge is to prevent a rise in nonperforming loans in countries with unrest, to spur greater financial development by removing barriers to entry and exit and, in some cases, to reduce state banking system ownership. Addressing the high number of nonperforming loans in a number of economies is another priority.

## Box 2.1. Unwinding External Imbalances in the European Union Periphery

The Great Recession forced a painful adjustment in external imbalances in the periphery of the European Union. Current account deficits soared in the years leading up to the crisis, with rapid growth in credit and domestic demand and strong increases in unit labor costs relative to the euro area. By 2007, the current account deficit averaged 10.0 percent of GDP in Greece, Ireland, Portugal, and Spain and 17.7 percent of GDP in the Baltic economies of Estonia, Latvia, and Lithuania. Because the nominal exchange rate is fixed, these economies have had to unwind the large imbalances through demand contraction and a decline in inflation and wage growth relative to their trading partners, a process known as internal devaluation. To shed light on how this process is proceeding, this box compares the experience of the Baltics with that of the other economies and discusses some challenges ahead.

### Estonia, Latvia, and Lithuania

These Baltic economies have eliminated their current account deficits, but the contraction in economic activity has been unusually large. GDP contracted by an average of 15.5 percent in 2009, and the unemployment rate rose by 12.8 percentage points during 2007–10. In terms of external adjustment, these economies' current accounts swung from a deficit averaging 17.7 percent of GDP in 2007 to a surplus averaging 5.8 percent of GDP in 2009, which may be above the long-term level. Indeed, the current account surplus declined in 2010, and the challenge is now to sustain recent improvements in competitiveness to support growth in productive sectors. Unit labor costs also fell sharply relative to the euro area, by 18.1 percent from their peak. The sharp rises in unemployment, as well as the flexibility of these economies' labor markets and large cuts in both public sector and private sector wages, accelerated internal devaluation and the restoration of competitiveness.

The sharp recession meant that the adjustment initially occurred through a contraction of imports, but exports subsequently contributed to the rebalancing. In 2009, the ratio of imports to GDP fell by an average of 14.6 percentage points. In 2010, imports

The authors of this box are Florence Jaumotte and Daniel Leigh.

rebounded and exports rose above their 2007 level, possibly reflecting the decline in unit labor costs and the recovery in global trade. In terms of saving and investment, the adjustment has so far been due mainly to a contraction in investment. A decline in public saving, mainly due to decreased government revenue during the recession, has been partly offset by a rise in private saving to more sustainable levels.

### Greece, Ireland, Portugal, and Spain

A painful but more gradual process of external adjustment is under way in these economies. GDP contracted by an average of 4.0 percent in 2009, and the unemployment rate rose by an average of

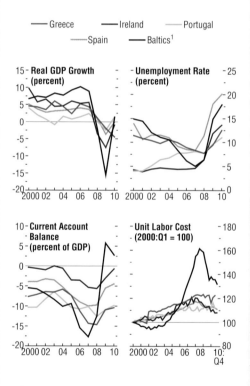

**Figure 2.1.1. Economic Activity and External Adjustment in the EU Periphery**

Sources: Haver Analytics; and IMF staff calculations.
[1]Baltics: Estonia, Latvia, and Lithuania. Aggregates for the Baltics are simple averages except for current account balance, which is calculated as the sum of the balances.

## Box 2.1 *(continued)*

7.0 percentage points during 2007–10. The external adjustment process started later than in the Baltic economies, with the ratio of the current account deficit to GDP falling by 4.3 percentage points—from 10.7 percent of GDP in 2008 to 6.4 percent of GDP in 2010. The current account deficits of Ireland and, to a lesser extent, Spain have moved toward more sustainable levels, but they remain excessively large in Greece and Portugal, at 10.4 and 9.9 percent of GDP, respectively, in 2010. The decline of unit labor costs relative to the euro area averaged 5.1 percent for these economies, but this is skewed by the 10.2 percent decline in Ireland; the decline was more modest in the other three countries.

There are signs of a turnaround in all four of these countries. They initially adjusted through import contraction, but exports started contributing to the adjustment in 2010. Reflecting the smaller contraction in income, the fall in the ratio of imports to GDP in 2009 was smaller than in the Baltics—an average of 4.8 percentage points compared with 14.6 percentage points. In 2010, there was a rebound in both imports and exports, but exports generally increased more, thus furthering the external adjustment process. Exports as a share of GDP rose by much more in Ireland, possibly reflecting the greater decline in unit labor costs there. In real terms, exports grew strongly in Ireland, Portugal, and especially Spain, largely as a rebound. In terms of saving and investment, the adjustment has so far consisted mainly of a contraction in investment, as in the Baltic economies, and the large fall in public saving has been partly offset by a rise in private saving. Wage moderation has played a relatively modest role in Greece, Portugal, and Spain, where labor markets are less flexible than in the Baltics.

A number of policies can contribute to the remaining adjustment that will be required, and many are already being implemented. In Greece and Ireland, they are an integral part of the authorities' adjustment programs, which are supported by the international community. The policies include measures on both the supply side and the demand side of the economy:

- Labor cost adjustment can be facilitated by promoting decentralized wage bargaining, removing

### Figure 2.1.2.  External Adjustment in the EU Periphery

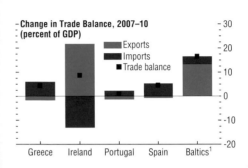

**Change in Trade Balance, 2007–10**
**(percent of GDP)**

Exports
Imports
Trade balance

Greece    Ireland    Portugal    Spain    Baltics[1]

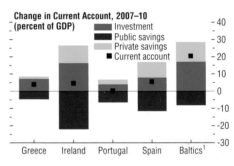

**Change in Current Account, 2007–10**
**(percent of GDP)**

Investment
Public savings
Private savings
Current account

Greece    Ireland    Portugal    Spain    Baltics[1]

Sources: Haver Analytics; and IMF staff calculations.
[1]Baltics: Estonia, Latvia, and Lithuania. Aggregates for the Baltics are calculated as sums of individual country data.

indexation mechanisms, and reducing dismissal costs. In addition, building a national consensus so that the burden of the adjustment is shared broadly through wage moderation can help prevent a protracted period of high unemployment.
- Reforms to increase productivity growth also contribute to improving competitiveness.
- The fiscal consolidation under way to address these economies' elevated government debt levels will also contribute to the external adjustment. In the short term, raising taxes or cutting government spending improves the current account balance by restraining domestic demand, including imports. Over the medium term, it would be helpful to create room to cut taxes, thereby supporting private investment and the supply side of the economy.

## References

Baldacci, Emanuele, Giovanni Callegari, David Coady, Ding Ding, Manmohan S. Kumar, Pietro Tommasino, and Jae-joon Woo, 2010, "Public Expenditures on Social Programs and Household Consumption in China," IMF Working Paper 10/69 (Washington: International Monetary Fund).

Bornhorst, Fabian, Nina Budina, Giovanni Callegari, Asmaa ElGanainy, Raquel Gomez Sirera, Andrea Lemgruber, Andrea Schaechter, and Joong Beom Shin, 2010, "A Status Update on Fiscal Exit Strategies," IMF Working Paper 10/272 (Washington: International Monetary Fund).

Dowling, Thomas, Marcello M. Estevão, and Evridiki Tsounta, 2010, "The Great Recession and Structural Unemployment," *United States: Selected Issues Paper*, IMF Country Report No. 10/248 (Washington: International Monetary Fund).

Estevão, Marcello M., and Evridiki Tsounta, 2011, "Has the Great Recession Raised U.S. Structural Unemployment?" IMF Working Paper (Washington: International Monetary Fund).

# OIL SCARCITY, GROWTH, AND GLOBAL IMBALANCES

*The persistent increase in oil prices over the past decade suggests that global oil markets have entered a period of increased scarcity. Given the expected rapid growth in oil demand in emerging market economies and a downshift in the trend growth of oil supply, a return to abundance is unlikely in the near term. This chapter suggests that gradual and moderate increases in oil scarcity may not present a major constraint on global growth in the medium to long term, although the wealth transfer from oil importers to exporters would increase capital flows and widen current account imbalances. Adverse effects could be much larger, depending on the extent and evolution of oil scarcity and the ability of the world economy to cope with increased scarcity. Sudden surges in oil prices could trigger large global output losses, redistribution, and sectoral shifts. There are two broad areas for policy action. First, given the potential for unexpected increases in the scarcity of oil and other resources, policymakers should review whether the current policy frameworks facilitate adjustment to unexpected changes in oil scarcity. Second, consideration should be given to policies aimed at lowering the risk of oil scarcity.*

After a year and a half of global recovery, natural resources are again in the headlines. The spot price of a barrel of Brent crude oil crossed the US$100 threshold in January 2011. The prices of many other commodities have risen to meet or surpass their precrisis peaks, and commodity futures markets point to further price increases in the next year or two. Commodity price strength mirrors buoyancy on the demand side. Consumption levels of many natural resources, including crude oil, have already risen above precrisis peaks, largely reflecting robust demand in emerging and developing economies.

At current high levels, commodity price developments and prospects can have important global economic repercussions (see Chapter 1). The pos-

sibility that rising energy prices will spill over into core inflation is just one example. But how unusual is the current situation? There are important linkages between global economic conditions and commodity prices, and large fluctuations in commodity prices over the global cycle are nothing new.[1] Cyclical factors and special factors seem to explain much recent commodity price behavior. Nevertheless, persistent commodity price increases in recent years point to a break with the experience of the 1980s and 1990s as well as with the experience of earlier commodity price booms.[2] Concern about resource scarcity is more widespread now than a decade or two ago.

This chapter considers the case of oil scarcity.[3] The main motivation is twofold. On the one hand, oil market prospects are central to the global economic outlook—the oil price assumption is one of the key assumptions underlying the forecasts in the *World Economic Outlook* (WEO). On the other hand, there is considerable uncertainty about how strong the tension will be between rapid growth in oil demand in emerging market economies and the downshift in oil supply trends. The baseline oil market outlook discussed in Chapter 1, which is based on current oil market pricing, assumes that the tension will be resolved with oil prices around current high levels.

Against this backdrop, this chapter analyzes the risks presented by several oil scarcity scenarios for the global outlook and the transition to a more robust and balanced global expansion. As indicated by the emphasis on scarcity, the focus is on the medium to long term, not on short-term risks.

Specifically, this chapter seeks to answer the following questions:

---

The main authors of this chapter are Thomas Helbling (team leader), Joong Shik Kang, Michael Kumhof, Dirk Muir, Andrea Pescatori, and Shaun Roache, with support from Min Kyu Song, Gavin Asdorian, Marina Rousset, and Nese Erbil.

[1]See Vansteenkiste (2009), Kilian (2009), or Helbling (forthcoming).

[2]See, for example, Radetzki (2006), who notes that earlier commodity price booms in the post–World War II period were short-lived.

[3]Appendix 2 of Chapter 1 provides an overview of recent developments and prospects for other commodities.

- What is oil scarcity? How is it measured? What is its current status?
- Will oil scarcity constrain the global economy in the medium to longer term? What are the risks that it will lower the feasible rate of global growth? Could it widen global imbalances?
- What are the policy implications?

A discussion of oil scarcity faces the challenge of any forward-looking analysis. Experience to date does not allow for strong predictions about the likely evolution of some of the factors that will determine the eventual extent and impact of oil scarcity. For example, technological developments will be crucial. These will affect the cost of extracting oil from reservoirs or deposits so far deemed uneconomical and will define the scope for efficiency and substitution. In the face of such uncertainty, which increases with the time horizon, the key objective of this chapter is to illustrate the potential global economic impact of various oil scarcity scenarios. At the same time, it marks the beginning of renewed efforts to give greater consideration to the role of oil and other natural resources in the IMF's modeling of the global economy, both as the source of shocks and in the transmission of other shocks.

## What Are the Main Findings?

- The increases in the trend component of oil prices suggest that the global oil market has entered a period of increased scarcity. The analysis of demand and supply prospects for crude oil suggests that the increased scarcity arises from continued tension between rapid growth in oil demand in emerging market economies and the downshift in oil supply trend growth. If the tension intensifies, whether from stronger demand, traditional supply disruptions, or setbacks to capacity growth, market clearing could force price spikes, as in 2007–08.
- As for the effects on the global economy, the simulation analysis suggests that the impact of increased oil scarcity on global growth could be relatively minor if it involves primarily a gradual downshift in oil supply growth rather than an absolute decline. In particular, a sizable downshift in oil supply trend growth of 1 percentage point

appears to slow annual global growth by less than ¼ percent in the medium and longer term. On the other hand, a persistent decline in oil supply levels could have sizable negative effects on output even if there is greater substitutability between oil and other primary energy sources. At the same time, in the medium term, the oil-induced wealth transfer from oil importers to exporters can increase capital flows, reduce the real interest rate, and widen current account imbalances.
- The analysis in this chapter suggests that oil scarcity will not inevitably be a strong constraint on the global economy. However, the risks it poses should not be underestimated either. Much will ultimately depend on the extent and evolution of oil scarcity, which remain uncertain. There is a potential for abrupt shifts, which would have much larger effects than more gradual shifts.
- The chapter concludes that policymakers should strengthen measures to reduce the risks from oil scarcity as a precautionary step and to facilitate adjustment if such shifts are larger than expected or materialize in an abrupt manner. Policies need to be complemented with efforts to strengthen social safety nets, because higher oil prices could lead to shifts in income distribution and to increased poverty.

This chapter is organized as follows. The first section defines oil scarcity, considers the extent of scarcity in the oil sector, and discusses the implications for the oil market outlook. The second section examines the effects of oil scarcity on global growth and global imbalances to determine whether it will constrain the global economy. The last section outlines some policy implications.

## Has Oil Become a Scarce Resource?

The implications of oil scarcity could be important and far-reaching. Oil is a key factor of production, including in the production of other commodities and in transportation, and is also a widely used consumption good. Oil is the most traded commodity, with world exports averaging US$1.8 trillion annually during 2007–09, which amounted to about 10 percent of total world exports in that period. This means that changes in oil market conditions have direct and indirect effects on the global economy, including on growth, inflation, external balances, and poverty. Since the late 1990s, oil prices have generally risen—notwithstanding cyclical fluctuations—and supply constraints are widely perceived to have contributed to this trend. This has raised concerns that the oil market is entering a period of increased scarcity.

## What Is Oil Scarcity?

Oil is considered scarce when its supply falls short of a specified level of demand. If supply cannot meet demand at the prevailing price, prices must rise to encourage more supply and to ration demand. In this sense, oil scarcity is reflected in the market price.

The price should reflect the opportunity cost of bringing an additional barrel of oil to market. It compensates the reserve owner for the cost of extraction and for the loss of one barrel of reserves that could have been sold in the future. In general, a high price level relative to the prices of other goods and services indicates scarcity, a low price indicates abundance, and changes in price over long periods signal changes in scarcity. Well-known models of commodity extraction also imply that the market price generally serves as a reliable guide to the opportunity cost, including the cost relative to expected future scarcity.[4]

In practice, it is important to distinguish between scarcity and other reasons for high oil prices. Scarcity usually refers to the declining availability of oil or other exhaustible natural resources in the long term. However, oil scarcity in the sense of high and increasing oil prices can also arise for other reasons over shorter horizons. Temporary supply shocks, for example, can lead to short-lived price spikes, as during the 1990–91 Gulf War. There can also be large cyclical fluctuations in oil prices, which largely reflect the interaction between cyclical—including some financial—factors and low short-term price elasticities of demand and supply.

[4]Hotelling (1931) shows that the price increases for a nonrenewable resource should track the interest rate (possibly including a risk premium) if marginal extraction costs remain constant. When the market learns gradually that a resource is becoming more scarce (or abundant), its price may rise at a faster pace (or remain flat or even decline).

Declining oil availability typically reflects technological and geological constraints or a shortfall in the required investment in capacity. Oil scarcity can be exacerbated by its low substitutability. Oil has unique physical properties that make rapid substitution difficult, meaning that the price may be determined largely by supply capacity. In contrast, if other, more abundant natural or synthetic resources can eventually replace oil in the production process, then relatively small increases in prices may redirect demand toward these substitutes.

## How Do We Measure Scarcity?

The following analysis focuses on long-term oil price developments as an indicator of scarcity and ignores short-term or periodic fluctuations such as the business cycle. Oil prices may also be subject to "super cycles" caused by long implementation lags for discovery, exploration, and capital investment in minerals industries (Cuddington and Jerrett, 2008). Sluggish supply responses to shifts in demand can then give rise to price cycles with a longer duration than the typical two- to eight-year business cycle (Slade, 1982).

Long-term variation is assessed by passing prices through two low-pass filters: the first filter excludes all price fluctuations with a cycle period of less than nine years (and therefore includes super cycles); the second considers periods of more than 30 years (Figure 3.1).[5] Including super cycles generates more volatility but similar long-term trends. To provide a broader perspective on energy markets, coal and natural gas are included in the analysis. One noticeable result is that real oil prices have not trended persistently up or down throughout the sample period.[6] Instead, prices have experienced slow-

[5]This analysis uses U.S. dollar price series deflated by the U.S. consumer price index over sample periods with starting dates going back to 1875. Low-frequency components were extracted by a Christiano-Fitzgerald (2003) asymmetric filter (see Appendix 3.1).

[6]In other words, real oil prices are stationary. Where prices are nonstationary, as in the case of natural gas, and follow a unit root process, the drift, or long-term trend, is typically small. This is consistent with the findings of Cashin, McDermott, and Scott (2002), who note that trends in real commodity prices are small and dominated by price variability.

### Figure 3.1. Energy Prices and Long-Term Price Trends

Following a period of increasing abundance during the 15 years through 2000, an upturn in long-term prices is evident across energy commodities.

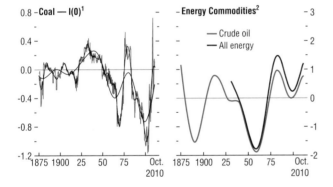

Sources: Global Financial Data; IMF Primary Commodity Price System; and IMF staff calculations.

[1]U.S.-dollar-denominated commodity prices are deflated by the U.S. consumer price index in log deviations from the sample mean. Deviation between filtered components and price is accounted for by noise, business cycle frequencies, and random walk drift where I(1).

[2]First-principal component (standard deviation from mean) normalized to have unit variance.

moving fluctuations around long-term averages. This suggests that periods of changing oil scarcity have been long-lasting but have come to an end, and that investment, technology, and discovery are eventually responsive to price signals.

Following a period of increasing abundance during the 15 years through 2000, an upturn in long-term prices is evident across energy commodities. The first principal component of the three filtered energy prices—which accounts for about two-thirds of total variance—confirms that the common factor in energy scarcity has been rising since 2000 and was not interrupted by the Great Recession (bottom right panel).

## What Lies behind the Apparent Increase in Oil Scarcity?

In the end, the signal from oil prices should reflect expectations of scarcity that must be considered in terms of underlying fundamentals. Understanding the signal from current market prices requires considering the prospects for demand and supply. Prospects for oil, as well as for other energy sources, are related strictly to primary energy demand. Therefore, this section first considers oil in the broader context of primary energy consumption before focusing on the supply and demand prospects for oil.

### What are the prospects for overall energy consumption?

Oil is the most important source of primary energy in the world, accounting for about 33 percent of the total; the other two main fossil fuels, coal and natural gas, account for 28 and 23 percent, respectively.[7] Renewable sources of energy are in a rapid growth phase, but they still account for only a small fraction of primary energy supply.

The context for much of the current concern about oil scarcity is the increase in the growth rate of global primary energy consumption in the past decade (Figure 3.2, top panel). This acceleration

[7]See U.S. Energy Information Administration (EIA), *International Energy Outlook*, 2009. Primary energy includes fossil fuels (coal, oil, natural gas); nuclear energy; and renewable energy (geothermal, hydropower, solar, wind).

primarily reflects an upward shift in the growth of energy consumption in China. As a result, China's share of world consumption of primary energy has risen rapidly (bottom panel), and China is now the largest energy consumer in the world (International Energy Agency—IEA, *World Energy Outlook,* 2010).

Future energy consumption will depend largely on the impact of continued rapid GDP growth in China and other fast-growing emerging market economies. To gauge the prospects for energy demand, the analysis in this section focuses on the relationship between per capita energy consumption and per capita real income and is based on a simple regression using a data set for 55 economies during 1980–2008 (see Appendix 3.2 for details).

The estimates suggest that the relationship between per capita energy consumption and per capita GDP is nonlinear. High-income economies can sustain GDP growth with little if any increase in energy consumption. Indeed, for some countries in the Organization for Economic Cooperation and Development (OECD), energy consumption has been flat in recent years (Figure 3.3). In contrast, in low- and middle-income economies energy demand growth has closely followed growth in per capita income. The income elasticity of energy demand is close to unity: a 1 percent increase in real per capita GDP is associated with a 1 percent increase in per capita energy consumption. The experience of Korea exemplifies this one-to-one relationship. China's energy demand has so far closely followed this pattern (Figure 3.4).

Given the empirical relationship estimated above and the most recent WEO forecast for China's per capita GDP, at current energy prices energy consumption in China is projected to double by 2017 and triple by 2025 from its 2008 level. But it remains to be seen whether China will be able to sustain such rapid growth. In fact, unlike Korea, China affects world market prices for primary energy sources, and rising prices might restrain economic growth and/or lead to a downward shift in the relationship between energy and income.

### What are the prospects for oil demand?

GDP growth has been a major driver of oil demand in emerging market economies. Figure

**Figure 3.2. Global Energy Demand, 1980–2008**

The rapid increase in global primary energy consumption, particularly in China, has raised concerns about oil scarcity.

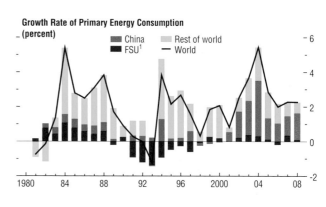

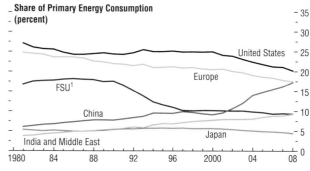

Source: International Energy Agency.
[1]FSU = former Soviet Union.

**Figure 3.3. Relationship between per Capita Energy Consumption and GDP Growth**

*(Hundred thousands of 2005 U.S. dollars on x-axis; billions of British thermal units on y-axis)*

Energy demand growth has closely followed growth in per capita income in low- and middle-income economies, whereas high-income economies can sustain GDP growth with little if any increase in energy consumption.

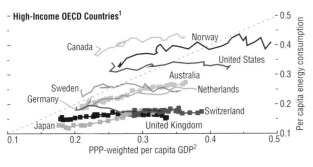

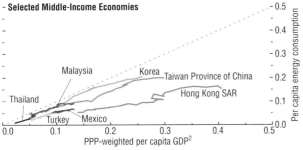

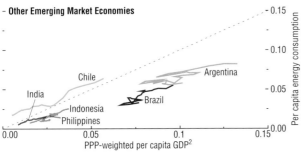

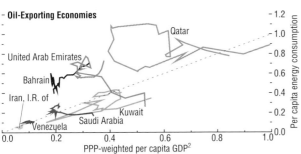

Sources: IMF, *International Financial Statistics;* International Energy Agency; World Bank, *World Development Indicators;* and IMF staff calculations.
[1]OECD = Organization for Economic Cooperation and Development.
[2]PPP = purchasing power parity.

3.5 shows how per capita oil consumption in the United States and other OECD economies has been broadly flat since the early 1980s, while it has risen rapidly in China. As a result, China's share in global oil consumption rose from 6 percent in 2000 to close to 11 percent in 2010. However, starting from a lower base, China's oil consumption is still only half as large as that of the United States (bottom panel).[8]

To gauge oil scarcity prospects, we first estimate oil consumption elasticities using a panel data approach.[9] Specifically, per capita oil consumption is regressed on its lagged value, real oil prices in local currency, a polynomial in real per capita GDP levels, the GDP growth rate, and a set of fixed effects (see Appendix 3.2). The data set starts in 1990 and includes 45 countries. The sample is divided into two groups, loosely named OECD and Non-OECD. Together, the two groups represented 84 percent of world oil consumption in 2009. (In addition, Appendix 3.2 examines a group of nine major oil-exporting economies and extends the sample to 1965.)[10]

The combined results for OECD and Non-OECD countries suggest very low short-term price elasticity, about –0.02 (Table 3.1).[11] This implies that a 10 percent increase in oil prices leads to a reduction in oil demand of only 0.2 percent. Although the long-term price elasticity is about four

[8]In 2008, coal accounted for 71 percent of total energy consumption in China, and oil and gas for only 19 and 3 percent, respectively. This is in contrast with the United States, where oil and gas accounted for 37 and 23 percent of total energy, respectively, and coal for 22 percent (U.S. EIA, *International Energy Outlook,* 2008).
[9]Other studies have attempted to estimate oil demand elasticities, such as Dargay and Gately (1995, 2010); Dargay, Gately, and Huntington (2007); Gately and Hillard (2002); Huntington (2002); and Cooper (2003), among others. Our framework is different, at least with respect to the sample period chosen, definition of country groups, and the overall econometric specification.
[10]The multicountry dimension helps overcome the downward bias problem that often arises when estimating demand price elasticities. Appendix 3.2 discusses identification issues in greater detail and presents robustness checks.
[11]The combined elasticities are the weighted averages of the group elasticities. The weights are the normalization of the last-10-year average oil consumption shares—which for OECD and Non-OECD countries stand at 0.55 and 0.31, respectively. Hence, the two groups combined represent 86 percent of world oil demand over the period.

times larger, the number is still small, which implies that a 10 percent permanent increase in oil prices reduces oil demand by about 0.7 percent after 20 years.

The short-term income elasticity is about 0.68, implying that a 1 percent increase in income is associated with an increase in oil demand of 0.68 percent. The long-term elasticity is considerably smaller, at 0.29. This result indicates that oil consumption has been considerably less income-elastic than primary energy demand, which means that the world economy has been (slowly) substituting away from oil.[12] In addition, the fact that income elasticity is higher in the short term than in the long term suggests that the response of oil consumption to an income shock involves some cyclical overshooting. Initial responses, such as those during the global recovery of 2009–10, therefore may not be representative of longer-term trends.

The growing importance of emerging market economies appears to have reduced world oil demand price elasticity (in absolute terms) and increased income elasticity. As shown in Table 3.1, the point estimate of the short-term price elasticity for the Non-OECD group is much lower than for OECD countries—though not as precisely estimated. Short-term income elasticity is only slightly higher than for OECD countries; however, long-term income elasticity is significantly higher for emerging market economies, at 0.39. Nevertheless, this value is substantially below the one found for energy, which is almost 1, and the weighted average of the two groups gives a combined elasticity of only 0.29. These results suggest that, instead of economies becoming more energy efficient, oil intensity has been declining substantially, even in emerging market economies—most probably as a result of the growing importance of other energy sources.

The surprisingly low price responsiveness of oil consumption in the OECD countries may reflect the lack of large-scale shifts in fuel use since the early 1990s. Most OECD countries saw a big switch away from oil in electric power generation in the early 1980s. After oil prices rose sharply compared

[12]In fact, the share of oil in total primary energy consumption has been decreasing since 1980, from 46 percent of the total in 1980 to 34 percent in 2009.

**Figure 3.4. Primary Energy Consumption**
*(Hundred thousands of 2005 U.S. dollars on x-axis; billions of British thermal units on y-axis)*

There has been a broadly one-to-one relationship between growth in per capita energy consumption and income in emerging market economies. China's energy demand has so far closely followed this pattern.

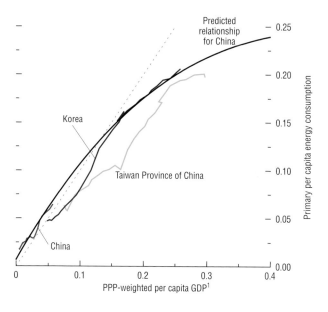

Sources: IMF, *International Financial Statistics;* International Energy Agency; World Bank, *World Development Indicators;* and IMF staff calculations.
[1]PPP = purchasing power parity.

### Figure 3.5. Oil Consumption in China and in Selected Advanced Economies

Per capita oil consumption in the United States and other OECD[1] economies has been broadly flat since the 1980s, while it has risen rapidly in China.

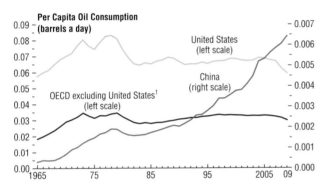

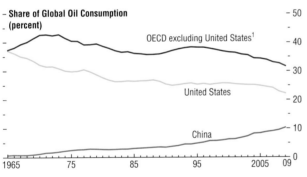

Sources: BP, *Statistical Review of World Energy,* June 2010; World Bank, *World Development Indicators;* and IMF staff calculations.
[1]OECD = Organization for Economic Cooperation and Development.

with the prices of other fossil fuels in the 1970s, the power sector switched from oil to other inputs (Figure 3.6): some countries went back to coal (for example, the United States); others increased their nuclear capacity (for example, France) or turned to alternative energy sources. In fact, when the sample period is extended to the 1960s, the estimated price elasticities are higher (see Appendix 3.2). Today, however, the power sector is no longer an important oil consumer in OECD or emerging market economies. In fact, the transportation sector currently accounts for about 50 percent of total oil consumption.[13] A substantial part of the remainder goes to the petrochemical industry and for other miscellaneous uses outside the power sector. Given current technologies, it is harder to substitute other factors for oil in these sectors, explaining the break in the estimated elasticities.

Even though there has not been any substantial substitution away from oil in recent years, new backstop technologies are emerging in the transportation sector. Predicting the scope for substitution using these technologies in the coming years is difficult, but a big switch cannot be ruled out over the medium term. Addressing logistical problems will pose a formidable challenge, but there should be a threshold at which alternative options become economically viable if oil prices are sustained above a particular level.[14] A mitigating factor in this respect is that in emerging market economies, a good part

---

[13]This includes jet fuel for aviation, bunker fuel as a naval propellant, and diesel fuel (used in trucks, industrial machinery, and cars).

[14]A simple calculation can give some insight regarding the price threshold. Assume that the current cost premium for a plug-in electric car is $2,000, amortized on an annual basis. Furthermore, assuming a driver values mileage limitations and other logistical problems specific to electric cars at $1,000 a year and summing up the costs, we have a total premium of $3,000 over gas-engine cars. The next step is to calculate the breakeven point, which is found when the difference in operating costs of an electric car versus a gas-engine car is equal to the premium. U.S. average fuel consumption per vehicle was about 600 gallons in 2008 (see Federal Highway Administration, 2008, Table VM-1), while the retail gasoline price is roughly 0.035 times the imported oil price plus taxes. If we set the retail price of electricity for cars at 20 percent of the 2008 gasoline price, we get a backstop price for imported oil in the United States at about $155. Other important factors could affect our back-of-the-envelope calculations—for example, on the downside, increasing marginal costs of ramping up production that starts at a very low level or, on

**Table 3.1. Oil Demand Price and Income Elasticities**
*(Subsample, 1990–2009)*

| | Short-Term Elasticity | | Long-Term Elasticity | |
|---|---|---|---|---|
| | Price | Income | Price | Income |
| Combined OECD[1] and Non-OECD | −0.019 [−0.028, −0.009] | 0.685 [0.562, 0.808] | −0.072 [−0.113, −0.032] | 0.294 [0.128, 0.452] |
| OECD | −0.025 [−0.035, −0.015] | 0.671 [0.548, 0.793] | −0.093 [−0.128, −0.057] | 0.243 [0.092, 0.383] |
| Non-OECD | −0.007 [−0.016, 0.002] | 0.711 [0.586, 0.836] | −0.035 [−0.087, 0.013] | 0.385 [0.193, 0.577] |

Source: IMF staff calculations.

Note: Median elasticities and confidence intervals showing 10th and 90th percentile of the distribution in brackets are estimated by Monte Carlo simulations. Long-term elasticities are calculated using a 20-year horizon.

[1]OECD = Organization for Economic Cooperation and Development.

of the infrastructure and distribution system is still under development and so, unlike in advanced economies, there will be less need to delay adoption of new technologies until current equipment and infrastructure become obsolete. Hence, it is conceivable that the (currently low) price responsiveness of oil demand could increase again, not only in OECD economies but also in emerging and developing economies.

### What are the prospects for oil supply?

Prospects for oil supply are strongly dependent on production constraints in some major producing economies stemming from their oil fields reaching maturity—the stage when field production plateaus or declines. These constraints became obvious when global crude oil production stagnated broadly during the global economic boom in the mid-2000s (Figure 3.7, top left panel).[15] Most maturity-related declines have emerged in economies that are not members of the Organization of Petroleum Exporting Countries (OPEC), including Russia, but some OPEC producers reportedly also face challenges from mature fields, including Saudi Arabia (Figure 3.7, top right panel).[16]

the upside, technological improvements and increasing returns to scale in the production of electric cars.

[15]Although market outcomes reflect both demand and supply developments, it would be difficult to attribute the stagnation entirely to factors other than new supply constraints, given the combination of rising prices and positive, albeit small, supply price elasticities as well as information about other factors (for example, conflict-related disruptions). See Hamilton (2009).

[16]See, for example, Sorrell and others (2010).

Maturing is part of the normal life cycle of oil fields (Box 3.1). What is novel since the late 1990s is that such maturing started to affect the supply from major producing countries, beginning with the North Sea fields. The resulting constraints on non-OPEC production became evident in the early 2000s, when oil demand began to grow unexpectedly and OPEC's spare capacity declined.

The key question for the future is how the larger and likely growing number of maturing oil fields will affect the global oil supply outlook. In particular, is the broad stagnation in oil production over the past five years temporary or more permanent? The answer depends on how permanently the decline in production from maturing fields can be more than offset by increased production from newly discovered reservoirs, from known but undeveloped reservoirs, or from increased recovery from current fields, including the maturing ones (see IEA, *World Energy Outlook*, 2008). Realizing such an offset will require continued large-scale investment, which the experience of the past five years has shown to be a formidable challenge.

Information to date suggests that the challenge does not stem from a lack of desire to invest but rather from the lag between investment planning and delivery. Following sustained price increases, oil investment activity predictably turned around, partly involving the development of higher-cost oil from ultra-deep water or unconventional resources. Drilling activity—an integral part of exploration and development in the oil sector—rose noticeably over the past decade (Figure 3.7, bottom left panel). Similarly, Goldman Sachs (2010) estimates that peak production from the oil projects in its Top 280 energy projects will amount to about 28 million barrels a day in 2020.[17] If the projects are executed and completed, these amounts could more than offset the decline from fields currently in operation, up to an aggregate decline rate of about 5 percent (the current production-weighted decline rate is estimated at about 4 to 4½ percent).

Despite the increased investment activity, however, improvements in delivery have been slow. As noted, time-to-build lags can be 10 years or longer in the mining and oil industries, depending on the complexity of the project. The turnaround in oil investment during the early 2000s therefore did not result in immediate capacity improvements, while the decline in oil investment from the mid-1980s to the late 1990s still had legacy effects. The latter will dissipate only slowly, as some of the new projects started over the past few years will not increase capacity for another 5 to 10 years.

Investment delivery has also been hampered by a surge in investment costs and by unexpected bottlenecks in oil investment services. As shown in the bottom right panel of Figure 3.7, one indicator of investment cost—the U.S. producer price index for oil and gas well drilling—almost tripled between 2003 and 2005, suggesting relatively weaker investment incentives. Higher cost and bottleneck problems, in turn, led investors to take a wait-and-see approach, and project approvals declined during 2007–08. Investment costs declined after the Great Recession but are still much higher in real terms. Similarly, bottlenecks in oil investment services have become less severe. But they are still present and will likely unwind only gradually.

Capacity increases are also constrained by restrictions on oil investment other than those related to pollution or other environment-related externalities, which have limited the overall investment response to high prices.[18] First, many areas are essentially closed to participation by outside investors and are developed exclusively by national oil companies.

### Figure 3.6. The Big Switch: Oil Share in the Electric Power Sector[1]

*(Percent of total electricity production on y-axis)*

After oil prices rose sharply relative to those of other fossil fuels in the 1970s, the power sector in most Organization for Economic Cooperation and Development countries switched away from oil for power generation in early 1980s.

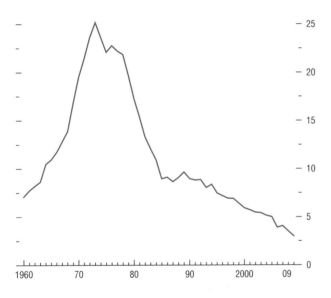

Sources: International Energy Agency; and IMF staff calculations.
[1]Electricity generated by oil divided by total electricity production.

[17]According to estimates by Goldman Sachs (2010), all projects achieve positive net present values with oil prices above $80 a barrel (in constant U.S. dollars).
[18]See Box 1.5 in the April 2008 *World Economic Outlook* for a detailed discussion.

While some national oil companies have ramped up capital expenditure in response to higher prices, others have been constrained by short-term budgetary revenue considerations. The lack of outside participation may also prevent the necessary upgrades in technology for exploration and development. Second, rising oil prices have also prompted changes in the regulatory environment, especially with respect to taxation and ownership, which have raised costs or reduced profitability and thereby slowed investment.

Against this backdrop, net capacity will likely build only gradually. A return to the trend growth of 1.8 percent in oil production experienced during 1981–2005 seems unlikely at this point despite the current investment effort, given continued field declines in some major producers.[19] In other words, prospects are for a downshift in the trend growth rate of oil supply. Current medium-term forecasts by the International Energy Agency (IEA, 2010a and 2010b), for example, suggest only modest increases in new net capacity over the next five years (Figure 3.8). Because capacity increases are the main drivers of supply growth—the short-term price elasticity of supply is very low, with most estimates ranging between 0.01 and 0.1—supply increases will likely be equally modest, except for the buffer provided by OPEC spare capacity.[20] The latter is currently estimated at some 6 million barrels a day. Assuming that between two-thirds and four-fifths of that spare capacity will eventually be tapped, cumulative oil supply growth during 2011–15 could amount to 6 to 8 percent, or 1¼ to 1½ percent annually on average, if the price of oil remains broadly constant in real terms.[21]

It is likely that part of the downshift in the oil supply trend has already been factored into current oil pricing. Nevertheless, predictions of the extent

[19]We exclude from the calculation all periods of turbulence in world oil markets, such as the early 1980s, and we also exclude the post-2005 period, which, as shown in Hamilton (2009), already exhibited a below-trend output growth rate. A downshift would also be consistent with the investment oil prediction from Goldman Sachs's Top 280 energy project inventory noted earlier.

[20]See, for example, Dées and others (2007) for recent estimates of supply elasticities.

[21]This assumes that OPEC keeps a spare capacity buffer of 2 million barrels a day, which is in line with its stated intentions.

### Figure 3.7. Global Oil Market Developments

Global crude oil production stagnated broadly during the global economic boom in the mid-2000s, notably in countries that are not members of the Organization of Petroleum Exporting Countries. The lag between investment planning and delivery seems to be the challenge in the medium term.

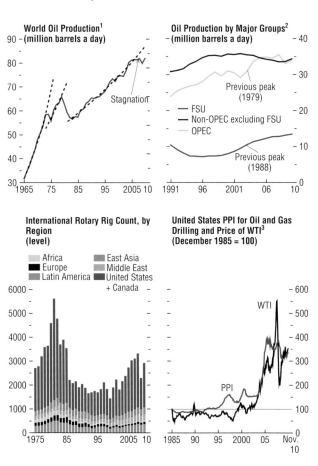

Sources: Bakker Hughes; BP, *Statistical Review of World Energy;* and Haver Analytics.
[1]Piecewise linear trend.
[2]FSU = former Soviet Union; OPEC = Organization of Petroleum Exporting Countries.
[3]PPI = producer price index; WTI = West Texas Intermediate.

**Figure 3.8. Projected Growth in Crude Oil Capacity**

*(Million barrels a day)*

Despite the current investment effort, new net capacity in oil production will increase only modestly in the medium term given continued field declines in some major producers.

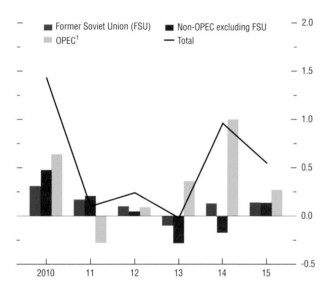

Sources: International Energy Agency, *Medium-Term Oil Market Report,* June 2010 and December 2010 update.

[1]Including spare capacity; OPEC = Organization of Petroleum Exporting Countries.

and speed of capacity buildup are usually characterized by a high amount of uncertainty. Indeed, project delivery was typically overestimated over the past few years, and some of the underlying risk factors are still present.

Such risk factors include uncertainty about time-to-build lags, potentially rising investment costs if the global economy continues on a brisk expansion, and risks to investment regimes. In addition, there is considerable uncertainty about the future paths of decline rates in maturing fields (see Box 3.1). Finally, geopolitical risks, both short- and long-term, remain, and changes in oil scarcity could be accompanied by changes in the market shares of large producers. Therefore, there is a risk of larger-than-anticipated oil scarcity. The possibilities range from larger downshifts in trend supply growth to an outright decline in oil production, either temporarily or more permanently.[22]

### What Are the Implications for Oil Scarcity?

The main reason behind continued, if not increased, oil scarcity is the tension between, on the one hand, the downshift in oil supply trends by some ¼ to ½ percent, with further downside risk, and, on the other hand, the strong momentum in oil demand growth stemming mainly from rapid income growth in emerging market economies.

The current WEO forecast is for an annual average world GDP growth rate of about 4.6 percent over the period 2011–15. The extent of market tension generated by these rates of global growth will depend on the income elasticity of oil demand. If a global short-term income elasticity of 0.68 (as estimated in the previous section) held throughout 2011–15, oil demand growth would remain above the growth in production at unchanged prices. Because price elasticities are very small, only substantial price increases would succeed in balancing the market, as described in the following example. At unchanged prices, if oil supply grows by 1.5 percent,

---

[22]For example, recent medium-term production forecasts by the U.S. EIA suggest annual oil production capacity growth of 0.9 percent over the period 2011–15. Other medium-term scenarios predicting low if any trend growth in oil production include British Petroleum (2011) and Shell (2011).

then oil demand growth will exceed that of supply by about 1.5 percentage points (4.6 × 0.68 – 1.5). With demand price elasticity at –0.02 and no supply response, the oil price should increase by 75 percent to rebalance the oil market.

The assumption of a zero supply response is clearly unrealistic. Moreover, as discussed earlier, there is strong evidence that longer-term income elasticities are lower than short-term ones.[23] The tension between moderate supply growth and continued high global economic growth could thus be resolved with smaller and, most likely, more gradual oil price increases, with some accompanying demand moderation. Nevertheless, with important downside risks to supply, oil scarcity risks will remain.

Oil scarcity risks must also be considered in the context of the overall energy market. If the supply of other primary energy sources continues to grow faster than the supply of oil, the past pattern of relatively slower oil demand growth in an environment of rapid GDP growth could be sustained. As of now, the situation seems promising. In particular, the so-called shale gas revolution may become a game changer and lay the foundation for a more global market for natural gas (Box 3.2). Natural gas could also become viable for applications that have so far relied almost exclusively on oil, including transportation.

## Oil Scarcity and the Global Economy

To assess the implications of greater oil scarcity for global economic growth and current account imbalances, this section uses simulation analysis based on the IMF's Global Integrated Monetary and Fiscal Model (GIMF), a multiregion dynamic general equilibrium model.[24] The GIMF includes several features found to be important for replicating real-world behavior, including households' and firms' finite planning horizons, gradual adjustment of prices and nominal wages to unexpected

changes, and macrofinancial linkages in the form of a financial accelerator. The version used here has six economic regions—oil exporters, the United States, the euro area, Japan, emerging Asia, and remaining countries. All regions are assumed to have flexible exchange rates.

The main simulation considers the effects of a downshift in the trend growth rate of world oil output in a controlled setting (Figure 3.9).[25] The motivation for the experiment follows from the analysis of oil demand and supply prospects in the previous sections. Because these prospects are subject to a great deal of uncertainty, the simulations assume that economic actors are surprised when the oil growth rate starts to decline.[26] This section also considers three sets of scenarios to examine the impact of changes in significant parameters.

## What Is the Model and How Is It Calibrated?

To understand the global economic impact of oil scarcity, we need to look at a few aspects of the model setup. The main difference between this application and the standard version of the GIMF is that oil is a third factor in an economy's production, in addition to capital and labor, and a second factor in final consumption, in addition to goods and services. The price and availability of oil therefore influence production as well as consumption possibilities.

The price responsiveness of oil demand, which reflects the degree to which other inputs can substitute for oil, is an important parameter determining the impact of changes in oil market conditions. In the benchmark simulation, the long-term price elasticity of oil demand in both production and consumption is assumed to equal 0.08, while the short-term elasticity is about 0.02. This is consistent with the estimates for the 1990–2009 sample in the previous section.

---

[23]In the present discussion of oil demand, the combined income elasticity is 0.29 over a 20-year horizon.

[24]For a presentation of the structure of the GIMF, see Kumhof, Muir, and Mursula (2010). For applications, see Kumhof and Laxton (2007, 2009), Freedman and others (2010), and Clinton and others (2010).

[25]Figure 3.9 also has a full listing of the countries included in each group.

[26]Actors are assumed to acquire full and immediate knowledge about the extent of the change in oil scarcity. In practice, information may be incomplete, and economic actors may learn only over time about the full extent of resource scarcity. The main effect of this delayed acquisition of knowledge would be smaller initial effects, but qualitatively the results remain broadly similar.

## Figure 3.9. Oil Scarcity and the Global Economy: Benchmark Scenario

*(Years on x-axis)*

This scenario considers the effects of a downshift in the trend growth rate of world oil output by 1 percentage point each year and the eventual return to the initial growth rate in year 25.

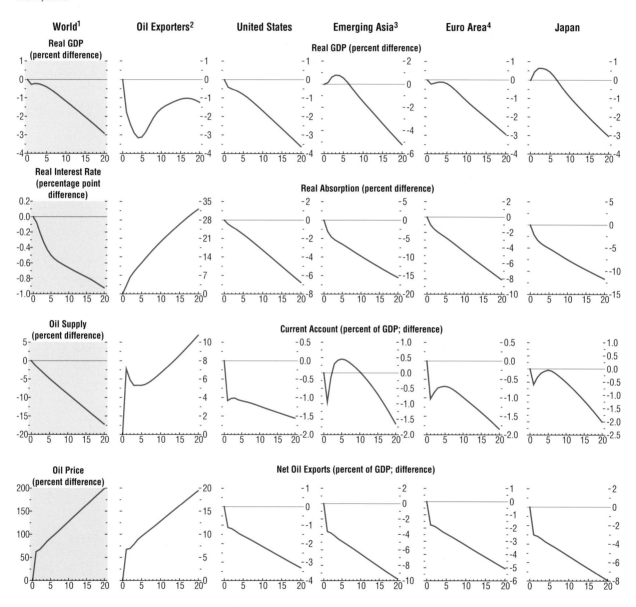

Source: Global Integrated Monetary and Fiscal Model.
[1]World: Total of all countries accounts for 78.78 percent of world GDP.
[2]Oil Exporters: Algeria, Angola, Azerbaijan, Bahrain, Canada, Republic of Congo, Equatorial Guinea, Iraq, Kuwait, Libya, Mexico, Nigeria, Norway, Oman, Qatar, Russia, Saudi Arabia, United Arab Emirates, and Venezuela.
[3]Emerging Asia: China, Hong Kong SAR, India, Indonesia, Korea, Malaysia, Philippines, Singapore, and Thailand.
[4]Euro area: Austria, Belgium, Cyprus, Finland, France, Germany, Greece, Ireland, Italy, Luxembourg, Malta, Netherlands, Portugal, Slovak Republic, Slovenia, and Spain.

Another important parameter is the contribution of oil to output, which in the benchmark will be determined by the oil cost share. Based on recent historical data, it has been calibrated at 2 to 5 percent, depending on the sector and region.

The supply side of oil has several elements. First, there is an exogenous endowment of oil. The growth in that endowment is assumed to fall below historical trends. This represents the constraints from maturing fields on global oil supply discussed earlier. The second element is a positive supply response to higher oil prices, but with a low price elasticity of 0.03. The third element is extraction cost. Here we assume that, initially, 40 percent of oil revenue must be used to pay for intermediate goods inputs; thereafter, the real extraction cost per barrel of oil increases at a constant annual rate of 2 percent.[27]

An important element in tracing the effects of oil scarcity is the use of the oil rent, the difference between the market price and extraction costs. This rent is distributed between the domestic private sector and the government. In advanced economies, the government is assumed to receive only a very small portion of these receipts, while in oil exporters it receives 90 percent. Critically, it is assumed that the government does not spend the additional funds immediately but accumulates them in a U.S.-dollar-based fund that is spent at a rate of 3 percent a year. One of the key effects of an increase in the oil price, therefore, is a dramatic increase in world savings due to governments' low propensity to consume out of oil revenues.

Finally, although the GIMF is well suited to medium- and long-term analysis, some complex factors that are not part of the model (for example, the nature of the oil shock, its transmission through financial markets, confidence effects) may be at play in the short term that amplify the initial output response to an oil scarcity shock. Box 3.3 explains in greater detail the nature of the problem and the most relevant amplification channels highlighted in the literature.

[27]Together, the second and third elements mimic the possibility of replacing crude oil from conventional sources with oil from higher-cost unconventional sources (see, for example, IEA, *World Energy Outlook,* 2008, p. 218).

## How Will Lower Oil Supply Trends Affect the Global Economy?

The benchmark simulation analyzes the impact of a decline in the average growth rate of world oil production by 1 percentage point below its historical trend starting in year 1 and an eventual return to its initial growth rate in year 25. Figure 3.9 shows the impact on a number of variables, expressed as deviations in percentage points (or percent) from a situation in which oil production grows at its historical trend rate of 1.8 percent.

Beginning with the global impact, the unexpected persistent reduction in oil supply growth leads to an immediate oil price spike of some 60 percent. This reflects the very low short-term oil demand elasticity. Because the decline in supply is persistent, the real oil price continues to increase thereafter, because market equilibrium requires some "demand destruction." Over a 20-year horizon, the cumulative oil price increase amounts to about 200 percent.

The reduced availability of oil and the resulting higher oil prices lead to a reduction in GDP levels in oil importers in the longer term. In the short to medium term, however, the global adjustment is shaped by the wealth transfer from oil importers to oil exporters, which has large effects on trade and capital flows. With rising oil prices, oil exporters experience sustained increases in income and wealth. As a result, their domestic demand (domestic absorption) increases ahead of GDP at more than 1.5 percent annually. The higher spending leads to upward domestic price pressures and a large real appreciation of the domestic currency. This reduces output in the tradables sector (other than oil), thereby reducing GDP by more than 3 percent over the first five years, followed by a recovery as government spending starts to consume a share of the growing oil fund. The current account improvement in this group of economies, which equals about 6 percent of GDP in the short term and more than 10 percent after 20 years, is due entirely to the higher value of oil exports. Goods exports fall relative to GDP, and the non-oil current account deteriorates. But the government's very low propensity to consume out of the oil fund means that the size of that deterioration remains moderate.

Domestic absorption by oil importers contracts over time as a result of lower oil availability, by 0.35 to 0.75 percent a year depending on the region. Their GDP also declines, but they initially experience two countervailing effects that support output. The first, and more important, is a surge in goods exports to oil importers to satisfy their increasing domestic demand. The second is a surge in investment demand in response to lower world real interest rates. This is because the oil exporters' additional oil revenue, which accrues primarily to governments, leads to higher saving, which reduces world real interest rates by almost 100 basis points over 20 years.[28] This effect is reminiscent of the international lending boom in the 1970s and early 1980s following large oil price increases. Regional differences among oil importers in this phase of the adjustment stem mostly from differences in the strength of their export links with oil exporters, with GDP in emerging Asia and Japan benefiting the most from the consumption boom in that region. In addition, emerging Asia also benefits more from lower world real interest rates, in view of the region's higher propensity to invest. Global imbalances worsen in this scenario over the short to medium term. The United States and euro area current accounts deteriorate as a result of costlier oil imports, while during a lengthy transition period the current accounts of surplus regions improve (emerging Asia), or remain nearly unchanged (Japan), as they export more goods to oil exporters. The long-term effects are not particularly large, however: oil importers' current accounts deteriorate by 1.5 to 2 percentage points of GDP by year 20. This is explained by oil's relatively low share in aggregate costs.

In the benchmark simulation, the longer-term output effects are not very severe. For oil importers, output falls cumulatively by between 3 percent (Japan, euro area) and 5 percent (emerging Asia) after 20 years, corresponding to about 0.15 to 0.25 percent a year, compared with a situation in which oil production follows past trends. The regional differences in the size of the long-term output effects reflect differences in the shares of oil in produc-

tion and consumption. For oil exporters, the initial real output loss due to lower oil production is also amplified by the deterioration of the non-oil trade balance due to appreciation in the real exchange value of the currency.

## Alternative Scenarios

This section explores the sensitivity of the benchmark results to three of the underlying assumptions—namely, the role played by oil's price elasticity of demand, the effect of a more sizable shock to oil supply trends, and the importance of oil for aggregate production. In the accompanying figures, the benchmark simulation results are shown as a solid blue line, and each alternative scenario is shown as a dashed red line.

### Scenario 1: greater substitution away from oil

A first alternative scenario considers a higher value for the long-term price elasticity of demand, consistent with greater substitution away from oil during periods of high oil prices. The scenario is based on a higher, more optimistic long-term elasticity of 0.3, almost five times as high as that used in the benchmark scenario. The feasibility of greater substitution is subject to uncertainty because it is difficult to predict the path of the technological developments required to bring it about.[29]

This alternative scenario has world oil prices increasing by only 100 percent after 20 years, rather than 200 percent as in the benchmark scenario (Figure 3.10). This reduces the drop in world output by two-thirds and by even more in oil importers. The longer-term current account developments are also much more favorable, mainly because easier substitution away from oil allows importers to keep the net oil import balance in check. This simulation highlights the fact that fairly high demand elasticities would be required to negate the effects of lower oil availability.

---

[28]They start to increase again soon after the 20-year horizon, as the government spends more and more of its accumulated oil funds.

[29]Hirsch, Bezdek, and Wendling (2005, 2010), for example, examine alternative fuels and technologies and conclude that substitution away from oil on a large scale would be extremely expensive and time-consuming. See also Ayres (2007).

## Figure 3.10. Alternative Scenario 1: Greater Substitution away from Oil
*(Years on x-axis)*

This scenario considers a higher value for the price elasticity of demand (0.3, compared with 0.08 in the baseline scenario), consistent with greater substitution away from oil.

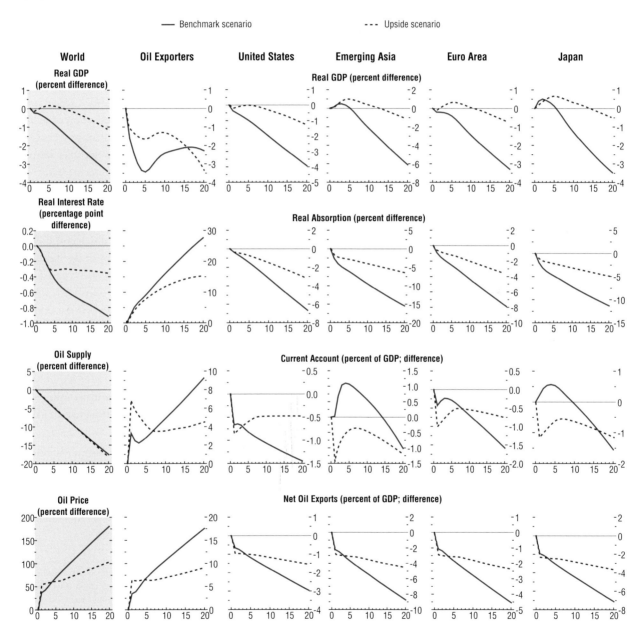

Source: Global Integrated Monetary and Fiscal Model.
Note: For the list of countries in each group, see Figure 3.9.

### Scenario 2: greater declines in oil production

Another alternative scenario considers the implications of a more pessimistic assumption for the declines in world oil output—3.8 percent rather than 1 percent annually—accompanied by a 4 percent annual increase in real extraction costs per barrel rather than 2 percent (Figure 3.11). This implies that, barring any increase due to the supply response to higher prices, oil production declines by 2 percent annually—a scenario that reflects the concerns of peak oil proponents, who argue that oil supplies have already peaked and will decline rapidly.[30] In this scenario, the longer-term output and current account effects are roughly three to four times as large as in the benchmark scenario, meaning they increase roughly in proportion to the size of the shock. Declines in absorption in oil importers are now on the order of 1.25 to 3 percent annually over the period shown, while in oil exporters, domestic absorption increases by more than 6 percent annually. Current account deterioration in oil importers is also much more serious, averaging 6 to 8 percentage points of GDP over the long term.

The most striking aspect of this scenario is, however, that supply reductions of this magnitude would require an increase of more than 200 percent in the oil price on impact and an 800 percent increase over 20 years. Relative price changes of this magnitude would be unprecedented and would likely have nonlinear effects on activity that the model does not adequately capture. Furthermore, the increase in world savings implied by this scenario is so large that several regions could, after the first few years, experience nominal interest rates that approach zero, which could make it difficult to carry out monetary policy.

### Scenario 3: greater economic role for oil

In the benchmark scenario, the output contribution of oil is equal to its cost share. Some researchers in the natural sciences have argued that this understates the importance of energy, including oil, for economic activity.[31] Economists have also identified

channels that amplify the effects of oil shocks.[32] To explore the implications of a potentially larger contribution by oil to output, the third alternative scenario assumes that part of total factor productivity represents technologies that are possible and remain usable only when there is a ready supply of oil. This effect is assumed to be external so that the beneficial effects of oil are not captured exclusively by the suppliers of oil but rather by all factors of production in proportion to their cost-share coefficients. The implication is that a negative oil supply shock resembles a negative technology shock.[33]

Figure 3.12 compares the benchmark scenario to a downside one in which the contribution of oil to output (either directly or as an enabler of technology) amounts to 25 percent in the tradables sector and 20 percent in the nontradables sector (rather than 5 percent and 2 percent). The simulations show that a higher output contribution by oil has small effects on current accounts: the main effects are on growth, with the deterioration in all regions' GDP larger by about a factor of two than in the baseline.

### Summary of the simulations

The alternative scenarios indicate that the extent to which oil scarcity will constrain global economic development depends critically on a small number of key factors. If, as in the benchmark scenario, the trend growth rate of oil output declined only modestly, world output would eventually suffer but the effect might not be dramatic. If higher oil prices

---

[30]Sorrell and others (2010) provide an overview, noting that several studies predict absolute global decline rates of at least 2 percent starting in the near future.

[31]Ayres and Warr (2005); and Kümmel, Henn, and Lindenberger (2002) have estimated aggregate production functions in

capital, labor, and energy for a number of industrialized countries and have found output contributions of energy that range from 30 percent to more than 60 percent. See also Ayres and Warr (2010), Kümmel (forthcoming), and Hall and Klitgaard (forthcoming). Because oil represents only a fraction, albeit large and critical, of aggregate energy inputs, values smaller than 30 to 60 percent are appropriate to illustrate this scenario.

[32]In Finn (2000), an oil shock can reduce capital utilization and induce a stronger drop in output than indicated by oil's cost share.

[33]There are many examples of such effects, such as the obsolescence of many private automotive transportation efficiencies and technologies if a large-scale switch to public transportation becomes necessary. But another important aspect is the fact, stressed by the IEA's *World Energy Outlook,* 2010, that in the future a much higher share of the world economy's investment funds and innovation potential will have to be devoted to the oil sector just to maintain current levels of production. It is not implausible to expect this to exert a downward drag on the growth of productivity elsewhere in the economy.

## Figure 3.11.  Alternative Scenario 2: Greater Decline in Oil Production
*(Years on x-axis)*

This scenario considers the implications of a more pessimistic assumption for the decline rate of oil production (3.8 percentage points annually, compared with 1 percentage point in the baseline scenario).

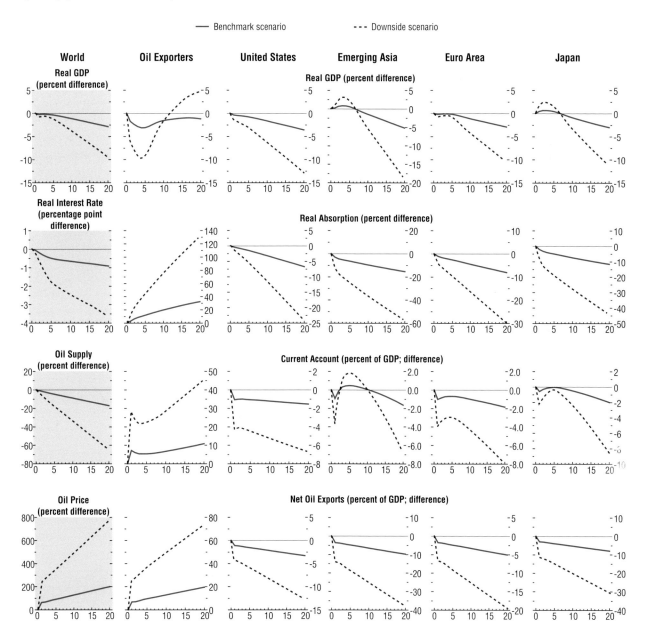

Source: Global Integrated Monetary and Fiscal Model.
Note: For the list of countries in each group, see Figure 3.9.

## Figure 3.12. Alternative Scenario 3: Greater Economic Role for Oil

*(Years on x-axis)*

This scenario considers a higher contribution of oil to output: 25 percent for the tradables sector (compared with 5 percent in the baseline scenario) and 20 percent in the nontradables sector (compared with 2 percent in the baseline scenario).

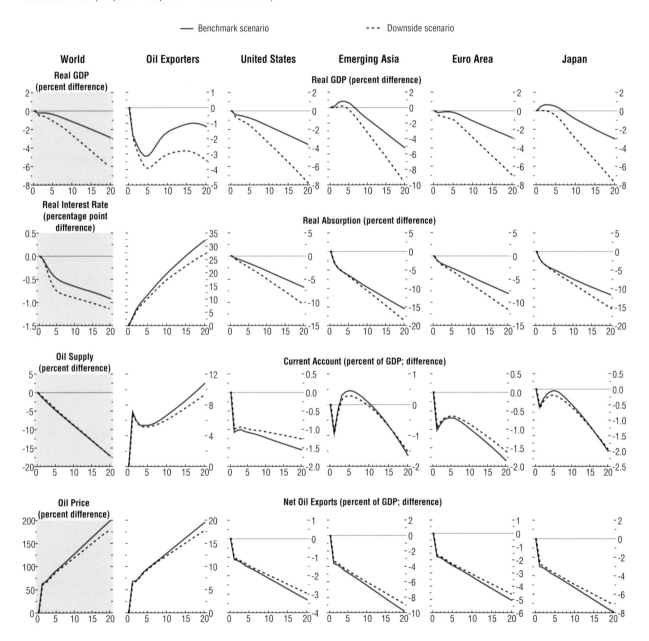

Source: Global Integrated Monetary and Fiscal Model.
Note: For the list of countries in each group, see Figure 3.9.

brought about easier substitution away from oil, not just temporarily but over a prolonged period, the effects could be even less severe. But if the reductions in oil output were in line with the more pessimistic studies of peak oil proponents or if the contribution of oil to output proved much larger than its cost share, the effects could be dramatic, suggesting a need for urgent policy action. In the longer term, the worst effects would be experienced by regions whose production is highly oil intensive, such as emerging Asia, and/or with weak export links to oil exporters, such as the United States.

### Additional Considerations

In each of the GIMF scenarios, the transition to a new equilibrium is, by assumption, a smooth process: consumers in oil-exporting economies easily absorb large surpluses in goods exports from oil importers, financial markets efficiently absorb and intermediate a flood of savings from oil exporters, businesses respond flexibly to higher oil prices by reallocating resources, and workers readily accept lower real wages. Some of these assumptions, however, may be too optimistic.

The experience of the 1970s suggests caution when it comes to the efficient intermediation of large net capital flows from oil exporters. If not efficiently allocated, risk premiums could increase in parts of the world where borrowers are vulnerable. This, in turn, could prevent borrowers from taking advantage of lower risk-free interest rates, which is an important mitigation mechanism in the face of oil scarcity. If private as well as public saving rates increase in oil-exporting economies, this problem could intensify.

A smooth reallocation of resources among inputs and across sectors as the economy adjusts to less oil is also a very strong assumption. Unlike in the model, real economies have many and highly interdependent industries. Several industries, including car manufacturing, airlines, trucking, long-distance trade, and tourism, would be affected by an oil shock much earlier and much more seriously than others.[34] The

[34]Even industries that could adapt to the increases in oil prices implied by the benchmark scenario might find it almost impossible to adjust to the 800 percent price increase implied by the second downside scenario.

adverse effects of large-scale bankruptcies in such industries could spread to the rest of the economy, either through corporate balance sheets (intercompany credit, interdependence of industries such as construction and tourism) or through bank balance sheets (lack of credit after loan losses).

In recent years, labor market flexibility has helped improve the absorption of oil shocks (Blanchard and Galí, 2007). In the case of larger and more persistent oil price increases, however, workers may resist a series of real wage cuts, which would significantly raise the output cost of the shock during the long transition period.

Finally, the simulations do not consider the possibility that some oil exporters might reserve an increasing share of their stagnating or decreasing oil output for domestic use, for example through fuel subsidies, in order to support energy-intensive industries (for example, petrochemicals) and also to forestall domestic unrest. If this were to happen, the amount of oil available to oil importers could shrink much faster than world oil output, with obvious negative consequences for growth in those regions.

### Implications for the Outlook and Policies

The analysis of energy prices in this chapter suggests that oil and other energy markets have entered a period of increased scarcity—a period of higher-than-average prices—as they have on earlier occasions. Past experience suggests that such periods can last a long time even if they eventually give way to periods of renewed abundance.

When it comes to crude oil scarcity, high prices reflect the tension between the increase in oil consumption growth, driven mainly by fast-growing emerging market economies, and the downshift in oil supply growth. Scarcity is reinforced by the low responsiveness of both oil demand and oil supply to price changes. However, the longer-term income elasticity of global demand for oil is below that of the demand for primary energy, which indicates that oil-saving efforts, technological change, and the move to a more service-based economy may all have an appreciable effect.

The analysis shows that the constraints on global growth in the medium to longer term from gradual and moderate increases in oil scarcity—those involving lower trend growth rather than sustained declines—could be relatively minor. In particular, a sizable downshift in oil supply trend growth of 1 percentage point appears to slow annual global growth by less than ¼ percent.

Such benign effects on output, however, should not be taken for granted. Important downside risks to oil investment and capacity growth, both above and below the ground, imply that oil scarcity could be more severe. Moreover, unexpected increases in oil scarcity and resource scarcity more broadly might not materialize as small, gradual changes but as larger, discrete changes. In practice, it will be difficult to draw a sharp distinction between unexpected changes in oil scarcity and more traditional temporary oil supply shocks, especially in the short term when many of the effects on the global economy will be similar. In addition, it is uncertain whether the world economy can really adjust as smoothly as the model envisages. Finally, there are risks related to the scope for the substitution away from oil, on both the upside and the downside. The adverse effects could be larger, especially if the availability of oil affects economy-wide productivity, for example by making some current production technologies redundant.

Therefore, the state of oil scarcity needs to be monitored carefully; the global economy is still in the early stages of the new era of maturity in major oil-producing economies.

What are the policy implications? Fundamentally, there are two broad areas for action. First, given the potential for unexpected increases in the scarcity of oil and other resources, policymakers should review whether current policy frameworks facilitate adjustment to unexpected changes in oil scarcity. Second, consideration should be given to policies aimed at lowering the risk of oil scarcity, including through the development of sustainable alternative sources of energy.

Macroeconomic and structural policies can help economies adjust to unexpected changes in oil scarcity. Real rigidities in product and labor markets may exacerbate the initial shock by preventing the smooth reallocation of resources. Policies aimed at easing adjustment in relative prices and resources would therefore be helpful. In labor markets, for example, relaxing employment protection policies in some circumstances could be useful, as too many restrictions can delay adjustment in real wages and hamper reallocation of jobs from sectors most affected by scarcity to sectors that are less affected.

In this respect, increased oil scarcity will pose fiscal policy challenges. In the face of an oil scarcity shock, the trend toward increasing end-user subsidies for petroleum products in many economies would put fiscal positions in oil importers at risk because the fiscal cost of the subsidies could increase dramatically.[35] On the other hand, there is a need to protect the poor. Hence, the priority in many economies should be to reduce fuel and other subsidies, especially if they are not well targeted, while putting in place targeted and cost-effective social safety nets. Such a strategy would not only help protect fiscal positions, but would also strengthen the role of price signals in the use of energy resources and reduce greenhouse gas emissions.[36]

On the structural policy side, the focus should be on strengthening the role of price signals in the adjustment to increased scarcity. Such policies would increase the price responsiveness of supply and demand, thereby allowing for smaller price responses to unexpected changes in scarcity. On the supply side, oil companies should be able to respond to higher prices under predictable investment and tax regimes that take into account differences in extraction costs and allow investors to be compensated for taking technological and geological risks. On the demand side, as noted above, a reduction in fuel and other subsidies at a global level would also increase the price elasticity of oil demand (in absolute value terms), thereby facilitating oil market adjustment and reducing oil price volatility.

Regarding policies aimed at lowering the worst-case risks of oil scarcity, a widely debated issue is whether to preemptively reduce oil consumption—through taxes or support for the development and deployment of new, oil-saving technologies—and to foster alternative sources of energy. Proponents argue that such interventions, if well engineered,

---

[35]Coady and others (2010) analyze the recent trends in fuel subsidies and discuss policy options to protect vulnerable segments of the population while also protecting fiscal positions.
[36]See Jones and Keen (2009) for a discussion.

would smoothly reduce oil demand, rebalancing tensions between demand and supply, and thus would reduce the risk of worst-case scarcity itself.

There are, however, several issues that need to be addressed before policy interventions to reduce oil consumption are implemented. Such interventions come at a cost, and their net benefits need to be evaluated. For example, lowering oil consumption through higher taxes could reduce growth and welfare during the period before serious scarcity has emerged. The calculations to establish costs and benefits are complex. This is mainly because the net benefits ultimately depend on the probability of significantly higher scarcity and the present discounted value of expected costs that the higher scarcity would impose, which are hard to quantify.

Finally, the model simulations indicate that persistent oil supply shocks would imply a surge in global capital flows and a widening of current account imbalances. This makes it even more important to strengthen global cooperation to reduce the risks associated with growing current account imbalances and of large capital flows to emerging market economies. Continued progress with financial sector reform also has a very important role to play, since the efficient intermediation of these capital flows will be of paramount importance for financial stability.

## Appendix 3.1. Low-Frequency Filtering for Extracting Business Cycle Trends

Filtering methods allow for gradual change in long-term trends as well as cycles of different frequencies. The ideal band-pass filter, which isolates only specified frequencies, uses an infinite number of leads and lags when calculating the filter weights. However, a finite number of leads and lags must be used in practice, and so a truncation decision needs to be made. Christiano and Fitzgerald (2003) propose asymmetric filters, which have the advantage of computing cyclical components for all observations at the beginning and end of the data span.[37] Given our interest in whether a long-term cycle is emerging in the final years of our data sample, this asymmetric Christiano and Fitzgerald filter is used to calculate long-term components at the end of our data sample, with adjustments for I(1) series, including crude oil, natural gas, and coal.

## Appendix 3.2. The Energy and Oil Empirical Models

### The Energy Model

We estimate the following relationship, where $i$ denotes the country and $t$ denotes years:

$$e_{it} = \alpha_i + P(y_{it}) + u_{it}, \qquad (3.1)$$

where $e$ is energy per capita; $y$ is real per capita GDP; and $P(y)$ is a third-order polynomial; fixed effects are captured by $\alpha_i$.

### The Oil Model

We estimate the following oil demand:

$$o_{it} = \alpha_i + \lambda_t + \rho o_{it-1} + \beta \log(p_{it}) + \gamma \Delta \log(y_{it}) + P(y_{it}) + u_{it}, \qquad (3.2)$$

where $o$ is oil per capita; $y$ is real per capita GDP at purchasing power parity; $P()$ is a third-order polynomial; $p$ is the real price of oil in local currency; fixed

effects are captured by $\alpha_i$; and $\lambda_t$ represents time dummies.[38]

None of the results shown have used time dummies; however, dummies have been used as alternatives to split the sample into pre- and post-1990s periods to test for the big switch.

When estimating high versus low oil price environments we use log differences for both oil and prices. In this case, given the formulation on growth rates, no persistence is introduced.

### Identification Issues

As explained in the text, estimating a demand schedule has to overcome the pitfall of introducing a downward bias in the price elasticities. Here we address this problem, explaining how the cross-country dimension reduces the usual bias and describe the results of a robustness test.

The usual problem is that a shock in the demand equation, changing total quantity demanded, has an impact on price. This implies a positive correlation between price and the error term, biasing the estimate downward. However, we are not estimating the aggregate oil demand schedule but many demand schedules for each country. Most of those economies are small relative to the size of the oil market; hence, oil demand shocks in a generic country have only a minor impact on oil prices. More precisely, we can split the oil demand shock of a country $i$ into an idiosyncratic component (country specific) and a common component shared by all countries (common). Country-specific shocks have no effect on the oil price by construction. Some examples of those shocks are changes in energy regulation, tax codes, the composition of the industrial sector, and all sorts

[37]The above results are very robust even when we extend the data series with forecast series, based on the autoregressive integrated moving average (ARIMA) specification or random walk, and use more leads for filtering at the end of the actual sample periods.

[38]The Organization for Economic Cooperation and Development (OECD) comprises Australia, Austria, Belgium, Canada, Denmark, Finland, France, Germany, Greece, Ireland, Italy, Japan, Korea, Luxembourg, Netherlands, New Zealand, Portugal, Singapore, Spain, Sweden, Switzerland, United Kingdom, and United States. "Remaining countries" are OECD countries plus Argentina, Bangladesh, Brazil, Bulgaria, Chile, China, Colombia, Egypt, Hong Kong SAR, Hungary, India, Indonesia, Malaysia, Mexico, Pakistan, Peru, Philippines, Poland, Romania, South Africa, former Soviet Union, Taiwan Province of China, Thailand, and Turkey. The oil-exporting countries comprise Algeria, Islamic Republic of Iran, Kuwait, Norway, Qatar, Saudi Arabia, United Arab Emirates, and Venezuela.

**Table 3.2. Oil Demand Price and Income Elasticities, Including Oil-Exporting Economies**
*(Subsample, 1990–2009)*

| | Short-Term Elasticity | | Long-Term Elasticity | |
|---|---|---|---|---|
| | Price | Income | Price | Income |
| Combined OECD,[1] Non-OECD, and Major Oil-Exporting Economies | −0.017 [−0.028, −0.006] | 0.676 [0.551, 0.801] | −0.067 [−0.132, −0.005] | 0.474 [0.210, 0.753] |
| Major Oil-Exporting Economies | −0.001 [−0.028, 0.025] | 0.565 [0.424, 0.703] | −0.018 [−0.368, 0.337] | 2.751 [1.246, 4.552] |

Source: IMF staff calculations.

Note: Median elasticities and confidence intervals showing 10th and 90th percentile of the distribution in brackets are estimated by Monte Carlo simulations. Long-term elasticities are calculated using a 20-year horizon. For OECD and non-OECD data, see Table 3.1.

[1]OECD = Organization for Economic Cooperation and Development.

of energy subsidies. When those changes are unrelated across countries they constitute country-specific oil demand shocks. Common shocks do have an impact on oil prices and introduce a downward bias. However, because we control for GDP growth, it is not easy to think of other common shocks. A potential candidate is the precautionary demand shock, as stressed recently by Kilian (2009). However, those shocks are not supposed to be very persistent; hence, at an annual frequency, their effect on oil consumption is small. In other words, there are reasons to believe that common shocks apart from the global business cycle play a minor role. The downward bias in our estimates should therefore be small.

To corroborate this assumption, we reestimated our equation using the oil-supply-shock-based price series of Cavallo and Wu (2006) instead of actual oil prices.[39] This series was constructed using only oil supply shocks that were identified with a narrative approach examining daily oil-related events during 1984–2007. In principle, this approach eliminates price movements due to an oil demand shock, thus removing the downward bias previously described.

The reestimation of our model over the period 1990–2007 with the Cavallo-Wu price series (CW) and our regular series (old) suggests that the estimated coefficients are remarkably similar. The new and old price elasticities are not statistically different.[40] It is also worth noting that the CW price elasticity is more precisely estimated than ours,

which adds support to their identification strategy. If the CW narrative approach captured only meaningless noise, the estimated coefficient—and, thus, the oil price elasticity—would not have been statistically different from zero when using their series.

**The Role of Major Oil Exporters**

The share of world oil consumption for our oil-exporter region increased from 4 percent in 1980 to almost 9 percent in 2009. Given the special features of this region, if its share keeps increasing, the oil market prospects could deteriorate. In Table 3.2, we show the estimated elasticities for this group of economies. Price elasticities are not at all significant. This is not completely surprising: subsidized oil products and a strong wealth effect related to oil price movements alter the usual relationship between prices and demand. In fact, higher prices could easily lead to higher oil demand in an oil-exporting country.

Another striking difference from the other regions studied is the high value of long-term income elasticity: a 1 percent increase in income is associated with a 2.7 percent increase in oil consumption! This probably reflects those economies' scant incentives to introduce oil-saving technologies.

Overall, even though the oil consumption share of oil exporters is still small, the combined results for the three groups are clearly affected. In particular, the long-term income elasticity, while still lower than for the short term, stands now at 0.47, compared with the 0.29 found before. The median estimate of price elasticity is only mildly reduced, but the uncertainty of the estimate becomes much higher.

---

[39]The log changes of the oil price series were provided by Tao Wu.

[40]The 99 percent confidence intervals of both estimates overlap.

### Table 3.3. Oil Demand Price and Income Elasticities in the Extended Sample
*(Full sample, 1965–2009)*

| | Short-Term Elasticity | | Long-Term Elasticity | |
|---|---|---|---|---|
| | Price | Income | Price | Income |
| OECD[1] | −0.039 | 0.704 | −0.576 | −0.385 |
| | [−0.044, −0.033] | [0.603, 0.803] | [−0.673, −0.489] | [−0.567, −0.208] |
| Non-OECD | −0.010 | 0.741 | −0.131 | 0.589 |
| | [−0.015, −0.006] | [0.663, 0.818] | [−0.196, −0.070] | [0.382, 0.777] |

Source: IMF staff calculations.

Note: Median elasticities and confidence intervals showing 10th and 90th percentile of the distribution in brackets are estimated by Monte Carlo simulations. Long-term elasticities are calculated using a 20-year horizon.

[1]OECD = Organization for Economic Cooperation and Development.

### Extended Sample: 1965–2009

As Table 3.3 shows, price elasticities are higher, especially for OECD countries, which confirms the argument in the main text. Moreover, since the "big switch" happened during a period when many OECD countries experienced relatively high per capita GDP growth, we also observe a change of sign (from negative to positive) of the long-term income elasticity between the two samples: economic growth helped introduce oil-efficient capital goods and technologies. Similar results are obtained when we use time dummies for the early 1980s to control for the big switch.

### Low and High Oil Price Environments

To examine whether high oil prices are more conducive to substitution away from oil than low oil prices, we split the sample into periods of high and low oil prices (defined as oil prices above and below the sample average). The results (Table 3.4) suggest that during periods of low oil prices, price elasticity is not statistically different from zero; the only variable that matters in the oil demand schedule is GDP growth. In contrast, during periods of high oil prices,

### Table 3.4. Oil Demand Price and Income Short-Term Elasticities: High versus Low Oil Price Environments
*(Subsample, 1990–2009)*

| | Price | Income |
|---|---|---|
| High Oil Prices | −0.038 | 0.649 |
| | [−0.070, −0.006] | [0.466, 0.832] |
| Low Oil Prices | * | 0.786 |
| | | [0.667, 0.904] |

Source: IMF staff calculations.

Note: * indicates that the value is not statistically different from zero. Median elasticities and confidence intervals showing 10th and 90th percentile of the distribution in brackets are estimated by Monte Carlo simulations. Long-term elasticities are calculated using a 20-year horizon.

price elasticity is much higher, at 0.38, and is statistically significant. At the same time, short-term income elasticity is slightly lower.

This result also suggests that when oil prices are low, their fluctuation has only a minor impact on households' and businesses' decisions, given that they do not substantially affect their total expenditures. However, when prices are already high, a further increase may induce a much higher number of households and businesses to switch to more oil-efficient equipment and technologies and/or to change their behavior.

## Box 3.1. Life Cycle Constraints on Global Oil Production

Oil reservoirs have a life cycle with three main phases: youth, maturity, and decline. This box discusses these life cycle stages and the implications for global oil supply prospects.

After discovery and development, oil reservoirs enter a period of youth during which flow production increases. At maturity, production peaks and then starts to decline. Maturity patterns vary across fields. In some, production plateaus at its peak and decline sets in only much later.

The life cycle reflects a combination of geological, technological, and economic factors. From a geological point of view, there is the natural phenomenon of declining reservoir pressure or water breakthroughs once a substantial part of the oil in a reservoir has been extracted. Technological intervention can influence the timing of production peaks and the rate of decline through secondary and enhanced recovery methods, although applying these methods comes at a cost that generally increases with the extent of depletion.[1] At some point it becomes too costly to prevent decline through ever more intensive intervention.

Life cycle patterns have been well established for individual oil reservoirs and fields.[2] A widely debated issue is whether life cycle patterns are of more general relevance for regional and even global oil production. The proposition that global oil production has already peaked or will peak in the medium term is a generalization of the life cycle hypothesis. But such peak oil propositions are dependent on additional assumptions.

A first assumption is that large oil fields are discovered first. In part this seems to be supported by historical data (Figure 3.1.1, top panel). In fact, the "giant" fields in the United States, the Middle East, and Russia discovered before the 1970s have been the backbone of global oil production for decades (IEA, *World Energy Outlook,* 2008). Many of those

The author of this box is Thomas Helbling.

[1]The costs involve both capital costs—considerable investment is a prerequisite, especially for enhanced recovery—and operating costs, including the cost of the gas or water used in recovery.

[2]A field is a collection of reservoirs in geographical proximity based on a single geological structure. Sorrell and others (2010) provide a good overview of the evidence of life cycle patterns in oil production.

### Figure 3.1.1. Life Cycle of Global Oil Production

Many giant oil fields have reached maturity. However, the decline rate of oil production has been relatively low because the marginal return from additional drilling has been high enough to support continued exploration and oil investment.

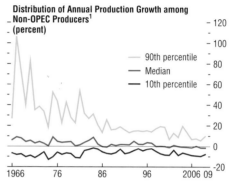

Distribution of Annual Production Growth among Non-OPEC Producers[1] (percent)

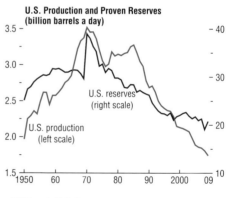

U.S. Production and Proven Reserves (billion barrels a day)

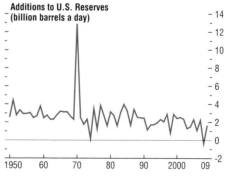

Additions to U.S. Reserves (billion barrels a day)

Sources: BP, *Statistical Review of World Energy,* June 2010; U.S. Energy Information Administration; and IMF staff calculations.
[1]OPEC = Organization of Petroleum Exporting Countries.

## Box 3.1 *(continued)*

fields have reached maturity, and so the peak oil argument goes as follows: since large fields are less likely to be discovered, to offset the decline of current large fields we need an unrealistically high rate of small-field discovery.

However, views on the scope for future discoveries differ considerably. The most recent assessments by the U.S. Geological Survey released in 2000—a standard reference—suggest that there are between 1 and 2.7 trillion barrels of conventional oil still in the ground that are technically recoverable. The range reflects different probabilities attached to the discovery of new reservoirs of oil that is technically recoverable and the growth of reserves in fields already in production.[3] The lower bound of the band reflects oil that is technically recoverable and consists mostly of current proven reserves. The fact that important oil discoveries continue to be made and that many promising areas have not yet been extensively explored suggests that this lower bound is likely pessimistic for a baseline projection.

The second assumption concerns the extent of the drag from declining production in mature fields. The main issue is whether past patterns in so-called observed decline rates provide a good basis for forecasts. There is a distinction between the natural decline rate, that is, the rate without any postpeak intervention, and the managed decline rate, with intervention after the peak. Some analysts see little scope for changing past patterns. In their view, production-weighted global decline rates, which are currently estimated at some 4 percent, are expected to increase further in the future as decline in large mature fields accelerates. However, observed decline rates are a function of technology and investment, factors that usually are not considered in the curve-fitting approaches used to predict decline rates. The use of secondary and enhanced recovery techniques is costly, and so investment in decline management will be a function of current and expected market conditions. Given that oil prices were low between the mid-1980s and the early 2000s, it is plausible that forecasts based on past patterns are not valid in a high-price environment. With prospects for continued high oil prices, field management and attempts to increase recovery rates are likely to play a more prominent role than in the past, implying lower global rates of decline. Moreover, technological developments have improved the scope for enhanced recovery at lower cost.

The experience with oil production in the United States provides some grounds for cautious optimism. U.S. oil production peaked in 1970, as some geologists had predicted it would (middle panel).[4] This corroborates the view that decline is difficult to overcome once it begins. Nevertheless, overall, U.S. oil production has declined by less than many predicted using curve fitting (see Lynch, 2002). The average rate of decline has been steady at about 1 percent a year since the 1970s.

The relatively low decline rate reflects a number of factors. Most important, the marginal return from additional drilling, as measured by reserve additions, has been high enough to support continued exploration and oil investment (bottom panel). This happened despite the presumption that discovery and development activity are increasingly less likely to result in reserve growth the more an area has already been explored and developed—as should be the case for the United States.[5] Finally, the U.S. experience also highlights the important influence of market conditions and incentives on exploration and investment and the importance of relatively low barriers to entry in the oil sector.[6] This has led

---

[3]Historically, the upgrading of reserve estimates because of increased knowledge about reservoir properties and the effectiveness of the installed capital after the beginning of production has been an important source of measured reserve growth. Cumulative production in many fields that are still producing is already well above initial reserve estimates.

[4]The prediction of a production peak between 1965 and 1970 in the lower 48 U.S. states by the late M. King Hubbert is well known.

[5]In the well-known model of Pindyck (1978), additional drilling and development have positive marginal returns. But these benefits from additional investment must be weighed against increasing marginal costs from diminishing returns from all past exploration and developing efforts. These costs are believed to be increasing with the cumulative past efforts (see, for example, Uhler, 1976; or Pesaran, 1990).

[6]Kaufmann (1991) notes that oil market conditions explain a significant part of the deviations of actual oil production from the levels predicted by so-called Hubbert curves.

## Box 3.1 *(continued)*

exploration and subsequent reservoir development to respond strongly to price signals.[7] In fact, exploration activity has remained higher in the United States than in some areas with more potential.

The conclusion is that there are constraints on global oil production from life cycle patterns in oil production. The main reasons for these constraints

are the broadly synchronized maturing of major large oil fields that have been the backbone of global oil production. Nevertheless, there remain important questions about the strength of these constraints. The U.S. experience suggests that managed decline is possible, especially in areas with many and large fields, including for example Saudi Arabia. It also underscores the risks of restricting investment in the oil sector, which can hamper the process of exploration and development.

[7]Dahl and Duggan (1998) survey the evidence.

## Box 3.2. Unconventional Natural Gas: A Game Changer?

Shale gas has emerged as a major new source of natural gas in the United States and could become a new source of supply elsewhere, with major implications for gas markets across the globe. This new energy source accounted for about half of total U.S. gas production in 2010 (Figure 3.2.1) and for three-quarters of global unconventional gas output (U.S. EIA, *International Energy Outlook*, 2010). This box discusses the potential and limitations of the recent "shale gas revolution."

Natural gas resources are classified as conventional or unconventional depending on the technology necessary for exploitation. Conventional gas is found either in easily accessible gas reservoirs or in oil wells. Unconventional natural gas resources include tight gas sands, coalbed methane, and shale gas, and these require more advanced extraction technology. Shale gas is natural gas trapped deep in sedimentary rock and diffused over a relatively large area. The existence of unconventional gas reservoirs has long been recognized. However, the technology to produce economically viable unconventional gas on a large scale emerged only in the past decade.[1]

The authors of this box are Reda Cherif and Ananthakrishnan Prasad.

[1]Unconventional gas extraction typically involves horizontal drilling and hydraulic fracturing (making fractures in the rock and injecting a fluid to increase permeability).

The global resource base for unconventional gas, which includes gas reservoirs that have not yet been developed or found and which is more uncertain with regard to recoverability, is considerably larger and exceeds that of conventional natural gas (Table 3.2.1).[2] In terms of production share, unconventional gas amounted to 12 percent of 2008 total global natural gas production, and the International Energy Agency expects it to rise to 15 percent by 2030 (IEA, *World Energy Outlook*, 2009). Yet there are sufficient resources for much larger expansion. At current global production rates, today's worldwide proven reserves (conventional and unconventional) could sustain current production for 58 years (IEA, *World Energy Outlook*, 2009),[3] whereas the combined resources equal 250 years of current production.

Shale gas extraction has so far been confined to the United States, but there is growing interest in exploiting unconventional sources of gas across the globe. In fact, a number of countries have started

[2]About 380 trillion cubic meters (tcm) of unconventional resources are estimated to have highly likely recoverability (IEA, *World Energy Outlook*, 2010). The remaining recoverable conventional gas resources are estimated at 400 tcm.

[3]The Middle East and North Africa region has more than 40 percent of the world's proven gas reserves, with scope for new discoveries. The Islamic Republic of Iran, Qatar, and Russia hold about half of global proven gas reserves.

### Table 3.2.1. Unconventional Natural Gas Resources, 2009
*(Trillions of cubic meters)*

|  | Tight Gas | Coalbed Methane | Shale Gas | Total |
|---|---|---|---|---|
| Middle East and North Africa | 23 | 0 | 72 | 95 |
| Sub-Saharan Africa | 22 | 1 | 8 | 31 |
| Former Soviet Union | 25 | 112 | 18 | 155 |
| Asia-Pacific | 52 | 48 | 174 | 274 |
|    Central Asia and China | 10 | 34 | 100 | 144 |
|    OECD[1] Pacific | 20 | 13 | 65 | 98 |
|    South Asia | 6 | 1 | 0 | 7 |
|    Other Asia-Pacific | 16 | 0 | 9 | 25 |
| North America | 39 | 85 | 109 | 233 |
| Latin America | 37 | 1 | 60 | 98 |
| Europe | 12 | 7 | 15 | 34 |
|    Central and Eastern Europe | 2 | 3 | 1 | 6 |
|    Western | 10 | 4 | 14 | 28 |
| World | 210 | 254 | 456 | 920 |

Source: International Energy Agency, *World Energy Outlook*, 2009.

[1]OECD = Organization for Economic Cooperation and Development.

**Box 3.2 (continued)**

**Figure 3.2.1.  U.S. Natural Gas Supply, 1998–2009**
*(Billions of cubic meters)*

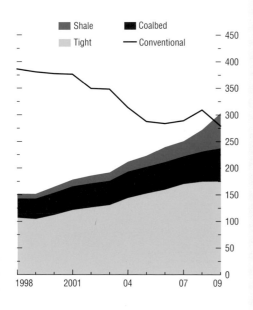

Sources: International Energy Agency; U.S. Energy Information Administration; and IMF staff calculations.

exploring potentially large shale gas resources, including Australia, Austria, Canada, China, Germany, Hungary, India, Poland, Saudi Arabia, and the United Kingdom.

In some countries assessing the commercial viability of reserves and developing the resource base could take up to a decade. There are a number of technical and political challenges: shale gas recovery requires large drilling areas that in some cases may cross borders, affect a large number of residents, and ultimately draw opposition on environmental grounds because of the risk of groundwater contamination with fracture fluids. For example, Europe, with high population density and many national borders, could face difficulties in regulating exploitation permits. Nevertheless, some eastern European countries, particularly Poland, are actively exploring their potential. China is targeting shale

gas production of 30 billion cubic meters a year, which is about half the country's 2009 natural gas consumption.

Long-term marginal costs and the role of shale gas in the energy mix are difficult to project. Shale gas production is characterized by high initial production rates followed by a rapid decline.[4] The market price therefore needs to cover relatively high operating costs (when compared with conventional natural gas production) and provide for fast investment amortization. A Massachusetts Institute of Technology study (MIT, 2010) estimates that the breakeven price for the exploitation of shale gas is in the range of $4 to $8 per million cubic feet (at constant 2007 prices). So far, the U.S. benchmark (Henry Hub) natural gas spot price has fluctuated within this breakeven range, even though it remains well below precrisis levels. As a result, production has continued to grow rapidly despite concerns about the impact of current low prices.

The rapid increase in shale gas supply partly explains the recent decoupling of natural gas prices from oil prices in the United States. If prices per unit of energy were the same, the price of natural gas would be one-sixth the oil price per barrel. Figure 3.2.2 shows that this parity held broadly in the U.S. spot market until late 2005. Since then, gas has become cheaper than oil, suggesting that arbitrage remains limited given that gas and oil are not good substitutes in many applications—transportation being a prime example.

Increased shale gas supply in the United States has led to a redirection of liquefied natural gas (LNG) supplies to other markets, notably Europe and Asia, which has raised questions about traditional contract pricing arrangements. In Europe and Asia, gas prices remained indexed to oil prices in long-term contracts (Table 3.2.2), but the combination of increased U.S. shale gas production and increased LNG supply and distribution capacity outside North America could lead to a decoupling of oil and gas prices as in the United States. This pressure on contract arrangements

[4]The average decline rate (weighted by production) of the Barnett shale horizontal wells is 39 percent in the second year and 50 percent in the third year relative to the first year (IEA, *World Energy Outlook*, 2009).

**Box 3.2** *(continued)*

**Figure 3.2.2. U.S. Natural Gas versus Oil Spot Prices**
*(U.S. dollars per million British thermal units)*

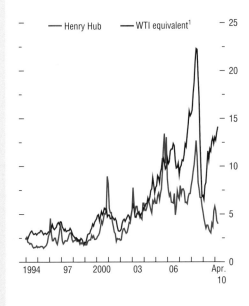

Source: Dow Jones & Company.
[1]WTI = West Texas Intermediate.

**Table 3.2.2. Composition of Wholesale Gas Transactions: United States and Europe, 2007**
*(Percent)*

|  | Spot Market Prices | Oil-Indexed Prices | Other |
|---|---|---|---|
| North America | 98.7 | 0 | 1.3 |
| Europe | 22 | 72.2 | 5.8 |

Source: International Energy Agency, *World Energy Outlook* (2009).

has led to the emergence of spot price markets similar to those in the United States. Greater LNG transportation capacity has also facilitated price arbitrage between markets.

In conclusion, shale gas has the potential to change prospects for natural gas as a source of primary energy, but it remains difficult to predict the extent to which this potential can be realized. Lower relative prices for gas will probably lead to a greater market share of natural gas in total primary energy, with the power sector likely the main beneficiary. But large-scale shale gas production will have to start outside the United States for this energy source to realize its full potential.

## Box 3.3. Short-Term Effects of Oil Shocks on Economic Activity

The short-term impact of large, unexpected oil price changes—typically referred to as oil shocks—on economic activity is hard to quantify and can be quite different from the impact over the long term. Both the nature of the oil price shock and the mix of short-term transmission channels at work can contribute to such differences. This box considers these issues and describes how the short-term impact of oil shocks may differ from the model simulations presented in this chapter.

The nature of the oil price shock is the most important determinant of its eventual impact on economic activity. If an unexpected increase in oil prices is driven by an unexpected boom in world economic growth (a demand shock), oil prices and GDP growth are likely to move together initially: the higher prices moderate the initial boom but do not cause a downturn. However, supply shocks due to factors such as a temporary disruption in oil production caused by geopolitical events or a permanent decline in the availability of oil are likely to raise oil prices regardless of global economic conditions and, depending on the magnitude of the supply disruption, may cause a loss of output.[1]

The expected duration of a supply shock is also likely to shape its macroeconomic effects. Producers and consumers base their decisions, in part, on expectations of future prices. As a result, a shock that is expected to be temporary (for example, supply disruptions due to short-lived geopolitical disturbances) should affect these plans less than a shock that is very persistent.

The analysis in this chapter considers an unexpected permanent supply reduction and suggests a relatively benign macroeconomic impact over

the medium to long term. This should not be surprising; over this horizon, the share of oil in the cost of production should shape most of the GDP impact of an oil price shock. In particular, although oil is either a direct or an indirect factor of production for many final and intermediate goods (from perfume to jet fuel), oil's overall cost share as a proportion of GDP is quite small, ranging from 2 to 5 percent depending on the country. In principle, for an oil importer, the elasticity of GDP with respect to an oil price change induced by a supply shock should be about equal to that of the cost share—that is, quite small. Moreover, for the entire world—which includes oil exporters where higher oil prices stimulate demand for goods and services—the impact can be even smaller.

In the short term, however, other factors and amplification channels may significantly affect the response of output to an unexpected oil price hike. These channels are, however, hard to consider in a large-scale model, and they may not play a significant role in all instances in practice.

A first channel is related to the possibility that oil price spikes (particularly those associated with geopolitical events) make both firms and households more risk-averse.[2] Higher uncertainty regarding future economic prospects can cause firms and households to postpone decisions that are difficult to reverse, such as hiring, investing, and buying durable goods. Financial markets may exacerbate these effects if imperfect information or herd behavior in markets contributes to a sharp decline in liquidity and a sharp adjustment in asset prices.

A second channel is the reallocation of the factors of production. Industries and firms that produce oil-intensive goods or use them as inputs

The main authors of this box are Andrea Pescatori, Shaun Roache, and Joong Shik Kang.
[1]Precautionary demand can exacerbate the oil price effects of small oil supply disruptions or supply concerns (Kilian, 2009).

[2]Studies have noted how small increases in the probability of very unlikely but catastrophic events (such as oil shortages, political turmoil, and the shutdown of some industries) can have dramatic effects on human behavior.

## Box 3.3 *(continued)*

are particularly vulnerable to oil price increases. Some of these industries and firms may no longer be profitable if oil prices stay high for long. This can either depress their profit margins or decrease demand for their products when the oil price increases are passed on to consumers.[3] At a macroeconomic level, the exit of such firms involves reallocation of capital and labor to other industries, a process that can take some time and involve large sunk costs.[4] More generally, the adverse effects of large-scale bankruptcies in hard-hit industries can spread to the rest of the economy through either corporate or bank balance sheets.

Policy mistakes can also exacerbate the effects of an oil supply shock. For instance, monetary policy can contribute to destabilizing output by mistakenly fighting a temporary oil-induced surge in headline inflation.[5] Price controls can lead to rationing and shortages, which may have played a role in amplifying the effects of the 1973 oil shock.[6]

Quantifying the short-term impact on growth of oil shocks has been a daunting challenge in the empirical literature (Table 3.3.1). It can be difficult to determine the nature of the shock—whether induced by demand or supply—and the interplay of the

---

[3]For example, the U.S. auto industry was hit hard by the 2007–08 gasoline price increase.

[4]Reallocating labor usually involves a loss of human capital, given that some skills are job-specific. One firm's capital goods may be less productive in another firm or just too costly to move.

[5]The role played by monetary policy in amplifying the initial oil shock is still debated (see Hamilton, 1996; Bernanke, Gertler, and Watson, 1997; and Hamilton and Herrera, 2004).

[6]In particular for gasoline (see Ramey and Vine, 2010).

**Table 3.3.1. Annualized Percent Impact of a 10 Percent Oil Price Increase on Real U.S. GDP Growth after One Year**

|  | GDP Peak Response (percent) | Sample Period |
|---|---|---|
| *Older Sample Period* | | |
| Rotemberg-Woodford (1996) | −2.00 | 1948–80 |
| Hamilton (1996) | −0.75 | 1948–73 |
| Blanchard-Galí (2007) | −0.40 | 1970–83 |
| *Recent Sample Period* | | |
| Hamilton (1996) | −0.20 | 1974–94 |
| Kilian (2009)[1] | < −1.00 | 1975–2007 |
| Blanchard-Galí (2007) | −0.15 | 1984–2007 |
| Cavallo-Wu (2006) | −0.40 | 1984–2007 |

Sources: Blanchard and Galí (2007); Cavallo and Wu (2006); Hamilton (1996); Rotemberg and Woodford (1996); and IMF staff calculations.

Note: The oil price series used may differ across studies. In all studies, oil price changes are meant to be induced by oil supply shocks and not driven by global demand.

[1]IMF staff calculations are based on Kilian (2009) results.

amplification channels described above. But another challenge arises from recent structural changes in economies. For example, there is general agreement that recent oil price hikes have affected output less than those during the 1970s. Some possible explanations include that recent increases were driven mainly by demand, that monetary policy forestalled damaging second-round effects on wages, that real wage rigidities have diminished, and that the oil intensity of advanced economies has fallen a lot.[7] Disentangling demand from supply shocks is the key challenge facing empirical work that tries to quantify the relationship between oil prices and activity.

---

[7]See Blanchard and Galí (2007) and Nakov and Pescatori (2010).

# References

Adelman, Morris A., 1986, "Scarcity and World Oil Prices," *Review of Economics and Statistics*, Vol. 68 (August), pp. 387–97 (Cambridge, Massachusetts: MIT Press).

———, and G. C. Watkins, 2008, "Reserve Prices and Mineral Resource Theory," *The Energy Journal*, International Association for Energy Economics, Vol. 29 (Special Issue), pp. 1–16.

Ayres, Robert U., 2007, "On the Practical Limits to Substitution," *Ecological Economics*, Vol. 61, No. 1, pp. 115–28.

———, and Benjamin Warr, 2005, "Accounting for Growth: The Role of Physical Work," *Structural Change and Economic Dynamics,* Vol. 16, No. 2, pp. 181–209.

———, 2010, *The Economic Growth Engine: How Energy and Work Drive Material Prosperity* (Cheltenham, United Kingdom: Edward Elgar).

Bernanke, Ben, Mark Gertler, and Mark Watson, 1997, "Systemic Monetary Policy and the Effects of Oil Price Shocks," *Brookings Papers on Economic Activity: 1,* Brookings Institution, pp. 91–142.

Blanchard, Olivier, and Jordi Galí, 2007, "The Macroeconomic Effects of Oil Shocks: Why Are the 2000s So Different from the 1970s?" NBER Working Paper No. 13368 (Cambridge, Massachusetts: National Bureau of Economic Research).

British Petroleum, 2010, *Statistical Review of World Energy* (London, June).

———, 2011, *Energy Outlook 2030* (London, January).

Cashin, Paul, C., John McDermott, and Alasdair Scott, 2002, "Booms and Slumps in World Commodity Prices," *Journal of Development Economics*, Vol. 69 (October 1), pp. 277–296.

Cavallo, Michele, and Tao Wu, 2006, "Measuring Oil-Price Shocks Using Market-Based Information," Federal Reserve Bank of San Francisco Working Paper 2006-28 (San Francisco: Federal Reserve Bank of San Francisco). Available at www.frbsf.org/publications/economics/papers/2006/wp06-28bk.pdf.

Christiano, Lawrence J., and Terry J. Fitzgerald, 2003, "The Band Pass Filter," *International Economic Review*, Vol. 44, No. 2, pp. 435–65.

Clinton, Kevin, Michael Kumhof, Douglas Laxton, and Susanna Mursula, 2010, "Deficit Reduction: Short-Term Pain for Long-Term Gain," *European Economic Review*, Vol. 55, No. 1, pp. 118–39.

Coady, David, Justin Tyson, John M. Piotrowski, Robert Gillingham, Rolando Ossowski, and Shamsuddin Tareqand, 2010, "Petroleum Product Subsidies: Costly, Inequitable, and on the Rise," IMF Staff Position Note10/05 (Washington: International Monetary Fund).

Cooper, John, 2003, "Price Elasticity of Demand for Crude Oil: Estimates for 23 Countries," *OPEC Review*, Vol. 27, No. 1, pp. 1–8.

Cuddington, John T., and Daniel Jerrett, 2008, "Super Cycles in Real Metals Prices?" *IMF Staff Papers,* Vol. 55, No. 4, pp. 541–65.

Dahl, Carol A., and Thomas, E. Duggan, 1998, "Survey of Price Elasticities from Economic Exploration Models of US Oil and Gas Supply," *Journal of Energy Finance and Development*, Vol. 3, No. 2, pp. 129–69.

Dargay, Joyce M., and Dermot Gately, 1995, "The Response of World Energy and Oil Demand to Income Growth and Changes in Oil Prices," *Annual Review of Energy and the Environment*, Vol. 20, pp. 145–78.

———, 2010, "World Oil Demand's Shift toward Faster Growing and Less Price-Responsive Products and Regions," *Energy Policy*, Vol. 38, pp. 6621–77.

———, and Hillard Huntington, 2007, "Price and Income Responsiveness of World Oil Demand by Product" (unpublished; New York: New York University Department of Economics). Available at www.econ.nyu.edu/dept/courses/gately/OilDemand.pdf.

Dées, Stephane, Pavlos Karadeloglou, Robert K. Kaufmann, and Marcelo Sanchez, 2007, "Modelling the World Oil Market: Assessment of a Quarterly Econometric Model," *Energy Policy,* Vol. 35, No. 1, pp. 178–91.

Federal Highway Administration, 2008, *Highway Statistics* (Washington: U.S. Department of Transportation).

Finn, Mary G., 2000, "Perfect Competition and the Effects of Energy Price Increases on Economic Activity," *Journal of Money, Credit and Banking*, Vol. 32, No. 3, pp. 400–16.

Freedman, Charles, Michael Kumhof, Douglas Laxton, Dirk Muir, and Susanna Mursula, 2010, "Global Effects of Fiscal Stimulus During the Crisis," *Journal of Monetary Economics*, Vol. 57, No. 5, pp. 506–26.

Gately, Dermot, and Hillard Huntington, 2002, "The Asymmetric Effects of Changes in Price and Income on Energy and Oil Demand," *Energy Journal*, Vol. 23, No. 1, pp. 19–55.

Goldman Sachs, 2010, *Global Energy: 280 Projects to Change the World.* (London: Goldman Sachs Group—Global Investment Research).

Hall, Charles A. S., and Kent A. Klitgaard, forthcoming, *Energy and the Wealth of Nations: Understanding the Biophysical Economy* (Hamburg: Springer Verlag).

Hamilton, James D., 1996, "This Is What Happened to the Oil Price-Macroeconomy Relationship," *Journal of Monetary Economics*, Vol. 38, pp. 215–20.

———, 2009, "Causes and Consequences of the Oil Shock of 2007–08," *Brookings Papers on Economic Activity* (Spring), pp. 215–61.

———, and Herrera, Ana M., 2004, "Oil Shocks and Aggregate Macroeconomic Behavior: The Role of Monetary Policy: A Comment," *Journal of Money, Credit, and Banking*, Vol. 36, No. 2 (March), pp. 265–86.

Helbling, Thomas, forthcoming, "Commodity Prices and the Global Economy—A Retrospective," IMF Working Paper (Washington: International Monetary Fund).

Hirsch, Robert L., Roger Bezdek, and Robert Wendling, 2005, *Peaking of World Oil Production: Impacts, Mitigation, and Risk Management* (Washington: U.S. Department of Energy).

———, 2010, *The Impending World Energy Mess* (Washington: Griffin Media Group, Apogee Prime).

Hotelling, Harold, 1931, "The Economics of Exhaustible Resources," *The Journal of Political Economy*, Vol. 39, No. 2, pp. 137–75.

Huntington, Hillard, 2010, "Short- and Long-Run Adjustments in U.S. Petroleum Consumption," *Energy Economics*, Vol. 32, No. 1, pp. 63–72.

International Energy Agency (IEA), *World Energy Outlook*, various years (Paris).

———, 2010a, *Medium-Term Oil Market Report* (Paris: June, July).

———, 2010b, *Medium-Term Oil Market Report, Update* (Paris, December).

Jones Benjamin, and Michael Keen, 2009, "Climate Policy and the Recovery," IMF Staff Position Note 09/28 (Washington: International Monetary Fund).

Kaufmann, Robert K., 1991, "Oil Production in the Lower 48 States: Reconciling Curve Fitting and Econometric Models," *Resources and Energy*, Vol. 13, No. 1, pp. 111–27.

Kilian, Lutz, 2009, "Not All Oil Price Shocks Are Alike: Disentangling Demand and Supply Shocks in the Crude Oil Market," *American Economic Review*, Vol. 99, No. 3, pp. 1053–69.

Kumhof, Michael, and Douglas Laxton, 2007, "A Party without a Hangover? On the Effects of U.S. Government Deficits," IMF Working Paper 07/202 (Washington: International Monetary Fund).

———, 2009, "Fiscal Deficits and Current Account Deficits," IMF Working Paper 09/237 (Washington: International Monetary Fund).

Kumhof, Michael, Dirk Muir, and Susanna Mursula, 2010, "The Global Integrated Monetary and Fiscal Model (GIMF)—Theoretical Structure," IMF Working Paper 10/34 (Washington: International Monetary Fund).

Kümmel, Reiner, forthcoming, *The Second Law of Economics: Energy, Entropy, and the Origins of Wealth* (Hamburg: Springer Verlag).

———, Julian Henn, and Dietmar Lindenberger, 2002, "Capital, Labor, Energy and Creativity: Modeling Innovation Diffusion," *Structural Change and Economic Dynamics*, Vol. 13, No. 4, pp. 415–33.

Lynch, Michael C., 2002, "Forecasting Oil Supply: Theory and Practice," *The Quarterly Review of Economics and Finance*, Vol. 42, No. 2, pp. 373–89.

Massachusetts Institute of Technology, 2010, *The Future of Natural Gas: Interim Report* (Cambridge, Massachusetts).

Nakov, Anton A., and Andrea Pescatori, 2010, "Oil and the Great Moderation," *The Economic Journal*, Vol. 120, No. 543, pp. 131–56.

Pesaran, M. Hashem, 1990, "An Econometric Analysis of Exploration and Extraction of Oil in the U.K. Continental Shelf," *The Economic Journal*, Vol. 100, No. 401, pp. 367–90.

———, and Hossein Samiei, 1995, "Forecasting Ultimate Resource Recovery," *International Journal of Forecasting*, Vol. 11, No. 4, pp. 543–55.

Pindyck, Robert S., 1978, "The Optimal Exploration and Production of Nonrenewable Resources," *Journal of Political Economy*, Vol. 86, No. 5, pp. 841–61.

Radetzki, Marian, 2006, "The Anatomy of Three Commodity Booms," *Resources Policy*, Vol. 31, No. 1, pp. 56–64.

Ramey, Valerie A., and Daniel J. Vine, 2010, "Oil, Automobiles, and the U.S. Economy: How Much Have Things Really Changed?" *NBER Macroeconomics Annual 2010*, Vol. 25 (Cambridge, Massachusetts: National Bureau of Economic Research).

Rotemberg, Julio J., and Michael Woodford, 1996, "Imperfect Competition and the Effects of Energy Price Increases on Economic Activity," *Journal of Money, Credit and Banking*, Vol. 28, No. 4, pp. 549–77.

Shell, 2011, *Signals and Signposts: Energy Scenario to 2050* (The Hague: Royal Dutch Shell).

Sillitoe, Richard H., 2000, "Exploration and Discovery of Base- and Precious-Metal Deposits in the Circum-Pacific Region—A Late 1990s Update," *Resource Geology Special Issue*, No. 21.

Slade, Margaret E., 1982, "Cycles in Natural-Resource Commodity Prices: An Analysis of the Frequency Domain," *Journal of Environmental Economics and Management*, Vol. 9, No. 2, pp. 138–48.

Sorrell, Steve, Richard Miller, Roger Bentley, and Jamie Speirs, 2010, "Oil Futures: A Comparison of Global Supply Forecasts," *Energy Policy*, Vol. 38, No. 9, pp. 4990–5003.

Uhler, Russell S., 1976, "Costs and Supply in Petroleum Exploration: The Case of Alberta," *The Canadian Journal of Economics*, Vol. 9, No. 1, pp. 72–90.

U.S. Energy Information Administration (EIA), *International Energy Outlook*, various years (Washington).

Vansteenkiste, Isabel, 2009, "How Important Are Common Factors in Driving Non-Fuel Commodity Prices? A Dynamic Factor Analysis," ECB Working Paper No. 1072 (Frankfurt: European Central Bank).

# INTERNATIONAL CAPITAL FLOWS: RELIABLE OR FICKLE?

*This chapter analyzes international capital flows over the past 30 years to assess their predictability and their likely response to changes in the global macroeconomic environment. It finds that capital flows exhibit low persistence and that their volatility has increased over time. Across economies, net flows to emerging market economies are somewhat more volatile than those to advanced economies; across types of flow, debt-creating flows are somewhat more volatile and less persistent than others. Net capital flows to emerging market economies have been strongly correlated with changes in global financing conditions, rising sharply during periods with relatively low global interest rates and low risk aversion (or greater appetite for risk) and falling afterward. Furthermore, economies that have a direct foreign financial exposure to the United States experience an additional decline in their net capital flows in response to U.S. monetary tightening over and above what is experienced by economies that have no such direct U.S. financial exposure. This negative additional effect is larger when the U.S. rate hike is unanticipated and sharper for emerging market economies that are more integrated with global financial and foreign exchange markets, but smaller for economies with greater financial depth and relatively strong growth performance. Finally, the additional response to U.S. monetary tightening is deeper in an environment of low global interest rates and low risk aversion. These findings suggest that the eventual unwinding of globally accommodative financing conditions will, on the margin, dampen net flows to emerging market economies that have a direct financial exposure to the United States relative to those that do not, although strong growth performance in these economies can offset this negative additional effect. Thus, as economies further integrate with global financial markets, it is important to adopt policies to preserve domestic economic and financial strength to cope with variable capital flows.*

The main authors of this chapter are John Bluedorn, Rupa Duttagupta (team leader), Jaime Guajardo, and Petia Topalova, with support from Angela Espiritu, Murad Omoev, Andy Salazar, and Jessie Yang.

International capital flows have been on an unprecedented roller-coaster ride in recent years.[1] After a remarkable surge in the run-up to the global crisis, gross inflows dropped precipitously in its wake (Milesi-Ferretti and Tille, 2010), but soon regained their upward momentum (Figure 4.1). The fluctuations in net flows were much sharper for emerging market economies (EMEs) compared with advanced economies (AEs)—in the latter, gross outflows largely offset gross inflows, generating smoother movements in net flows (Figure 4.2). By contrast, in EMEs, gross inflows and net flows both fell dramatically during the crisis and rebounded sharply afterward. For many EMEs, net flows in the first three quarters of 2010 had already outstripped the averages reached during 2004–07 (Figure 4.3) but were still lower than their precrisis highs.

Policymakers in many EMEs have eyed the recent turnaround in capital flows with mixed enthusiasm. Although external capital can provide the financing and/or spur the currency appreciation needed to strengthen domestic demand in recipient economies, net flows may increase at a pace that policymakers find difficult to manage, or they may fluctuate unpredictably, exacerbating domestic economic or financial boom-bust cycles.

Consequently, a key question confronting policymakers is what will happen to capital flows when easy global financing conditions characterized by

[1]The chapter uses "capital flows" to describe cross-border financial transactions recorded in economies' external financial accounts, as described in the sixth edition of the IMF's *Balance of Payments and International Investment Position Manual.* Consistent with the manual, inflows arise when external liabilities are incurred by the recipient economy (inflows with a positive sign) and external liabilities are reduced (inflows with a negative sign). Outflows are purchases of external assets from the viewpoint of the purchasing economy (outflows with a negative sign), as well as the deleveraging of its assets (outflows with a positive sign). Net flows are the sum of gross inflows and outflows, where outflows are recorded with a negative sign. Reserve asset accumulation, which may be influenced by non-market-driven factors, is excluded from the computation of net flows as defined in this chapter.

**Figure 4.1. The Collapse and Recovery of Cross-Border Capital Flows**

*(Percent of aggregate GDP)*

After an unprecedented rise during the run-up to the financial crisis and a precipitous fall in its wake, international capital flows rebounded to both advanced and emerging market economies.

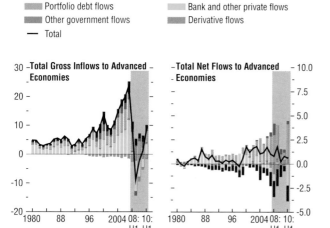
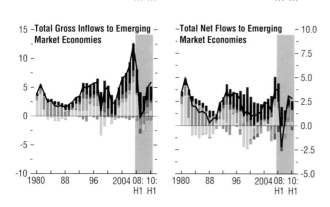

Sources: CEIC; Haver Analytics; IMF, *Balance of Payments Statistics;* national sources; and IMF staff calculations.

Note: See Appendix 4.1 for a list of the economies included in the advanced and emerging market economy aggregates. Data are plotted on an annual basis until 2007 and on a semiannual basis thereafter (indicated by gray shading). Semiannual data are calculated as the sum of capital flows over the two relevant quarters divided by the sum of nominal GDP (both in U.S. dollars) for the same period. Total flows may not equal the sum of the individual components because of a lack of data on the underlying composition for some economies.

low global interest rates and low risk aversion come to an end. Will capital flows reverse course with the resumption of monetary tightening in the United States or in other major AEs?

To inform this debate, this chapter analyzes the nature of net private cross-border capital flows over the past 30 years across advanced, emerging market, and other developing economies.[2] It examines how variable such flows are and how likely they are to respond to changes in the global macroeconomic environment. Its core focus is the behavior of net flows to EMEs, comparing the EME experience with that of other economies. In particular, this chapter addresses the following questions:

- After the global crisis, what was the nature of the capital flow recovery across advanced and emerging market economies? In terms of its size and composition, how did the postcrisis upturn in flows to EMEs compare with the surge before the crisis and with historical trends? Was the recovery in net flows broadly similar across regions, economies, and types of flow?

- How volatile and variable are net flows? Are flows to some economies more volatile or less persistent than flows to others? Have these statistical properties changed over time and do they vary by type of flow?

[2]A growing body of literature considers gross rather than net capital flows to uncover the extent to which cross-border capital movement is driven by foreign investors or domestic residents (see Forbes and Warnock, 2010). Although the behavior of gross inflows and outflows is interesting, an analysis of their determinants would require careful modeling of the nonstationarities that are pervasive in the gross flows data. This chapter focuses on net flows, which are both stationary and a natural counterpart to the current account, which lies at the heart of the external rebalancing debate. As in Chapter 4 of the October 2007 *World Economic Outlook,* we focus on net "private" capital flows, defined from the point of view of the recipient sector. Thus, capital flows as considered here exclude all flows to the general government and monetary authorities within the "other investment" component of the financial account given that the latter is expected to be largely driven by nonmarket factors (such as bilateral sovereign loans or transactions with the IMF). However, this concept of capital flows still includes portfolio flows to the government. For the full list of economies included in the advanced, emerging market, and other developing economy groups, see Appendix 4.1. We exclude offshore financial centers (also listed in Appendix 4.1) from the main analysis given that capital flows to these economies may reflect factors unrelated to the domestic economy.

- How did net flows, and their components, behave during previous episodes of low global interest rates and low risk aversion? How much of the variation in net flows can be explained by common—such as global or regional—versus domestic factors?

- Does an economy's direct financial exposure to the United States affect the sensitivity of its net capital flows to U.S. monetary policy changes? To what extent is this sensitivity associated with the structural and economic characteristics of the recipient economy, such as its degree of global financial integration, domestic financial depth, exchange rate regime, and growth performance? Does this sensitivity vary by the type of flow or the underlying global economic and financial environment?

In answering these questions, this chapter makes several contributions to the voluminous literature on capital flows. First, in its descriptive analysis, it expands on earlier work on the volatility and persistence of capital flows (for example, Becker and Noone, 2009; Levchenko and Mauro, 2007; Claessens, Dooley, and Warner, 1995) for a large sample of economies over a longer and more recent time period. Second, it examines how net flows to EMEs behaved during and in the aftermath of periods when the global economic environment was similar to today's: loose global monetary conditions and relatively low risk aversion. This is the foremost economic scenario in many policymakers' minds, but it has not been adequately explored.[3] Third, the chapter identifies how differences in economies' direct financial exposure to the United States affect the responses of their capital flows to changes in U.S. monetary policy, while taking into account all possible global factors. This is accomplished by means of two innovations:

- The existing literature that examines the "push" (global) and "pull" (domestic) drivers of capital flows has generally attempted to estimate the total effect on capital flows of a selected set of global

---

[3]Exceptions include Calvo and others (2001), who document the pattern of capital flows to EMEs during various U.S. growth and monetary policy cycles, and the IMF's May 2010 *Regional Economic Outlook* for the Western Hemisphere, which contrasts the behavior of capital inflows to Latin America during periods of low global interest rates and low risk aversion.

**Figure 4.2. The Evolution of Gross and Net Capital Flows**
*(Percent of aggregate GDP)*

Emerging market economies experienced much sharper fluctuations in net capital flows than advanced economies, despite the similarity in the behavior of gross capital inflows and outflows for the two groups.

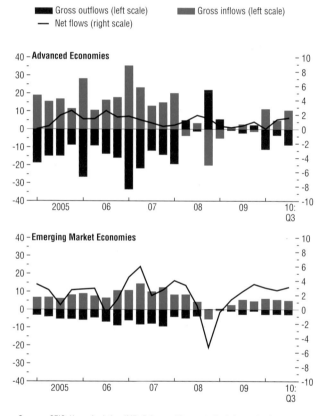

Sources: CEIC; Haver Analytics; IMF, *Balance of Payments Statistics;* national sources; and IMF staff calculations.
Note: Net flows, which do not include reserve accumulation, may not equal the sum of gross inflows and gross outflows because of a lack of data on gross flows for some economies.

**Figure 4.3. The Recovery of Net Private Capital Flows**

*(Change in net private capital flows in percent of GDP between 2010:Q1–Q3 and 2004–07 average unless noted otherwise)*

Net private capital flows in the first three quarters of 2010 in many emerging market economies already outstripped the averages reached during 2004–07.

■ Net private capital flows higher in 2010:Q1–Q3 than 2004–07 average
■ Net private capital flows lower in 2010:Q1–Q3 than 2004–07 average
☐ Insufficient data

Sources: CEIC; Haver Analytics; IMF, *Balance of Payments Statistics*; national sources; and IMF staff calculations.
Note: Net private capital flows are defined as the sum of net foreign direct investment, net portfolio, net derivative, and net other investment flows, excluding other investment flows to the general government and monetary authorities. The 2004–07 average is computed as the average of net private flows as a percent of GDP across the four years based on annual data. The 2010:Q1–Q3 number is derived from quarterly data as the sum of net private capital flows over the relevant quarters divided by the sum of nominal GDP (both in U.S. dollars). Due to data limitations, the calculations for several of the economies for which quarterly data are available are based on net total capital flows (including other investment flows to the official sector). These economies are China, Costa Rica, Ecuador, Egypt, India, Jordan, Malaysia, Morocco, New Zealand, Singapore, the Slovak Republic, and Uruguay. The postcrisis capital flows data for Peru are for 2010:H1 due to a lack of data for 2010:Q3.

drivers, such as U.S. interest rates, risk aversion, and so on. This type of analysis may fall short because it cannot control for every possible global factor affecting cross-border capital movements. Instead of trying to identify all push factors or the overall effect of U.S. monetary policy changes, this chapter tries to identify the difference in the effect of U.S. monetary policy on net flows to economies according to their direct financial exposure to the United States. At the same time, the estimation controls for all possible global factors that may affect capital movements equally across economies at each point in time.

- The literature also typically treats U.S. monetary policy as exogenous to capital flows to other economies. Although U.S. policy is not set in response

to net flows to other economies, the impact of U.S. interest rate changes on net flows elsewhere may depend on when information about a U.S. move is available to the market. Capital flows may occur at the time news arrives about the change in U.S. monetary policy rather than at the time of the actual change. Moreover, if U.S. monetary policy responds countercyclically to U.S. economic developments (which likely exert an independent influence on global flows), capital flows may be muted in response to U.S. interest rate changes. As a result, the estimated effect of realized changes in the interest rate on capital flows may underestimate the magnitude of the effect of U.S. monetary policy. This chapter draws on the approach of Kuttner (2001) in an attempt to isolate the unanticipated component of U.S. monetary policy changes. Throughout the estimation analysis, the chapter distinguishes between the difference in the effect on capital flows of an unanticipated and exogenous change in the U.S. policy rate as opposed to an actual (realized) change.

## What Are the Main Findings?

- The postcrisis recovery in net capital flows was more impressive in terms of its pace than its level. Nevertheless, for many EMEs that were not at the center of the global crisis, levels were comparable with those during previous episodes of large net flows. The composition of the upturn was somewhat different, however, with a higher share of debt-creating flows and a lower share of foreign direct investment (FDI) compared with historical trends.

- Net flows have become slightly more volatile for all economies over time. They also exhibit low persistence. The volatility of net flows is generally higher in EMEs and other developing economies (ODEs) than in AEs. By contrast, there are no obvious differences in the persistence of net flows across economies. Bank and other private flows have typically been the most volatile, and portfolio debt the least persistent, but the differences in volatility and persistence across types of flow are not always statistically significant for all economies. FDI is only slightly more stable and more persistent than debt-creating flows to EMEs.

- Historically, net flows to EMEs have tended to be higher under low global interest rates, low global risk aversion, and stronger growth performance in EMEs compared with AEs. The pattern is most pronounced when global interest rates and risk aversion are both low. Nevertheless, common factors—both global and regional—account for a relatively small share of the total variation in net flows to EMEs, highlighting the importance of domestic factors.

- Advanced and emerging market economies that are directly financially exposed to the United States face an additional decline in their net capital flows in response to U.S. monetary policy tightening over and above what is experienced by economies with no such U.S. direct financial exposure. The

negative additional effect of a hike in the U.S. rate that is unanticipated is larger than that of a realized rate increase. Thus, positive U.S. monetary policy surprises may induce investors to revise up their expectations for future U.S. monetary policy, thereby resulting in a sharper retrenchment of their positions in economies that are directly financially exposed to the United States than under actual U.S. monetary policy changes that were partly or wholly anticipated. This negative additional effect for financially exposed EMEs is larger for EMEs that are more integrated with global financial markets and those with relatively flexible exchange rate regimes, but smaller for EMEs with greater domestic financial depth and strong growth performance. Finally, of particular relevance to today's environment is the finding that the negative additional effect on net flows to financially exposed EMEs due to U.S. monetary policy tightening is larger during periods of low global interest rates and low global risk aversion. This may reflect the fact that cross-border investors are more likely to chase returns when global financial asset returns are low and risk appetite is high.

The chapter's findings suggest that capital flows are generally fickle—from the point of view of the recipient economy—and sensitive to AEs' monetary policy changes, which are outside the control of domestic policymakers. While the general perception that capital flows toward EMEs broadly represent a secular trend is likely true (see Figure 4.1), the main findings of the chapter point to the sensitivity of capital flows to the global cycle, such as changes in global financial conditions. Drawing on event studies, it is reasonable to expect that future U.S. monetary tightening would be associated with a dampening of net flows to EMEs. Moreover, the regression analysis indicates that economies with greater direct financial exposure to the United States will experience greater additional declines in net flows because of U.S. monetary tightening, compared with economies with lesser U.S. financial exposure. It is important to note that the chapter does not address whether higher capital flow volatility induces higher macroeconomic volatility across EMEs, nor does it try to identify the source of capital flow volatility—whether it is driven by specific types of market participants (for example, banks, insurance and pension funds, or hedge funds). However, the analysis does indicate that the variability of capital flows is as much an issue for AEs as for EMEs. Moreover, despite increasing globalization and major changes in international capital market structures over the past two decades, the intrinsic variability of net flows has not shifted much over time.[4] Thus, as EMEs further integrate with global financial markets, it is key that they maintain domestic economic and financial strength and stability—via strong macroeconomic policies, prudential regulation of the financial sector, and other macrofinancial measures—to better manage capital flow variability.

The rest of the chapter is organized as follows. The first section describes how the postcrisis recovery in net flows to EMEs until the first three quarters of 2010 compared with previous capital flow upturns. It then documents the historical evolution of the volatility and persistence of net capital flows and compares these trends across economies. The second section discusses the behavior of net flows to EMEs during periods of low global interest rates and low risk aversion. It then uses a global factor model to compute the relative importance of common factors versus economy-specific factors in explaining the variation in net flows across economies. The third section presents a regression analysis of the difference in the effect of U.S. monetary policy changes on net flows between economies that are directly financially exposed to the United States and those that are not. The fourth section summarizes the findings and discusses the key policy lessons from the analysis.

## Trends in Net Capital Flows: Size, Composition, Volatility, and Persistence

To set the stage, this section describes the resurgence of net capital flows to EMEs in the wake of the global financial crisis. Did net capital flows recover equally across regions and across types of flow? How did the recovery compare with previous episodes of large net capital flows to EMEs? Next, the section discusses how the volatility and persistence of net flows have evolved over time and across economies.

## What Is Different about the Recent Recovery?

Net capital flows to EMEs staged a strong comeback beginning in mid-2009 but more in pace than in level (Figure 4.4). All EMEs experienced a sharp recovery in net flows in a strikingly short span of time. Nevertheless, unlike during the run-up to the crisis, when net flows rushed to all EME regions, the strength of the postcrisis recovery was uneven. To compare the recent recovery against historical experience, we identify two periods of strong net capital flows to EMEs—before the Asian crisis (1991–97) and before the recent global crisis (2004–07).[5] Although aggregate net flows to emerging Asia and Latin America during the first three quarters of 2010 were already above the precrisis (2004–07) averages, these levels did not always exceed record highs (Figure 4.5). For example, postcrisis net flows to Latin America were weaker than during 1991–97, when these economies financed larger current account deficits. For emerging Europe, which was hit hard by the crisis, as well as other emerging economies (from the Commonwealth of Independent States, the Middle East, and Africa), recent net flows have been anemic compared with either 2004–07 or 1991–97 averages.

Interestingly, the disaggregated data indicate that the recovery was stronger in larger economies, pulling up the regional aggregates (Figure 4.6). Net flows rose in a fairly broad-based manner to emerging Asia and the newly industrialized Asian economies (NIEs), but the experience was mixed for Latin America and other emerging economies. As noted, net flows were depressed for most of emerging Europe compared with 2004–07 averages, with a few exceptions.

In terms of composition, the recovery was driven primarily by portfolio debt flows and, for emerging Asia and Latin America, also by bank and other private flows (see Figure 4.5). The share of FDI in net flows fell during the first three quarters of 2010 compared with previous episodes of large net flows to EMEs (1991–97 and 2004–07). The relatively smaller share of bank and other private flows compared with portfolio debt flows for most regions may reflect ongoing deleveraging in external asset posi-

---

[4]For instance, Chapter 2 of the April 2007 *Global Financial Stability Report* documents the growing role of institutional investors in international asset allocation since the mid-1990s.

[5]These periods were characterized by net capital flows to EMEs that were higher than the 1990–2009 median level (see also Chapter 4 of the October 2007 *World Economic Outlook*).

tions by the AE banks that were at the epicenter of the global financial crisis.[6] In the absence of recent data, it is difficult to tell, however, whether this trend has continued into 2011.

If the recent pattern continues, it would imply a shift away from the historical trend of a declining share of debt-creating flows, especially in EMEs (Figures 4.7 and 4.8).[7] More specifically, the importance of bank and other private flows has fallen over the past three decades for all economies. This could reflect, in part, a natural shift toward nonbank means of financing as a result of deepening domestic capital markets and greater financial integration. Although the share of portfolio debt did increase over time, this did not offset the decline in bank and other private flows until after the global crisis.[8]

## How Stable Are Net Capital Flows?

This section investigates the volatility and persistence properties of capital flows. If capital flows were steady and persistent, they would likely be easier to predict. Following the literature, we measure volatility with the standard deviation of net flows scaled by GDP over a 10-year rolling window using annual data, while gauging their persistence through a regression of net flows scaled by GDP on their past level (that is, the AR(1) coefficient), also over a 10-year rolling window.[9]

---

[6]Chuhan, Perez-Quiros, and Popper (1996) also document that bank flows generally remain depressed for several years following a financial crisis.

[7]Following Becker and Noone (2009), we calculate the relative importance of a particular type of flow as the absolute value of the net flows of that type divided by the sum of the absolute value of the net flows of all types of flow.

[8]The historically declining share of debt-creating flows supports the findings of Faria and others (2007) and Dell'Ariccia and others (2007), who note a shift in recent years in the composition of external assets and liabilities of high- and middle-income economies away from debt instruments.

[9]An alternative measure of volatility, namely the coefficient of variation, which divides the standard deviation by the mean, is not appropriate to use in this context because the mean of net flows can be zero or negative. However, to account for the effect that a potential trend increase in net flows might have on their standard deviation, we also compute the standard deviation of the detrended series. The results are broadly unchanged with this alternative measure.

## Figure 4.4. The Recovery of Net Capital Flows and Their Composition

*(Percent of aggregate GDP, four-quarter moving average)*

The postcrisis rebound in net private capital flows was uneven across regions, with the pace of recovery faster for regions that were more resilient in the recent crisis (Asia, Latin America) than others.

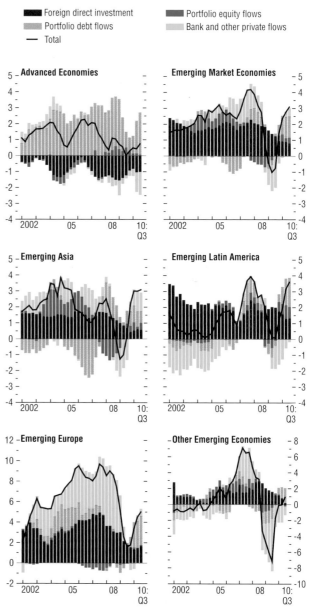

Sources: CEIC; Haver Analytics; IMF, *Balance of Payments Statistics;* national sources; and IMF staff calculations.
Note: See Appendix 4.1 for a list of the economies included in the regional aggregates. The group and regional aggregates exclude offshore financial centers. Total net private capital flows do not equal the sum of the plotted components, because net derivative flows are not plotted and there is a lack of data on the underlying composition for some economies.

## *Are net flows volatile?*

Net flows have become marginally more volatile over time across all economies, with volatility in EMEs higher than in AEs (Figure 4.9, left panel). The rise in the median volatility of net private flows has been most pronounced in AEs, although the pattern of a slow rise in volatility is also evident for both EMEs and ODEs. The standard deviation of net flows to EMEs has been about 30 percent higher than of those to AEs, although the differences in the medians are generally not statistically significant.[10]

In terms of composition, bank and other private flows have been the most volatile in all economies (Figure 4.9, right panel).[11] However, it is hard to discern systematic differences in volatility among the remaining components. In AEs, both bank and other private and portfolio debt flows appear equally volatile, whereas FDI and portfolio equity flows are somewhat less so, with the differences between the latter two (and the former two) generally not statistically significant. Similarly, in EMEs, the standard deviations of FDI versus portfolio debt flows are not statistically different from each other. In general, the increase in the volatility of the overall net financial account has been accompanied by an upward trend in the volatility of all individual components, although much more prominently for AEs than for others.[12]

Note, however, that despite higher volatility of the individual components of net flows in AEs compared with EMEs, alternative flows have served as broad substitutes for AEs, helping lower their total

### Figure 4.5. The Size and Composition of Net Private Capital Flows during Waves of Large Capital Flows to Emerging Market Economies

*(Percent of aggregate GDP)*

The recent recovery was led by portfolio debt flows, followed by bank and other private flows. In contrast with previous periods, the share of foreign direct investment was smaller.

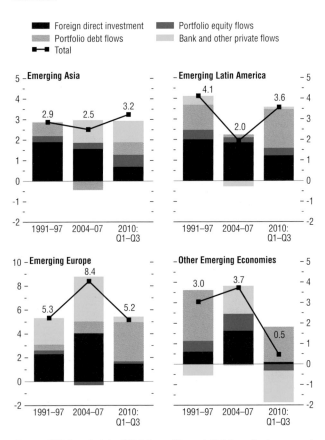

Sources: CEIC; Haver Analytics; IMF, *Balance of Payments Statistics;* national sources; and IMF staff calculations.
Note: The 1991–97 and 2004–07 numbers are computed as the sum of net flows over the relevant years divided by the sum of regional nominal GDP during the same period using annual data. The 2010:Q1–Q3 numbers are calculated as the sum of net flows over the three relevant quarters divided by the sum of regional nominal GDP during the same period. The total does not equal the sum of the plotted components, because net derivative flows are not plotted and there is a lack of data on the underlying composition for some economies. Waves of large capital flows to emerging market economies are defined as periods during which capital flows are larger than the 1990–2009 median. The regional aggregates exclude offshore financial centers.

---

[10]These estimates are slightly lower than what has been found in recent studies, such as Becker and Noone (2009), Levchenko and Mauro (2007), Broner and Rigobon (2006), and Prasad and others (2003). The volatility of net capital flows was also computed for the median EME across alternative regions (see Appendix 4.2). There appears to be little systematic difference in the volatility of total flows across the emerging market regions, although there is some suggestive evidence that the volatility of flows to emerging Europe is slightly higher and that the volatility of flows to other emerging market economies has risen in recent periods.

[11]These findings relate to the literature that stresses that an economy's propensity to experience a crisis is dependent on the composition of its capital flows and external liabilities (Frankel and Rose, 1996; Frankel and Wei, 2005; Levchenko and Mauro, 2007; Tong and Wei, 2010; and Ghosh, Ostry, and Tsangarides, 2010).

[12]The results for equity flows for this and subsequent sections should be treated with caution because very few EMEs and ODEs report any data on these flows prior to the 2000s.

volatility (Figure 4.10). This mutual substitutability is negligible for EMEs and ODEs.

### Are net flows persistent?

The persistence of net flows is generally low, and it is only marginally higher in AEs than in EMEs and ODEs (Figure 4.11, left panel). There are no significant differences in persistence between these economies, even though there appears to be a cyclical component in persistence over time, especially for net flows to AEs.[13] Portfolio debt flows are the least persistent across all economies (Figure 4.11, right panel). Persistence is somewhat higher for FDI than for other flows, although it has fallen since the early 2000s for AEs and EMEs. In AEs, the persistence among various types of flow is essentially indistinguishable.

The findings in this section suggest that the accepted wisdom about the stability of some kinds of capital flows, such as FDI, compared with others should be regarded with caution, especially for EMEs (for example, Sarno and Taylor, 1999; Chuhan, Perez-Quiros, and Popper, 1996). Bank and other private flows were found to be the most volatile and portfolio debt flows the least persistent. However, FDI is only slightly more stable than other types of flow—for EMEs, the differences in volatility between FDI and portfolio debt flows, and the differences in persistence between FDI and bank and other private flows, are not generally statistically significant. Moreover, like other types of flow, FDI volatility has increased and persistence has fallen over time, although this pattern is more evident in AEs than in EMEs. This could reflect changing FDI characteristics. For instance, the share of financial FDI—direct borrowing by a subsidiary from a parent bank or firm—may have increased relative to nonfinancial FDI, raising its total volatility.[14] Moreover, for all economies—

[13]The persistence of total net private capital flows also does not vary substantially across the four emerging market regions (see Appendix 4.2). Although net flows to emerging Asia appear to have been the most persistent and net flows to the "other emerging market" economies the least persistent, these differences are not statistically significant and have become smaller over time.

[14]See ECB (2004) and BCGFS (2004) for evidence of an increase in financial FDI in EMEs, and Ostry and others (2010) for the impact of a rising share of financial FDI on macroeconomic volatility.

**Figure 4.6. Regional Variation in Net Private Capital Flows to Emerging Market Economies**
*(Percent of GDP)*

The nature of the recovery was diverse within each region. Net flows rose strongly in a majority of economies within emerging Asia, while falling short of precrisis averages in most economies within emerging Europe. The experience was more mixed for Latin America and other emerging market economies.

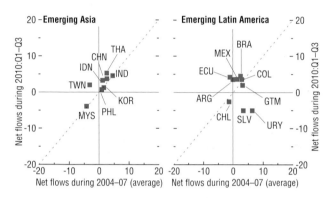

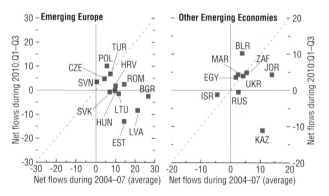

Sources: CEIC; Haver Analytics; IMF, *Balance of Payments Statistics;* national sources; and IMF staff calculations.

Note: Emerging Asia (CHN: China; IND: India; IDN: Indonesia; KOR: Korea; MYS: Malaysia; PHL: Philippines; TWN: Taiwan Province of China; THA: Thailand). Emerging Latin America (ARG: Argentina; BRA: Brazil; CHL: Chile; COL: Colombia; ECU: Ecuador; GTM: Guatemala; MEX: Mexico; SLV: El Salvador; URY: Uruguay). Emerging Europe (BGR: Bulgaria; CZE: Czech Republic; EST: Estonia; HRV: Croatia; HUN: Hungary; LVA: Latvia; LTU: Lithuania; POL: Poland; ROM: Romania; SVK: Slovak Republic; SVN: Slovenia; TUR: Turkey). Other Emerging Economies (BLR: Belarus; EGY: Egypt; JOR: Jordan; ISR: Israel; KAZ: Kazakhstan; MAR: Morocco; RUS: Russia; UKR: Ukraine; ZAF: South Africa).

despite the trend decline in debt-creating flows—net flows have still become more volatile and continue to exhibit low persistence.

## Capital Flows and the Global Environment

Do net capital flows exhibit regular patterns in response to the global environment? To answer this question, we first examine how net capital flows to EMEs behaved when global conditions were similar to today's economic environment of relatively low global interest rates, falling risk aversion, and strong growth performance in EMEs.[15] Next, we assess the relative strength of common (global and regional) as compared with economy-specific factors in explaining the variation in EME capital flows across economies.

### Are Net Capital Flows Correlated with Underlying Global Conditions?

Historically, most periods of loose global monetary conditions have overlapped with periods of high growth disparity between EMEs and AEs, but not with periods of low global risk aversion (Figure 4.12).[16] This seems to indicate that monetary policy has been largely countercyclical or that accommodative monetary policy has coincided with weak economic prospects and/or low expected inflation in AEs (see Calvo and others, 2001). In contrast, during the recent global crisis, risk appetite did not always move in tandem with low interest rates, especially under conditions of financial stress. There

### Figure 4.7. The Relative Importance of Various Types of Flow
*(Percent of total)*

The importance of bank and other private flows has declined over time and across advanced, emerging market, and other developing economies in favor of rising portfolio and foreign direct investment flows. Bank and other private flows, however, remain a substantial component of the net financial account.

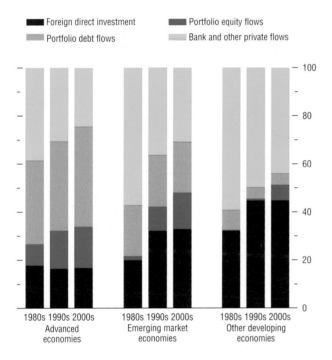

Sources: IMF, *Balance of Payments Statistics;* national sources; and IMF staff calculations.
Note: The relative importance of a particular type of flow is calculated as the absolute value of the net flows of that type to the economies of the group divided by the sum of the absolute value of the net flows of all four types of instruments to the economies in the group. Ratios are calculated for each decade with annual data, computing both numerator and denominator over the years in each decade. Derivative flows, which comprise a very small share of the financial account, are excluded from the calculation. The group aggregates exclude offshore financial centers.

[15]However, common patterns between capital flows and underlying conditions should not be interpreted as causal links.

[16]Periods of low global interest rates, low global risk aversion, and strong EME growth performance are defined as periods when the global real interest rate, risk aversion, and growth differential between AEs and EMEs are lower than their median values over the entire 1980–2009 period (see also the IMF's May 2010 *Regional Economic Outlook* for the Western Hemisphere). The global real interest rate is computed as the GDP-weighted average of the real European Central Bank financing rate (and the Bundesbank base rate prior to 1999) and the U.S. real federal funds rate. Risk aversion is proxied by the Chicago Board of Options Exchange Volatility Index (VIX) level. The growth differential between emerging market and advanced economies is the difference between the weighted average real GDP growth rates of each group (excluding offshore financial centers).

were two relatively long periods when all three conditions coincided: (1) the run-up to the Asian crisis (1991–96, excluding 1994 due to a lower growth differential and 1995 due to higher global interest rates) and (2) the run-up to the recent global crisis (2004–07). With falling risk aversion since late 2010, the period ahead may also yield a similar confluence of the above three conditions.

Total net capital flows to EMEs during each type of episode were larger than the year before or after and largest when all three types of episodes coincided (Figure 4.13).[17] The sharpest increase (and decline) occurred around periods of low risk aversion—net flows increased by 2¼ percentage points of GDP from the year preceding the period and fell by 1¼ percentage points afterward. Conversely, the increase was smaller when the underlying condition was characterized by only low global interest rates. Net flows to EMEs tended to be strongest when global interest rates and risk aversion were both low (Figure 4.14), whereas when risk aversion was high but global interest rates were low, net flows were only marginally above where they were when both conditions were tight.

The stated dynamics in capital flows around alternative events were driven mostly by bank and other private flows (see Figures 4.13 and 4.14). The rise in these flows was typically the sharpest during the event and declined most dramatically afterward. In particular, bank and other private flows appear to be strongly correlated with changes in global risk aversion. Although all other types of flow tended to increase during the alternative events, their behavior in the aftermath varied. Portfolio debt and equity flows typically remained elevated at the end of periods characterized by a relatively strong growth performance in EMEs, but fell at the end of easy global financing conditions (that is, low global interest rate and low risk aversion). This could reflect the countercyclical nature of portfolio flows to EMEs: higher net flows at the end of strong growth performance may have helped meet recipient economies' larger financing needs. Conversely, FDI generally remained strong even after the end of loose global financing conditions, but

[17]Net flows are averaged across years for multiyear events.

### Figure 4.8. Historical Trends: A Shift away from Debt-Creating Flows
*(Percent of total)*

Debt-creating flows have become relatively less important over time across all economies, reflecting the decline in net bank and other private flows.

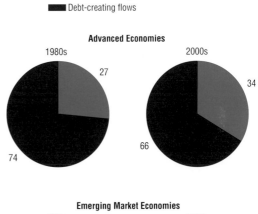
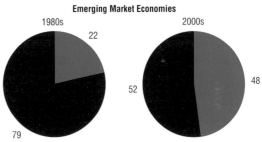
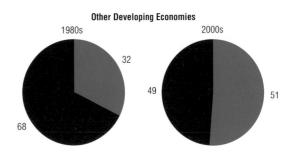

Sources: IMF, *Balance of Payments Statistics;* national sources; and IMF staff calculations,

Note: Debt-creating flows include portfolio debt and bank and other private flows. The relative importance of a particular type of flow is calculated as the absolute value of the net flows of that type divided by the sum of the absolute value of the net flows of all four types of instruments. Ratios are calculated for each decade with annual data, computing both numerator and denominator over the years in each decade. The group aggregates exclude offshore financial centers. The sum of the shares may not equal 100 because decimals are rounded.

## Figure 4.9. The Volatility of Net Private Capital Flows

*(Standard deviation of net capital flows in percent of GDP)*

The volatility of net private capital flows has been creeping up over time across all economies and across most types of flow. Emerging market and other developing economies have generally experienced higher volatility in their net financial account than advanced economies. Net bank and other private flows have consistently been the most volatile type of flow.

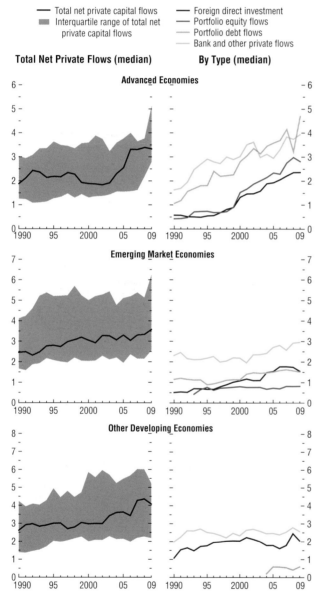

Sources: IMF, *Balance of Payments Statistics;* national sources; and IMF staff calculations.

Note: Using annual data, the volatility of any particular flow is computed as its standard deviation over the prior 10-year window for each economy (for example, the 1990 value corresponds to the standard deviation during 1981–90). The median is plotted only if the standard deviation for the particular 10-year window and type of flow can be calculated for at least one-fifth of the economies in the group. The groups exclude offshore financial centers.

fell at the end of strong growth episodes in EMEs. Overall, the rise and fall in FDI during and after alternative events appear less prominent than the rise and fall in other types of flow.[18]

To summarize, the event studies demonstrate an inverted V-shaped pattern of net capital flows to EMEs around events outside the policymakers' control, underscoring the fickle nature of capital flows from the perspective of the recipient economy. Thus, net flows to EMEs have tended to be temporarily higher during periods with low global interest rates and low risk aversion. Moreover, the rise in net flows to EMEs has been much greater during periods characterized by both low global interest rates and low risk aversion. The dynamics in net flows appear to be driven largely by bank and other private flows. Other types of flow also tended to increase during the events but did not always fall at the end of events.

### How Much of the Variation in Net Capital Flows Is Due to Global and Regional Factors?

A global factor model is used to discern the relative importance of common factors—global and regional—versus economy-specific factors in explaining the variation in net flows to EMEs. A large or growing share of the total variation of net flows explained by common factors would imply that capital flows are increasingly determined outside the domestic economy.

The estimated model underscores the dominance of economy-specific factors, captured by the model residual, in explaining the variation in capital flow movements in EMEs (Figure 4.15).[19] However, it also shows that the share explained by common factors was higher in the past two decades—increasing from less than 15 percent in the 1980s, to about 23 percent in the 1990s, and to more than 30 percent

---

[18]A number of robustness checks—for example, excluding the 10 largest EMEs or including offshore financial centers—did not change this picture. The similarity in the pattern of net capital flows across all EME regions suggests that the association between global events and capital flows to EMEs is not driven by only a few systemically important economies.

[19]Appendix 4.3 describes the specifics of the model.

in the 2000s.[20] As a comparison, for AEs, the share explained by common factors is much smaller, hovering at about 10 percent, and lower in the past decade compared with the 1990s.

Within the set of common factors in EMEs, the relative importance of regional factors appears to have increased since the mid-1990s. This could be related to widespread liberalization of capital accounts in many EMEs during the 1990s, the subsequent Asian crisis in the late 1990s, increasing cross-border financial links within emerging Europe since the mid-1990s, and the overall surge in global capital flows since the 1990s, which has had a strong regional component. In particular, the larger weight of regional factors in EMEs than in AEs emphasizes greater sensitivity on the part of cross-border investors to regional differences among EMEs than among AEs.

In conclusion, although common factors appear to be more important for EMEs than AEs in explaining the variation in net flows, the variation is still predominantly explained by economy-specific factors. This provides suggestive evidence in favor of a secular trend of capital flows to recipient economies driven by the economies' structural characteristics. Thus, any formal analysis of the role of global cyclical variables as causes of capital flows must control for these economy-specific characteristics.

## Does Direct Financial Exposure Affect the Response of Net Private Capital Flows to Changes in U.S. Monetary Policy?

This section attempts to estimate how direct financial exposure to the United States affects the impact of U.S. monetary policy changes on net private capital flows to EMEs. Following the literature, we focus on the U.S. policy interest rate as a proxy for global monetary conditions given the systemic importance of the United States in the global economy.[21]

---

[20]These estimates are similar to the findings of Levchenko and Mauro (2007) for a diverse group of EMEs but are lower than those of Calvo, Leiderman, and Reinhart (1993) for Latin America.

[21]That said, a key robustness test separately controls for the changes in the euro area interest rate in the baseline regression (see Appendix 4.4 for details).

**Figure 4.10.  Correlations between Net Flows of Various Types and the Rest of the Financial Account**

*(Pearson correlation coefficient of different flow types in percent of GDP)*

In advanced economies, various types of flow have served as broad substitutes within the financial account—helping dampen the volatility of total net flows. This has not been the case in emerging market and other developing economies.

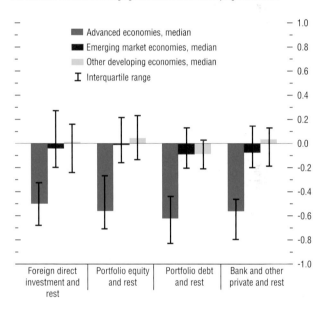

Sources: IMF, *Balance of Payments Statistics;* national sources; and IMF staff calculations.
Note: The vertical bars represent the median correlation (across economies) between the net flows in percent of GDP of a particular type of flow and the remainder of the financial account computed with annual data during 1980–2009. The groups exclude offshore financial centers.

## Figure 4.11. The Persistence of Net Private Capital Flows

*(AR(1) regression coefficients of net private capital flows in percent of GDP)*

The persistence of net private capital flows is generally low, with no significant differences across economy groups. Among the various types, net portfolio debt flows appear to be the least persistent.

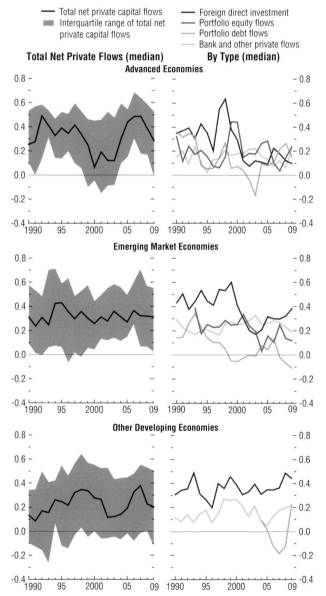

Sources: IMF, *Balance of Payments Statistics;* national sources; and IMF staff calculations.

Note: Using annual data, the persistence of any particular flow is its AR(1) regression coefficient computed over the prior 10-year window for each economy (for example, the 1990 value corresponds to the AR(1) coefficient during 1981–90). The median is plotted only if the AR(1) coefficient for the particular 10-year window and type of flow can be calculated for at least one-fifth of the economies in the group. The groups exclude offshore financial centers.

## Methodology

We adopt a panel regression framework with fixed effects that controls for all time-invariant economy-level idiosyncrasies and structural characteristics. The sample comprises 50 economies (30 EMEs and 20 AEs), with data on capital flows at a quarterly frequency during 1989:Q1–2010:Q3.[22] Although many studies have examined the role of U.S. monetary policy (among other global factors) in driving capital flows to other economies, this chapter builds on the existing literature in two prominent ways.

• It identifies how differences in economies' direct financial exposure to the United States affect the impact of U.S. monetary policy changes on their net capital flows, after controlling for all common events, including any common effect of U.S. monetary policy changes. Previous studies have attempted to estimate the total effect of U.S. monetary policy on capital flows simply by including U.S. interest rates in a selected set of global control variables. By opting to explicitly outline the set of global variables considered, such studies preclude the use of time dummies as a proxy for a general, global common factor.[23] This exposes these analyses to an omitted-variables problem: how can the effects of common events that could have large impacts on capital flows (for example, 1989 Brady Plan, 1997–98 Asian crisis, September 11 terrorist attacks) be distinguished from U.S. monetary policy changes with which they may have coincided? To get around this issue, we first include in the regression time dummies that capture the average effect of all global factors on net flows (including U.S. monetary policy), without identifying what these factors might be. We then exploit the fact that certain economies are more directly financially exposed to the United States than others (see Appendix 4.4), to focus on the narrower question of how differences in direct financial exposure translate into differences in the effect of U.S. monetary policy. Specifically, the change in

[22]The sample size drops due to the unavailability of data on quarterly capital flows, GDP, or domestic explanatory variables for some economies.

[23]Inclusion of both time dummies that control for all time-specific events and other global variables that vary only across time but not across economies would subject the panel regression to a perfect collinearity problem.

U.S. interest rate is multiplied by a measure of each economy's direct U.S. financial exposure to identify the difference in the effect of U.S. monetary policy changes on net flows to financially exposed versus unexposed economies. An economy's U.S. direct financial exposure is measured by the share of its U.S. assets plus liabilities in total external assets plus liabilities.

- The chapter distinguishes between realized and unanticipated changes in U.S. real interest rates, a distinction not yet made in this literature.[24] Because the actual or realized U.S. monetary policy change may be partly anticipated, capital flows may adjust at the time of information arrival—reflecting investors' forward-looking behavior—rather than at the time of the actual (realized) rate change, which would attenuate any estimated effect of monetary policy changes on capital flows. Moreover, if U.S. monetary policy responds countercyclically to U.S. economic developments (which likely exert an independent influence on global flows), then capital flows may be muted in response to U.S. interest rate changes. In order to overcome this problem, we construct a series of unanticipated U.S. monetary policy changes using the approach in Kuttner (2001), aggregating them to quarterly frequency using the method in Bluedorn and Bowdler (2011).[25] To further ensure that the changes in U.S. monetary policy are not confounded with the effects of growth innovations, we also control for surprise in U.S. growth changes.[26]

[24]In the related international finance literature, the effects of U.S. monetary policy volatility or surprises on a variety of variables have been analyzed. These include world stock prices (see Laeven and Tong, 2010), emerging market bond spreads (see Hartelius, Kashiwase, and Kodres, 2008), U.S. capital flows (see Fratzscher, Saborowski, and Straub, 2010), and domestic monetary and exchange rate policies (see Miniane and Rogers, 2007; Bluedorn and Bowdler, 2010).

[25]Specifically, the change in the federal funds futures price (dependent on market expectations of U.S. policy) around scheduled meetings of the Federal Open Market Committee yields the "surprise" or unanticipated component of the realized U.S. policy rate change. These daily changes are then mapped to quarters (see Appendix 4.4 for the details).

[26]To compute the surprise U.S. growth component, we take the difference between the U.S. growth outcome in a given quarter and the one-step-ahead forecast growth taken from the Survey of Professional Forecasters in the previous quarter. These are weighted by the bilateral trade share of each economy with the United States.

**Figure 4.12. Historical Periods of Easy External Financing and High Growth Differential between Emerging Market and Advanced Economies**
*(Deviations from median in percentage points)*

There are two long periods during which easy external financing conditions—low interest rates in the advanced economies and low risk aversion—coincided with high growth differential between emerging market and advanced economies: the run-up to the Asian crisis (1991–96, excluding 1994–95) and the run-up to the global financial crisis (2004–07).

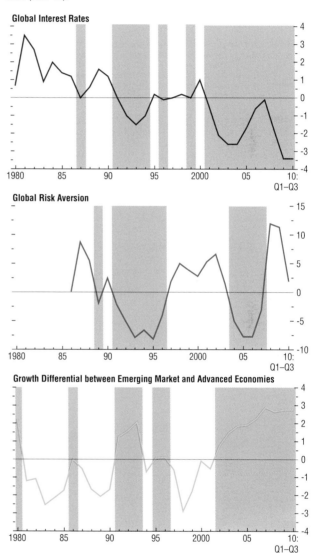

Sources: Haver Analytics; and IMF staff calculations.
Note: Global interest rates are proxied by a GDP-weighted average of the real European Central Bank financing rate (the Bundesbank base rate prior to 1999) and the real U.S. federal funds rate. One-year-ahead expected inflation is subtracted from the nominal rates of each economy to measure the ex ante real interest rates. Global risk aversion is measured by the level of the Chicago Board of Options Exchange Volatility Index (VIX), which proxies for the market's expectation of stock market volatility over the following 30 days. The growth differential between emerging market and advanced economies is measured as the difference between the weighted average real GDP growth rate of each group (excluding offshore financial centers), where the weights are the economy's share in the group aggregate nominal GDP in U.S. dollars. Shaded areas represent periods of easy external financing or high growth differential.

Our baseline reduced-form specification is thus

$$y_{i,t} = \alpha_i + \alpha_t + \sum_{s=0}^{8} \beta_s(\omega_i \times \Delta r_{us,t-s}) \\ + \sum_{s=0}^{8} \lambda_s(\delta_i \times \Delta g_{us,t-s}) + X_{i,t-1}'\gamma + \varepsilon_{i,t}, \qquad (4.1)$$

where $i$ indexes economies and $t$ indexes time (quarterly date); $y_{i,t}$ is the ratio of net capital flows to GDP; $\alpha_i$ represents economy-specific fixed effects and $\alpha_t$ time-fixed effects; $\omega_i$ denotes the U.S. direct financial exposure weight; $\Delta r_{us,t}$ is the U.S. monetary policy change measure—here, either the realized or the unanticipated rate change; $\delta_i$ represents U.S. direct trade exposure weights; $\Delta g_{us,t}$ is the U.S. growth forecast error; $X_{i,t-1}$ is a vector of lagged additional controls including the domestic short-term real (ex post) interest rate, domestic real GDP growth, *International Country Risk Guide* (ICRG) composite risk level, log nominal GDP to control for size and domestic aggregate demand, liquid liabilities to GDP to control for domestic financial market depth (Beck, Demirgüç-Kunt, and Levine, 2000 and 2009), a de facto pegged exchange rate regime indicator (Reinhart and Rogoff, 2004; Ilzetzki, Reinhart, and Rogoff, 2008), and an index of the economy's de jure capital account openness (Chinn and Ito, 2006 and 2008; Aizenman, Chinn, and Ito, 2010); and $\varepsilon_{i,t}$ is a mean zero error term. Therefore, $\beta_0 \times \omega$ represents the difference in the immediate effect of a U.S. monetary policy change on net flows to an economy that has a direct financial exposure of $\omega$ to the United States versus an economy with no direct financial exposure.

## Are Net Capital Flows to Economies with Direct Financial Exposure to the United States Sensitive to U.S. Monetary Policy?

A key finding is that economies with direct financial exposure to the United States experience a negative additional effect on their net flows due to U.S. monetary tightening, over and above what is experienced by economies with no direct U.S. financial exposure. This means the relative impact of U.S. monetary policy changes is stronger (weaker) for economies with greater (lesser) direct financial exposure to the United States. This difference in the effect of U.S. monetary policy is referred to as the "additional" effect throughout, as it is always measured vis-à-vis an economy with no direct U.S. financial

## Figure 4.13. Net Private Capital Flows during Periods of Easy External Financing and High Growth Differential between Emerging Market and Advanced Economies

*(Percent of GDP)*

Net private capital flows to emerging market economies peaked during periods when three conditions prevailed: low global interest rates, low global risk aversion, and high growth differential between emerging market and advanced economies. Flows were generally larger than the year before or after and were largest when all three conditions coincided. The sharpest increase (and subsquent decline) occurred around periods of low risk aversion.

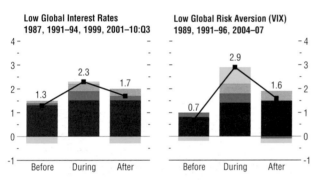

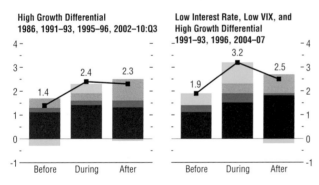

Sources: IMF, *Balance of Payments Statistics*; national sources; and IMF staff calculations.

Note: Net private capital flows exclude derivative flows. The values for each bar correspond to the average across years for each multiyear period during which the condition prevailed, where the annual data are calculated as the sum of net capital flows across economies divided by the sum of nominal GDP (both in U.S. dollars) across the same group of economies. The group aggregates exclude offshore financial centers.

exposure. Moreover, the additional impact of monetary policy estimated using unanticipated changes is larger than the corresponding impact estimated using an equivalent realized rate change (Figure 4.16). For the full sample, for an economy with average direct financial exposure to the United States (about 16 percent), a 1 standard deviation unanticipated rise in the U.S. real interest rate—approximately equivalent to 5 basis points—causes a statistically significant additional reduction in net flows on the order of ½ percentage point of GDP in the first quarter. When cumulated, this increases to 1¼ percentage points of GDP after two years.[27] The cumulated effect shows the cumulative difference in the dynamic effects of a permanent U.S. rate hike on net flows for an economy with average financial exposure to the United States relative to an economy with no direct financial exposure. These additional effects are much weaker for an equivalent realized rate change (12 basis point increase), reducing relative net flows by less than one-tenth of a percentage point of GDP on impact and about ½ percentage point of GDP after two years. The reason may be that, when U.S. monetary policy changes come as a surprise, forward-looking investors may undertake a greater reassessment of the prospective returns from alternative cross-border investments because of changing expectations about the future path of U.S. policy and its economy. Such surprise policy changes thus trigger a sharper portfolio rebalancing (and hence a sharper change in net flows)

---

[27]The uncumulated impulse responses show the additional effect of a temporary U.S. policy rate rise on net flows for an economy at the sample's average direct financial exposure to the United States (0.16 for the full sample, 0.17 for EMEs, and 0.14 for AEs) relative to an economy with no direct financial exposure. The cumulated responses show the cumulative difference in the effect when the U.S. rate hike is permanent over the next eight quarters (for the economy with average direct financial exposure to the United States relative to an economy with no direct financial exposure). Given that U.S. interest rates are currently at historically low levels, the cumulated additional response corresponding to a permanent U.S. rate change appear more relevant, and these are therefore the focus of the remaining part of the regression analysis. That said, the long-term additional effect of a U.S. monetary policy change is considered significant when the sum of the partial coefficients corresponding to eight lags on the U.S. variable is statistically significant, whether driven by the statistical significance of each individual quarter leading up to two years or driven by only some of them.

**Figure 4.14.  Net Private Flows to Emerging Market Economies under Alternative Financing Conditions**
*(Percent of GDP)*

Net capital flows to emerging market economies tended to be strongest when global monetary and risk conditions were both slack, whereas under high risk aversion (but low global interest rates), flows were only marginally above net flows when both conditions were tight.

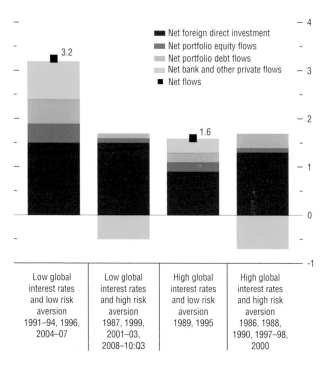

Sources: IMF, *Balance of Payments Statistics*; national sources; and IMF staff calculations.
Note: Net private capital flows exclude derivative flows. The values for each bar correspond to the average across years for each multiyear period during which the condition prevailed, where the annual data are calculated as the sum of net capital flows across economies divided by the sum of nominal GDP (both in U.S. dollars) across the same group of economies. The group aggregates exclude offshore financial centers.

## Figure 4.15. Common Factors Underlying the Variation in Net Private Capital Flows to Advanced and Emerging Market Economies

*(R–squared)*

Global and regional factors explain only a small share of the variation in net private capital flows to advanced and emerging market economies, underscoring the importance of economy-specific factors. However, the share explained by regional factors in emerging market economies has increased over time, suggesting a greater sensitivity on the part of foreign investors to regional differences among emerging market economies than among advanced economies.

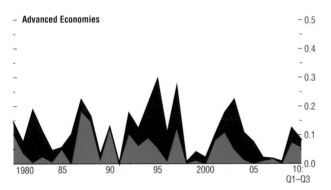

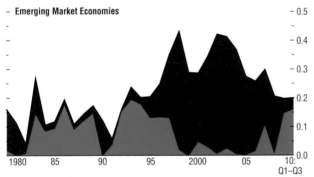

Sources: IMF, *Balance of Payments Statistics*; national sources; and IMF staff calculations.

Note: The blue area corresponds to the share of variation in net flows in percent of GDP across economies within each group that is explained by global factors (time dummies) relative to a specification with only a constant (without time dummies). The red area corresponds to the additional variation of net flows in percent of GDP explained by regional factors (regional time dummies). The black line is the total variation in net flows jointly explained by global and regional factors. Both samples exclude offshore financial centers. For additional information on the estimation procedure, see Appendix 4.3.

among economies that are directly financially exposed to the United States.

The negative additional effect of U.S. monetary policy tightening continues to hold for the subsample comprising only EMEs and the subsample with only AEs excluding the United States. In both subsamples, the additional effect of an unanticipated rate change exceeds that of a realized rate change, confirming that focusing only on realized rate changes results in an underestimation of the impact of U.S. monetary policy changes on net flows to economies that are directly financially exposed to the United States. For an EME with average direct financial exposure to the United States (17 percent), an unanticipated rate change entails an immediate additional fall of ½ percentage point of GDP, cumulating to 2 percentage points of GDP after two years (compared with an EME with no direct financial exposure to the United States). These short- and long-term additional effects are both statistically significant. Again, the cumulated additional effect is smaller (½ percentage point of GDP) for a realized rate change, although statistically significant after the first year. The immediate and cumulated additional effects on net flows to financially exposed AEs are similar to those for EMEs.

The above results hold up under a number of robustness tests, which are discussed in more detail in Appendix 4.4. These include estimating an explicitly dynamic model that includes lagged values of net capital flows as regressors; restricting the sample to the largest 10 economies; including offshore financial centers in the sample; adding more control variables (such as euro area growth forecast errors, euro area real interest rate changes, global risk-aversion changes); introducing a structural break in 1997; and estimating the model for the period before 2008. The core result continues to hold—there is a negative additional effect on capital flows to EMEs that are directly financially exposed to the United States from a tightening in U.S. monetary policy compared with those that have no direct U.S. financial exposure. In particular, this sensitivity holds up even after the late 1990s, a period that witnessed major changes in global capital markets (as documented in Chapter 2 of the April 2007 *Global Financial Stability Report*).

Some of the other notable relationships between capital flows to EMEs and the domestic control variables include a positive association between net flows and real GDP growth, size of the economy (which proxies for the role of domestic demand), financial depth, lower risk levels, and pegged regimes, although only the first two relationships are statistically significant (see Appendix 4.4). Surprisingly, net flows to EMEs are negatively correlated with real domestic interest rates. This could reflect EMEs' experience with sudden stops or reversals in capital flows that occur even when EME policymakers raise domestic interest rates to prevent a turnaround in net flows. Indeed, there is no negative relationship between net flows and domestic real interest rates for AEs, which have historically experienced fewer financial crises.[28]

### Does the Sensitivity of Capital Flows to U.S. Monetary Policy Depend on the Characteristics of the Recipient Economy?

This section investigates whether the additional effect of U.S. monetary policy changes on net flows to EMEs that are directly financially exposed to the United States is sensitive to the structural and economic characteristics of these economies. Specifically, we examine how the additional effects vary according to differences in integration with global financial markets, domestic financial depth, foreign exchange rate regime, and domestic economic growth. It is important to stress that the results should not be interpreted as assigning a causal role to these structural and economic characteristics on the sensitivity of net flows to EMEs to U.S. monetary policy. For each specific characteristic, the results show the additional effects (immediate

---

[28]Unlike studies that find an important role for U.S. real activity in driving flows to developing economies (see Mody, Taylor, and Kim, 2001), our results suggest that a U.S. growth surprise does not significantly affect net flows to economies with a direct trade exposure to the United States. This result continues to hold if the U.S. growth surprise is complemented by a growth forecast error from the euro area. This finding is more in line with Taylor and Sarno (1997) and Calvo, Leiderman, and Reinhart (1993), who find a bigger role for U.S. monetary policy than for U.S. real activity indicators.

### Figure 4.16. Difference in the Response of Net Private Capital Flows to U.S. Monetary Tightening across Economies
*(Percent of GDP)*

An unanticipated U.S. monetary tightening has an immediate and statistically significant negative additional effect on net flows to economies that are directly financially exposed to the United States compared with economies that are not. The additional impact under a realized U.S. rate hike is much smaller.

— Unanticipated rise in U.S. monetary policy rate
— Realized rise in U.S. monetary policy rate

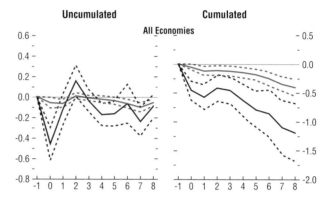

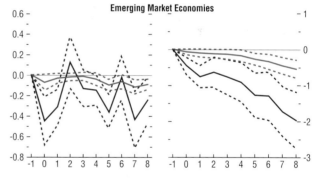

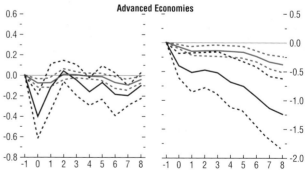

Source: IMF staff calculations.
Note: See Appendix 4.1 for the sample of economies included in the analysis. The dependent variable is total net private capital flows in percent of GDP. The x-axis shows the number of quarters after an impulse. Impulses at quarter zero are normalized to a 1 standard deviation unanticipated rate rise for the economy at the group's average financial exposure. The underlying impulse is indicated in the legend. Dashed lines indicate one standard error bands. The regression specification and the set of control variables are given in Appendix 4.4.

and cumulated) on net flows to an economy with average direct financial exposure to the United States compared with net flows to an economy that has no direct U.S. financial exposure.

### The role of financial globalization

The negative additional effect of an unanticipated tightening in U.S. monetary policy tends to be stronger for EMEs that are more integrated with global financial markets (Figure 4.17, first and second columns). Financial globalization is proxied by two measures—greater capital account openness and greater foreign penetration (holdings) in the domestic debt market. There is a sharp negative additional effect of U.S. rate hikes on financially integrated economies, whereas the additional effect on economies that are less globalized is not statistically significant.[29] Realized rate changes resemble unanticipated rate changes in terms of their additional effects on net flows but are of smaller magnitude.

### The role of domestic financial depth/ intermediation

Net flows to directly financially exposed EMEs with low domestic financial depth are more sensitive to U.S. rate changes than others (Figures 4.17, third column). For both types of economies—those with higher and lower financial depth—U.S. rate hikes have a negative additional impact on net flows. But this additional effect is statistically significant only for economies with lower financial depth. This result is surprising if one expects financial depth to be correlated with financial globalization. The sensitivity of net flows to U.S. rate hikes in financially shallow economies could reflect the behavior of domestic investors (that is, gross outflows) rather than foreign investors (gross inflows), given that the latter will likely be low in financially shallow economies (Calderon and Kubota, 2009). Note, however, that the measure for financial depth is not tantamount to financial openness but proxies the size of domestic financial intermediation (Beck, Demirgüç-Kunt, and Levine, 2000 and 2009). In fact, some large

economies—for example, China and India—with proportionately larger financial sectors (but closed capital accounts) also belong to this group.

### The role of the exchange rate regime

The additional response of net flows to U.S. monetary policy tightening in directly financially exposed economies with nonpegged exchange rate regimes is sharper than in those with pegged regimes (Figure 4.17, fourth column).[30] In particular, for relatively flexible regimes, an unanticipated U.S. rate hike has a negative additional effect on net flows that is significant in the long term. The corresponding effect of a realized rate increase is significant in the short and long term but is of a smaller magnitude. For pegged regimes, the initial and cumulated additional effects are never statistically significant, whether or not U.S. rate hikes are unanticipated.

The disparate experiences of peggers and others could reflect a number of factors. First, several economies in the sample that had relatively pegged exchange rate regimes over the sample period also had relatively more closed capital accounts during this period (for example, Argentina, Morocco, Russia, and a majority of Asian economies). Conversely, several of the nonpeggers also have relatively open capital accounts (for example, Brazil, Indonesia, Mexico). Second, as a caveat, a nonpegged regime need not imply that the exchange rate path itself is fully flexible—for instance, if the exchange rate is managed, then the lack of sufficient exchange rate adjustment could give rise to a one-way bet and exaggerate the consequent adjustment in capital flows.

### The role of domestic economic growth

Directly financially exposed economies with relatively weak growth performance appear to face a sharper negative additional effect of an unanticipated U.S. monetary tightening (Figure 4.17, right column). In contrast, the additional impact of unan-

[29]This result also supports the findings of Milesi-Ferretti and Tille (2010) that economies with a high degree of financial integration experienced deeper declines in capital inflows during the global financial crisis. Examples of economies in the sample with high financial openness using both measures include Hungary and Peru.

[30]Pegged regimes are defined as those without a separate legal tender or where the exchange rate is fixed by a currency board or a fixed or crawling peg arrangement under which the exchange rate (or the band around it) does not move more than ±2 percent. This corresponds to categories 1 and 2 in Reinhart and Rogoff's de facto exchange rate classification (2004). All other regimes, which are likely more flexible, are defined as nonpegged.

## Figure 4.17.  Difference in the Response of Emerging Market Economy Net Private Capital Flows to U.S. Monetary Tightening by Selected Economic Characteristics
*(Percent of GDP)*

The sensitivity of net flows to an unanticipated U.S. monetary tightening is greater for directly financially exposed emerging market economies that are more globally financially integrated and have shallower financial markets, more flexible exchange rates, or lower domestic growth (compared with financially unexposed economies). A similar pattern holds for the sensitivity of net flows in response to a realized U.S. monetary tightening.

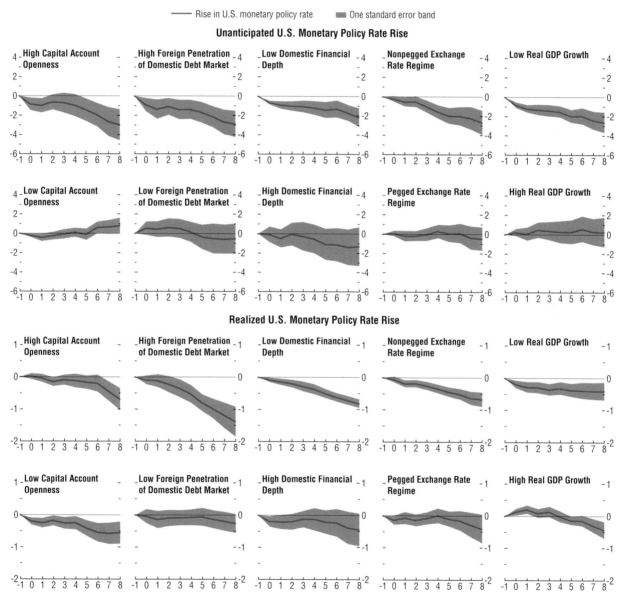

Source: IMF staff calculations.
  Note: See Appendix 4.1 for the sample of emerging market economies. The dependent variable is total net private capital flows in percent of GDP, for emerging market economies with the selected characteristic. Sample splits are based on being above or below the median for the characteristic. The x-axis shows the number of quarters after an impulse. The impulse at quarter zero is a permanent U.S. monetary policy rate rise, normalized to a 1 standard deviation unanticipated rate rise for the economy at the group's average financial exposure. The regression specification and the set of control variables are given in Appendix 4.4.

ticipated U.S. rate hikes on net capital flows is not significant for directly financially exposed economies with strong growth performance. Economies with strong growth may be adopting the right mix of macroeconomic and prudential policies to attract capital flows, which offsets the negative additional effect of U.S. unanticipated rate hikes. The opposite may be true for low-growth economies.

These findings illustrate how the average additional effect of U.S. rate hikes on net flows to EMEs that are directly financially exposed to the United States masks important differences within the sample. Unlike AEs—which are more homogeneous in terms of their structural characteristics (with most economies characterized as having open financial markets, flexible exchange rate regimes, and financial depth)—EMEs are much more diverse. That diversity, combined with the differences in their direct financial exposure to the United States, yields the differential responses to U.S. monetary policy changes.

### Do Different Types of Flow Respond Differently to U.S. Monetary Policy?

The negative additional effect of an increase in the U.S. interest rate on net capital flows is most pronounced for portfolio debt flows and statistically significant in the short and long term with the unanticipated rate change (Figure 4.18). For FDI and bank and other private flows, the additional impact of U.S. monetary tightening on net flows to directly financially exposed EMEs is negative but not always statistically significant. Finally, equity flows are not sensitive to changes in U.S. monetary policy. The relatively higher sensitivity of FDI to U.S. monetary policy, after portfolio debt flows, could reflect an increasing share of financial FDI over time in directly financially exposed economies, which behaves more like debt-creating flows (Ostry and others, 2010).

### Does the Global Economic Environment Affect the Impact of U.S. Monetary Policy on Net Flows to Directly Financially Exposed Economies?

A finding most relevant to the world's current circumstances is that the additional effect of U.S. interest rate changes on capital flows to economies

**Figure 4.18. Difference in the Response of Emerging Market Economy Net Private Capital Flows to U.S. Monetary Tightening by Type of Flow**

*(Percent of GDP)*

The negative additional effect of an unanticipated U.S. monetary tightening on net flows to directly financially exposed emerging market economies is most evident for portfolio debt flows and absent for portfolio equity flows. Foreign direct investment shows a strong additional response, whereas the responses of bank and other private flows are delayed. For a realized U.S. monetary tightening, only foreign direct investment shows a strong additional response.

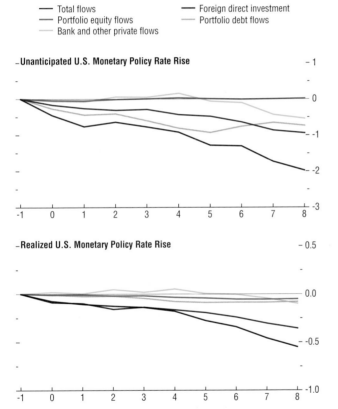

Source: IMF staff calculations.
Note: See Appendix 4.1 for the sample of emerging market economies. The dependent variable is total net private capital flows in percent of GDP. The x-axis shows the number of quarters after an impulse. The impulse at quarter zero is a permanent U.S. monetary policy rate rise, normalized to a 1 standard deviation unanticipated rate rise for the economy at the group's average financial exposure. The regression specification and the set of control variables are given in Appendix 4.4.

that are directly financially exposed to the United States is deeper when global financial conditions—both interest rates and risk aversion—are relatively easy. For a typical EME with an average direct financial exposure, the additional effect of an unanticipated U.S. rate increase in a low-interest-rate environment is more protracted than under the baseline (Figure 4.19). This result implies that the current global economic environment, whereby loose U.S. monetary conditions—sustained via interest rate cuts and quantitative easing—would induce greater sensitivity of net capital flows to financially exposed EMEs to U.S. monetary policy changes. During periods of low risk aversion, the effect is even sharper and statistically significant in the short and long term. Finally, the additional impact of U.S. rate hikes on net flows is deepest in an underlying environment of both low global interest rates and low risk aversion, with the effect again statistically significant in the short and long term. These results could reflect the fact that capital flows are more prone to respond to return-chasing incentives when global financial asset returns are generally low while the appetite for taking risks is high (low risk aversion) and relate to the recent literature highlighting the role of global risk perception in driving capital flow volatility and sudden stops and surges.[31] The additional effects of a realized rate change are also similar under the alternative circumstances, although with smaller magnitudes and significant only in the long term.

In summary, economies directly financially exposed to the United States experience a negative additional impact on their net capital flows because of U.S. monetary tightening that is proportional to their level of exposure. The estimated additional effect is larger when the U.S. policy change is measured by the unanticipated component of the corresponding U.S. interest rate move, while the effect is underestimated when U.S. policy changes are proxied with the actual or realized rate change. The additional negative effect of a U.S. rate hike may be stronger in the current environment of relatively

[31]For example, see Forbes and Warnock (2010) and the IMF's May 2010 *Regional Economic Outlook* for the Western Hemisphere.

### Figure 4.19. Difference in the Response of Emerging Market Economy Net Private Capital Flows to U.S. Monetary Tightening under Alternative Global Economic Conditions

*(Percent of GDP)*

The underlying macroeconomic background plays an important role in determining the responsiveness of net flows to U.S. rate hikes for emerging markets with direct financial exposure to the United States. Compared with the baseline, the additional fall in net flows is deeper during periods with low global interest rates, even more during periods of low global risk aversion, and finally, the deepest when both global interest rates and risk aversion are low.

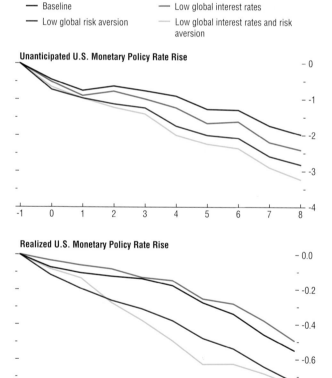

Source: IMF staff calculations.
Note: See Appendix 4.1 for the sample of emerging market economies. The dependent variable is total net private capital flows in percent of GDP. The *x*-axis shows the number of quarters after an impulse. The impulse at quarter zero is a permanent U.S. monetary policy rate rise, normalized to a 1 standard deviation unanticipated rate rise for the economy at the group's average financial exposure. The regression specification and the set of control variables are given in Appendix 4.4. The low global interest rates and low risk aversion periods are taken from Figure 4.12. See the main text for full details on the selection of the periods.

loose global monetary conditions and low global risk aversion. Also, differences in financial openness, financial depth, exchange rate regime, and economic growth among directly financially exposed EMEs are associated with different sensitivities of net flows to U.S. monetary policy changes.

## Policy Implications and Conclusions

Net capital flows are generally fickle from domestic policymakers' point of view. Flows have become more volatile over time, and their persistence has generally been low. EMEs tend to experience greater overall capital flow volatility than AEs. Bank and other private flows across economies are the most volatile and portfolio debt the least persistent, but the statistical properties across the remaining types of flow are not distinguishable. Historically, changes in global financing conditions were associated with temporary tides of net flows to EMEs, with flows rising during periods of low global interest rates and risk aversion and falling afterward. Finally, using a novel identification strategy, the analysis indicates that economies that have a direct foreign financial exposure to the United States experience an additional decline in their net capital flows in response to U.S. monetary tightening over and above what is experienced by economies that have no such exposure. This additional impact is larger when the changes in the U.S. policy rate are unanticipated and if they occur in an environment of low global interest rates and low risk aversion.

How should the above results inform policymakers' expectations? First, given the direct financial exposure of most economies vis-à-vis the United States (some large, some small), it is reasonable to expect that eventual monetary tightening in the United States will have a negative additional impact on their capital flows, especially in an environment of low global interest rates and risk aversion. The extent of the impact will depend on the degree of their direct financial exposure to the United States. Second, the variability of capital flows is pervasive across all economies and will likely continue in a climate of increasing financial globalization. Whether and by how much net

flows to economies would actually change at any given time will depend on the overall effect of all other drivers, including any common effect of U.S. monetary policy change, and on whether or not the change in U.S. monetary policy is anticipated.

How should policymakers manage volatile capital flows? Notwithstanding the benefits of financial globalization, the recent literature stresses its associated risks (Kose and others, 2006) and also highlights the importance of deep and liquid domestic financial markets (*Global Financial Stability Report,* October 2007), greater exchange rate flexibility and prudential regulation (*Global Financial Stability Report,* April 2010), fiscal restraint (*World Economic Outlook,* October 2007), and strong institutions (Papaioannou, 2009) to reduce these risks. In the face of variable capital flows, as documented in this chapter, the key is to ameliorate their impact on domestic economic and financial stability. In particular, as discussed in Chapter 1 of this *World Economic Outlook* and in IMF (2011), it is important to adopt strong macroeconomic policies, prudential financial supervision, and other macroprudential measures to sustain strong growth and better cope with the restive nature of capital flows.

## Appendix 4.1. Classification of Economies and Data Sources

### Classification of Economies

We started with the largest possible sample of economies with data on capital flows (see below for sources). Economies are included in the annual (quarterly) sample if they have at least 10 (5) years of data on capital flows and GDP. The advanced economies (AEs) in the sample correspond to the IMF 1990 *World Economic Outlook* (WEO) definition of industrial economies. For emerging market economies (EMEs), in the absence of an official definition, we take the same sample of emerging market and developing economies used in the regional analysis in Chapter 2 of the *World Economic Outlook* under emerging Asia, emerging Europe, Latin America and the Caribbean, Commonwealth of Independent States (CIS), Middle East and North Africa, and sub-Saharan Africa, but exclude relatively low-income economies (eligible for assistance under the IMF's Poverty Reduction and Growth Trust) and those that are relatively small (with nominal GDP in U.S. dollars averaged over 1990–2009 of less than the median GDP based on all developing and emerging market economies in the sample). This results in a sample of EMEs that are largely covered by the universe of external sources, such as Morgan Stanley Capital International, *The Economist,* and Dow Jones & Company. In addition, economies that are classified as AEs today but were not in 1990 are included in the sample of EMEs. These economies include Cyprus, the Czech Republic, Malta, Estonia, the Slovak Republic, Slovenia, and the newly industrialized Asian economies. All non-emerging-market and non-advanced economies are defined as other developing economies. The statistical analyses, event studies, and regressions exclude offshore financial centers as defined by the Financial Stability Forum (Table 2 in IMF, 2000). These economies include Antigua and Barbuda, Bahrain, Barbados, Belize, Costa Rica, Cyprus, Hong Kong SAR, Lebanon, Luxembourg, Malta, Mauritius, Panama, Seychelles, Singapore, St. Kitts and Nevis, St. Lucia, St. Vincent and the Grenadines, Switzerland, and Vanuatu. To ensure comparability over time, the descriptive analysis, event studies, and global factor model are based on a constant set of economies, with the exception of central and eastern European and CIS economies, which are included starting in 1994. Because data availability differs depending on the time horizon and frequency level, the set of economies included in the various figures may differ slightly. The analytical and regional groupings of economies are presented in Table 4.1.

## Data Sources

The chapter uses primarily the IMF's Balance of Payments Statistics (BPS), WEO, and International Financial Statistics (IFS) databases. Additional data sources are listed in Table 4.2.

Annual data on capital flows are taken from the IMF BPS database. In particular, net private capital flows correspond to the sum of net foreign direct investment flows (line 4500), net portfolio flows (line 4600), net derivative flows (line 4910), and net other investment flows (line 4700), excluding other investment flows to the general government and monetary authorities. Gross and net capital flows, as well as their components, are reported in nominal U.S. dollars and are normalized by nominal GDP in U.S. dollars. The latter series is taken from the World Bank World Development Indicators database and extended with data from the WEO database.

Quarterly data on capital flows are also primarily taken from the IMF BPS database and extended with data from other sources, such as Haver Analytics, the CEIC EMED database, and national sources (China and Australia). Quarterly nominal GDP (not seasonally adjusted) series in local currency and the average nominal exchange rate vis-à-vis the U.S. dollar are extracted from the IFS and are extended with alternative sources when needed.

Global real interest rates are proxied by a GDP-weighted average of the real European Central Bank financing rate (and the Bundesbank base rate prior to 1999) and the real U.S. federal funds rate, all taken from Haver Analytics. The one-quarter-ahead expected inflation rate used to construct the ex ante real rate for the United States corresponds to the forecasts of the GDP deflator change from the Survey of Professional Forecasters, published by the Federal Reserve Bank of Philadelphia, whereas the ex ante real rate for Europe is calculated using the one-year-ahead forecast of consumer price index inflation from *Consensus Forecasts.* Global risk aversion is measured by the Chicago Board of Options Exchange Volatility Index level.

We use two measures to track changes in U.S. monetary policy: the realized changes are constructed from the St. Louis Federal Reserve's FRED database, series DFF at a daily frequency, and the unanticipated changes are constructed from data on the daily settlement prices of the Chicago Board of Trade's federal funds futures contracts from Datastream, series CFF. The change in one-quarter-ahead expected inflation from the Survey of Professional Forecasters is subtracted from the realized nominal rate change to derive the real rate change used. See Appendix 4.4 for more details on

## Table 4.1. Economy Groupings

| Advanced Economies | Emerging Asia | Other Emerging Economies | Other Developing Economies |
|---|---|---|---|
| United States (111)* | Sri Lanka (524) | South Africa (199)*† | Bolivia (218) |
| United Kingdom (112)*† | Taiwan Province of China (528)* | Israel (436)*† | Haiti (263) |
| Austria (122)*† | Hong Kong SAR (532)* | Jordan (439)*† | Honduras (268) |
| Belgium (124)*† | India (534)*† | Kuwait (443) | Nicaragua (278) |
| Denmark (128)*† | Indonesia (536)*† | Lebanon (446) | Paraguay (288) |
| France (132)*† | Korea (542)*† | Oman (449) | Antigua and Barbuda (311) |
| Germany (134)*† | Malaysia (548)*† | Saudi Arabia (456) | Barbados (316) |
| Italy (136)*† | Philippines (566)*† | Syrian Arab Republic (463) | Dominica (321) |
| Luxembourg (137)* | Singapore (576)* | United Arab Emirates (466) | Grenada (328) |
| Netherlands (138)*† | Thailand (578)*† | Egypt (469)*† | Jamaica (343) |
| Norway (142)*† | China (924)*† | Pakistan (564) | St. Kitts and Nevis (361) |
| Sweden (144)*† | | Algeria (612) | St. Lucia (362) |
| Switzerland (146)* | **Emerging Latin America** | Libya (672) | St. Vincent and the Grenadines (364) |
| Canada (156)*† | Argentina (213)*† | Morocco (686)*† | Suriname (366) |
| Japan (158)*† | Brazil (223)*† | Tunisia (744) | Bahrain (419) |
| Finland (172)*† | Chile (228)*† | Azerbaijan (912) | Bangladesh (513) |
| Greece (174)*† | Colombia (233)*† | Belarus (913)* | Maldives (556) |
| Iceland (176)*† | Costa Rica (238)* | Kazakhstan (916)* | Nepal (558) |
| Ireland (178)*† | Dominican Republic (243) | Russia (922)*† | Vietnam (582) |
| Portugal (182)*† | Ecuador (248)*† | Ukraine (926)*† | Botswana (616) |
| Spain (184)*† | El Salvador (253)*† | | Cameroon (622) |
| Australia (193)*† | Guatemala (258)*† | | Cape Verde (624) |
| New Zealand (196)*† | Mexico (273)*† | | Ethiopia (644) |
| | Panama (283) | | Ghana (652) |
| | Peru (293)*† | | Côte d'Ivoire (662) |
| | Uruguay (298)*† | | Kenya (664) |
| | Venezuela (299) | | Lesotho (666) |
| | | | Mauritius (684) |
| | **Emerging Europe** | | Mozambique (688) |
| | Malta (181)* | | Nigeria (694) |
| | Turkey (186)*† | | Rwanda (714) |
| | Cyprus (423)* | | Seychelles (718) |
| | Bulgaria (918)*† | | Sierra Leone (724) |
| | Czech Republic (935)*† | | Swaziland (734) |
| | Slovak Republic (936)* | | Tanzania (738) |
| | Estonia (939)* | | Uganda (746) |
| | Latvia (941)* | | Solomon Islands (813) |
| | Hungary (944)*† | | Fiji (819) |
| | Lithuania (946)* | | Papua New Guinea (853) |
| | Croatia (960)* | | Albania (914) |
| | Slovenia (961)* | | |
| | Poland (964)*† | | |
| | Romania (968)*† | | |

Note: See Appendix 4.1 for details on the economy groupings. The numbers in parentheses after the economy name denote the economy's IFS code. * indicates advanced and emerging market economies included in the analysis at a quarterly frequency. † indicates economies included in the quarterly regression sample (smaller due to unavailability of domestic explanatory variables for some economies).

## Table 4.2. Data Sources

| Variable | Source |
| --- | --- |
| Annual | |
| Capital Flows (net; gross assets and liabilities) | Balance of Payments Statistics (BPS) Database, National Sources |
| Nominal GDP in U.S. Dollars | World Bank World Development Indicators (WDI) Database, World Economic Outlook (WEO) Database |
| Liquid Liabilities | Beck, Demirgüç-Kunt, and Levine (2000, 2009) |
| Bilateral Exports and Imports | Direction of Trade Statistics Database |
| Capital Account Openness Index | Chinn and Ito (2006, 2008) |
| Exchange Rate Regime Indicator | Reinhart and Rogoff (2004); Ilzetzki, Reinhart, and Rogoff (2008) |
| Foreign Penetration in Debt Market | Bank for International Settlements Database |
| External Assets and Liabilities | BPS Database: IMF International Investment Position Statistics |
| Quarterly | |
| Capital Flows (net; gross assets and liabilities) | BPS Database, Haver Analytics, CEIC, National Sources |
| Nominal GDP in U.S. Dollars | International Financial Statistics (IFS) Database, Haver Analytics, CEIC EMED Database, National Sources |
| Real GDP growth (year over year) | WEO database |
| Federal Funds Futures Contract Settlement Prices | Chicago Board of Trade, Datastream (series CFF) |
| Realized U.S. Interest Rate | Federal Reserve (FRED series DFF) |
| U.S. Growth Forecast | Federal Reserve Bank of Philadelphia Survey of Professional Forecasters |
| U.S. External Assets and Liabilities on a Bilateral Basis | U.S. Treasury International Capital System Database, Bureau of Economic Analysis Foreign Direct Investment Statistics |
| Short-Term Interest Rate | Haver Analytics (G-10, EMERGE, IFS), Eurostat, Datastream |
| Consumer Price Index | IFS Database |
| Composite Risk Level | PRS Group International Country Risk Guide |
| Investors' Risk Aversion | Chicago Board of Options Exchange Volatility Index, Haver Analytics |
| European Central Bank Financing Rate | Haver Analytics |
| Bundesbank Base Rate | Haver Analytics |

the construction of the unanticipated and realized changes in the U.S. federal funds rate.

Data on direct financial exposure to the United States, used to construct economy-specific weights (which are interacted with U.S. monetary policy measures for the regression analysis), are from three sources: (1) the U.S. Treasury International Capital System (TICS) database on bilateral assets and liabilities of the United States vis-à-vis other countries; (2) U.S. Bureau of Economic Analysis (BEA) Foreign Direct Investment (FDI) Statistics; and (3) the IMF's International Investment Position (IIP) statistics from the BPS database. The U.S. TICS database contains information on the U.S. bilateral international asset and liability positions for all instruments covered in the BPS, except for FDI information, which is collected by the BEA. These bilateral series are used to construct the numerator of the weight; the denominator is constructed using the external asset and liability positions by economy, taken from the IMF IIP. See

Appendix 4.4 for full details on how the weights are constructed.

Two series are used to compute the U.S. growth forecast error. For any given quarter, the U.S. growth forecast corresponds to the median forecast from the previous quarter for the current quarter's seasonally adjusted, quarter-over-quarter real GDP growth rate from the Survey of Professional Forecasters. The actual seasonally adjusted, real quarter-over-quarter GDP growth rate is taken from the WEO database. Direct trade exposure to the United States (which is interacted with growth surprises in the United States) is constructed from the IMF Direction of Trade Statistics (DOTS) database. It is the sum of an economy's exports to and imports from the United States divided by total imports and exports of the economy. The trade exposure weights used in the regression analysis correspond to the average of the above weights between 2000 and 2009.

Domestic short-term nominal interest rates are from Haver Analytics (G-10, EMERGE, IFS), Eurostat, Datastream, and IMF IFS databases. Year-over-year inflation is calculated from consumer price indices in the IMF IFS database and subtracted from the short-term rates to derive an ex post real rate. Nominal interest rate series are adjusted to exclude periods during which interest rates appeared to be set administratively. In addition, periods of hyperinflation, defined as year-over-year consumer price index growth rates greater than 100 percent, are not included in the analysis. The domestic year-over-year real GDP growth series are taken from the WEO database, and the composite risk rating of the country is the average of the political, economic, and financial risk rating from the *International Country Risk Guide*. The liquid liabilities series are taken from the Financial Structure Database (Beck, Demirgüç-Kunt, and Levine, 2000 and 2009) and extended until 2010 using the growth rate of broad money from the IMF IFS database and other sources. The degree of capital account openness is measured using the Chinn and Ito (2008) index of openness of capital account transactions, constructed from the IMF's *Annual Report on Exchange Arrangements and Exchange Restrictions*. The de facto exchange rate regime is taken from Reinhart and Rogoff (2004), updated with Ilzetzki, Reinhart, and Rogoff (2008). The series on capital account openness and exchange rate regime were available until 2008 and 2007, respectively, and were extended until 2009 under the assumption that there were no changes from their last recorded values. Finally, the series of foreign penetration in domestic debt markets is measured as the ratio of domestically issued debt held by foreigners divided by the sum of total domestically issued debt from the Bank for International Settlements database (Tables 11 and 16A).[32]

---

[32]We thank Gian Maria Milesi-Ferretti for sharing the data on foreign penetration in domestic debt markets.

## Appendix 4.2. Composition, Volatility, and Persistence of Net Private Capital Flows across Emerging Market Regions

We examine the composition, volatility, and persistence of net capital flows over time across the different emerging market regions, as defined in Appendix 4.1. These are measured as discussed in the main text.

### Composition

The trend decline in net bank and other private flows that was observed for emerging market economies—EMEs (see Figure 4.7) is more prominent in emerging Asia and, to some extent, Latin America (Figure 4.20). In emerging Europe, the share of net bank and other private flows actually increased in the 2000s, whereas in other emerging economies, it increased in the 1990s but fell in the 2000s.

### Volatility

Historically, there have been no systematic differences in the volatility of total net private capital flows across the various emerging market regions (Figure 4.21). Flows to emerging Asia appear to have had the lowest volatility over the past 30 years relative to those of the remaining regions, but the differences in volatility are not statistically significant. Only recently (starting in 1996) does there appear to be a relative rise in the volatility of total net flows to the other emerging economies, perhaps related to their relatively gradual shift away from debt-creating flows. The rise in the volatility of net flows to these economies, as well as the marginally higher volatility of net flows to emerging Europe, appears to underlie the small increase in volatility of net flows to EMEs discussed in the text and illustrated in Figure 4.9.

### Persistence

The persistence of total net flows, measured as the AR(1) regression coefficient of total net private capital flows in percent of GDP, also does not appear to vary substantially across the four emerging market regions (Figure 4.22). Net flows to emerging Asian economies appear to have been the most persistent, whereas net flows to the other emerging economies have been the least persistent, but these differences are not statistically significant. Most notably, the persistence of flows to the median economy in each region has become more similar over time.

## Appendix 4.3. Global Factor Model

The following two models are estimated using cross-sectional ordinary least squares to identify the influence of (1) global factors and (2) global and regional factors on the variation in net capital flows to emerging market economies (EMEs) in any given year:[33]

$$\text{Global factor model:} \quad y_{i,t} = \alpha_t + \varepsilon_{i,t} \qquad (4.2)$$

Global and regional factor model:
$$y_{i,t} = \alpha_t + \sum_{j=1}^{4} \beta_t^{(j)} D_j + \varepsilon_{i,t}, \qquad (4.3)$$

where $y_{i,t}$ is the level of net capital flows (scaled by GDP) in economy $i$ at time $t$; $\alpha_t$ is a time dummy capturing the common global factor across all EMEs ($i$) at time $t$; $\beta_t^{(j)}$ is the regional factor common to all economies within region ($j$) at time $t$; $D_j$ is a dummy for region $j$; and $\varepsilon_{i,t}$ is a mean zero error term.

The models are estimated for a sample of 20 AEs in each year: the 23 economies listed in Table 4.1, excluding Belgium because of lack of data, and the financial centers, Luxembourg and Switzerland. For EMEs, the models are estimated for each year between 1980 and 1993 for 36 economies—the 59 economies listed in Table 4.2, excluding eastern Europe, the Commonwealth of Independent States (CIS), the financial centers, and other countries for which data are lacking.[34] For every year after 1994,

---

[33]This section draws on Abiad (1996). EMEs are divided into four geographic regions—Asia, Latin America, Europe, and other (mainly CIS, Middle Eastern, and African economies) as listed in Table 4.2.

[34]The excluded eastern European and CIS economies are Belarus, Bulgaria, Croatia, Czech Republic, Estonia, Hungary, Latvia, Lithuania, Poland, Romania, Russia, Slovak Republic, Slovenia, and Ukraine. The excluded financial centers are Costa Rica, Cyprus, Hong Kong SAR, Lebanon, Malta, Panama, and Singapore. The economies excluded because of a lack of data are Angola, Azerbaijan, the Islamic Republic of Iran, Iraq, Kazakhstan, Qatar, Serbia, Trinidad, and Turkmenistan.

### Figure 4.20. The Relative Importance of Various Types of Flow across Emerging Market Regions
*(Percent of total)*

The decline in the importance of bank and other private flows has been most pronounced in emerging Asian and Latin American economies. In emerging Europe, the share of bank and other private flows actually went up in the 2000s, while in other emerging market economies, it increased in the 1990s before falling in the 2000s.

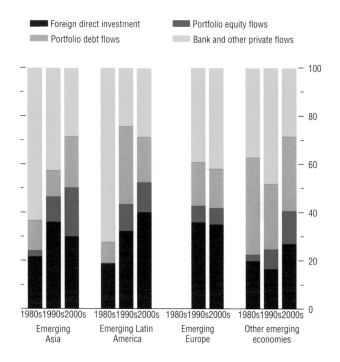

Sources: IMF, *Balance of Payments Statistics;* national sources; and IMF staff calculations.
Note: The relative importance of a particular type of flow is calculated as the absolute value of the net flows of that type to the economies of the group divided by the sum of the absolute value of the net flows of all four types of instruments to the economies of the group. Ratios are calculated for each decade with annual data, computing both numerator and denominator over the years in each decade. Derivative flows, which comprise a very small share of the financial account, are excluded from the calculation. The group aggregates exclude offshore financial centers.

**Figure 4.21. The Volatility of Net Private Capital Flows across Emerging Market Regions**

*(Standard deviation of net private capital flows in percent of GDP)*

The volatility of total net private capital flows to different emerging market regions has been broadly similar. In recent periods, flows to other emerging market economies appear to have become relatively more volatile, which is perhaps related to the greater importance of debt-creating flows for these economies. However, the differences with respect to the remaining emerging market regions are generally not statistically significant.

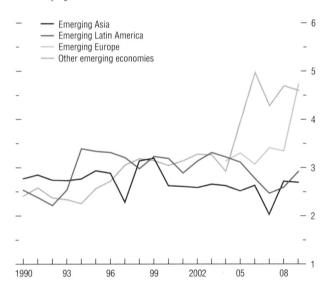

— Emerging Asia
— Emerging Latin America
  Emerging Europe
······ Other emerging economies

1990    93    96    99    2002    05    08

Sources: IMF, *Balance of Payments Statistics;* national sources; and IMF staff calculations.

Note: Using annual data, the volatility of any particular flow is computed as its standard deviation over the prior 10-year window for each economy (for example, the 1990 value corresponds to the standard deviation during 1981–90). The median is plotted only if the standard deviation for the particular 10-year window and type of flow can be calculated for at least one-fifth of the economies in the group. The groups exclude offshore financial centers.

the sample includes eastern Europe and the CIS, and thus the models are estimated for the 50 EMEs listed in Table 4.1, excluding the financial centers and other countries for which data are lacking. The sum of the regional dummies is equal to the time dummy in the second model, and so instead of dropping one of the regional dummies, we restrict the coefficients to sum to zero, $\sum_{j=1}^{4} \beta_t^{(j)} = 0$ at every $t$, so that the coefficients $\beta_t^{(j)}$ represent the over- or underperformance of the region relative to the global factor in all periods.

The residuals from the first model correspond to the portion of the cross-country dispersion in net capital flows that cannot be explained by global factors and are thus related to regional or economy-specific factors. Similarly, the residuals from the second model correspond to the portion of the cross-country dispersion in net capital flows that cannot be explained by global or regional factors and are thus related to economy-specific factors. To calculate the fraction of the dispersion in net capital flows across EMEs that is explained by global and regional factors, we compare the residuals from the two models above with those from a simple constant ($\alpha$) model:

$$y_{i,t} = \alpha + \varepsilon_{i,t}. \qquad (4.4)$$

The share of the variation of net flows across countries explained by global and global and regional factors at each point in time corresponds to the following $R^2$ statistics:

$$\text{Global factor model: } R_t^{G2} = 1 - \frac{\sum_{i=1}^{N} (y_{it} - \hat{y}_{it}^{G})^2}{\sum_{i=1}^{N} (y_{it} - \hat{y}_{it}^{C})^2} \qquad (4.5)$$

Global and regional factors model:

$$R_t^{G\&R2} = 1 - \frac{\sum_{i=1}^{N} (y_{it} - \hat{y}_{it}^{G\&R})^2}{\sum_{i=1}^{N} (y_{it} - \hat{y}_{it}^{C})^2} \qquad (4.6)$$

$R^{G2}$ is the variation in net capital flows that is explained by global factors only (relative to the simple constant model), $\hat{y}_{it}^{G}$ is the fitted value from the global factor model, and $\hat{y}_{it}^{C}$ is the fitted value from the simple constant model. $R^{G\&R2}$ is the variation in net capital flows that is jointly explained by global and regional factors (relative to the simple constant model), and $\hat{y}_{it}^{G\&R}$ is the fitted value from the global and regional factors model.

## Appendix 4.4. Regression Methodology and Robustness Checks

This appendix provides further details regarding the statistical methods used and the robustness of the regression results. It first describes the baseline regression model and estimation strategy. Next, it outlines the construction of the U.S. direct financial exposure weights. Third, it describes the approach used to isolate the component of changes in U.S. monetary policy rates that are unanticipated from the market's perspective. Fourth, it discusses a variety of robustness checks that have been undertaken regarding the core results.

### Model Specification and Estimation

The baseline specification is a cross section and time fixed-effects panel data model:

$$y_{i,t} = \alpha_i + \alpha_t + \sum_{s=0}^{8} \beta_s(\omega_i \times \Delta r_{us,t-s}) + \sum_{s=0}^{8} \lambda_s(\delta_i \times \Delta g_{us,t-s}) + X_{i,t-1}\gamma + \varepsilon_{i,t}, \qquad (4.7)$$

where $i$ indexes economies; $t$ indexes time (quarterly date); $y_{i,t}$ is the ratio of net capital flows to GDP; $\alpha_i$ and $\alpha_t$ are economy and time fixed effects, respectively; $\omega_i$ denotes the U.S. direct financial exposure weights (described below); $\Delta r_{us,t}$ is the U.S. monetary policy change measure—here, based on either the realized or the unanticipated rate; $\delta_i$ denotes U.S. direct trade exposure weights; $\Delta g_{us,t}$ is the U.S. growth forecast error; $X_{i,t-1}$ is a vector of additional controls, including the lagged level in domestic short-term real rate, lagged level in domestic real GDP growth, lagged *International Country Risk Guide* composite risk level (whereby a higher value indicates lower risk), lagged log nominal GDP, a lagged binary exchange rate regime indicator (representing 1 for all pegged regimes and zero for nonpegged regimes), the fourth lag of the Chinn-Ito capital account openness measure, and the fourth lag of the liquid-liabilities-to-GDP ratio (Beck, Demirgüç-Kunt, and Levine, 2000 and 2009); and $\varepsilon_{i,t}$ is a mean zero error term.

### Figure 4.22. The Persistence of Net Private Capital Flows across Emerging Market Regions

*(AR(1) regression coefficients of net private capital flows in percent of GDP)*

The persistence of total net private capital flows does not vary substantially across emerging market regions. Net flows to emerging Asian economies appear to have been the most persistent historically, while net flows to other emerging market economies have been the least, but these differences are not statistically significant and have declined over time.

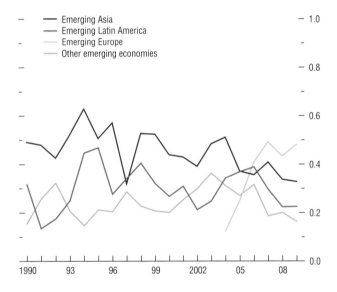

Sources: IMF, *Balance of Payments Statistics;* national sources; and IMF staff calculations.

Note: Using annual data, the persistence of any particular flow is its AR(1) regression coefficient computed over the prior 10-year window for each economy (for example, the 1990 value corresponds to the AR(1) coefficient during 1981–90). The median is plotted only if the AR(1) coefficient for the particular 10-year window and type of flow can be calculated for at least one-fifth of the economies in the group. The groups exclude offshore financial centers.

The additional effect of U.S. monetary policy changes on net capital flows to directly financially exposed economies is disentangled from the time fixed effect (capturing all global factors) by interacting the U.S. monetary policy measure with the exposure weight, as seen in the term ($\omega_i \times \Delta r_{us,t-s}$). Because the interaction varies across both economy and time, its effects (denoted by the set of $\beta$s) are separately identifiable from the economy- and time-fixed effects.

Following the recommendations of Stock and Watson (2008) for fixed-effect panels, the underlying standard errors are clustered at the economy level. This allows for heteroscedasticity across economies and arbitrary autocorrelation of the error term within each economy. Figure 4.16 shows both the uncumulated and cumulated difference in the effect of a U.S. monetary policy change on economies with average direct financial exposure to the United States compared with those with no such exposure. The latter, for a given horizon S, is calculated as $\sum_{s=0}^{S} \beta_s$, multiplied by the mean exposure for the relevant sample and then multiplied by the size of the impulse. Conceptually, it is akin to the additional effect on net capital flows of a permanent change in the U.S. monetary policy stance for an economy with mean exposure. See Table 4.3 for the results from the baseline model, with their associated standard errors. As detailed below, the broad conclusions are unchanged if an explicitly dynamic panel model is used.

### Construction of U.S. Direct Financial Exposure Weights

The economy-specific weight applied to the U.S. monetary policy measure for economy $i$ in the baseline specification is defined as

$$\omega_i = \left( \frac{\sum_{k=1}^{K} (A_{US,i}^k + L_{US,i}^k)}{A_i + L_i} \right), \qquad (4.8)$$

where $i$ refers to economy $i$; $k$ indexes instruments or capital types (securities, bank loans, and so on); $A_{US,i}^k$ denotes economy $i$'s U.S. asset holdings of type $k$; $L_{US,i}^k$ denotes economy $i$'s liabilities of type $k$ to the United States; $A_i$ denotes economy $i$'s international external asset position; and $L_i$ denotes economy $i$'s international external liability position.

As indicated in Appendix 4.1, the components of the weights draw from three sources: (1) the U.S. Treasury International Capital System (TICS) database on bilateral assets and liabilities of the United States vis-à-vis other countries; (2) the U.S. Bureau of Economic Analysis Foreign Direct Investment Statistics; and (3) the IMF's International Investment Position (IIP) Statistics. The time coverage of the complete U.S. TICS data is irregular, with consistent coverage occurring only within the past decade. Accordingly, the average of the numerator terms is taken over the years 1994 and 2003–07 for each economy.[35] This is then divided by the sum of economy $i$'s average IIP asset and liability position over the same years to derive the weight. See Table 4.4 for the calculated weights for the economies in the full regression sample.

### Identification of U.S. Monetary Policy Changes

This section describes the steps used to estimate the unanticipated component of U.S. monetary policy changes. We follow a modified version of the approach in Kuttner (2001). He argues that this can be measured using changes in the price of federal funds rate futures (derivatives based on the market's expectations of U.S. monetary policy) that occur around the time of policy decisions by the Federal Reserve Open Market Committee (FOMC). The federal funds futures market was established in October 1988 by the Chicago Board of Trade, with the set of contracts written on a monthly basis. They are settled based on the history of the effective federal funds rate within the contract month. As of the inception of these funds, Kuttner (2001) uses the daily change in the market price of the current-month futures contract around Federal Reserve monetary policy interventions to infer the size of the surprise component of U.S. monetary policy changes. Because the settlement price is a function of the monthly average federal funds rate, the

---

[35]1994 is the first year that comprehensive benchmarking of the U.S. external, bilateral asset, and liability positions was undertaken. There is then a gap of several years before a similar degree of coverage is achieved, leading to the set of years detailed here. An economy is dropped if more than 75 percent of the data that underlie the numerator average used in the weight calculation are missing.

## Table 4.3. Baseline Results

| Explanatory Variable | Full Sample (1) Unanticipated | Full Sample (2) Realized | Emerging Market Economies (3) Unanticipated | Emerging Market Economies (4) Realized | Advanced Economies (5) Unanticipated | Advanced Economies (6) Realized |
|---|---|---|---|---|---|---|
| USMP Rate Change | −0.457*** | −0.058 | −0.449* | −0.073 | −0.404* | −0.079* |
| | [0.158] | [0.052] | [0.235] | [0.078] | [0.213] | [0.040] |
| USMP Rate Change Lag 1 | −0.121 | −0.065* | −0.311* | −0.032 | −0.116 | −0.076 |
| | [0.149] | [0.038] | [0.176] | [0.048] | [0.227] | [0.046] |
| USMP Rate Change Lag 2 | 0.158 | 0.009 | 0.124 | −0.020 | 0.041 | 0.007 |
| | [0.153] | [0.031] | [0.254] | [0.035] | [0.102] | [0.053] |
| USMP Rate Change Lag 3 | −0.040 | −0.011 | −0.131 | −0.013 | −0.047 | 0.003 |
| | [0.107] | [0.024] | [0.181] | [0.041] | [0.153] | [0.027] |
| USMP Rate Change Lag 4 | −0.173 | −0.024 | −0.147 | −0.040 | −0.161 | −0.012 |
| | [0.109] | [0.035] | [0.147] | [0.061] | [0.133] | [0.027] |
| USMP Rate Change Lag 5 | −0.164 | −0.037 | −0.363** | −0.098* | −0.072 | −0.016 |
| | [0.119] | [0.035] | [0.169] | [0.055] | [0.164] | [0.034] |
| USMP Rate Change Lag 6 | −0.066 | −0.067 | −0.020 | −0.064 | −0.186 | −0.072 |
| | [0.189] | [0.042] | [0.213] | [0.069] | [0.210] | [0.058] |
| USMP Rate Change Lag 7 | −0.239* | −0.102** | −0.435 | −0.117* | −0.198* | −0.096* |
| | [0.141] | [0.047] | [0.275] | [0.069] | [0.096] | [0.053] |
| USMP Rate Change Lag 8 | −0.092 | −0.056* | −0.245 | −0.092* | −0.101 | −0.044 |
| | [0.113] | [0.033] | [0.222] | [0.052] | [0.125] | [0.033] |
| US Growth Innovation | −0.054 | −0.049 | −0.049 | −0.038 | −0.030 | −0.019 |
| | [0.057] | [0.057] | [0.081] | [0.073] | [0.059] | [0.060] |
| US Growth Inn. Lag 1 | 0.086 | 0.074 | 0.012 | −0.003 | 0.117 | 0.114 |
| | [0.056] | [0.056] | [0.045] | [0.058] | [0.095] | [0.085] |
| US Growth Inn. Lag 2 | 0.025 | 0.068 | −0.058 | −0.010 | 0.045 | 0.074* |
| | [0.039] | [0.044] | [0.053] | [0.054] | [0.031] | [0.038] |
| US Growth Inn. Lag 3 | 0.025 | 0.033 | 0.073 | 0.080 | −0.041 | −0.028 |
| | [0.043] | [0.047] | [0.058] | [0.070] | [0.051] | [0.055] |
| US Growth Inn. Lag 4 | 0.027 | 0.042 | −0.108** | −0.034 | 0.061 | 0.046 |
| | [0.046] | [0.043] | [0.048] | [0.056] | [0.046] | [0.031] |
| US Growth Inn. Lag 5 | −0.017 | −0.018 | 0.058 | 0.059 | −0.038 | −0.022 |
| | [0.047] | [0.041] | [0.042] | [0.053] | [0.048] | [0.039] |
| US Growth Inn. Lag 6 | 0.001 | 0.039 | 0.049 | 0.074 | −0.011 | 0.010 |
| | [0.045] | [0.051] | [0.079] | [0.067] | [0.045] | [0.049] |
| US Growth Inn. Lag 7 | 0.026 | 0.084 | −0.041 | 0.061 | 0.071 | 0.111 |
| | [0.049] | [0.054] | [0.067] | [0.078] | [0.065] | [0.077] |
| US Growth Inn. Lag 8 | −0.056 | −0.027 | 0.047 | 0.052 | −0.043 | 0.008 |
| | [0.047] | [0.048] | [0.085] | [0.071] | [0.057] | [0.077] |
| Domestic Real GDP Growth Lag 1 | 0.382*** | 0.374*** | 0.318*** | 0.316*** | 0.525 | 0.506 |
| | [0.112] | [0.112] | [0.074] | [0.073] | [0.342] | [0.337] |
| Domestic Real Short Rate Lag 1 | −0.098** | −0.102*** | −0.121*** | −0.124*** | 0.117 | 0.124 |
| | [0.037] | [0.038] | [0.028] | [0.029] | [0.436] | [0.425] |
| Domestic Risk Index Lag 1 | 0.078 | 0.091 | 0.047 | 0.053 | 0.150 | 0.169 |
| | [0.077] | [0.078] | [0.089] | [0.092] | [0.301] | [0.296] |
| Domestic Log NGDP Lag 1 | 4.576** | 4.430** | 4.667** | 4.157** | 7.762 | 7.601 |
| | [1.858] | [1.821] | [1.790] | [1.806] | [5.570] | [5.475] |
| Domestic Fin. Depth Lag 4 | 4.010 | 3.876 | 1.315 | 0.829 | 6.843 | 6.772 |
| | [3.250] | [3.107] | [3.973] | [3.835] | [6.724] | [6.544] |
| Domestic FX Regime Lag 1 | −0.461 | −0.542 | −0.027 | 0.156 | −2.316 | −2.704 |
| | [0.852] | [0.854] | [1.122] | [1.139] | [2.115] | [1.939] |
| Domestic KA Openness Lag 4 | −0.469 | −0.519 | −0.551 | −0.562 | 0.619 | 0.438 |
| | [0.327] | [0.315] | [0.386] | [0.382] | [1.207] | [1.155] |
| $R^2$ | 0.2295 | 0.2320 | 0.4007 | 0.4063 | 0.1851 | 0.1869 |
| N | 3,008 | 3,008 | 1,581 | 1,581 | 1,427 | 1,427 |
| N Economies | 50 | 50 | 30 | 30 | 20 | 20 |

Source: IMF staff calculations.

Note: The dependent variable is total net private capital flows in percent of GDP. Standard errors are in brackets underneath each estimate. *, **, and *** denote significance at the 10 percent, 5 percent, and 1 percent level, respectively. Offshore financial centers are excluded from the analysis. The estimates for the effects of U.S. monetary policy (USMP) and U.S. growth innovation are evaluated at the average values of U.S. direct financial exposure and U.S. bilateral trade weights for each sample. The monetary effects are also normalized to a 1 standard deviation unanticipated rate rise. The average financial exposures by sample are 0.159 for all economies, 0.173 for emerging market economies, and 0.138 for advanced economies. The bilateral trade weights by sample are 0.154 for all economies, 0.179 for emerging market economies, and 0.116 for advanced economies. NGDP = national gross domestic product. FX = foreign exchange. KA openness measures financial openness.

## Table 4.4. U.S. Direct Financial Exposure Weight

*(Proportion of total external assets and liabilities that are U.S. assets and/or liabilities)*

| Economy and IFS Code | U.S. Direct Financial Exposure | Economy and IFS Code | U.S. Direct Financial Exposure |
|---|---|---|---|
| Canada (156) | 0.470 | Sweden (144) | 0.138 |
| Mexico (273) | 0.451 | Indonesia (536) | 0.135 |
| Uruguay (298) | 0.328 | Belgium (124) | 0.133 |
| China (924) | 0.302 | South Africa (199) | 0.130 |
| Korea (542) | 0.289 | Russia (922) | 0.130 |
| Israel (436) | 0.289 | Hungary (944) | 0.127 |
| Brazil (223) | 0.276 | Ireland (178) | 0.126 |
| Guatemala (258) | 0.274 | Poland (964) | 0.108 |
| Japan (158) | 0.273 | Finland (172) | 0.104 |
| Colombia (233) | 0.246 | Turkey (186) | 0.102 |
| Chile (228) | 0.234 | Germany (134) | 0.100 |
| United Kingdom (112) | 0.234 | France (132) | 0.094 |
| Australia (193) | 0.233 | Denmark (128) | 0.085 |
| Philippines (566) | 0.218 | Iceland (176) | 0.076 |
| El Salvador (253) | 0.206 | Czech Republic (935) | 0.066 |
| Peru (293) | 0.182 | Spain (184) | 0.059 |
| Thailand (578) | 0.182 | Italy (136) | 0.051 |
| Netherlands (138) | 0.178 | Austria (122) | 0.043 |
| India (534) | 0.168 | Romania (968) | 0.041 |
| Norway (142) | 0.160 | Jordan (439) | 0.039 |
| Egypt (469) | 0.156 | Ukraine (926) | 0.038 |
| Malaysia (548) | 0.152 | Greece (174) | 0.036 |
| Argentina (213) | 0.141 | Bulgaria (918) | 0.028 |
| Ecuador (248) | 0.139 | Morocco (686) | 0.025 |
| New Zealand (196) | 0.139 | Portugal (182) | 0.023 |

Sources: U.S. Treasury International Capital System Database; U.S. Bureau of Economic Analysis Foreign Direct Investment Statistics; IMF International Investment Position Statistics; and IMF staff calculations.

Note: The economies listed here coincide with those included in the full regression sample. In a robustness check, we also include offshore financial centers for which data are available. They and their U.S. exposures are Costa Rica (238) at 0.241, Hong Kong SAR (532) at 0.082, Singapore (576) at 0.216, and Switzerland (146) at 0.224. The underlying data and construction of the weights are described in Appendix 4.4.

procedure requires scaling the day-to-day difference in closing prices for the current-month futures contract on the day of a Federal Reserve intervention. Specifically, the unanticipated (surprise) component is calculated as

$$u_{t,s} = -\left(\frac{D_s}{D_s - t + 1}\right)(f_{t,s} - f_{t-1,s}), \qquad (4.9)$$

where the intervention occurs on day $t$ in month/year $s$; $D_s$ is the number of days in month/year $s$; $f_{t,s}$ is the closing price of the federal funds futures contract for month/year $s$; and $u_{t,s}$ is the unanticipated component of the intervention.

Near the end of the month, the scaling factor grows extremely large, potentially magnifying the influence of any noise in price movements. Based on the findings of Hamilton (2008) regarding the influence of noise on federal funds futures prices, the chapter takes the unscaled change in the next-month contract price whenever the date of an intervention occurs during the last fifth of a month.[36]

[36]In the original 2001 article, Kuttner addresses this issue by using the unscaled change in the next month's federal funds futures contract whenever the date of an intervention occurs on the last three days of the month.

This analysis makes two modifications to Kuttner's approach. First, it considers only U.S. monetary policy actions (or inactions) that are associated with scheduled FOMC meetings. Second, the dates when monetary policy actions are revealed to the market are determined according to the method described in Bernanke and Kuttner (2005). Roughly speaking, during the period October 1988–January 1994, this means that the analysis uses the scaled difference between the closing price from the day after the concluding date of an FOMC meeting and the price from the FOMC meeting's concluding date. After February 1994, the analysis uses the scaled difference between the closing price from the day of the concluding date of an FOMC meeting and the price from the day before the FOMC meeting's concluding date.[37]

Because the net capital flows data are quarterly, the unanticipated U.S. monetary policy change series at the FOMC meeting frequency (which is daily) must be mapped to a quarterly frequency. To ensure that the contemporaneous and lagged effects of such identified U.S. monetary policy changes are correctly estimated, the analysis follows a version of the aggregation method in Bluedorn and Bowdler (2011). For the contemporaneous effect, the analysis takes the sum of the daily weighted U.S. monetary policy changes within the quarter. In each case, the daily weight is the number of days remaining in the quarter at the time of a U.S. monetary policy change divided by the total number of days in the quarter. For the lagged effect, the unweighted sum of the policy changes within the quarter is used. The same aggregation method is also applied to calculate the quarterly realized rate change, using daily data on the effective federal funds rate. The realized nominal rate changes are transformed into real rate changes by subtracting the corresponding change in the Survey of Professional Forecasters one-quarter-ahead forecast of inflation.

Figure 4.23 compares the contemporaneous realized and unanticipated real rate change series over time. From the figure, it is clear that the realized rate change contains a host of components other than

[37]FOMC policy decisions at a meeting have been publicly announced since February 1994.

**Figure 4.23. Realized and Unanticipated Changes in U.S. Monetary Policy over Time**
*(Percentage points)*

Realized changes in U.S. monetary policy rates contain a host of components other than the unanticipated component. The unanticipated component accounts for only a small part of the variation of realized rate changes.

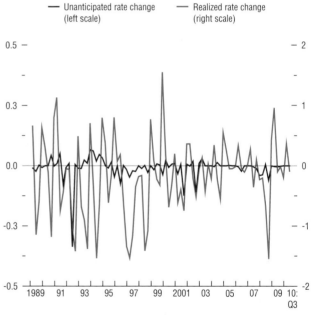

Sources: Datastream; Federal Reserve; and IMF staff calculations.
Note: The underlying data and construction of the realized and unanticipated, time-weighted changes in the U.S. policy rate are described in Appendix 4.4.

**Figure 4.24. Robustness Checks for the Difference in Response of Net Private Capital Flows to Directly Financially Exposed Emerging Market Economies**
*(Percent of GDP)*

The main result of a negative additional effect of U.S. monetary tightening on net flows to emerging market economies that are directly financially exposed to the United States (relative to those that are not) continues to hold under alternative robustness checks.

— Baseline
— Dynamic model
— Change in volatility index
— Largest 10 emerging market economies
— European Monetary Union/ German growth innovation
— Including offshore financial centers
— Pre-1998
— Post-1997
— Pre-2008
— Change in European Economic and Monetary Union/German real interest rates

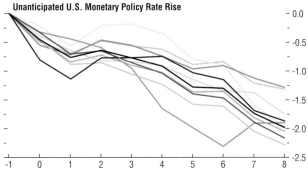

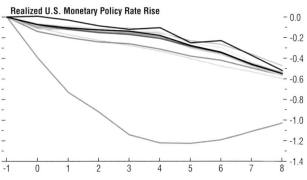

Source: IMF staff calculations.
Note: The dependent variable is total net private capital flows in percent of GDP. The x-axis shows the number of quarters after an impulse. The impulse at quarter zero is a permanent U.S. monetary policy rate rise, normalized to a 1 standard deviation unanticipated rate rise for the economy at the group's average financial exposure. Discussion of the various robustness checks is in Appendix 4.4.

the unanticipated rate change. Possible confounders include changes in inflation expectations unrelated to monetary policy, the endogenous response of real rates to a productivity boom, the endogenous response of real rates to a rise in aggregate demand, and so on.

Finally, as noted in the main text, the impulse responses are presented for a 1 standard deviation unanticipated rate rise (calculated during 1989:Q1–2010:Q3). In the case of the unanticipated rate change, this is approximately a 4.8 basis point impulse. For the realized U.S. rate change, the corresponding impulse is approximately 11.8 basis points, as revealed by a simple univariate regression of the realized rate change on the unanticipated rate change. Thus, a within-quarter realized rate change of 12 basis points corresponds to about a 5 basis point unanticipated rate change. The effect of unanticipated changes on realized changes is greater than one for one, which arises from the fact that each unanticipated rate change also changes the anticipated path of rates later in the quarter.

## Robustness Checks

A variety of robustness checks were undertaken for the baseline results of the additional impact of U.S. monetary policy rate changes on net flows to directly financially exposed EMEs (Figure 4.24). These include:

- A dynamic fixed-effects (economy and time) panel model: A single one-quarter lag of the dependent variable was added to the baseline specification (standard autocorrelation tests indicated this lagged specification as sufficient). The impulse responses generated from this model then take into account the additional dynamics introduced by the lagged dependent variable.
- A broader set of global growth indicators: We augmented the baseline specification with European Economic and Monetary Union (post-1998) and German (pre-1999) growth innovations at a quarterly frequency (contemporaneous and eight lags). To disentangle the additional effect of direct trade exposure to Europe from the general global factor, we weighted the growth innovations with their

respective economy-specific bilateral trade shares (similar to the U.S. growth innovations). The EMU/German growth innovations are the one-year-ahead growth forecasts errors for each quarter. (One-quarter-ahead errors were not available.)

- A measure of global risk aversion: We augmented the baseline specification with the Chicago Board Options Exchange Volatility Index (VIX) changes at a quarterly frequency (contemporaneous and eight lags). Again, to disentangle its additional effect on internationally financially exposed economies from the global factor, we weighted the VIX changes with each economy's international financial exposure, as measured by the sum of an economy's external assets plus liabilities divided by domestic GDP.
- Euro area real interest rate: We augmented the baseline specification with the euro area real interest rate (constructed as described in the main text) changes at a quarterly frequency (contemporaneous and eight lags). Similar to the global risk-aversion measure robustness check, we weighted these real interest rate changes with each economy's international financial exposure, as measured by the sum of an economy's external assets plus liabilities divided by domestic GDP.
- Estimation using only pre-2008 observations, prior to the global financial crisis.
- Estimation using only observations from before 1998, prior to the Asian crisis.
- Estimation using only observations from 1998 onward, a period that witnessed major changes in global capital markets.
- Estimation including offshore financial centers (OFCs).[38]
- Estimation using only the 10 largest emerging market economies in the baseline regression sample.[39]

As shown in Figure 4.24, the overall qualitative pattern of the additional response of net flows for directly financially exposed economies to a 1 standard deviation unanticipated U.S. policy rate rise is roughly the same across the robustness checks. There

[38]See Appendix 4.1 for a listing of the OFCs.
[39]The 10 largest EMEs in the baseline regression sample are Argentina, Brazil, China, India, Indonesia, Korea, Mexico, Poland, Russia, and Turkey.

is typically a downward trend over time, starting from a negative additional impact effect. All responses are negative across the robustness checks at quarter 8, with a long-term effect lying between 1.25 and 2.5 percent of GDP. The additional response of net flows for directly financially exposed economies to a realized rate change of comparable size is similarly robust, exhibiting a downward trend toward a long-term effect of about 0.5 percent of GDP. The only marked outlier here is the response estimated only over the pre-1998 sample for EMEs. It shows a much stronger initial additional effect before settling on a long-term additional effect that is about 1 percent of GDP.

## References

Abiad, Abdul, 1996, "Common and Country-Specific Components in Currency Movements: What's Holding the Forint Up?" in *Hungary: Selected Issues,* IMF Country Report No. 06/367 (Washington: International Monetary Fund).

Aizenman, Joshua, Menzi Chinn, and Hiro Ito, 2010, "The Financial Crisis, Rethinking of the Global Financial Architecture, and the Trilemma," ADBI Working Papers No. 213 (Tokyo: Asian Development Bank Institute).

Basel Committee on the Global Financial System (BCGFS), 2004, "Foreign Direct Investment in the Financial Sector of Emerging Market Economies," CGFS Publication No. 22 (Basel: Bank for International Settlements, March).

Beck, Thorsten, Asli Demirgüç-Kunt, and Ross Levine, 2000 (revised October 17, 2007), "A New Database on Financial Development and Structure," *World Bank Economic Review*, Vol. 14 (September), pp. 597–605.

———, 2009, "Financial Institutions and Markets Across Countries and Over Time: Data and Analysis," Policy Research Working Paper No. 4943 (Washington: World Bank, May).

Becker, Chris, and Clare Noone, 2009, "Volatility and Persistence of Capital Flows," Reserve Bank of Australia Research Discussion Paper No. 2009-09 (Sydney: Reserve Bank of Australia). www.rba.gov.au/publications/rdp/2009/pdr/rdp2009-09.pdf.

Bernanke, Ben S., and Kenneth N. Kuttner, 2005, "What Explains the Stock Market's Reaction to Federal Reserve Policy?" *Journal of Finance*, Vol. 60, No. 3, pp. 1221–58.

Bluedorn, John C., and Christopher Bowdler, 2010, "The Empirics of International Monetary Transmission: Identification and the Impossible Trinity," *Journal of Money, Credit and Banking*, Vol. 42, No. 4, pp. 679–713.

———, 2011, "The Open Economy Consequences of U.S. Monetary Policy," *Journal of International Money and Finance*, Vol. 30, No. 2, pp. 289–392.

Broner, Fernando, and Roberto Rigobon, 2006, "Why Are Capital Flows So Much More Volatile in Emerging than in Developing Countries?" in *External Vulnerability and Preventive Policies,* ed. by Ricardo Caballero, César Calderón, and Luis Céspedes (Santiago: Central Bank of Chile).

Calderon, Cesar, and Megumi Kubota, 2011, "Sudden Stops: Are Global and Local Investors Alike?" World Bank Policy Research Working Paper No. 5569 (Washington: World Bank).

Calvo, Guillermo A., Eduardo Fernández-Arias, Carmen Reinhart, and Ernesto Talvi, 2001, "The Growth-Interest Rate Cycle in the United States and its Consequences for Emerging Markets," Research Department Working Paper No. 458 (Washington: Inter-American Development Bank). www.iadb.org/res/publications/pubfiles/pubWP-458.pdf.

Calvo, Guillermo, Leonardo Leiderman, and Carmen M. Reinhart, 1993, "Capital Inflows and Real Exchange Rate Appreciation in Latin America: The Role of External Factors," *IMF Staff Papers*, Vol. 40, No. 1, pp. 108–51.

Chinn, Menzie, and Hiro Ito, 2006, "What Matters for Financial Development? Capital Controls, Institutions, and Interactions," *Journal of Development Economics,* Vol. 81, No. 1, pp. 163–92.

———, 2008, "A New Measure of Financial Openness," *Journal of Comparative Policy Analysis*, Vol. 10, No. 3, pp. 307–20.

Chuhan, Punam, Gabriel Perez-Quiros, and Helen Popper, 1996, "International Capital Flows: Do Short-Term Investment and Direct Investment Differ?" Policy Research Working Paper No. 1669 (Washington: World Bank).

Claessens, Stijn, Michael Dooley, and Andrew Warner, 1995, "Portfolio Capital Flows: Hot or Cold?" *World Bank Economic Review*, Vol. 9, No. 1, pp. 153–74.

Dell'Ariccia, Giovanni, Julian di Giovanni, André Faria, M. Ayhan Kose, Paolo Mauro, Martin Schindler, Marco Terrones, and Jonathan Ostry, 2007, *Reaping the Benefits of Financial Globalization,* IMF Occasional Paper 264 (Washington: International Monetary Fund).

European Central Bank (ECB), 2004, "Financial FDI to the EU Accession Countries," Working Paper No. 04/78 (Frankfurt).

Faria, André, Philip Lane, Paolo Mauro, and Gian Maria Milesi-Ferretti, 2007, "The Shifting Composition of External Liabilities," *Journal of the European Economic Association*, Vol. 5, No. 2–3, pp. 480–90.

Forbes, Kristin J., and Francis E. Warnock, 2010, "Capital Flow Waves: Surges, Stops, Flight, and Retrenchment" (unpublished; Cambridge, Massachusetts: Massachusetts Institute of Technology, December).

Frankel, Jeffrey, and Andrew Rose, 1996, "Currency Crashes in Emerging Markets: An Empirical Treatment," *Journal of International Economics*, Vol. 41, No. 3/4, pp. 351–66.

Frankel, Jeffrey, and Shang-Jin Wei, 2005, "Managing Macroeconomic Crises: Policy Lessons," in *Managing Macroeconomic Volatility and Crises: A Practitioner's Guide,* ed. by Joshua Aizenman and Brian Pinto (New York: Cambridge University Press).

Fratzscher, Marcel, Christian Saborowski, and Roland Straub, 2010, "Monetary Policy Shocks and Portfolio Choice," CEPR Discussion Paper No. 8099 (London: Centre for Economic Policy Research).

Ghosh, Atish R., Jonathan D. Ostry, and Charalambos Tsangarides, 2010, *Exchange Rate Regimes and the Stability of the International Monetary System,* IMF Occasional Paper No. 270 (Washington: International Monetary Fund).

Hamilton, James D., 2008, "Assessing Monetary Policy Effects Using Daily Federal Funds Futures Contracts," *Federal Reserve Bank of St. Louis Review*, Vol. 90, No. 4, pp. 377–93.

Hartelius, Kristian, Kenichiro Kashiwase, and Laura E. Kodres, 2008, "Emerging Market Spread Compression: Is It Real or Is It Liquidity?" IMF Working Paper 08/10 (Washington: International Monetary Fund).

Ilzetzki, Ethan, Carmen M. Reinhart, and Kenneth S. Rogoff, 2008, "The Country Chronologies and Background Material to Exchange Rate Arrangements in the 21st Century: Which Anchor Will Hold?" (unpublished; College Park, Maryland: University of Maryland). http://terpconnect.umd.edu/~creinhar/Papers/ERA-Country%20chronologies.pdf.

International Monetary Fund (IMF), 2000, "Offshore Financial Centers," IMF Background Paper (Washington). www.imf.org/external/np/mae/oshore/2000/eng/back.htm.

———, 2011, "Recent Experiences in Managing Capital Flows: Cross-Cutting Themes and Proposed Guidelines for Emerging Markets," IMF Board Paper prepared by the Strategy, Policy, and Review Department (Washington).

Kose, M. Ayhan, Eswar Prasad, Kenneth Rogoff, and Shang-Jin Wei, 2006, "Financial Globalization: A Reappraisal," IMF Working Paper 06/189 (Washington: International Monetary Fund).

Kuttner, Kenneth, 2001, "Monetary Policy Surprises and Interest Rates: Evidence from the Fed Funds Futures Market," *Journal of Monetary Economics,* Vol. 47, No. 3, pp. 523–44.

Laeven, Luc, and Hui Tong, 2010, "U.S. Monetary Shocks and Global Stock Prices," IMF Working Paper 10/278 (Washington: International Monetary Fund).

Levchenko, Andrei, and Paolo Mauro, 2007, "Do Some Forms of Financial Flows Help Protect Against Sudden Stops?" *World Bank Economic Review*, Vol. 21, No. 3, pp. 389–411.

Milesi-Ferretti, Gian Maria, and Cédric Tille, 2010, "The Great Retrenchment: International Capital Flows During the Global Financial Crisis" (unpublished; Washington: International Monetary Fund; forthcoming, *Economic Policy)*.

Miniane, Jacques, and John H. Rogers, 2007, "Capital Controls and the International Transmission of U.S. Monetary Shocks," *Journal of Money, Credit and Banking*, Vol. 39, No. 5, pp. 1003–35.

Mody, Ashoka, Mark Taylor, and Jung Yeon Kim, 2001, "Modeling Economic Fundamentals for Forecasting Capital Flows to Emerging Markets," *International Journal of Finance and Economics*, Vol. 6, No. 3, pp. 201–16.

Ostry, Jonathan D., Atish R. Ghosh, Karl Habermeier, Marcos Chamon, Mahvash S. Qureshi, and Dennis B.S. Reinhardt, 2010, "Capital Inflows: The Role of Controls," IMF Staff Position Note 10/04 (Washington: International Monetary Fund).

Papaioannou, Elias, 2009, "What Drives International Financial Flows? Politics, Institutions, and Other Determinants," *Journal of Development Economics,* Vol. 88, No. 2, pp. 269–81.

Prasad, Eswar, Kenneth S. Rogoff, Shang-Jin Wei, and Ayhan Kose, 2003, *Effects of Financial Globalization on Developing Countries: Some Empirical Evidence,* IMF Occasional Paper No. 220 (Washington: International Monetary Fund).

Reinhart, Carmen M., and Kenneth S. Rogoff, 2004, "The Modern History of Exchange Rate Arrangements: A Reinterpretation," *The Quarterly Journal of Economics*, Vol. 119 (February), pp. 1–48.

Sarno, Lucio, and Mark Taylor, 1999, "Hot Money, Accounting Labels and the Permanence of Capital Flows to Developing Countries: An Empirical Investigation," *Journal of Development Economics*, Vol. 59, No. 2, pp. 337–64.

Stock, James H., and Mark W. Watson, 2008, "Heteroskedasticity-Robust Standard Errors for Fixed Effects Panel Data Regression," *Econometrica,* Vol. 76, No. 1, pp. 155–74.

Taylor, Mark P., and Lucio Sarno, 1997, "Capital Flows to Developing Countries: Long- and Short-Term Determinants," *The World Bank Economic Review*, Vol. 11, No. 3, pp. 451–70.

Tong, Hui, and Shang-Jin Wei, 2010, "The Composition Matters: Capital Inflows and Liquidity Crunch During a Global Economic Crisis," forthcoming, *Review of Financial Studies* (published online September 26, 2010).

# IMF EXECUTIVE BOARD DISCUSSION OF THE OUTLOOK, MARCH 2011

*The following remarks by the Acting Chair were made at the conclusion of the Executive Board's discussion of the* World Economic Outlook *on March 28, 2011.*

Executive Directors noted that the global recovery is gaining strength, though at varying speeds across countries. Many advanced economies that had been at the center of the global crisis and/or had large precrisis imbalances continue to experience relatively sluggish growth and elevated unemployment rates. Growth in many emerging market and developing economies has been robust, with signs of overheating in a number of countries. While remaining vulnerabilities have yet to be fully addressed, new challenges are emerging, pointing to the urgency of pursuing more vigorously the policies needed to build a more balanced and robust global economy.

Directors observed that, while the prospects for global recovery have solidified, downside risks continue to prevail. These emanate from high unemployment, still-weak sovereign and financial balance sheets, and vulnerable real estate markets in many advanced economies. Meanwhile, rising oil, food, and commodity prices, developments in the Middle East and North Africa, and the recent earthquake in Japan have further amplified the challenges. On the upside, a stronger pickup in corporate sector activity in some advanced economies and, over the near term, buoyant demand in emerging market and developing economies could propel global growth further.

Directors underscored the importance of faster progress in strengthening government and financial sector balance sheets in many advanced and some developing economies. Improving economic conditions provide a good opportunity to implement fiscal consolidation plans and entitlement reforms—supported by strong fiscal frameworks and institutions—and place public debt on a sustainable path. With the pace of fiscal consolidation slower than

anticipated for 2011 in key advanced economies, clearer, more detailed medium-term adjustment strategies are all the more important to reestablish fiscal credibility. Financial sector repair and reform also need to be accelerated on all fronts to restore confidence. The focus should be on rigorous stress testing, further bank restructuring and recapitalization, and rebuilding stronger mortgage credit and securitization markets. A further priority is to fill persistent gaps in financial sector supervisory and regulatory frameworks, addressing risks posed by shadow banking systems and "too-important-to-fail" institutions and inadequate cross-border resolution frameworks.

Directors generally agreed that, in advanced economies with strong central bank credibility and well-anchored inflation expectations, monetary policy could remain accommodative while the much needed fiscal consolidation and financial sector reforms proceed. In some countries, however, risks to price stability deserve closer attention. While unconventional measures designed to deal with specific financial market tensions could continue to be maintained in the near term, their implications for bank restructuring should be carefully assessed.

Directors emphasized that many emerging market and developing economies need to be vigilant for overheating pressures and inflation risks stemming from food and energy prices, which weigh heavily in consumption baskets, as well as from the rapid recovery in domestic credit. For countries with external surpluses and no fiscal concerns, the priority would be to unwind monetary accommodation and allow stronger currencies to anchor inflation expectations, which will also assist external rebalancing. Those with external deficits should tighten both fiscal and monetary policies. In addition to macroeconomic adjustment, economies experiencing booms in credit and asset markets could adopt macroprudential policies to maintain financial sector strength and stability, complemented by other measures to manage capital inflows where deemed necessary.

Directors recognized that, because countries are at different stages of recovery and cyclical positions, their monetary policy responses necessarily differ, widening interest rate differentials among countries. Beyond domestic factors, global financial conditions help explain the variability of cross-border capital flows. Directors noted the IMF staff's conclusion that, as long as accommodative monetary policies help stabilize output in advanced economies, spillovers to emerging and developing economies would be, on the net, beneficial. At the same time, many Directors drew attention to the effects of prolonged loose monetary policy in major advanced economies, and risks of a sudden reversal, on global capital flows. They viewed these developments as further complicating macroeconomic policymaking in many capital-recipient countries, underscoring, in the view of some Directors, the case for international monetary coordination.

Directors noted that the persistent rise in oil prices reflects both increased scarcity of supply and rapid growth in oil consumption. Although gradual and moderate increases in oil scarcity are not expected to pose a major constraint on global growth in the medium to long term, uncertainty remains high and the potential for abrupt shifts cannot be ruled out. Directors saw merit in further analysis and discussion on the range of policy options to facilitate adjustment. They stressed the need for policymakers to pay attention to social challenges arising from elevated prices of food and commodities, with the first priority being the development of well-targeted social safety nets to protect the poor.

Directors underscored that the continuing improvement in global economic and financial health should not diminish the urgency for completing the policy reform agenda. Decisive further progress in fiscal and financial sector adjustment, the removal of distortions that hold back global demand rebalancing, and tighter macroeconomic policies where inflation pressures are building are all key to sustaining healthier, more balanced global growth. While these policies are in the interest of each individual country and action should not be delayed, continued coordination and joint initiatives will facilitate more ambitious policy adjustments and stronger outcomes.

# STATISTICAL APPENDIX

The Statistical Appendix presents historical data as well as projections. It comprises five sections: Assumptions, What's New, Data and Conventions, Classification of Countries, and Statistical Tables.

The assumptions underlying the estimates and projections for 2011–12 and the medium-term scenario for 2013–16 are summarized in the first section. The second section presents a brief description of changes to the database and statistical tables. The third section provides a general description of the data and of the conventions used for calculating country group composites. The classification of countries in the various groups presented in the *World Economic Outlook* is summarized in the fourth section.

The last, and main, section comprises the statistical tables. (Statistical Appendix A is included here; Statistical Appendix B is available online.) Data in these tables have been compiled on the basis of information available through late March 2011. The figures for 2011 and beyond are shown with the same degree of precision as the historical figures solely for convenience; because they are projections, the same degree of accuracy is not to be inferred.

## Assumptions

Real effective *exchange rates* for the advanced economies are assumed to remain constant at their average levels during the period February 8–March 8, 2011. For 2011 and 2012, these assumptions imply average U.S. dollar/SDR conversion rates of 1.565 and 1.562, U.S. dollar/euro conversion rates of 1.369 and 1.362, and yen/U.S. dollar conversion rates of 82.3 and 82.5, respectively.

It is assumed that the *price of oil* will average $107.16 a barrel in 2011 and $108.00 a barrel in 2012.

Established *policies* of national authorities are assumed to be maintained. The more specific policy

assumptions underlying the projections for selected economies are described in Box A1.

With regard to *interest rates,* it is assumed that the London interbank offered rate (LIBOR) on six-month U.S. dollar deposits will average 0.6 percent in 2011 and 0.9 percent in 2012, that three-month euro deposits will average 1.7 percent in 2011 and 2.6 percent in 2012, and that six-month yen deposits will average 0.6 percent in 2011 and 0.3 percent in 2012.

With respect to *introduction of the euro,* on December 31, 1998, the Council of the European Union decided that, effective January 1, 1999, the irrevocably fixed conversion rates between the euro and currencies of the member states adopting the euro are as follows.

| 1 euro | = | 13.7603 | Austrian schillings |
|--------|---|---------|---------------------|
| | = | 40.3399 | Belgian francs |
| | = | 0.585274 | Cyprus pound[1] |
| | = | 1.95583 | Deutsche mark |
| | = | 15.6466 | Estonian krooni[2] |
| | = | 5.94573 | Finnish markkaa |
| | = | 6.55957 | French francs |
| | = | 340.750 | Greek drachma[3] |
| | = | 0.787564 | Irish pound |
| | = | 1,936.27 | Italian lire |
| | = | 40.3399 | Luxembourg francs |
| | = | 0.42930 | Maltese lira[4] |
| | = | 2.20371 | Netherlands guilders |
| | = | 200.482 | Portuguese escudos |
| | = | 30.1260 | Slovak koruna[5] |
| | = | 239.640 | Slovenian tolars[6] |
| | = | 166.386 | Spanish pesetas |

[1]Established on January 1, 2008.
[2]Established on January 1, 2011.
[3]Established on January 1, 2001.
[4]Established on January 1, 2008.
[5]Established on January 1, 2009.
[6]Established on January 1, 2007.

See Box 5.4 of the October 1998 *World Economic Outlook* for details on how the conversion rates were established.

## What's New

- On January 1, 2011, Estonia became the 17th country to join the euro area. Data for Estonia are not included in the euro area aggregates because the database has not yet been converted to euros but are included in data aggregated for advanced economies.
- Starting with the April 2011 *World Economic Outlook,* the data for Tuvalu are included in the emerging and developing economy aggregates.
- The country group composites for fiscal data are calculated as the sum of the U.S dollar values for the relevant individual countries. This differs from the calculations in the October 2010 and earlier issues of the *World Economic Outlook,* for which the composites were weighted by GDP valued at purchasing power parities (PPPs) as a share of total world GDP.
- WEO aggregated data excludes Libya for projection years due to the uncertain political situation.
- Except for GDP growth and inflation, projections for Côte d'Ivoire are not shown due to the uncertain political situation.

## Data and Conventions

Data and projections for 184 economies form the statistical basis for the *World Economic Outlook* (the WEO database). The data are maintained jointly by the IMF's Research Department and regional departments, with the latter regularly updating country projections based on consistent global assumptions.

Although national statistical agencies are the ultimate providers of historical data and definitions, international organizations are also involved in statistical issues, with the objective of harmonizing methodologies for the compilation of national statistics, including analytical frameworks, concepts, definitions, classifications, and valuation procedures used in the production of economic statistics. The WEO database reflects information from both national source agencies and international organizations.

Most countries' macroeconomic data presented in the *World Economic Outlook* conform broadly to

the 1993 version of the *System of National Accounts* (SNA). The IMF's sector statistical standards—the *Balance of Payments Manual, Fifth Edition* (BPM5), the *Monetary and Financial Statistics Manual* (MFSM 2000), and the *Government Finance Statistics Manual 2001* (GFSM 2001)—have all been aligned with the 1993 SNA. These standards reflect the IMF's special interest in countries' external positions, financial sector stability, and public sector fiscal positions. The process of adapting country data to the new standards begins in earnest when the manuals are released. However, full concordance with the manuals is ultimately dependent on the provision by national statistical compilers of revised country data; hence, the *World Economic Outlook* estimates are only partially adapted to these manuals. Nonetheless, for many countries the impact of conversion to the updated standards will be small on major balances and aggregates. Many other countries have partially adopted the latest standards and will continue implementation over a period of years.

Consistent with the recommendations of the 1993 SNA, several countries have phased out their traditional *fixed-base-year* method of calculating real macroeconomic variable levels and growth by switching to a *chain-weighted* method of computing aggregate growth. The chain-weighted method frequently updates the weights of price and volume indicators. It allows countries to measure GDP growth more accurately by reducing or eliminating the downward biases in volume series built on index numbers that average volume components using weights from a year in the moderately distant past.

Composite data for country groups in the *World Economic Outlook* are either sums or weighted averages of data for individual countries. Unless noted otherwise, multiyear averages of growth rates are expressed as compound annual rates of change.[7] Arithmetically weighted averages are used for all data for the emerging and developing economies group except inflation and money growth, for which geometric averages are used. The following conventions apply.

[7] Averages for real GDP and its components, employment, per capita GDP, inflation, factor productivity, trade, and commodity prices, are calculated based on the compound annual rate of change, except for the unemployment rate, which is based on the simple arithmetic average.

- Country group composites for exchange rates, interest rates, and growth rates of monetary aggregates are weighted by GDP converted to U.S. dollars at market exchange rates (averaged over the preceding three years) as a share of group GDP.
- Composites for other data relating to the domestic economy, whether growth rates or ratios, are weighted by GDP valued at purchasing power parity (PPP) as a share of total world or group GDP.[8]
- Composites for data relating to the domestic economy for the euro area (16 member countries throughout the entire period unless noted otherwise)[9] are aggregates of national source data using GDP weights. Annual data are not adjusted for calendar-day effects. For data prior to 1999, data aggregations apply 1995 European currency unit exchange rates.
- Composites for fiscal data are sums of individual country data after conversion to U.S. dollars at the average market exchange rates in the years indicated.
- Composite unemployment rates and employment growth are weighted by labor force as a share of group labor force.
- Composites relating to the external economy are sums of individual country data after conversion to U.S. dollars at the average market exchange rates in the years indicated for balance of payments data and at end-of-year market exchange rates for debt denominated in currencies other than U.S. dollars. Composites of changes in foreign trade volumes and prices, however, are arithmetic averages of percent changes for individual countries weighted by the U.S. dollar value of exports or imports as a share of total world or group exports or imports (in the preceding year).
- Unless noted otherwise, group composites are computed if 90 percent or more of the share of group weights is represented.

[8] See Box A2 of the April 2004 *World Economic Outlook* for a summary of the revised PPP-based weights and Annex IV of the May 1993 *World Economic Outlook*. See also Anne-Marie Gulde and Marianne Schulze-Ghattas, "Purchasing Power Parity Based Weights for the *World Economic Outlook*," in *Staff Studies for the World Economic Outlook* (Washington: International Monetary Fund, December 1993), pp. 106–23.

[9] Data for Estonia are not included in the euro area aggregates because the database has not yet been converted to euros.

## Classification of Countries
### Summary of the Country Classification

The country classification in the *World Economic Outlook* divides the world into two major groups: advanced economies, and emerging and developing economies.[10] This classification is not based on strict criteria, economic or otherwise, and it has evolved over time. The objective is to facilitate analysis by providing a reasonably meaningful method for organizing data. Table A provides an overview of the country classification, showing the number of countries in each group by region and summarizing some key indicators of their relative size (GDP valued by PPP, total exports of goods and services, and population).

Some countries remain outside the country classification and therefore are not included in the analysis. Cuba and the Democratic People's Republic of Korea are not IMF members, and their economies therefore are not monitored by the IMF. San Marino is omitted from the group of advanced economies for lack of a fully developed database. Likewise, the Marshall Islands, the Federated States of Micronesia, Palau, and Somalia are omitted from the emerging and developing economies group composites because of data limitations.

## General Features and Composition of Groups in the *World Economic Outlook* Classification
### Advanced Economies

The 34 advanced economies are listed in Table B. The seven largest in terms of GDP—the United States, Japan, Germany, France, Italy, the United Kingdom, and Canada—constitute the subgroup of *major advanced economies,* often referred to as the Group of Seven (G7). The members of the *euro area* and the *newly industrialized Asian economies* are also distinguished as subgroups. Composite data shown in the tables for the euro area cover the current members for all years, even though the membership has increased over time.[11]

[10] As used here, the terms "country" and "economy" do not always refer to a territorial entity that is a state as understood by international law and practice. Some territorial entities included here are not states, although their statistical data are maintained on a separate and independent basis.

[11] Data for Estonia are not included in the euro area aggregates because the database has not yet been converted to euros.

Table C lists the member countries of the European Union, not all of which are classified as advanced economies in the *World Economic Outlook*.

## Emerging and Developing Economies

The group of emerging and developing economies (150 countries) includes all those that are not classified as advanced economies.

The *regional breakdowns* of emerging and developing economies are *central and eastern Europe (CEE), Commonwealth of Independent States (CIS), developing Asia, Latin America and the Caribbean (LAC), Middle East and North Africa (MENA), and sub-Saharan Africa (SSA)*.

Emerging and developing economies are also classified according to *analytical criteria*. The analytical criteria reflect the composition of countries' export earnings and other income from abroad; a distinction between net creditor and net debtor countries; and, for the net debtor countries, financial criteria based on external financing sources and experience with external debt servicing. The detailed composition of emerging and developing economies in the regional and analytical groups is shown in Tables D and E.

The analytical criterion by *source of export earnings* distinguishes between categories: *fuel* (Standard International Trade Classification—SITC 3) and *nonfuel* and then focuses on *nonfuel primary products* (SITCs 0, 1, 2, 4, and 68). Countries are categorized into one of these groups when their main source of

export earnings exceeds 50 percent of total exports on average between 2005 and 2009.

The financial criteria focus on *net creditor economies, net debtor economies,* and *heavily indebted poor countries* (HIPCs). Countries are categorized as net debtors when their current account balance accumulations from 1972 (or earliest data available) to 2009 are negative. Net debtor countries are further differentiated on the basis of two additional financial criteria: *official external financing* and *experience with debt servicing.*[12] Countries are placed in the official external financing category when 65 percent or more of their total debt, on average between 2005 and 2009, is financed by official creditors.

The HIPC group comprises the countries that are or have been considered by the IMF and the World Bank for participation in their debt initiative known as the HIPC Initiative, which aims to reduce the external debt burdens of all the eligible HIPCs to a "sustainable" level in a reasonably short period of time.[13] Many of these countries have already benefited from debt relief and graduated from the initiative.

---

[12]During 2005–09, 44 countries incurred external payments arrears or entered into official or commercial-bank debt-rescheduling agreements. This group of countries is referred to as *economies with arrears and/or rescheduling during 2005–09.*

[13]See David Andrews, Anthony R. Boote, Syed S. Rizavi, and Sukwinder Singh, *Debt Relief for Low-Income Countries: The Enhanced HIPC Initiative,* IMF Pamphlet Series, No. 51 (Washington: International Monetary Fund, November 1999).

## Table A. Classification by *World Economic Outlook* Groups and Their Shares in Aggregate GDP, Exports of Goods and Services, and Population, 2010[1]

*(Percent of total for group or world)*

| | Number of Countries | GDP | | Exports of Goods and Services | | Population | |
|---|---|---|---|---|---|---|---|
| | | Advanced Economies | World | Advanced Economies | World | Advanced Economies | World |
| **Advanced Economies** | **34** | **100.0** | **52.3** | **100.0** | **63.7** | **100.0** | **15.0** |
| United States | | 37.7 | 19.7 | 15.4 | 9.8 | 30.4 | 4.5 |
| Euro Area[2] | 16 | 27.8 | 14.6 | 40.9 | 26.1 | 32.1 | 4.8 |
| Germany | | 7.6 | 4.0 | 12.6 | 8.0 | 8.0 | 1.2 |
| France | | 5.5 | 2.9 | 5.5 | 3.5 | 6.2 | 0.9 |
| Italy | | 4.6 | 2.4 | 4.6 | 2.9 | 5.9 | 0.9 |
| Spain | | 3.5 | 1.8 | 3.1 | 2.0 | 4.5 | 0.7 |
| Japan | | 11.1 | 5.8 | 7.3 | 4.6 | 12.5 | 1.9 |
| United Kingdom | | 5.6 | 2.9 | 5.6 | 3.5 | 6.1 | 0.9 |
| Canada | | 3.4 | 1.8 | 3.9 | 2.5 | 3.3 | 0.5 |
| Other Advanced Economies | 14 | 14.3 | 7.5 | 27.0 | 17.2 | 15.5 | 2.3 |
| *Memorandum* | | | | | | | |
| Major Advanced Economies | 7 | 75.5 | 39.5 | 54.8 | 34.9 | 72.4 | 10.8 |
| Newly Industrialized Asian Economies | 4 | 7.4 | 3.9 | 15.4 | 9.8 | 8.3 | 1.2 |

| | Number of Countries | Emerging and Developing Economies | World | Emerging and Developing Economies | World | Emerging and Developing Economies | World |
|---|---|---|---|---|---|---|---|
| **Emerging and Developing Economies** | **150** | **100.0** | **47.7** | **100.0** | **36.3** | **100.0** | **85.0** |
| **Regional Groups** | | | | | | | |
| Central and Eastern Europe | 14 | 7.2 | 3.4 | 9.4 | 3.4 | 3.0 | 2.6 |
| Commonwealth of Independent States[3] | 13 | 8.9 | 4.2 | 10.1 | 3.7 | 4.8 | 4.1 |
| Russia | | 6.3 | 3.0 | 6.7 | 2.4 | 2.4 | 2.1 |
| Developing Asia | 27 | 50.4 | 24.0 | 43.6 | 15.8 | 61.5 | 52.3 |
| China | | 28.6 | 13.6 | 26.0 | 9.4 | 23.1 | 19.7 |
| India | | 11.3 | 5.4 | 4.8 | 1.7 | 21.0 | 17.8 |
| Excluding China and India | 25 | 10.5 | 5.0 | 12.9 | 4.7 | 17.4 | 14.8 |
| Latin America and the Caribbean | 32 | 18.0 | 8.6 | 14.7 | 5.3 | 9.8 | 8.3 |
| Brazil | | 6.2 | 2.9 | 3.4 | 1.2 | 3.3 | 2.8 |
| Mexico | | 4.4 | 2.1 | 4.6 | 1.7 | 1.9 | 1.6 |
| Middle East and North Africa | 20 | 10.4 | 5.0 | 16.8 | 6.1 | 7.1 | 6.0 |
| Sub-Saharan Africa | 44 | 5.1 | 2.4 | 5.4 | 2.0 | 13.8 | 11.7 |
| Excluding Nigeria and South Africa | 42 | 2.5 | 1.2 | 2.8 | 1.0 | 10.2 | 8.7 |
| **Analytical Groups** | | | | | | | |
| **By Source of Export Earnings** | | | | | | | |
| Fuel | 27 | 17.9 | 8.5 | 26.6 | 9.6 | 11.4 | 9.7 |
| Nonfuel | 123 | 82.1 | 39.1 | 73.4 | 26.6 | 88.6 | 75.3 |
| Of Which, Primary Products | 20 | 2.3 | 1.1 | 2.6 | 1.0 | 4.8 | 4.1 |
| **By External Financing Source** | | | | | | | |
| Net Debtor Economies | 121 | 50.4 | 24.0 | 42.9 | 15.6 | 62.0 | 52.7 |
| Of Which, Official Financing | 28 | 2.5 | 1.2 | 1.8 | 0.6 | 9.7 | 8.2 |
| **Net Debtor Economies by Debt-Servicing Experience** | | | | | | | |
| Economies with Arrears and/or Rescheduling during 2004–08 | 44 | 4.9 | 2.4 | 4.4 | 1.6 | 9.6 | 8.1 |
| Other Net Debtor Economies | 77 | 45.5 | 21.7 | 38.5 | 14.0 | 52.4 | 44.5 |
| **Other Groups** | | | | | | | |
| Heavily Indebted Poor Countries | 39 | 2.4 | 1.2 | 1.9 | 0.7 | 10.7 | 9.1 |

[1]The GDP shares are based on the purchasing-power-parity valuation of countries' GDP. The number of countries comprising each group reflects those for which data are included in the group aggregates.

[2]Euro area data do not include Estonia, but Estonia is included in data aggregated for advanced economies.

[3]Georgia and Mongolia, which are not members of the Commonwealth of Independent States, are included in this group for reasons of geography and similarities in economic structure.

## Table B. Advanced Economies by Subgroup

### Major Currency Areas

United States
Euro Area
Japan

### Euro Area[1]

| | | |
|---|---|---|
| Austria | Greece | Portugal |
| Belgium | Ireland | Slovak Republic |
| Cyprus | Italy | Slovenia |
| Finland | Luxembourg | Spain |
| France | Malta | |
| Germany | Netherlands | |

### Newly Industrialized Asian Economies

| | |
|---|---|
| Hong Kong SAR[2] | Singapore |
| Korea | Taiwan Province of China |

### Major Advanced Economies

| | | |
|---|---|---|
| Canada | Italy | United States |
| France | Japan | |
| Germany | United Kingdom | |

### Other Advanced Economies

| | | |
|---|---|---|
| Australia | Iceland | Singapore |
| Czech Republic | Israel | Sweden |
| Denmark | Korea | Switzerland |
| Estonia | New Zealand | Taiwan Province of China |
| Hong Kong SAR[2] | Norway | |

[1]Data for Estonia are not included in the euro area aggregates because the database has not yet been converted to euros.

[2]On July 1, 1997, Hong Kong was returned to the People's Republic of China and became a Special Administrative Region of China.

## Table C. European Union

| | | |
|---|---|---|
| Austria | Germany | Netherlands |
| Belgium | Greece | Poland |
| Bulgaria | Hungary | Portugal |
| Cyprus | Ireland | Romania |
| Czech Republic | Italy | Slovak Republic |
| Denmark | Latvia | Slovenia |
| Estonia | Lithuania | Spain |
| Finland | Luxembourg | Sweden |
| France | Malta | United Kingdom |

## Table D. Emerging and Developing Economies by Region and Main Source of Export Earnings

| | Fuel | Nonfuel Primary Products |
|---|---|---|
| **Commonwealth of Independent States[1]** | | |
| | Azerbaijan | Mongolia |
| | Kazakhstan | Uzbekistan |
| | Russia | |
| | Turkmenistan | |
| **Developing Asia** | | |
| | Brunei Darussalam | Papua New Guinea |
| | Timor-Leste | Solomon Islands |
| **Latin America and the Caribbean** | | |
| | Ecuador | Chile |
| | Trinidad and Tobago | Guyana |
| | Venezuela | Peru |
| | | Suriname |
| **Middle East and North Africa** | | |
| | Algeria | Mauritania |
| | Bahrain | |
| | Islamic Republic of Iran | |
| | Iraq | |
| | Kuwait | |
| | Libya | |
| | Oman | |
| | Qatar | |
| | Saudi Arabia | |
| | Sudan | |
| | United Arab Emirates | |
| | Republic of Yemen | |
| **Sub-Saharan Africa** | | |
| | Angola | Burkina Faso |
| | Chad | Burundi |
| | Republic of Congo | Democratic Republic of Congo |
| | Equatorial Guinea | Guinea |
| | Gabon | Guinea-Bissau |
| | Nigeria | Malawi |
| | | Mali |
| | | Mozambique |
| | | Sierra Leone |
| | | Zambia |
| | | Zimbabwe |

[1]Mongolia, which is not a member of the Commonwealth of Independent States, is included in this group for reasons of geography and similarities in economic structure.

## Table E. Emerging and Developing Economies by Region, Net External Position, and Status as Heavily Indebted Poor Countries

| | Net External Position | | Heavily Indebted Poor Countries[2] | | Net External Position | | Heavily Indebted Poor Countries[2] |
|---|---|---|---|---|---|---|---|
| | Net Creditor | Net Debtor[1] | | | Net Creditor | Net Debtor[1] | |
| **Central and Eastern Europe** | | | | Kiribati | * | | |
| Albania | | * | | Lao People's Democratic Republic | | * | |
| Bosnia and Herzegovina | | * | | Malaysia | * | | |
| Bulgaria | | * | | Maldives | | * | |
| Croatia | | * | | Myanmar | | * | |
| Hungary | | * | | Nepal | | • | |
| Kosovo | | * | | Pakistan | | * | |
| Latvia | | * | | Papua New Guinea | * | | |
| Lithuania | | * | | Philippines | | * | |
| Former Yugoslav Republic of Macedonia | | * | | Samoa | | • | |
| Montenegro | | * | | Solomon Islands | | * | |
| Poland | | * | | Sri Lanka | | * | |
| Romania | | * | | Thailand | | * | |
| Serbia | | * | | Timor-Leste | * | | |
| Turkey | | * | | Tonga | | * | |
| **Commonwealth of Independent States[3]** | | | | Tuvalu | | • | |
| Armenia | | * | | Vanuatu | | * | |
| Azerbaijan | * | | | Vietnam | | * | |
| Belarus | | * | | **Latin America and the Caribbean** | | | |
| Georgia | | * | | Antigua and Barbuda | | * | |
| Kazakhstan | | * | | Argentina | | * | |
| Kyrgyz Republic | | • | * | The Bahamas | | * | |
| Moldova | | * | | Barbados | | * | |
| Mongolia | | • | | Belize | | * | |
| Russia | * | | | Bolivia | * | | • |
| Tajikistan | | * | | Brazil | | * | |
| Turkmenistan | * | | | Chile | | * | |
| Ukraine | | * | | Colombia | | * | |
| Uzbekistan | * | | | Costa Rica | | * | |
| **Developing Asia** | | | | Dominica | | * | |
| Islamic Republic of Afghanistan | | • | • | Dominican Republic | | * | |
| Bangladesh | | • | | Ecuador | | • | |
| Bhutan | | * | | El Salvador | | * | |
| Brunei Darussalam | * | | | Grenada | | * | |
| Cambodia | | * | | Guatemala | | * | |
| China | * | | | Guyana | | • | • |
| Fiji | | * | | Haiti | | • | • |
| India | | * | | Honduras | | * | • |
| Indonesia | * | | | Jamaica | | * | |
| | | | | Mexico | | * | |

## Table E (concluded)

| | Net External Position | | Heavily Indebted Poor Countries[2] | | Net External Position | | Heavily Indebted Poor Countries[2] |
|---|---|---|---|---|---|---|---|
| | Net Creditor | Net Debtor[1] | | | Net Creditor | Net Debtor[1] | |
| Nicaragua | | * | • | Cameroon | | * | • |
| Panama | | * | | Cape Verde | | * | |
| Paraguay | | * | | Central African Republic | | • | • |
| Peru | | * | | Chad | | * | * |
| St. Kitts and Nevis | | * | | Comoros | | • | * |
| St. Lucia | | * | | Democratic Republic of Congo | | • | • |
| St. Vincent and the Grenadines | | • | | Republic of Congo | | • | • |
| Suriname | | • | | Côte d'Ivoire | | * | * |
| Trinidad and Tobago | * | | | Equatorial Guinea | | * | |
| Uruguay | | * | | Eritrea | | • | * |
| Venezuela | * | | | Ethiopia | | • | • |
| **Middle East and North Africa** | | | | Gabon | * | | |
| | | | | The Gambia | | • | • |
| Algeria | * | | | Ghana | | • | • |
| Bahrain | * | | | Guinea | | * | * |
| Djibouti | | * | | Guinea-Bissau | | * | • |
| Egypt | | * | | Kenya | | * | |
| Islamic Republic of Iran | * | | | Lesotho | | * | |
| Iraq | * | | | Liberia | | * | • |
| Jordan | | * | | Madagascar | | • | • |
| Kuwait | * | | | Malawi | | * | • |
| Lebanon | | * | | Mali | | • | • |
| Libya | * | | | Mauritius | | * | |
| Mauritania | | * | • | Mozambique | | * | • |
| Morocco | | * | | Namibia | * | | |
| Oman | * | | | Niger | | * | • |
| Qatar | * | | | Nigeria | * | | |
| Saudi Arabia | * | | | Rwanda | | • | • |
| Sudan | | * | * | São Tomé and Príncipe | | * | • |
| Syrian Arab Republic | | • | | Senegal | | * | • |
| Tunisia | | * | | Seychelles | | * | |
| United Arab Emirates | * | | | Sierra Leone | | * | • |
| Republic of Yemen | | * | | South Africa | | * | |
| **Sub-Saharan Africa** | | | | Swaziland | | * | |
| Angola | * | | | Tanzania | | * | • |
| Benin | | * | • | Togo | | • | • |
| Botswana | * | | | Uganda | | * | • |
| Burkina Faso | | • | • | Zambia | | * | • |
| Burundi | | • | • | Zimbabwe | | • | |

[1]Dot instead of star indicates that the net debtor's main external finance source is official financing.

[2]Dot instead of star indicates that the country has reached the completion point.

[3]Georgia and Mongolia, which are not members of the Commonwealth of Independent States, are included in this group for reasons of geography and similarities in economic structure.

## Box A1. Economic Policy Assumptions Underlying the Projections for Selected Economies

*Fiscal Policy Assumptions*

The short-term fiscal policy assumptions used in the *World Economic Outlook* (WEO) are based on officially announced budgets, adjusted for differences between the national authorities and the IMF staff regarding macroeconomic assumptions and projected fiscal outturns. The medium-term fiscal projections incorporate policy measures that are judged likely to be implemented. In cases where the IMF staff has insufficient information to assess the authorities' budget intentions and prospects for policy implementation, an unchanged structural primary balance is assumed unless indicated otherwise. Specific assumptions used in some of the advanced economies follow (see also Tables B5, B6, B7, and B9 in the online section of the Statistical Appendix for data on fiscal net lending/borrowing and structural balances).[1]

*Argentina:* The 2011 forecasts are based on the 2010 outturn and IMF staff assumptions. For the outer years, the IMF staff assumes unchanged policies.

*Australia:* Fiscal projections are based on IMF staff projections and the 2010–11 Mid-Year Economic and Fiscal Outlook.

*Austria:* The historical figures and the projections for general government deficit and debt do not yet fully reflect the most recent revisions by Statistik Austria in the context of their fiscal notification to Eurostat.

*Belgium:* The estimates for 2010 are preliminary estimates by the National Bank of Belgium. IMF staff projections for 2011 and beyond are based on unchanged policies. The 2011 projections, however,

include some of the planned measures for the 2011 federal budget still under preparation and the 2011 budgetary targets for the regions and communities and the social security administration. For local governments, unchanged policies imply continuation of their electoral cycle.

*Brazil:* The 2010 forecasts are based on the budget law and IMF staff assumptions. For the outer years, the IMF staff assumes unchanged policies, with a further increase in public investment in line with the authorities' intentions.

*Canada:* Projections use the baseline forecasts in the latest Budget 2011—A Low-Tax Plan for Jobs and Growth. The IMF staff makes some adjustments to this forecast for differences in macroeconomic projections. The IMF staff forecast also incorporates the most recent data releases from Finance Canada (Update of Economic and Fiscal Projections, October 2010) and Statistics Canada, including federal, provincial, and territorial budgetary outturns through the end of 2010:Q4.

*China:* For 2010–11, the government is assumed to continue and complete the stimulus program announced in late 2008, although the lack of details published on this package complicates IMF staff analysis. Specifically, the IMF staff assumes the stimulus is not withdrawn in 2010, and so there is no significant fiscal impulse. Stimulus is withdrawn in 2011, resulting in a negative fiscal impulse of about 1 percent of GDP (reflecting both higher revenue and lower spending).

*Denmark:* Projections for 2010–11 are aligned with the latest official budget estimates and the underlying economic projections, adjusted where appropriate for the IMF staff's macroeconomic assumptions. For 2012–16, the projections incorporate key features of the medium-term fiscal plan as embodied in the authorities' 2009 Convergence Program submitted to the European Union.

*France:* Estimates for the general government in 2010 are preliminary estimates from the 2011 budget and, for the central government, reflect the actual outturn. Projections for 2011 and beyond reflect the authorities' 2011–14 multiyear budget, adjusted for differences about assumptions regarding macroeconomic and financial variables and revenue projections.

[1]The output gap is actual minus potential output, as a percent of potential output. Structural balances are expressed as a percent of potential output. The structural balance is the actual net lending/borrowing that would be observed if the level of actual output coincided with potential output. Changes in the structural balance consequently include effects of temporary fiscal measures, the impact of fluctuations in interest rates and debt-service costs, and other noncyclical fluctuations in net lending/borrowing. The computations of structural balances are based on IMF staff estimates of potential GDP and revenue and expenditure elasticities (see the October 1993 *World Economic Outlook*, Annex I). Net debt is defined as gross debt minus financial assets of the general government, which include assets held by the social security insurance system. Estimates of the output gap and of the structural balance are subject to significant margins of uncertainty.

## Box A1 *(continued)*

*Germany:* The estimates for 2010 are preliminary estimates from the Federal Statistical Office of Germany. The IMF staff's projections for 2011 and beyond reflect the authorities' adopted core federal government budget plan adjusted for the differences in the IMF staff's macroeconomic framework and staff assumptions about fiscal developments in state and local governments, the social insurance system, and special funds. The estimate of gross debt at end-2010 includes the transfer of liabilities of bad banks to the government balance sheet.

*Greece:* Macroeconomic and fiscal projections for 2011 and the medium term are consistent with the policies that the IMF has agreed to support in the context of the Stand-By Arrangement. Fiscal projections assume a strong front-loaded fiscal adjustment, which already started in 2010 and will be followed by further measures in 2011–13. Growth is expected to bottom out in late 2010 and to gradually rebound thereafter, coming into positive territory in 2012. The data include fiscal data revisions for 2006–09. These revisions rectify a number of shortfalls with earlier statistics. First, government-controlled enterprises whose sales cover less than 50 percent of production costs have been reclassified as part of the general government sector, in line with Eurostat guidelines. A total of 17 entities were affected, including a number of large loss-making entities. The debt of these entities (7¼ percent of GDP) is now included in headline general government debt data, and their annual losses increase the annual deficit (to the extent that their called guarantees were not reflected in previous deficit data). Second, the revisions reflect better information on arrears (including for tax refunds, lump sum payments to retiring civil service pensioners, and payments to health sector suppliers) and revised social security balances that reflect corrections for imputed interest payments, double counting of revenues, and other inaccuracies. Finally, newly available information on swaps also helps explain the upward revision in debt data.

*Hong Kong SAR:* Projections are based on the authorities' medium-term fiscal projections.

*Hungary:* Fiscal projections include IMF staff assumptions about the macroeconomic framework and the impact of existing legislated measures and fiscal policy plans announced by end-December 2010.

*India:* Historical data are based on budgetary execution data. Projections are based on available information on the authorities' fiscal plans, with adjustments for IMF staff assumptions. Subnational data are incorporated with a lag of up to two years; general government data are thus finalized well after central government data. IMF presentation differs from Indian national accounts data, particularly regarding divestment and license auction proceeds, net versus gross recording of revenues in certain minor categories, and some public sector lending.

*Indonesia:* The 2010 deficit was lower than expected (0.6 percent of GDP), reflecting underspending, particularly for public investment. The 2011 deficit is estimated at 1.5 percent of GDP, lower than the budget estimate of 1.8 percent of GDP. While higher oil prices will have a negative budgetary impact in the absence of fuel subsidy reform, this effect is likely to be offset by underspending, in particular on public investment, given significant budgeted increases. Fiscal projections for 2012–16 are built around key policy reforms needed to support economic growth, namely enhancing budget implementation to ensure fiscal policy effectiveness, reducing energy subsidies through gradual administrative price increases, and continuous revenue mobilization efforts to increase room for infrastructure development.

*Ireland:* The fiscal projections are based on the 2011 budget and the medium-term adjustment envisaged in the December 2010 EU/IMF Program. This includes €15 billion in consolidation measures over 2011–14, with €6 billion in savings programmed for 2011. The projections are adjusted for differences between the macroeconomic projections of the IMF staff and those of the Irish authorities. The new government that assumed office in early March 2011 has also committed to the 2011–12 fiscal program and to further consolidation in the medium term.

*Italy:* The fiscal projections incorporate the impact of the 2010 budget law and fiscal adjustment measures for 2011–13 as approved by the government in May 2010 and modified during parliamentary approval in June–July 2010. The estimates for 2010 are the preliminary outturn data from the Italian

## Box A1 *(continued)*

National Institute of Statistics (Istat). The IMF staff projections are based on the authorities' estimates of the policy scenario, including the above-mentioned medium-term fiscal consolidation package and adjusted mainly for differences in macroeconomic assumptions and for less optimistic assumptions concerning the impact of revenue administration measures (to combat tax evasion). After 2013, a constant structural primary balance (net of one-time items) is assumed.

*Japan:* The 2011 projections assume fiscal measures already announced by the government and reconstruction spending of around 1 percent of GDP. The medium-term projections typically assume that expenditure and revenue of the general government are adjusted in line with current underlying demographic and economic trends (excluding fiscal stimulus).

*Korea:* The fiscal projections assume that fiscal policies will be implemented in 2011 as announced by the government. The projection for 2010 is mainly based on the outturn as of November 2010, assuming that the first 11 months had collected/used about 92 percent of total revenue/expenditure. As a result, the fiscal impulse is projected to be –3 percent of GDP in 2010. Expenditure numbers for 2011 are broadly in line with the government's budget. Revenue projections reflect the IMF staff's macroeconomic assumptions, adjusted for the tax measures included in the multiyear stimulus package introduced in 2009 and discretionary revenue-raising measures included in the 2010 budget. The medium-term projections assume that the government will continue with its consolidation plans and balance the budget (excluding social security funds) by 2013.

*Mexico:* Fiscal projections are based on (1) the IMF staff's macroeconomic projections; (2) the modified balanced budget rule under the Fiscal Responsibility Legislation, including the use of the exceptional clause; and (3) the authorities' projections for spending, including for pensions and health care, and for wage restraint. For 2010–11, projections take into account departure from the balanced budget target under the exceptional clause of the fiscal framework, which allows for a small deficit that reflects cyclical deterioration in revenues.

*Netherlands:* Fiscal projections for the period 2010–15 are based on the Bureau for Economic Policy Analysis budget projections, after adjusting for differences in macroeconomic assumptions. For 2016, the projection assumes that fiscal consolidation continues at the same pace as for 2015.

*New Zealand:* Fiscal projections are based on the authorities' 2010 budget and IMF staff estimates. The New Zealand fiscal accounts switched to generally accepted accounting principles beginning in fiscal year 2006/07, with no comparable historical data.

*Portugal:* 2010 data are preliminary. For 2011 and beyond, the IMF staff incorporates all the approved fiscal measures (thus excluding the measures proposed in March 2011, which were rejected by Parliament). The fiscal numbers also incorporate the impact of the IMF staff's macroeconomic projections.

*Russia:* Projections for 2011–13 are based on the non-oil deficit in percent of GDP implied by the draft medium-term budget and on the IMF staff's revenue projections. The IMF staff assumes an unchanged non-oil federal government balance in percent of GDP during 2013–16.

*Saudi Arabia:* The authorities adopt a conservative assumption for oil prices—the 2011 budget is based on a price of $54 a barrel—with the result that fiscal outcomes often differ significantly from the budget. IMF staff projections of oil revenues are based on WEO baseline oil prices discounted by 5 percent, reflecting the higher sulfur content in Saudi crude oil. Regarding non-oil revenues, customs receipts are assumed to grow in line with imports, investment income in line with the London interbank offered rate (LIBOR), and fees and charges as a function of non-oil GDP. On the expenditure side, wages are assumed to rise above the natural rate of increase, reflecting a salary increase of 15 percent distributed during 2008–10, and goods and services are projected to grow in line with inflation over the medium term. In 2010 and 2013, 13th-month pay is awarded based on the lunar calendar. Interest payments are projected to decline in line with the authorities' policy of repaying public debt. Capital spending in 2010 is projected to be higher than in the budget by about 32 percent and in line with the authorities' announcement of $400 billion in spending over the

## Box A1 *(concluded)*

medium term. The pace of spending is projected to slow over the medium term, leading to a tightening of the fiscal stance.

*Singapore:* For fiscal year 2011/12, projections are based on budget numbers. For the remainder of the projection period, the IMF staff assumes unchanged policies.

*South Africa:* Fiscal projections are based on the authorities' 2011 budget and policy intentions stated in the Budget Review, published February 23, 2011.

*Spain:* The 2010 numbers are the authorities' estimated outturns for the general government for the year. For 2011 and beyond, the projections are based on the 2011 budget and the authorities' medium-term plan, adjusted for the IMF staff's macroeconomic projections.

*Sweden:* Fiscal projections for 2010 are in line with the authorities' projections. The impact of cyclical developments on the fiscal accounts is calculated using the OECD's latest semi-elasticity.

*Switzerland:* Projections for 2009–15 are based on IMF staff calculations, which incorporate measures to restore balance in the federal accounts and strengthen social security finances.

*Turkey:* Fiscal projections assume the authorities adhere to their budget balance targets as set out in the 2011–2013 Medium-Term Program.

*United Kingdom:* Fiscal projections are based on the authorities' 2011 budget announced in March 2011 and Economic and Fiscal Outlook by the Office for Budget Responsibility published along with the Budget. These projections incorporate the announced medium-term consolidation plans from 2011 onward. The projections are adjusted for differences in forecasts of macroeconomic and financial variables.

*United States:* Fiscal projections are based on the president's draft FY2012 budget adjusted for the IMF staff's assessment of policies likely adopted by Congress. Compared with the president's budget, the IMF staff assumes more front-loaded discretionary spending cuts, a further extension of emergency unemployment benefits, and delayed action on the proposed revenue-raising measures. IMF staff estimates of fiscal deficits also exclude certain measures yet to be specified by the authorities and are adjusted for a different accounting treatment of financial sector support. The resulting projections are adjusted to reflect IMF staff forecasts of key macroeconomic and financial variables and are converted to the general government basis.

### Monetary Policy Assumptions

Monetary policy assumptions are based on the established policy framework in each country. In most cases, this implies a nonaccommodative stance over the business cycle: official interest rates will increase when economic indicators suggest that inflation will rise above its acceptable rate or range, and they will decrease when indicators suggest that prospective inflation will not exceed the acceptable rate or range, that prospective output growth is below its potential rate, and that the margin of slack in the economy is significant. On this basis, the LIBOR on six-month U.S. dollar deposits is assumed to average 0.6 percent in 2011 and 0.9 percent in 2012 (see Table 1.1). The rate on three-month euro deposits is assumed to average 1.7 percent in 2011 and 2.6 percent in 2012. The interest rate on six-month Japanese yen deposits is assumed to average 0.6 percent in 2011 and 0.3 percent in 2012.

## List of Tables

## Table A1. Summary of World Output[1]

*(Annual percent change)*

| | Average 1993–2002 | 2003 | 2004 | 2005 | 2006 | 2007 | 2008 | 2009 | 2010 | Projections 2011 | 2012 | 2016 |
|---|---|---|---|---|---|---|---|---|---|---|---|---|
| **World** | **3.3** | **3.6** | **4.9** | **4.6** | **5.2** | **5.4** | **2.9** | **−0.5** | **5.0** | **4.4** | **4.5** | **4.7** |
| **Advanced Economies** | **2.8** | **1.9** | **3.1** | **2.7** | **3.0** | **2.7** | **0.2** | **−3.4** | **3.0** | **2.4** | **2.6** | **2.4** |
| United States | 3.4 | 2.5 | 3.6 | 3.1 | 2.7 | 1.9 | 0.0 | −2.6 | 2.8 | 2.8 | 2.9 | 2.7 |
| Euro Area[2] | 2.1 | 0.8 | 2.2 | 1.7 | 3.1 | 2.9 | 0.4 | −4.1 | 1.7 | 1.6 | 1.8 | 1.7 |
| Japan | 0.8 | 1.4 | 2.7 | 1.9 | 2.0 | 2.4 | −1.2 | −6.3 | 3.9 | 1.4 | 2.1 | 1.2 |
| Other Advanced Economies[3] | 3.8 | 2.6 | 4.1 | 3.4 | 3.9 | 4.0 | 1.1 | −2.3 | 4.3 | 3.2 | 3.3 | 3.1 |
| **Emerging and Developing Economies** | **4.1** | **6.2** | **7.5** | **7.3** | **8.2** | **8.8** | **6.1** | **2.7** | **7.3** | **6.5** | **6.5** | **6.8** |
| **Regional Groups** | | | | | | | | | | | | |
| Central and Eastern Europe | 3.3 | 4.8 | 7.3 | 5.9 | 6.4 | 5.5 | 3.2 | −3.6 | 4.2 | 3.7 | 4.0 | 3.9 |
| Commonwealth of Independent States[4] | −1.2 | 7.7 | 8.1 | 6.7 | 8.9 | 9.0 | 5.3 | −6.4 | 4.6 | 5.0 | 4.7 | 4.3 |
| Developing Asia | 7.1 | 8.1 | 8.6 | 9.5 | 10.4 | 11.4 | 7.7 | 7.2 | 9.5 | 8.4 | 8.4 | 8.6 |
| Latin America and the Caribbean | 2.7 | 2.1 | 6.0 | 4.7 | 5.6 | 5.7 | 4.3 | −1.7 | 6.1 | 4.7 | 4.2 | 3.9 |
| Middle East and North Africa | 3.3 | 7.3 | 6.0 | 5.4 | 5.8 | 6.2 | 5.1 | 1.8 | 3.8 | 4.1 | 4.2 | 5.1 |
| Sub-Saharan Africa | 3.7 | 4.9 | 7.1 | 6.2 | 6.4 | 7.2 | 5.6 | 2.8 | 5.0 | 5.5 | 5.9 | 5.4 |
| *Memorandum* | | | | | | | | | | | | |
| European Union | 2.4 | 1.5 | 2.6 | 2.2 | 3.5 | 3.2 | 0.7 | −4.1 | 1.8 | 1.8 | 2.1 | 2.1 |
| **Analytical Groups** | | | | | | | | | | | | |
| **By Source of Export Earnings** | | | | | | | | | | | | |
| Fuel | 1.3 | 7.2 | 7.9 | 6.7 | 7.5 | 7.7 | 5.2 | −1.9 | 3.8 | 4.9 | 4.4 | 4.4 |
| Nonfuel | 4.9 | 6.0 | 7.4 | 7.4 | 8.4 | 9.1 | 6.3 | 3.8 | 8.0 | 6.9 | 6.9 | 7.2 |
| Of Which, Primary Products | 3.9 | 4.1 | 5.5 | 6.1 | 6.2 | 6.6 | 6.6 | 1.5 | 7.0 | 6.7 | 5.7 | 5.6 |
| **By External Financing Source** | | | | | | | | | | | | |
| Net Debtor Economies | 3.5 | 4.5 | 6.6 | 5.9 | 6.7 | 6.8 | 4.6 | 0.9 | 6.8 | 5.3 | 5.3 | 5.6 |
| Of Which, Official Financing | 3.5 | 3.3 | 6.3 | 6.4 | 5.9 | 5.8 | 6.3 | 5.2 | 5.1 | 6.2 | 5.9 | 6.1 |
| **Net Debtor Economies by Debt-Servicing Experience** | | | | | | | | | | | | |
| Economies with Arrears and/or Rescheduling during 2005–09 | 2.4 | 6.1 | 7.5 | 7.8 | 7.7 | 7.7 | 6.1 | 2.2 | 6.5 | 5.3 | 5.0 | 4.9 |
| *Memorandum* | | | | | | | | | | | | |
| **Median Growth Rate** | | | | | | | | | | | | |
| Advanced Economies | 3.2 | 2.2 | 4.0 | 3.1 | 3.8 | 4.1 | 0.9 | −3.5 | 2.4 | 2.4 | 2.4 | 2.5 |
| Emerging and Developing Economies | 3.8 | 4.7 | 5.4 | 5.4 | 5.6 | 6.3 | 5.1 | 1.8 | 4.3 | 4.6 | 4.7 | 4.7 |
| **Output per Capita** | | | | | | | | | | | | |
| Advanced Economies | 2.1 | 1.2 | 2.4 | 2.0 | 2.3 | 2.0 | −0.5 | −4.0 | 2.4 | 1.7 | 2.0 | 1.8 |
| Emerging and Developing Economies | 2.8 | 5.0 | 6.4 | 6.1 | 7.1 | 7.6 | 4.9 | 1.6 | 6.3 | 5.5 | 5.5 | 5.8 |
| **World Growth Rate Based on Market Exchange** | **2.7** | **2.7** | **3.9** | **3.5** | **4.0** | **3.9** | **1.6** | **−2.1** | **3.9** | **3.5** | **3.7** | **3.8** |
| **Value of World Output (billions of U.S. dollars)** | | | | | | | | | | | | |
| At Market Exchange Rates | 30,111 | 37,416 | 42,119 | 45,562 | 49,349 | 55,702 | 61,268 | 57,920 | 62,909 | 68,652 | 72,486 | 90,452 |
| At Purchasing Power Parities | 37,220 | 48,797 | 52,655 | 56,729 | 61,583 | 66,715 | 70,038 | 70,124 | 74,265 | 78,291 | 82,913 | 105,546 |

[1]Real GDP.
[2]Excludes Estonia.
[3]In this table, Other Advanced Economies means advanced economies excluding the United States, Euro Area countries, and Japan but including Estonia.
[4]Georgia and Mongolia, which are not members of the Commonwealth of Independent States, are included in this group for reasons of geography and similarities in economic structure.

## Table A2. Advanced Economies: Real GDP and Total Domestic Demand[1]

*(Annual percent change)*

| | Average 1993–2002 | 2003 | 2004 | 2005 | 2006 | 2007 | 2008 | 2009 | 2010 | Projections 2011 | Projections 2012 | Projections 2016 | Fourth Quarter[2] 2010:Q4 | Fourth Quarter[2] Projections 2011:Q4 | Fourth Quarter[2] Projections 2012:Q4 |
|---|---|---|---|---|---|---|---|---|---|---|---|---|---|---|---|
| **Real GDP** | | | | | | | | | | | | | | | |
| **Advanced Economies** | **2.8** | **1.9** | **3.1** | **2.7** | **3.0** | **2.7** | **0.2** | **−3.4** | **3.0** | **2.4** | **2.6** | **2.4** | **2.7** | **2.6** | **2.5** |
| United States | 3.4 | 2.5 | 3.6 | 3.1 | 2.7 | 1.9 | 0.0 | −2.6 | 2.8 | 2.8 | 2.9 | 2.7 | 2.7 | 3.0 | 2.7 |
| Euro Area[3] | 2.1 | 0.8 | 2.2 | 1.7 | 3.1 | 2.9 | 0.4 | −4.1 | 1.7 | 1.6 | 1.8 | 1.7 | 2.0 | 1.5 | 2.1 |
| Germany | 1.5 | −0.2 | 0.7 | 0.9 | 3.6 | 2.8 | 0.7 | −4.7 | 3.5 | 2.5 | 2.1 | 1.3 | 4.0 | 1.9 | 2.5 |
| France | 2.0 | 1.1 | 2.3 | 2.0 | 2.4 | 2.3 | 0.1 | −2.5 | 1.5 | 1.6 | 1.8 | 2.1 | 1.5 | 1.7 | 2.0 |
| Italy | 1.6 | 0.0 | 1.5 | 0.7 | 2.0 | 1.5 | −1.3 | −5.2 | 1.3 | 1.1 | 1.3 | 1.4 | 1.5 | 1.3 | 1.2 |
| Spain | 3.2 | 3.1 | 3.3 | 3.6 | 4.0 | 3.6 | 0.9 | −3.7 | −0.1 | 0.8 | 1.6 | 1.7 | 0.6 | 1.1 | 1.9 |
| Netherlands | 2.9 | 0.3 | 2.2 | 2.0 | 3.4 | 3.9 | 1.9 | −3.9 | 1.7 | 1.5 | 1.5 | 1.8 | 2.1 | 0.6 | 2.8 |
| Belgium | 2.3 | 0.8 | 3.1 | 2.0 | 2.7 | 2.8 | 0.8 | −2.7 | 2.0 | 1.7 | 1.9 | 1.9 | 1.6 | 1.9 | 2.1 |
| Austria | 2.2 | 0.8 | 2.5 | 2.5 | 3.6 | 3.7 | 2.2 | −3.9 | 2.0 | 2.4 | 2.3 | 1.8 | 3.1 | 1.3 | 3.1 |
| Greece | 2.7 | 5.9 | 4.4 | 2.3 | 5.2 | 4.3 | 1.0 | −2.0 | −4.5 | −3.0 | 1.1 | 2.9 | −6.6 | −0.6 | 1.6 |
| Portugal | 2.7 | −0.9 | 1.6 | 0.8 | 1.4 | 2.4 | 0.0 | −2.5 | 1.4 | −1.5 | −0.5 | 1.2 | 1.2 | −2.0 | 0.3 |
| Finland | 3.5 | 2.0 | 4.1 | 2.9 | 4.4 | 5.3 | 0.9 | −8.2 | 3.1 | 3.1 | 2.5 | 2.0 | 5.0 | 1.4 | 3.5 |
| Ireland | 7.7 | 4.4 | 4.6 | 6.0 | 5.3 | 5.6 | −3.5 | −7.6 | −1.0 | 0.5 | 1.9 | 3.4 | −0.6 | 2.6 | 1.9 |
| Slovak Republic | ... | 4.8 | 5.1 | 6.7 | 8.5 | 10.5 | 5.8 | −4.8 | 4.0 | 3.8 | 4.2 | 4.2 | 3.4 | 3.9 | 4.2 |
| Slovenia | 4.1 | 2.8 | 4.3 | 4.5 | 5.9 | 6.9 | 3.7 | −8.1 | 1.2 | 2.0 | 2.4 | 1.9 | 1.9 | 3.9 | 2.2 |
| Luxembourg | 4.7 | 1.5 | 4.4 | 5.4 | 5.0 | 6.6 | 1.4 | −3.7 | 3.4 | 3.0 | 3.1 | 3.1 | 3.2 | 2.7 | 3.7 |
| Estonia | ... | 7.6 | 7.2 | 9.4 | 10.6 | 6.9 | −5.1 | −13.9 | 3.1 | 3.3 | 3.7 | 3.6 | 6.8 | 1.7 | 4.8 |
| Cyprus | 4.1 | 1.9 | 4.2 | 3.9 | 4.1 | 5.1 | 3.6 | −1.7 | 1.0 | 1.7 | 2.2 | 2.7 | 2.6 | 1.7 | 2.2 |
| Malta | ... | −0.3 | 1.1 | 4.7 | 2.1 | 4.4 | 5.3 | −3.4 | 3.6 | 2.5 | 2.2 | 2.4 | 4.0 | 5.1 | 2.0 |
| Japan | 0.8 | 1.4 | 2.7 | 1.9 | 2.0 | 2.4 | −1.2 | −6.3 | 3.9 | 1.4 | 2.1 | 1.2 | 2.5 | 2.5 | 1.3 |
| United Kingdom | 3.1 | 2.8 | 3.0 | 2.2 | 2.8 | 2.7 | −0.1 | −4.9 | 1.3 | 1.7 | 2.3 | 2.6 | 1.5 | 2.2 | 2.4 |
| Canada | 3.5 | 1.9 | 3.1 | 3.0 | 2.8 | 2.2 | 0.5 | −2.5 | 3.1 | 2.8 | 2.6 | 1.9 | 3.2 | 2.8 | 2.5 |
| Korea | 6.1 | 2.8 | 4.6 | 4.0 | 5.2 | 5.1 | 2.3 | 0.2 | 6.1 | 4.5 | 4.2 | 4.0 | 4.9 | 4.6 | 4.2 |
| Australia | 4.0 | 3.3 | 3.8 | 3.1 | 2.6 | 4.6 | 2.6 | 1.3 | 2.7 | 3.0 | 3.5 | 3.0 | 2.7 | 3.5 | 3.2 |
| Taiwan Province of China | 5.0 | 3.7 | 6.2 | 4.7 | 5.4 | 6.0 | 0.7 | −1.9 | 10.8 | 5.4 | 5.2 | 4.9 | 5.6 | 8.3 | 3.7 |
| Sweden | 2.6 | 2.3 | 4.2 | 3.2 | 4.3 | 3.3 | −0.6 | −5.3 | 5.5 | 3.8 | 3.5 | 3.4 | 7.2 | 1.8 | 5.7 |
| Switzerland | 1.3 | −0.2 | 2.5 | 2.6 | 3.6 | 3.6 | 1.9 | −1.9 | 2.6 | 2.4 | 1.8 | 1.8 | 3.2 | 1.8 | 1.8 |
| Hong Kong SAR | 3.0 | 3.0 | 8.5 | 7.1 | 7.0 | 6.4 | 2.3 | −2.7 | 6.8 | 5.4 | 4.2 | 4.3 | 6.0 | 5.7 | 2.9 |
| Singapore | 6.1 | 4.6 | 9.2 | 7.4 | 8.7 | 8.8 | 1.5 | −0.8 | 14.5 | 5.2 | 4.4 | 4.0 | 13.7 | 6.3 | 3.3 |
| Czech Republic | ... | 3.6 | 4.5 | 6.3 | 6.8 | 6.1 | 2.5 | −4.1 | 2.3 | 1.7 | 2.9 | 3.2 | 2.6 | 1.4 | 4.4 |
| Norway | 3.4 | 1.0 | 3.9 | 2.7 | 2.3 | 2.7 | 0.8 | −1.4 | 0.4 | 2.9 | 2.5 | 2.1 | 1.5 | 2.7 | 2.5 |
| Israel | 4.5 | 1.5 | 5.1 | 4.9 | 5.7 | 5.3 | 4.2 | 0.8 | 4.6 | 3.8 | 3.8 | 3.3 | 5.6 | 2.4 | 4.7 |
| Denmark | 2.4 | 0.4 | 2.3 | 2.4 | 3.4 | 1.6 | −1.1 | −5.2 | 2.1 | 2.0 | 2.0 | 1.9 | 2.7 | 2.3 | 2.1 |
| New Zealand | 3.8 | 4.2 | 4.5 | 3.3 | 1.0 | 2.8 | −0.2 | −2.1 | 1.5 | 0.9 | 4.1 | 2.4 | 0.8 | 2.0 | 4.4 |
| Iceland | 3.3 | 2.4 | 7.7 | 7.5 | 4.6 | 6.0 | 1.4 | −6.9 | −3.5 | 2.3 | 2.9 | 3.0 | 0.0 | 3.3 | 2.3 |
| *Memorandum* | | | | | | | | | | | | | | | |
| Major Advanced Economies | 2.5 | 1.8 | 2.9 | 2.4 | 2.6 | 2.2 | −0.2 | −3.7 | 2.8 | 2.3 | 2.5 | 2.2 | 2.6 | 2.5 | 2.3 |
| Newly Industrialized Asian Economies | 5.4 | 3.2 | 5.9 | 4.8 | 5.8 | 5.9 | 1.8 | −0.8 | 8.4 | 4.9 | 4.5 | 4.3 | 6.1 | 5.9 | 3.8 |
| **Real Total Domestic Demand** | | | | | | | | | | | | | | | |
| **Advanced Economies** | **2.8** | **2.2** | **3.2** | **2.7** | **2.8** | **2.3** | **−0.2** | **−3.7** | **2.8** | **2.0** | **2.3** | **2.4** | **2.8** | **2.4** | **2.4** |
| United States | 3.8 | 2.8 | 4.0 | 3.2 | 2.6 | 1.3 | −1.1 | −3.6 | 3.2 | 2.4 | 2.7 | 2.9 | 3.1 | 2.8 | 2.7 |
| Euro Area[3] | ... | 1.4 | 1.9 | 1.9 | 2.9 | 2.6 | 0.4 | −3.4 | 0.9 | 0.8 | 1.3 | 1.6 | 1.4 | 1.1 | 1.6 |
| Germany | 1.0 | 0.6 | −0.1 | 0.0 | 2.4 | 1.3 | 1.2 | −1.9 | 2.5 | 1.3 | 1.6 | 1.2 | 3.4 | 1.5 | 1.7 |
| France | 1.9 | 1.8 | 3.1 | 2.8 | 2.7 | 3.3 | 0.4 | −2.4 | 1.1 | 1.5 | 1.8 | 2.1 | 0.9 | 1.7 | 1.9 |
| Italy | 1.3 | 0.8 | 1.3 | 0.9 | 2.0 | 1.3 | −1.4 | −3.9 | 1.6 | 1.4 | 0.9 | 1.2 | 2.3 | 0.9 | 1.3 |
| Spain | 3.1 | 3.8 | 4.8 | 5.1 | 5.2 | 4.1 | −0.6 | −6.0 | −1.1 | −0.1 | 1.3 | 1.5 | −0.6 | 1.1 | 1.4 |
| Japan | 0.8 | 0.8 | 1.9 | 1.7 | 1.2 | 1.3 | −1.4 | −4.8 | 2.1 | 1.8 | 2.0 | 1.0 | 2.1 | 2.7 | 1.1 |
| United Kingdom | 3.3 | 2.9 | 3.5 | 2.1 | 2.5 | 3.1 | −0.7 | −5.5 | 2.4 | 0.9 | 1.6 | 2.3 | 2.8 | 0.5 | 2.1 |
| Canada | 2.9 | 4.5 | 4.1 | 5.0 | 4.4 | 3.9 | 2.5 | −2.6 | 5.2 | 2.8 | 2.5 | 1.8 | 4.1 | 3.1 | 2.5 |
| Other Advanced Economies[4] | 3.9 | 2.0 | 4.6 | 3.3 | 4.0 | 4.7 | 1.6 | −2.9 | 5.7 | 4.1 | 3.8 | 3.8 | 4.9 | 4.0 | 4.5 |
| *Memorandum* | | | | | | | | | | | | | | | |
| Major Advanced Economies | 2.6 | 2.2 | 3.0 | 2.5 | 2.4 | 1.7 | −0.6 | −3.6 | 2.8 | 2.0 | 2.2 | 2.2 | 2.8 | 2.3 | 2.1 |
| Newly Industrialized Asian Economies | 4.7 | 0.8 | 4.8 | 2.9 | 4.2 | 4.3 | 1.7 | −3.2 | 7.9 | 4.8 | 4.3 | 4.5 | 5.5 | 5.2 | 5.1 |

[1]When countries are not listed alphabetically, they are ordered on the basis of economic size.
[2]From the fourth quarter of the preceding year.
[3]Excludes Estonia.
[4]In this table, Other Advanced Economies means advanced economies excluding the United States, Euro Area countries, and Japan but including Estonia.

## Table A3. Advanced Economies: Components of Real GDP
*(Annual percent change)*

| | Averages | | 2003 | 2004 | 2005 | 2006 | 2007 | 2008 | 2009 | 2010 | Projections | |
| --- | --- | --- | --- | --- | --- | --- | --- | --- | --- | --- | --- | --- |
| | 1993–2002 | 2003–12 | | | | | | | | | 2011 | 2012 |
| **Private Consumer Expenditure** | | | | | | | | | | | | |
| **Advanced Economies** | **3.0** | **1.7** | **2.0** | **2.7** | **2.7** | **2.6** | **2.5** | **0.2** | **−1.1** | **1.7** | **2.0** | **2.1** |
| United States | 3.8 | 2.0 | 2.8 | 3.5 | 3.4 | 2.9 | 2.4 | −0.3 | −1.2 | 1.8 | 2.9 | 2.2 |
| Euro Area[1] | ... | 1.1 | 1.2 | 1.6 | 1.8 | 2.1 | 1.7 | 0.4 | −1.1 | 0.8 | 1.1 | 1.3 |
| Germany | 1.5 | 0.5 | 0.1 | 0.1 | 0.3 | 1.4 | −0.2 | 0.7 | −0.2 | 0.4 | 1.2 | 1.1 |
| France | 2.0 | 1.8 | 2.1 | 2.4 | 2.5 | 2.6 | 2.5 | 0.5 | 0.6 | 1.7 | 1.4 | 1.6 |
| Italy | 1.3 | 0.6 | 1.0 | 0.7 | 1.1 | 1.2 | 1.1 | −0.8 | −1.8 | 1.0 | 1.4 | 1.4 |
| Spain | 2.8 | 1.8 | 2.9 | 4.2 | 4.2 | 3.8 | 3.7 | −0.6 | −4.2 | 1.2 | 1.3 | 1.4 |
| Japan | 1.2 | 0.7 | 0.4 | 1.6 | 1.3 | 1.5 | 1.6 | −0.7 | −1.9 | 1.8 | −0.2 | 1.6 |
| United Kingdom | 3.6 | 1.2 | 3.0 | 3.1 | 2.2 | 1.8 | 2.2 | 0.4 | −3.2 | 0.6 | 0.4 | 1.5 |
| Canada | 3.1 | 3.1 | 3.0 | 3.3 | 3.7 | 4.2 | 4.6 | 2.9 | 0.4 | 3.4 | 3.2 | 2.6 |
| Other Advanced Economies[2] | 4.2 | 3.0 | 1.8 | 3.7 | 3.5 | 3.7 | 4.7 | 1.2 | 0.2 | 3.4 | 3.7 | 3.7 |
| *Memorandum* | | | | | | | | | | | | |
| Major Advanced Economies | 2.8 | 1.6 | 2.0 | 2.6 | 2.5 | 2.4 | 2.0 | 0.0 | −1.2 | 1.6 | 1.9 | 1.9 |
| Newly Industrialized Asian Economies | 5.5 | 3.1 | 0.6 | 3.0 | 3.9 | 3.8 | 4.7 | 1.0 | 0.5 | 4.2 | 4.6 | 4.4 |
| **Public Consumption** | | | | | | | | | | | | |
| **Advanced Economies** | **2.0** | **1.4** | **2.2** | **1.7** | **1.3** | **1.6** | **1.9** | **2.3** | **2.4** | **1.4** | **−0.2** | **−0.5** |
| United States | 1.7 | 0.8 | 2.2 | 1.4 | 0.6 | 1.0 | 1.3 | 2.5 | 1.9 | 1.0 | −1.7 | −2.0 |
| Euro Area[1] | ... | 1.5 | 1.7 | 1.6 | 1.6 | 2.2 | 2.2 | 2.4 | 2.4 | 0.7 | −0.1 | −0.1 |
| Germany | 1.4 | 1.2 | 0.4 | −0.7 | 0.4 | 1.0 | 1.6 | 2.3 | 2.9 | 2.3 | 1.1 | 0.6 |
| France | 1.3 | 1.5 | 2.0 | 2.2 | 1.2 | 1.3 | 1.5 | 1.6 | 2.8 | 1.4 | 0.5 | 0.5 |
| Italy | 0.5 | 0.8 | 1.9 | 2.2 | 1.9 | 0.5 | 0.9 | 0.5 | 1.0 | −0.6 | 0.1 | −0.3 |
| Spain | 3.1 | 3.2 | 4.8 | 6.3 | 5.5 | 4.6 | 5.5 | 5.8 | 3.2 | −0.7 | −1.1 | −1.6 |
| Japan | 2.9 | 1.5 | 2.3 | 1.9 | 1.6 | 0.4 | 1.5 | 0.5 | 3.0 | 2.3 | 1.2 | 0.6 |
| United Kingdom | 1.6 | 1.3 | 3.4 | 3.0 | 2.0 | 1.4 | 1.3 | 1.6 | 1.0 | 0.8 | −0.5 | −1.3 |
| Canada | 1.1 | 2.7 | 3.1 | 2.0 | 1.4 | 3.0 | 2.7 | 3.9 | 3.5 | 3.4 | 2.9 | 1.1 |
| Other Advanced Economies[2] | 2.9 | 2.6 | 2.4 | 1.9 | 2.0 | 3.2 | 3.1 | 2.9 | 3.2 | 2.9 | 2.3 | 2.0 |
| *Memorandum* | | | | | | | | | | | | |
| Major Advanced Economies | 1.7 | 1.1 | 2.1 | 1.5 | 1.0 | 1.0 | 1.4 | 2.0 | 2.2 | 1.3 | −0.4 | −0.9 |
| Newly Industrialized Asian Economies | 3.8 | 3.2 | 2.2 | 2.4 | 2.4 | 3.9 | 4.0 | 3.3 | 4.2 | 3.7 | 2.9 | 2.8 |
| **Gross Fixed Capital Formation** | | | | | | | | | | | | |
| **Advanced Economies** | **3.4** | **1.4** | **2.1** | **4.5** | **4.3** | **3.9** | **2.2** | **−2.5** | **−12.1** | **2.5** | **4.2** | **6.2** |
| United States | 5.6 | 1.2 | 3.1 | 6.2 | 5.3 | 2.5 | −1.2 | −4.5 | −14.8 | 3.2 | 5.3 | 9.7 |
| Euro Area[1] | ... | 0.8 | 1.3 | 2.3 | 3.2 | 5.4 | 4.7 | −0.8 | −11.4 | −0.7 | 1.9 | 3.0 |
| Germany | 0.2 | 1.8 | −0.3 | −0.3 | 0.9 | 8.0 | 4.7 | 2.5 | −10.1 | 6.0 | 4.2 | 3.7 |
| France | 2.1 | 1.6 | 2.2 | 3.3 | 4.4 | 4.5 | 6.0 | 0.5 | −7.1 | −1.6 | 1.5 | 2.6 |
| Italy | 1.9 | −0.3 | −1.2 | 2.3 | 0.8 | 2.9 | 1.7 | −3.8 | −11.9 | 2.5 | 2.6 | 2.6 |
| Spain | 4.4 | 0.0 | 5.9 | 5.1 | 7.0 | 7.2 | 4.5 | −4.8 | −16.0 | −7.6 | −2.7 | 4.0 |
| Japan | −1.2 | −0.3 | −0.5 | 1.4 | 3.1 | 0.5 | −1.2 | −3.6 | −11.7 | −0.2 | 6.3 | 4.3 |
| United Kingdom | 4.5 | 1.4 | 1.1 | 5.1 | 2.4 | 6.4 | 7.8 | −5.0 | −15.4 | 3.0 | 3.9 | 6.4 |
| Canada | 4.2 | 3.7 | 6.2 | 7.8 | 9.3 | 7.1 | 3.5 | 1.4 | −11.7 | 8.3 | 3.2 | 3.3 |
| Other Advanced Economies[2] | 4.3 | 3.7 | 2.8 | 6.2 | 4.7 | 5.8 | 6.7 | −0.3 | −5.9 | 7.2 | 5.5 | 5.5 |
| *Memorandum* | | | | | | | | | | | | |
| Major Advanced Economies | 3.3 | 1.1 | 1.8 | 4.4 | 4.2 | 3.4 | 1.0 | −3.0 | −13.0 | 2.8 | 4.7 | 6.8 |
| Newly Industrialized Asian Economies | 4.1 | 3.3 | 1.9 | 6.2 | 2.2 | 3.9 | 4.6 | −3.0 | −3.9 | 11.4 | 5.8 | 5.2 |

## Table A3. Advanced Economies: Components of Real GDP (concluded)

| | Averages | | | | | | | | | | Projections | |
|---|---|---|---|---|---|---|---|---|---|---|---|---|
| | 1993–2002 | 2003–12 | 2003 | 2004 | 2005 | 2006 | 2007 | 2008 | 2009 | 2010 | 2011 | 2012 |
| **Final Domestic Demand** | | | | | | | | | | | | |
| **Advanced Economies** | **2.8** | **1.6** | **2.0** | **2.9** | **2.8** | **2.7** | **2.3** | **0.0** | **−2.7** | **1.8** | **2.1** | **2.3** |
| United States | 3.8 | 1.7 | 2.8 | 3.6 | 3.3 | 2.5 | 1.5 | −0.6 | −3.1 | 1.8 | 2.5 | 2.6 |
| Euro Area[1] | . . . | 1.1 | 1.3 | 1.8 | 2.1 | 2.8 | 2.4 | 0.6 | −2.6 | 0.5 | 1.0 | 1.3 |
| Germany | 1.2 | 0.9 | 0.1 | −0.1 | 0.4 | 2.6 | 1.1 | 1.4 | −1.8 | 1.9 | 1.9 | 1.6 |
| France | 1.9 | 1.7 | 2.1 | 2.5 | 2.6 | 2.7 | 3.0 | 0.7 | −0.5 | 1.0 | 1.2 | 1.5 |
| Italy | 1.3 | 0.5 | 0.7 | 1.4 | 1.2 | 1.4 | 1.2 | −1.2 | −3.4 | 0.9 | 1.4 | 1.3 |
| Spain | 3.2 | 1.6 | 4.0 | 4.8 | 5.2 | 4.9 | 4.2 | −0.7 | −6.0 | −1.2 | −0.1 | 1.4 |
| Japan | 0.8 | 0.6 | 0.5 | 1.6 | 1.9 | 1.1 | 1.0 | −1.1 | −3.4 | 1.5 | 1.4 | 2.0 |
| United Kingdom | 3.3 | 1.2 | 2.8 | 3.4 | 2.2 | 2.5 | 2.9 | −0.3 | −4.3 | 1.0 | 0.8 | 1.6 |
| Canada | 2.8 | 3.1 | 3.7 | 3.9 | 4.4 | 4.6 | 4.0 | 2.8 | −1.8 | 4.4 | 3.1 | 2.4 |
| Other Advanced Economies[2] | 3.9 | 3.1 | 2.1 | 3.9 | 3.4 | 4.0 | 4.9 | 1.2 | −0.7 | 4.2 | 3.9 | 3.8 |
| *Memorandum* | | | | | | | | | | | | |
| Major Advanced Economies | 2.7 | 1.4 | 2.0 | 2.7 | 2.6 | 2.3 | 1.7 | −0.3 | −2.9 | 1.7 | 2.0 | 2.2 |
| Newly Industrialized Asian Economies | 4.8 | 3.2 | 1.2 | 3.7 | 3.2 | 3.9 | 4.7 | 0.4 | 0.0 | 5.7 | 4.6 | 4.3 |
| **Stock Building[3]** | | | | | | | | | | | | |
| **Advanced Economies** | **0.0** | **0.0** | **0.1** | **0.3** | **−0.1** | **0.1** | **0.0** | **−0.2** | **−1.0** | **1.0** | **0.0** | **0.1** |
| United States | 0.0 | 0.0 | 0.1 | 0.4 | −0.1 | 0.1 | −0.2 | −0.5 | −0.7 | 1.4 | −0.1 | 0.1 |
| Euro Area[1] | . . . | 0.0 | 0.1 | 0.2 | −0.2 | 0.1 | 0.2 | −0.2 | −0.8 | 0.4 | −0.2 | 0.0 |
| Germany | −0.2 | 0.0 | 0.5 | 0.0 | −0.4 | −0.2 | −0.1 | −0.2 | 0.1 | 0.5 | −0.8 | 0.0 |
| France | 0.1 | −0.1 | −0.3 | 0.6 | 0.2 | 0.0 | 0.4 | −0.3 | −1.9 | 0.1 | 0.3 | 0.2 |
| Italy | 0.0 | 0.1 | 0.1 | −0.1 | −0.3 | 0.5 | 0.1 | −0.2 | −0.6 | 0.9 | 0.0 | 0.0 |
| Spain | −0.1 | 0.0 | −0.1 | 0.0 | −0.1 | 0.3 | −0.1 | 0.1 | 0.0 | 0.1 | 0.0 | 0.0 |
| Japan | 0.0 | 0.0 | 0.2 | 0.3 | −0.1 | 0.2 | 0.3 | −0.2 | −1.5 | 0.6 | 0.3 | 0.0 |
| United Kingdom | 0.1 | 0.0 | 0.2 | 0.1 | 0.0 | 0.0 | 0.1 | −0.5 | −1.2 | 1.4 | 0.3 | 0.0 |
| Canada | 0.1 | 0.0 | 0.7 | 0.1 | 0.5 | −0.2 | −0.1 | −0.2 | −0.9 | 0.8 | −0.3 | 0.1 |
| Other Advanced Economies[2] | 0.0 | 0.0 | −0.1 | 0.6 | −0.1 | 0.0 | −0.2 | 0.3 | −2.0 | 1.3 | 0.3 | 0.1 |
| *Memorandum* | | | | | | | | | | | | |
| Major Advanced Economies | 0.0 | 0.0 | 0.1 | 0.3 | −0.1 | 0.1 | 0.0 | −0.4 | −0.8 | 1.0 | 0.0 | 0.1 |
| Newly Industrialized Asian Economies | −0.1 | 0.0 | −0.2 | 0.8 | −0.2 | 0.2 | −0.3 | 1.0 | −3.0 | 1.9 | 0.2 | 0.0 |
| **Foreign Balance[3]** | | | | | | | | | | | | |
| **Advanced Economies** | **−0.1** | **0.2** | **−0.3** | **−0.1** | **−0.1** | **0.2** | **0.4** | **0.5** | **0.4** | **0.2** | **0.4** | **0.3** |
| United States | −0.5 | 0.1 | −0.5 | −0.7 | −0.3 | −0.1 | 0.6 | 1.2 | 1.3 | −0.4 | 0.3 | 0.0 |
| Euro Area[1] | . . . | 0.1 | −0.6 | 0.3 | −0.2 | 0.2 | 0.3 | 0.1 | −0.7 | 0.8 | 0.8 | 0.4 |
| Germany | 0.5 | 0.4 | −0.8 | 1.3 | 0.7 | 1.1 | 1.6 | −0.1 | −3.2 | 1.2 | 1.3 | 0.6 |
| France | 0.1 | −0.4 | −0.7 | −0.8 | −0.8 | −0.3 | −1.0 | −0.3 | −0.2 | 0.4 | 0.1 | 0.0 |
| Italy | 0.3 | −0.2 | −0.8 | 0.2 | −0.3 | 0.0 | 0.2 | 0.1 | −1.3 | −0.5 | −0.2 | 0.4 |
| Spain | −0.1 | 0.0 | −0.8 | −1.7 | −1.7 | −1.4 | −0.8 | 1.5 | 2.7 | 1.0 | 0.9 | 0.2 |
| Japan | 0.1 | 0.4 | 0.7 | 0.8 | 0.3 | 0.8 | 1.1 | 0.2 | −1.5 | 1.8 | −0.3 | 0.2 |
| United Kingdom | −0.3 | 0.1 | −0.1 | −0.7 | 0.0 | 0.2 | −0.5 | 0.7 | 0.9 | −1.0 | 0.6 | 0.7 |
| Canada | 0.6 | −1.2 | −2.3 | −0.8 | −1.6 | −1.4 | −1.5 | −1.9 | 0.2 | −2.2 | −0.2 | 0.0 |
| Other Advanced Economies[2] | 0.3 | 0.7 | 0.6 | 0.4 | 1.0 | 0.9 | 0.8 | 0.2 | 1.7 | 0.5 | 0.3 | 0.2 |
| *Memorandum* | | | | | | | | | | | | |
| Major Advanced Economies | −0.2 | 0.1 | −0.4 | −0.2 | −0.2 | 0.1 | 0.4 | 0.5 | 0.1 | 0.0 | 0.2 | 0.2 |
| Newly Industrialized Asian Economies | 0.4 | 1.5 | 2.0 | 1.3 | 2.1 | 1.9 | 2.2 | 0.5 | 2.0 | 1.5 | 0.8 | 0.7 |

[1]Excludes Estonia.
[2]In this table, Other Advanced Economies means advanced economies excluding the G7 and Euro Area countries but including Estonia.
[3]Changes expressed as percent of GDP of the preceding period.

## Table A4. Emerging and Developing Economies: Real GDP[1]

*(Annual percent change)*

| | Average 1993–2002 | 2003 | 2004 | 2005 | 2006 | 2007 | 2008 | 2009 | 2010 | Projections 2011 | Projections 2012 | Projections 2016 |
|---|---|---|---|---|---|---|---|---|---|---|---|---|
| **Central and Eastern Europe[2]** | **3.3** | **4.8** | **7.3** | **5.9** | **6.4** | **5.5** | **3.2** | **–3.6** | **4.2** | **3.7** | **4.0** | **3.9** |
| Albania | 6.7 | 5.8 | 5.7 | 5.8 | 5.4 | 5.9 | 7.7 | 3.3 | 3.5 | 3.4 | 3.6 | 4.5 |
| Bosnia and Herzegovina | . . . | 3.5 | 6.3 | 4.0 | 6.1 | 6.1 | 5.7 | –3.1 | 0.8 | 2.2 | 4.0 | 5.0 |
| Bulgaria | –1.2 | 5.5 | 6.7 | 6.4 | 6.5 | 6.4 | 6.2 | –5.5 | 0.2 | 3.0 | 3.5 | 4.0 |
| Croatia | 2.9 | 5.0 | 4.2 | 4.2 | 4.7 | 5.5 | 2.4 | –5.8 | –1.4 | 1.3 | 1.8 | 3.0 |
| Hungary | 3.1 | 4.0 | 4.5 | 3.5 | 3.3 | 0.8 | 0.8 | –6.7 | 1.2 | 2.8 | 2.8 | 3.2 |
| Kosovo | . . . | 5.4 | 2.6 | 3.8 | 3.4 | 6.3 | 6.9 | 2.9 | 4.0 | 5.5 | 5.2 | 4.5 |
| Latvia | 2.9 | 7.2 | 8.7 | 10.6 | 12.2 | 10.0 | –4.2 | –18.0 | –0.3 | 3.3 | 4.0 | 4.0 |
| Lithuania | . . . | 10.2 | 7.4 | 7.8 | 7.8 | 9.8 | 2.9 | –14.7 | 1.3 | 4.6 | 3.8 | 3.6 |
| Former Yugoslav Republic of Macedonia | 0.0 | 2.8 | 4.6 | 4.4 | 5.0 | 6.1 | 5.0 | –0.9 | 0.7 | 3.0 | 3.7 | 4.0 |
| Montenegro | . . . | 2.5 | 4.4 | 4.2 | 8.6 | 10.7 | 6.9 | –5.7 | 1.1 | 2.0 | 3.5 | 3.8 |
| Poland | 4.6 | 3.9 | 5.3 | 3.6 | 6.2 | 6.8 | 5.1 | 1.7 | 3.8 | 3.8 | 3.6 | 3.9 |
| Romania | 1.7 | 5.2 | 8.5 | 4.2 | 7.9 | 6.3 | 7.3 | –7.1 | –1.3 | 1.5 | 4.4 | 4.0 |
| Serbia | . . . | 2.4 | 8.3 | 5.6 | 5.2 | 6.9 | 5.5 | –3.1 | 1.8 | 3.0 | 5.0 | 5.0 |
| Turkey | 3.0 | 5.3 | 9.4 | 8.4 | 6.9 | 4.7 | 0.7 | –4.7 | 8.2 | 4.6 | 4.5 | 4.0 |
| **Commonwealth of Independent States[2,3]** | **–1.2** | **7.7** | **8.1** | **6.7** | **8.9** | **9.0** | **5.3** | **–6.4** | **4.6** | **5.0** | **4.7** | **4.3** |
| Russia | –0.9 | 7.3 | 7.2 | 6.4 | 8.2 | 8.5 | 5.2 | –7.8 | 4.0 | 4.8 | 4.5 | 4.0 |
| Excluding Russia | –2.0 | 9.1 | 10.8 | 7.6 | 10.6 | 10.0 | 5.5 | –3.1 | 6.0 | 5.5 | 5.1 | 5.1 |
| Armenia | 4.4 | 14.0 | 10.5 | 13.9 | 13.2 | 13.7 | 6.9 | –14.2 | 2.6 | 4.6 | 4.3 | 4.0 |
| Azerbaijan | –1.4 | 10.5 | 10.2 | 26.4 | 34.5 | 25.0 | 10.8 | 9.3 | 5.0 | 2.8 | 2.5 | 2.8 |
| Belarus | 0.8 | 7.0 | 11.4 | 9.4 | 10.0 | 8.6 | 10.2 | 0.2 | 7.6 | 6.8 | 4.8 | 4.5 |
| Georgia | . . . | 11.1 | 5.9 | 9.6 | 9.4 | 12.3 | 2.4 | –3.8 | 6.4 | 5.5 | 4.8 | 4.7 |
| Kazakhstan | 0.3 | 9.3 | 9.6 | 9.7 | 10.7 | 8.9 | 3.2 | 1.2 | 7.0 | 5.9 | 5.6 | 6.4 |
| Kyrgyz Republic | –0.9 | 7.0 | 7.0 | –0.2 | 3.1 | 8.5 | 7.6 | 2.9 | –1.4 | 5.0 | 6.0 | 5.0 |
| Moldova | –3.8 | 6.6 | 7.4 | 7.5 | 4.8 | 3.0 | 7.8 | –6.0 | 6.9 | 4.5 | 4.8 | 4.5 |
| Mongolia | 2.7 | 7.0 | 10.6 | 7.3 | 18.8 | 10.2 | 8.9 | –1.3 | 6.1 | 9.8 | 7.1 | 15.6 |
| Tajikistan | –1.7 | 10.2 | 10.6 | 6.7 | 7.0 | 7.8 | 7.9 | 3.9 | 6.5 | 5.8 | 5.0 | 5.0 |
| Turkmenistan | 1.6 | 17.1 | 14.7 | 13.0 | 11.0 | 11.1 | 14.7 | 6.1 | 9.2 | 9.0 | 6.4 | 6.9 |
| Ukraine | –5.0 | 9.6 | 12.1 | 2.7 | 7.4 | 7.9 | 1.9 | –14.8 | 4.2 | 4.5 | 4.9 | 4.0 |
| Uzbekistan | 1.9 | 4.2 | 7.4 | 7.0 | 7.5 | 9.5 | 9.0 | 8.1 | 8.5 | 7.0 | 7.0 | 6.0 |

## Table A4. Emerging and Developing Economies: Real GDP *(continued)*

| | Average 1993–2002 | 2003 | 2004 | 2005 | 2006 | 2007 | 2008 | 2009 | 2010 | Projections 2011 | 2012 | 2016 |
|---|---|---|---|---|---|---|---|---|---|---|---|---|
| **Developing Asia** | **7.1** | **8.1** | **8.6** | **9.5** | **10.4** | **11.4** | **7.7** | **7.2** | **9.5** | **8.4** | **8.4** | **8.6** |
| Islamic Republic of Afghanistan | . . . | 8.4 | 1.1 | 11.2 | 5.6 | 13.7 | 3.6 | 20.9 | 8.2 | 8.0 | 7.5 | 9.6 |
| Bangladesh | 5.0 | 5.8 | 6.1 | 6.3 | 6.5 | 6.3 | 6.0 | 5.8 | 6.0 | 6.3 | 6.6 | 7.0 |
| Bhutan | 6.2 | 4.0 | 8.0 | 7.0 | 6.4 | 20.1 | 3.0 | 8.7 | 6.7 | 6.5 | 6.0 | 17.4 |
| Brunei Darussalam | 2.1 | 2.9 | 0.5 | 0.4 | 4.4 | 0.2 | −1.9 | −1.8 | 4.1 | 3.1 | 2.6 | 3.4 |
| Cambodia | 7.0 | 8.5 | 10.3 | 13.3 | 10.8 | 10.2 | 6.7 | −2.0 | 6.0 | 6.5 | 6.5 | 6.7 |
| China | 9.8 | 10.0 | 10.1 | 11.3 | 12.7 | 14.2 | 9.6 | 9.2 | 10.3 | 9.6 | 9.5 | 9.5 |
| Fiji | 2.8 | 1.0 | 5.5 | 0.6 | 1.9 | −0.5 | −0.1 | −3.0 | 0.1 | 1.3 | 1.2 | 2.6 |
| India | 5.8 | 6.9 | 8.1 | 9.2 | 9.7 | 9.9 | 6.2 | 6.8 | 10.4 | 8.2 | 7.8 | 8.1 |
| Indonesia | 3.4 | 4.8 | 5.0 | 5.7 | 5.5 | 6.3 | 6.0 | 4.6 | 6.1 | 6.2 | 6.5 | 7.0 |
| Kiribati | 4.4 | 2.3 | 2.2 | 3.9 | 1.9 | 0.4 | −1.1 | −0.7 | 1.8 | 3.0 | 3.5 | 2.0 |
| Lao People's Democratic Republic | 6.1 | 6.2 | 7.0 | 6.8 | 8.6 | 7.8 | 7.8 | 7.6 | 7.7 | 7.5 | 7.3 | 7.3 |
| Malaysia | 5.8 | 5.8 | 6.8 | 5.3 | 5.8 | 6.5 | 4.7 | −1.7 | 7.2 | 5.5 | 5.2 | 5.0 |
| Maldives | 7.1 | 14.0 | 12.4 | −7.1 | 21.4 | 12.6 | 12.8 | −4.8 | 8.0 | 6.0 | 5.0 | 3.5 |
| Myanmar | 8.6 | 13.8 | 13.6 | 13.6 | 13.1 | 12.0 | 3.6 | 5.1 | 5.3 | 5.5 | 5.5 | 5.7 |
| Nepal | 4.5 | 3.9 | 4.7 | 3.5 | 3.4 | 3.4 | 6.1 | 4.9 | 4.6 | 4.5 | 3.8 | 5.0 |
| Pakistan | 3.1 | 4.9 | 7.4 | 7.7 | 6.1 | 5.6 | 1.6 | 3.4 | 4.8 | 2.8 | 4.0 | 6.0 |
| Papua New Guinea | 2.5 | 4.4 | 0.6 | 3.9 | 2.3 | 7.2 | 6.6 | 5.5 | 7.0 | 8.0 | 5.0 | 5.0 |
| Philippines | 3.7 | 4.9 | 6.4 | 5.0 | 5.3 | 7.1 | 3.7 | 1.1 | 7.3 | 5.0 | 5.0 | 5.0 |
| Samoa | 4.2 | 3.8 | 4.2 | 7.0 | 2.2 | 2.1 | 5.1 | −5.1 | −0.0 | 2.8 | 2.1 | 3.0 |
| Solomon Islands | −0.4 | 6.5 | 4.9 | 5.4 | 6.9 | 10.7 | 7.3 | −1.3 | 5.6 | 5.8 | 5.9 | 5.8 |
| Sri Lanka | 4.5 | 5.9 | 5.4 | 6.2 | 7.7 | 6.8 | 6.0 | 3.8 | 9.1 | 6.9 | 6.5 | 6.5 |
| Thailand | 3.6 | 7.1 | 6.3 | 4.6 | 5.1 | 5.0 | 2.5 | −2.3 | 7.8 | 4.0 | 4.5 | 5.0 |
| Timor-Leste | . . . | 0.1 | 4.2 | 6.2 | −5.8 | 9.1 | 11.0 | 12.9 | 6.0 | 7.3 | 8.6 | 7.9 |
| Tonga | 1.9 | 1.8 | 0.0 | −0.4 | −0.4 | 0.9 | 1.3 | −0.3 | 0.3 | 1.4 | 1.7 | 1.8 |
| Tuvalu | . . . | −3.3 | −1.5 | −3.9 | 3.3 | 4.8 | 7.0 | −1.7 | 0.2 | 0.0 | 0.6 | 1.8 |
| Vanuatu | 1.7 | 3.7 | 4.5 | 5.2 | 7.4 | 6.5 | 6.2 | 3.5 | 2.2 | 3.8 | 4.2 | 4.0 |
| Vietnam | 7.5 | 7.3 | 7.8 | 8.4 | 8.2 | 8.5 | 6.3 | 5.3 | 6.8 | 6.3 | 6.8 | 7.5 |

**Table A4. Emerging and Developing Economies: Real GDP** *(continued)*

| | Average 1993–2002 | 2003 | 2004 | 2005 | 2006 | 2007 | 2008 | 2009 | 2010 | Projections 2011 | 2012 | 2016 |
|---|---|---|---|---|---|---|---|---|---|---|---|---|
| **Latin America and the Caribbean** | **2.7** | **2.1** | **6.0** | **4.7** | **5.6** | **5.7** | **4.3** | **−1.7** | **6.1** | **4.7** | **4.2** | **3.9** |
| Antigua and Barbuda | 3.4 | 4.3 | 5.4 | 5.0 | 12.9 | 6.5 | 1.8 | −8.9 | −4.1 | 3.1 | 2.5 | 4.6 |
| Argentina[4] | 0.6 | 9.0 | 8.9 | 9.2 | 8.5 | 8.6 | 6.8 | 0.8 | 9.2 | 6.0 | 4.6 | 4.0 |
| The Bahamas | 3.6 | 0.7 | 1.6 | 5.0 | 3.5 | 1.9 | −1.7 | −4.3 | 0.5 | 1.3 | 2.3 | 2.3 |
| Barbados | 1.8 | 2.0 | 4.8 | 3.9 | 3.6 | 3.8 | −0.2 | −4.7 | −0.5 | 2.0 | 2.5 | 3.5 |
| Belize | 4.7 | 9.3 | 4.6 | 3.0 | 4.7 | 1.2 | 3.8 | 0.0 | 2.0 | 2.3 | 2.5 | 2.5 |
| Bolivia | 3.5 | 2.7 | 4.2 | 4.4 | 4.8 | 4.6 | 6.1 | 3.4 | 4.2 | 4.5 | 4.5 | 4.5 |
| Brazil | 2.9 | 1.1 | 5.7 | 3.2 | 4.0 | 6.1 | 5.2 | −0.6 | 7.5 | 4.5 | 4.1 | 4.2 |
| Chile | 5.0 | 4.0 | 6.0 | 5.5 | 4.6 | 4.6 | 3.7 | −1.7 | 5.3 | 5.9 | 4.9 | 4.3 |
| Colombia | 2.5 | 3.9 | 5.3 | 4.7 | 6.7 | 6.9 | 3.5 | 1.5 | 4.3 | 4.6 | 4.5 | 4.5 |
| Costa Rica | 4.5 | 6.4 | 4.3 | 5.9 | 8.8 | 7.9 | 2.7 | −1.3 | 4.2 | 4.3 | 4.4 | 4.5 |
| Dominica | 0.7 | 0.1 | 3.0 | 3.3 | 4.8 | 2.5 | 3.2 | −0.3 | 1.0 | 1.6 | 2.5 | 3.0 |
| Dominican Republic | 5.7 | −0.3 | 1.3 | 9.3 | 10.7 | 8.5 | 5.3 | 3.5 | 7.8 | 5.5 | 5.5 | 6.0 |
| Ecuador | 2.2 | 3.3 | 8.8 | 5.7 | 4.8 | 2.0 | 7.2 | 0.4 | 3.2 | 3.2 | 2.8 | 2.3 |
| El Salvador | 3.9 | 2.3 | 1.9 | 3.3 | 4.2 | 4.3 | 2.4 | −3.5 | 0.7 | 2.5 | 3.0 | 4.0 |
| Grenada | 3.9 | 7.1 | −5.7 | 11.0 | −2.3 | 4.9 | 2.2 | −7.6 | −1.4 | 1.0 | 2.8 | 4.0 |
| Guatemala | 3.5 | 2.5 | 3.2 | 3.3 | 5.4 | 6.3 | 3.3 | 0.5 | 2.6 | 3.0 | 3.2 | 3.5 |
| Guyana | 3.9 | −0.7 | 1.6 | −1.9 | 5.1 | 7.0 | 2.0 | 3.3 | 3.6 | 4.7 | 5.9 | 3.1 |
| Haiti | 0.3 | 0.4 | −3.5 | 1.8 | 2.2 | 3.3 | 0.8 | 2.9 | −5.1 | 8.6 | 8.8 | 5.7 |
| Honduras | 3.0 | 4.5 | 6.2 | 6.1 | 6.6 | 6.2 | 4.1 | −2.1 | 2.8 | 3.5 | 4.0 | 4.0 |
| Jamaica | 0.6 | 3.5 | 1.4 | 1.1 | 3.0 | 1.4 | −0.9 | −3.0 | −1.1 | 1.6 | 2.4 | 3.8 |
| Mexico | 2.7 | 1.4 | 4.0 | 3.2 | 5.2 | 3.2 | 1.5 | −6.1 | 5.5 | 4.6 | 4.0 | 3.2 |
| Nicaragua | 3.9 | 2.5 | 5.3 | 4.3 | 4.2 | 3.1 | 2.8 | −1.5 | 4.5 | 3.5 | 3.7 | 4.0 |
| Panama | 4.0 | 4.2 | 7.5 | 7.2 | 8.5 | 12.1 | 10.1 | 3.2 | 7.5 | 7.4 | 7.2 | 5.0 |
| Paraguay | 1.4 | 3.8 | 4.1 | 2.9 | 4.3 | 6.8 | 5.8 | −3.8 | 15.3 | 5.6 | 4.5 | 4.0 |
| Peru | 4.3 | 4.0 | 5.0 | 6.8 | 7.7 | 8.9 | 9.8 | 0.9 | 8.8 | 7.5 | 5.8 | 5.7 |
| St. Kitts and Nevis | 4.0 | −1.2 | 7.3 | 5.2 | 2.6 | 4.2 | 4.6 | −9.6 | −1.5 | 1.5 | 1.5 | 2.0 |
| St. Lucia | 1.1 | 3.5 | 3.6 | 5.0 | 4.4 | 1.5 | 0.7 | −3.6 | 0.8 | 4.2 | 3.9 | 3.1 |
| St. Vincent and the Grenadines | 2.5 | 2.8 | 6.8 | 2.6 | 7.6 | 8.0 | −0.6 | −1.1 | −2.3 | 2.5 | 2.5 | 4.0 |
| Suriname | 1.1 | 6.3 | 8.5 | 4.5 | 3.8 | 5.1 | 4.7 | 3.1 | 4.4 | 5.0 | 5.0 | 5.4 |
| Trinidad and Tobago | 5.6 | 14.4 | 7.9 | 6.2 | 13.2 | 4.8 | 2.4 | −3.5 | 0.0 | 2.2 | 2.4 | 2.6 |
| Uruguay | 0.7 | 2.3 | 4.6 | 6.8 | 4.3 | 7.3 | 8.6 | 2.6 | 8.5 | 5.0 | 4.2 | 4.0 |
| Venezuela | 0.0 | −7.8 | 18.3 | 10.3 | 9.9 | 8.2 | 4.8 | −3.3 | −1.9 | 1.8 | 1.6 | 1.8 |
| **Middle East and North Africa** | **3.3** | **7.3** | **6.0** | **5.4** | **5.8** | **6.2** | **5.1** | **1.8** | **3.8** | **4.1** | **4.2** | **5.1** |
| Algeria | 2.3 | 6.9 | 5.2 | 5.1 | 2.0 | 3.0 | 2.4 | 2.4 | 3.3 | 3.6 | 3.2 | 3.5 |
| Bahrain | 4.8 | 7.2 | 5.6 | 7.9 | 6.7 | 8.4 | 6.3 | 3.1 | 4.1 | 3.1 | 5.1 | 5.4 |
| Djibouti | −0.8 | 3.2 | 3.0 | 3.2 | 4.8 | 5.1 | 5.8 | 5.0 | 4.5 | 4.8 | 5.7 | 5.8 |
| Egypt | 4.8 | 3.2 | 4.1 | 4.5 | 6.8 | 7.1 | 7.2 | 4.7 | 5.1 | 1.0 | 4.0 | 6.5 |
| Islamic Republic of Iran | 3.2 | 7.2 | 5.1 | 4.7 | 5.8 | 7.8 | 1.0 | 0.1 | 1.0 | 0.0 | 3.0 | 4.3 |
| Iraq | . . . | . . . | . . . | −0.7 | 6.2 | 1.5 | 9.5 | 4.2 | 0.8 | 9.6 | 12.6 | 9.8 |
| Jordan | 4.3 | 4.2 | 8.6 | 8.1 | 7.9 | 8.5 | 7.6 | 2.3 | 3.1 | 3.3 | 3.9 | 5.5 |
| Kuwait | 4.8 | 17.4 | 11.2 | 10.4 | 5.3 | 4.5 | 5.0 | −5.2 | 2.0 | 5.3 | 5.1 | 5.4 |
| Lebanon | 4.0 | 3.2 | 7.5 | 1.0 | 0.6 | 7.5 | 9.3 | 8.5 | 7.5 | 2.5 | 5.0 | 4.0 |
| Libya[5] | −1.6 | 13.0 | 4.4 | 10.3 | 6.7 | 7.5 | 2.3 | −2.3 | 4.2 | . . . | . . . | . . . |
| Mauritania | 2.9 | 5.6 | 5.2 | 5.4 | 11.4 | 1.0 | 3.5 | −1.2 | 4.7 | 5.2 | 5.8 | 5.5 |
| Morocco | 3.2 | 6.3 | 4.8 | 3.0 | 7.8 | 2.7 | 5.6 | 4.9 | 3.2 | 3.9 | 4.6 | 5.0 |
| Oman | 3.8 | 0.3 | 3.4 | 4.0 | 5.5 | 6.7 | 12.9 | 1.1 | 4.2 | 4.4 | 4.1 | 4.4 |
| Qatar | 7.4 | 6.3 | 17.7 | 7.6 | 18.6 | 26.8 | 25.4 | 8.6 | 16.3 | 20.0 | 7.1 | 4.3 |
| Saudi Arabia | 1.4 | 7.7 | 5.3 | 5.6 | 3.2 | 2.0 | 4.2 | 0.6 | 3.7 | 7.5 | 3.0 | 4.9 |
| Sudan | 5.5 | 7.1 | 5.1 | 6.3 | 11.3 | 10.2 | 6.8 | 6.0 | 5.1 | 4.7 | 5.6 | 5.9 |
| Syrian Arab Republic | 3.4 | −2.0 | 6.9 | 6.2 | 5.0 | 5.7 | 4.5 | 6.0 | 3.2 | 3.0 | 5.1 | 5.5 |
| Tunisia | 4.2 | 5.5 | 6.0 | 4.0 | 5.7 | 6.3 | 4.5 | 3.1 | 3.7 | 1.3 | 5.6 | 6.5 |
| United Arab Emirates | 4.5 | 16.4 | 10.1 | 8.6 | 8.8 | 6.5 | 5.3 | −3.2 | 3.2 | 3.3 | 3.8 | 4.2 |
| Republic of Yemen | 5.0 | 3.7 | 4.0 | 5.6 | 3.2 | 3.3 | 3.6 | 3.9 | 8.0 | 3.4 | 4.0 | 4.7 |

## Table A4. Emerging and Developing Economies: Real GDP *(concluded)*

| | Average 1993–2002 | 2003 | 2004 | 2005 | 2006 | 2007 | 2008 | 2009 | 2010 | Projections 2011 | 2012 | 2016 |
|---|---|---|---|---|---|---|---|---|---|---|---|---|
| **Sub-Saharan Africa** | **3.7** | **4.9** | **7.1** | **6.2** | **6.4** | **7.2** | **5.6** | **2.8** | **5.0** | **5.5** | **5.9** | **5.4** |
| Angola | 3.5 | 3.3 | 11.2 | 20.6 | 19.5 | 23.9 | 13.8 | 2.4 | 1.6 | 7.8 | 10.5 | 5.8 |
| Benin | 4.9 | 4.0 | 3.0 | 2.9 | 3.8 | 4.6 | 5.0 | 2.7 | 2.5 | 3.4 | 4.3 | 5.0 |
| Botswana | 6.3 | 6.3 | 6.0 | 1.6 | 5.1 | 4.8 | 3.1 | −3.7 | 8.6 | 6.0 | 6.6 | 3.4 |
| Burkina Faso | 5.5 | 7.8 | 4.5 | 8.7 | 5.5 | 3.6 | 5.2 | 3.2 | 5.8 | 5.5 | 5.6 | 6.5 |
| Burundi | −1.7 | −1.2 | 4.8 | 0.9 | 5.1 | 3.6 | 4.5 | 3.5 | 3.9 | 4.5 | 4.8 | 5.0 |
| Cameroon[6] | 2.9 | 4.0 | 3.7 | 2.3 | 3.2 | 3.4 | 2.6 | 2.0 | 3.0 | 3.5 | 4.5 | 4.5 |
| Cape Verde | 7.5 | 4.7 | 4.3 | 6.5 | 10.1 | 8.6 | 6.2 | 3.6 | 5.4 | 5.5 | 6.8 | 5.5 |
| Central African Republic | 1.5 | −7.1 | 1.0 | 2.4 | 3.8 | 3.7 | 2.0 | 1.7 | 3.3 | 4.1 | 5.0 | 5.7 |
| Chad | 3.5 | 14.7 | 33.6 | 7.9 | 0.2 | 0.2 | −0.4 | 0.3 | 5.1 | 4.1 | 6.0 | 2.7 |
| Comoros | 1.6 | 2.5 | −0.2 | 4.2 | 1.2 | 0.5 | 1.0 | 1.8 | 2.1 | 2.4 | 3.5 | 4.0 |
| Democratic Republic of Congo | −3.6 | 5.8 | 6.6 | 7.8 | 5.6 | 6.3 | 6.2 | 2.8 | 7.2 | 6.5 | 6.0 | 6.1 |
| Republic of Congo | 1.8 | 0.8 | 3.5 | 7.8 | 6.2 | −1.6 | 5.6 | 7.5 | 9.1 | 7.8 | 4.7 | 5.5 |
| Côte d'Ivoire | 3.2 | −1.7 | 1.6 | 1.9 | 0.7 | 1.6 | 2.3 | 3.8 | 2.6 | −7.5 | 6.0 | 6.0 |
| Equatorial Guinea | 36.7 | 14.0 | 38.0 | 9.7 | 1.3 | 21.4 | 10.7 | 5.7 | −0.8 | 7.2 | 4.0 | −3.4 |
| Eritrea | 5.1 | −2.7 | 1.5 | 2.6 | −1.0 | 1.4 | −9.8 | 3.9 | 2.2 | 7.9 | 6.1 | 1.9 |
| Ethiopia | 5.6 | −2.1 | 11.7 | 12.6 | 11.5 | 11.8 | 11.2 | 10.0 | 8.0 | 8.5 | 8.0 | 8.0 |
| Gabon | 1.6 | 2.5 | 1.4 | 3.0 | 1.2 | 5.6 | 2.3 | −1.4 | 5.7 | 5.6 | 3.3 | 3.4 |
| The Gambia | 3.8 | 6.9 | 7.0 | 0.3 | 3.4 | 6.0 | 6.3 | 6.7 | 5.7 | 5.5 | 5.5 | 5.5 |
| Ghana | 4.6 | 5.2 | 5.4 | 6.2 | 4.6 | 6.5 | 8.4 | 4.7 | 5.7 | 13.7 | 7.3 | 4.4 |
| Guinea | 4.4 | 1.2 | 2.3 | 3.0 | 2.5 | 1.8 | 4.9 | −0.3 | 1.9 | 4.0 | 4.5 | 5.1 |
| Guinea-Bissau | 0.4 | 0.4 | 2.8 | 4.3 | 2.1 | 3.2 | 3.2 | 3.0 | 3.5 | 4.3 | 4.5 | 4.7 |
| Kenya | 2.2 | 2.8 | 4.6 | 6.0 | 6.3 | 7.0 | 1.6 | 2.6 | 5.0 | 5.7 | 6.5 | 6.6 |
| Lesotho | 3.5 | 4.7 | 2.3 | 2.4 | 4.7 | 4.5 | 4.7 | 3.0 | 2.4 | 3.1 | 4.1 | 5.0 |
| Liberia | . . . | −31.3 | 2.6 | 5.3 | 7.8 | 9.4 | 7.1 | 4.6 | 5.1 | 5.9 | 9.8 | 5.0 |
| Madagascar | 1.5 | 9.8 | 5.3 | 4.6 | 5.0 | 6.2 | 7.1 | −3.7 | −2.0 | 0.6 | 4.7 | 5.1 |
| Malawi | 3.0 | 5.5 | 5.5 | 2.6 | 7.7 | 5.8 | 8.6 | 7.6 | 6.6 | 6.1 | 5.7 | 5.0 |
| Mali | 4.5 | 7.6 | 2.3 | 6.1 | 5.3 | 4.3 | 5.0 | 4.5 | 4.5 | 6.0 | 5.4 | 5.0 |
| Mauritius | 4.8 | 4.3 | 5.5 | 1.5 | 4.5 | 5.9 | 5.5 | 3.0 | 4.0 | 4.1 | 4.2 | 4.5 |
| Mozambique | 8.5 | 6.5 | 7.9 | 8.4 | 8.7 | 7.3 | 6.8 | 6.3 | 7.0 | 7.5 | 7.8 | 7.3 |
| Namibia | 3.0 | 4.3 | 12.3 | 2.5 | 7.1 | 5.4 | 4.3 | −0.8 | 4.4 | 4.8 | 4.5 | 4.4 |
| Niger | 2.8 | 7.1 | −0.8 | 8.4 | 5.8 | 3.3 | 9.3 | −0.9 | 7.5 | 5.5 | 15.4 | 9.7 |
| Nigeria | 4.7 | 10.3 | 10.6 | 5.4 | 6.2 | 7.0 | 6.0 | 7.0 | 8.4 | 6.9 | 6.6 | 6.0 |
| Rwanda | 2.2 | 2.2 | 7.4 | 9.4 | 9.2 | 5.5 | 11.2 | 4.1 | 6.5 | 6.5 | 7.0 | 6.5 |
| São Tomé and Príncipe | 2.7 | 5.4 | 6.6 | 5.7 | 6.7 | 6.0 | 5.8 | 4.0 | 4.5 | 5.0 | 6.0 | 5.6 |
| Senegal | 3.2 | 6.7 | 5.9 | 5.6 | 2.4 | 5.0 | 3.2 | 2.2 | 4.2 | 4.5 | 4.8 | 5.4 |
| Seychelles | 3.4 | −5.9 | −2.9 | 6.7 | 6.4 | 9.6 | −1.3 | 0.7 | 6.2 | 4.0 | 4.7 | 4.6 |
| Sierra Leone | −1.9 | 9.5 | 7.4 | 7.2 | 7.3 | 6.4 | 5.5 | 3.2 | 5.0 | 5.1 | 6.0 | 5.5 |
| South Africa | 2.8 | 2.9 | 4.6 | 5.3 | 5.6 | 5.6 | 3.6 | −1.7 | 2.8 | 3.5 | 3.8 | 4.5 |
| Swaziland | 2.7 | 3.9 | 2.5 | 2.2 | 2.9 | 2.8 | 3.1 | 1.2 | 2.0 | 0.5 | 1.5 | 2.5 |
| Tanzania | 4.0 | 6.9 | 7.8 | 7.4 | 7.0 | 6.9 | 7.3 | 6.7 | 6.5 | 6.4 | 6.6 | 6.9 |
| Togo | 1.0 | 5.0 | 2.1 | 1.2 | 4.1 | 2.3 | 2.4 | 3.2 | 3.4 | 3.6 | 4.0 | 4.2 |
| Uganda | 7.2 | 6.5 | 6.8 | 6.3 | 10.8 | 8.4 | 8.7 | 7.2 | 5.2 | 6.0 | 6.5 | 7.0 |
| Zambia | 0.5 | 5.1 | 5.4 | 5.3 | 6.2 | 6.2 | 5.7 | 6.4 | 7.6 | 6.8 | 7.4 | 7.3 |
| Zimbabwe[7] | . . . | −17.2 | −6.9 | −2.2 | −3.5 | −3.7 | −17.7 | 6.0 | 9.0 | 7.3 | 5.7 | 4.7 |

[1]For many countries, figures for recent years are IMF staff estimates. Data for some countries are for fiscal years.

[2]Data for some countries refer to real net material product (NMP) or are estimates based on NMP. For many countries, figures for recent years are IMF staff estimates. The figures should be interpreted only as indicative of broad orders of magnitude because reliable, comparable data are not generally available. In particular, the growth of output of new private enterprises of the informal economy is not fully reflected in the recent figures.

[3]Georgia and Mongolia, which are not members of the Commonwealth of Independent States, are included in this group for reasons of geography and similarities in economic structure.

[4]Private analysts are of the view that real GDP growth was significantly lower than the official estimates in 2008 and 2009, although the discrepancy between private and official estimates of real GDP growth narrowed in 2010.

[5]Libya's projections are excluded due to the uncertain political situation.

[6]The percent changes in 2002 are calculated over a period of 18 months, reflecting a change in the fiscal year cycle (from July–June to January–December).

[7]The Zimbabwe dollar ceased circulating in early 2009. Data are based on staff estimates of price and exchange rate developments in U.S. dollars. IMF staff estimates of U.S. dollar values may differ from authorities' estimates. Real GDP is in constant 2009 prices.

## Table A5. Summary of Inflation
*(Percent)*

| | Average 1993–2002 | 2003 | 2004 | 2005 | 2006 | 2007 | 2008 | 2009 | 2010 | Projections 2011 | 2012 | 2016 |
|---|---|---|---|---|---|---|---|---|---|---|---|---|
| **GDP Deflators** | | | | | | | | | | | | |
| **Advanced Economies** | **1.8** | **1.8** | **2.1** | **2.1** | **2.2** | **2.3** | **2.0** | **0.8** | **0.9** | **1.4** | **1.4** | **1.7** |
| United States | 1.9 | 2.2 | 2.8 | 3.3 | 3.3 | 2.9 | 2.2 | 0.9 | 1.0 | 1.1 | 1.4 | 1.8 |
| Euro Area[1] | 1.9 | 2.2 | 1.9 | 2.0 | 1.9 | 2.4 | 2.0 | 1.0 | 0.8 | 1.2 | 1.5 | 1.7 |
| Japan | −0.6 | −1.6 | −1.1 | −1.2 | −0.9 | −0.7 | −1.0 | −0.4 | −2.1 | −1.4 | −0.1 | 0.6 |
| Other Advanced Economies[2] | 2.4 | 2.1 | 2.4 | 1.9 | 2.2 | 2.7 | 2.9 | 0.8 | 2.3 | 3.4 | 2.0 | 2.0 |
| **Consumer Prices** | | | | | | | | | | | | |
| **Advanced Economies** | **2.2** | **1.8** | **2.0** | **2.3** | **2.4** | **2.2** | **3.4** | **0.1** | **1.6** | **2.2** | **1.7** | **1.9** |
| United States | 2.5 | 2.3 | 2.7 | 3.4 | 3.2 | 2.9 | 3.8 | −0.3 | 1.6 | 2.2 | 1.6 | 2.0 |
| Euro Area[1,3] | 2.1 | 2.1 | 2.2 | 2.2 | 2.2 | 2.1 | 3.3 | 0.3 | 1.6 | 2.3 | 1.7 | 1.9 |
| Japan | 0.2 | −0.3 | 0.0 | −0.3 | 0.3 | 0.0 | 1.4 | −1.4 | −0.7 | 0.2 | 0.2 | 1.0 |
| Other Advanced Economies[2] | 2.4 | 1.8 | 1.8 | 2.1 | 2.1 | 2.1 | 3.8 | 1.5 | 2.5 | 3.3 | 2.4 | 2.2 |
| **Emerging and Developing Economies** | **28.6** | **6.7** | **5.9** | **5.9** | **5.6** | **6.5** | **9.2** | **5.2** | **6.2** | **6.9** | **5.3** | **3.8** |
| **Regional Groups** | | | | | | | | | | | | |
| Central and Eastern Europe | 44.9 | 10.9 | 6.6 | 5.9 | 5.9 | 6.0 | 8.0 | 4.7 | 5.3 | 5.1 | 4.2 | 3.5 |
| Commonwealth of Independent States[4] | 108.2 | 12.3 | 10.4 | 12.1 | 9.5 | 9.7 | 15.6 | 11.2 | 7.2 | 9.6 | 8.1 | 6.0 |
| Developing Asia | 6.8 | 2.7 | 4.1 | 3.8 | 4.1 | 5.4 | 7.4 | 3.1 | 6.0 | 6.0 | 4.2 | 2.8 |
| Latin America and the Caribbean | 39.3 | 10.4 | 6.6 | 6.3 | 5.3 | 5.4 | 7.9 | 6.0 | 6.0 | 6.7 | 6.0 | 5.1 |
| Middle East and North Africa | 8.9 | 5.5 | 6.5 | 6.4 | 7.5 | 10.0 | 13.4 | 6.5 | 6.9 | 10.0 | 7.3 | 4.8 |
| Sub-Saharan Africa | 22.9 | 10.8 | 7.6 | 8.9 | 6.9 | 6.9 | 11.7 | 10.5 | 7.5 | 7.8 | 7.3 | 5.7 |
| *Memorandum* | | | | | | | | | | | | |
| European Union | 4.9 | 2.2 | 2.3 | 2.3 | 2.3 | 2.4 | 3.7 | 0.9 | 2.0 | 2.7 | 1.9 | 2.0 |
| **Analytical Groups** | | | | | | | | | | | | |
| **By Source of Export Earnings** | | | | | | | | | | | | |
| Fuel | 48.4 | 11.3 | 9.7 | 10.0 | 9.0 | 10.1 | 14.9 | 9.3 | 8.2 | 10.9 | 8.6 | 6.2 |
| Nonfuel | 23.6 | 5.6 | 5.0 | 4.9 | 4.7 | 5.6 | 7.9 | 4.3 | 5.8 | 6.0 | 4.6 | 3.3 |
| Of Which, Primary Products | 27.0 | 5.0 | 3.8 | 5.2 | 5.2 | 5.1 | 9.1 | 5.2 | 4.0 | 5.3 | 5.2 | 3.9 |
| **By External Financing Source** | | | | | | | | | | | | |
| Net Debtor Economies | 30.6 | 7.4 | 5.5 | 5.9 | 5.8 | 6.0 | 9.0 | 7.2 | 7.4 | 6.7 | 5.9 | 4.3 |
| Of Which, Official Financing | 21.1 | 8.5 | 6.3 | 7.6 | 7.5 | 7.8 | 12.9 | 9.3 | 6.5 | 7.7 | 6.7 | 5.2 |
| **Net Debtor Economies by Debt-Servicing Experience** | | | | | | | | | | | | |
| Economies with Arrears and/or Rescheduling during 2005–09 | 24.1 | 12.0 | 7.9 | 8.1 | 8.7 | 8.2 | 11.4 | 6.5 | 8.0 | 8.6 | 8.1 | 6.8 |
| *Memorandum* | | | | | | | | | | | | |
| **Median Inflation Rate** | | | | | | | | | | | | |
| Advanced Economies | 2.4 | 2.1 | 2.1 | 2.2 | 2.3 | 2.1 | 3.9 | 0.7 | 2.0 | 2.5 | 2.1 | 2.0 |
| Emerging and Developing Economies | 8.2 | 4.3 | 4.4 | 6.0 | 6.0 | 6.3 | 10.3 | 3.7 | 4.5 | 6.0 | 5.4 | 4.0 |

[1]Excludes Estonia.
[2]In this table, Other Advanced Economies means advanced economies excluding the United States, Euro Area countries, and Japan but including Estonia.
[3]Based on Eurostat's harmonized index of consumer prices.
[4]Georgia and Mongolia, which are not members of the Commonwealth of Independent States, are included in this group for reasons of geography and similarities in economic structure.

## Table A6. Advanced Economies: Consumer Prices
*(Annual percent change)*

| | Average 1993–2002 | 2003 | 2004 | 2005 | 2006 | 2007 | 2008 | 2009 | 2010 | Projections 2011 | Projections 2012 | Projections 2016 | End of Period[1] 2010 | Projections 2011 | Projections 2012 |
|---|---|---|---|---|---|---|---|---|---|---|---|---|---|---|---|
| **Consumer Prices** | | | | | | | | | | | | | | | |
| **Advanced Economies** | **2.2** | **1.8** | **2.0** | **2.3** | **2.4** | **2.2** | **3.4** | **0.1** | **1.6** | **2.2** | **1.7** | **1.9** | **1.9** | **2.1** | **1.6** |
| United States | 2.5 | 2.3 | 2.7 | 3.4 | 3.2 | 2.9 | 3.8 | −0.3 | 1.6 | 2.2 | 1.6 | 2.0 | 1.4 | 2.1 | 1.4 |
| Euro Area[2,3] | 2.1 | 2.1 | 2.2 | 2.2 | 2.2 | 2.1 | 3.3 | 0.3 | 1.6 | 2.3 | 1.7 | 1.9 | 2.2 | 2.1 | 1.7 |
| Germany | 1.7 | 1.0 | 1.8 | 1.9 | 1.8 | 2.3 | 2.8 | 0.2 | 1.2 | 2.2 | 1.5 | 2.0 | 1.9 | 2.2 | 1.5 |
| France | 1.6 | 2.2 | 2.3 | 1.9 | 1.9 | 1.6 | 3.2 | 0.1 | 1.7 | 2.1 | 1.7 | 1.9 | 1.7 | 2.1 | 1.7 |
| Italy | 3.1 | 2.8 | 2.3 | 2.2 | 2.2 | 2.0 | 3.5 | 0.8 | 1.6 | 2.0 | 2.1 | 2.0 | 1.9 | 2.0 | 2.1 |
| Spain | 3.3 | 3.1 | 3.1 | 3.4 | 3.6 | 2.8 | 4.1 | −0.2 | 2.0 | 2.6 | 1.5 | 1.8 | 2.9 | 2.1 | 1.4 |
| Netherlands | 2.6 | 2.2 | 1.4 | 1.5 | 1.7 | 1.6 | 2.2 | 1.0 | 0.9 | 2.3 | 2.2 | 1.8 | 1.8 | 2.2 | 2.1 |
| Belgium | 1.8 | 1.5 | 1.9 | 2.5 | 2.3 | 1.8 | 4.5 | −0.0 | 2.3 | 2.9 | 2.3 | 2.0 | 3.3 | 2.9 | 2.3 |
| Austria | 1.8 | 1.3 | 2.0 | 2.1 | 1.7 | 2.2 | 3.2 | 0.4 | 1.7 | 2.5 | 2.0 | 1.9 | 2.2 | 2.2 | 1.8 |
| Greece | 6.4 | 3.4 | 3.0 | 3.5 | 3.3 | 3.0 | 4.2 | 1.4 | 4.7 | 2.5 | 0.5 | 1.2 | 5.1 | 1.4 | 0.5 |
| Portugal | 3.5 | 3.3 | 2.5 | 2.1 | 3.0 | 2.4 | 2.7 | −0.9 | 1.4 | 2.4 | 1.4 | 1.8 | 2.4 | 1.4 | 2.1 |
| Finland | 1.7 | 1.3 | 0.1 | 0.8 | 1.3 | 1.6 | 3.9 | 1.6 | 1.7 | 3.0 | 2.1 | 2.0 | 2.8 | 2.2 | 2.2 |
| Ireland | 2.8 | 4.0 | 2.3 | 2.2 | 2.7 | 2.9 | 3.1 | −1.7 | −1.6 | 0.5 | 0.5 | 1.7 | −0.2 | 0.7 | 1.0 |
| Slovak Republic | ... | 8.4 | 7.5 | 2.8 | 4.3 | 1.9 | 3.9 | 0.9 | 0.7 | 3.4 | 2.7 | 2.8 | 1.3 | 3.4 | 2.9 |
| Slovenia | 12.1 | 5.6 | 3.6 | 2.5 | 2.5 | 3.6 | 5.7 | 0.9 | 1.8 | 2.2 | 3.1 | 2.4 | 1.9 | 3.0 | 2.7 |
| Luxembourg | 2.0 | 2.0 | 2.2 | 2.5 | 2.7 | 2.3 | 3.4 | 0.4 | 2.3 | 3.5 | 1.7 | 2.1 | 2.8 | 3.6 | 1.7 |
| Estonia | ... | 1.3 | 3.0 | 4.1 | 4.4 | 6.6 | 10.4 | −0.1 | 2.9 | 4.7 | 2.1 | 2.5 | 5.4 | 3.5 | 2.0 |
| Cyprus | 3.1 | 4.0 | 1.9 | 2.0 | 2.2 | 2.2 | 4.4 | 0.2 | 2.6 | 3.9 | 2.8 | 2.2 | 1.9 | 4.1 | 2.6 |
| Malta | 3.2 | 1.9 | 2.7 | 2.5 | 2.6 | 0.7 | 4.7 | 1.8 | 2.0 | 3.0 | 2.6 | 2.5 | 4.0 | 2.0 | 2.6 |
| Japan | 0.2 | −0.3 | 0.0 | −0.3 | 0.3 | 0.0 | 1.4 | −1.4 | −0.7 | 0.2 | 0.2 | 1.0 | 0.0 | 0.1 | 0.3 |
| United Kingdom[2] | 1.8 | 1.4 | 1.3 | 2.0 | 2.3 | 2.3 | 3.6 | 2.1 | 3.3 | 4.2 | 2.0 | 2.0 | 3.4 | 3.9 | 1.9 |
| Canada | 1.8 | 2.7 | 1.8 | 2.2 | 2.0 | 2.1 | 2.4 | 0.3 | 1.8 | 2.2 | 1.9 | 2.0 | 2.2 | 2.0 | 2.0 |
| Korea | 4.2 | 3.5 | 3.6 | 2.8 | 2.2 | 2.5 | 4.7 | 2.8 | 3.0 | 4.5 | 3.0 | 3.0 | 3.5 | 4.1 | 3.0 |
| Australia | 2.5 | 2.8 | 2.3 | 2.7 | 3.5 | 2.3 | 4.4 | 1.8 | 2.8 | 3.0 | 3.0 | 2.6 | 2.7 | 3.4 | 2.9 |
| Taiwan Province of China | 1.7 | −0.3 | 1.6 | 2.3 | 0.6 | 1.8 | 3.5 | −0.9 | 1.0 | 2.0 | 2.0 | 2.0 | 7.4 | 2.3 | 2.0 |
| Sweden | 1.7 | 2.3 | 1.0 | 0.8 | 1.5 | 1.7 | 3.3 | 2.0 | 1.9 | 2.0 | 2.0 | 2.0 | 2.1 | 1.7 | 2.0 |
| Switzerland | 1.1 | 0.6 | 0.8 | 1.2 | 1.1 | 0.7 | 2.4 | −0.5 | 0.7 | 0.9 | 1.0 | 1.0 | 0.7 | 0.9 | 1.0 |
| Hong Kong SAR | 2.8 | −2.6 | −0.4 | 0.9 | 2.0 | 2.0 | 4.3 | 0.5 | 2.4 | 5.8 | 4.4 | 2.5 | 3.1 | 4.0 | 4.4 |
| Singapore | 1.2 | 0.5 | 1.7 | 0.5 | 1.0 | 2.1 | 6.6 | 0.6 | 2.8 | 3.3 | 3.0 | 2.0 | 4.0 | 2.8 | 3.1 |
| Czech Republic | ... | 0.1 | 2.8 | 1.8 | 2.5 | 2.9 | 6.3 | 1.0 | 1.5 | 2.0 | 2.0 | 2.0 | 2.3 | 2.2 | 2.0 |
| Norway | 2.2 | 2.5 | 0.5 | 1.5 | 2.3 | 0.7 | 3.8 | 2.2 | 2.4 | 1.8 | 2.2 | 2.5 | 2.8 | 2.0 | 2.4 |
| Israel | 7.1 | 0.7 | −0.4 | 1.3 | 2.1 | 0.5 | 4.6 | 3.3 | 2.7 | 3.0 | 2.5 | 1.7 | 2.6 | 2.7 | 2.4 |
| Denmark | 2.1 | 2.1 | 1.2 | 1.8 | 1.9 | 1.7 | 3.4 | 1.3 | 2.3 | 2.0 | 2.0 | 2.0 | 2.9 | 2.1 | 2.0 |
| New Zealand | 1.9 | 1.7 | 2.3 | 3.0 | 3.4 | 2.4 | 4.0 | 2.1 | 2.3 | 4.1 | 2.7 | 2.1 | 4.0 | 0.7 | 4.7 |
| Iceland | 3.3 | 2.1 | 3.2 | 4.0 | 6.8 | 5.0 | 12.4 | 12.0 | 5.4 | 2.6 | 2.6 | 2.5 | 2.4 | 3.0 | 2.5 |
| *Memorandum* | | | | | | | | | | | | | | | |
| Major Advanced Economies | 1.9 | 1.7 | 2.0 | 2.3 | 2.4 | 2.2 | 3.2 | −0.1 | 1.4 | 2.0 | 1.5 | 1.8 | 1.5 | 1.9 | 1.4 |
| Newly Industrialized Asian Economies | 3.1 | 1.5 | 2.4 | 2.2 | 1.6 | 2.2 | 4.5 | 1.3 | 2.3 | 3.8 | 2.9 | 2.6 | 4.6 | 3.5 | 2.9 |

[1]December–December changes. Several countries report Q4–Q4 changes.
[2]Based on Eurostat's harmonized index of consumer prices.
[3]Excludes Estonia.

## Table A7. Emerging and Developing Economies: Consumer Prices[1]
*(Annual percent change)*

| | Average 1993–2002 | 2003 | 2004 | 2005 | 2006 | 2007 | 2008 | 2009 | 2010 | Projections 2011 | Projections 2012 | Projections 2016 | End of Period[2] 2010 | Projections 2011 | Projections 2012 |
|---|---|---|---|---|---|---|---|---|---|---|---|---|---|---|---|
| **Central and Eastern Europe[3]** | **44.9** | **10.9** | **6.6** | **5.9** | **5.9** | **6.0** | **8.0** | **4.7** | **5.3** | **5.1** | **4.2** | **3.5** | **5.1** | **5.2** | **3.8** |
| Albania | 17.0 | 2.3 | 2.9 | 2.4 | 2.4 | 2.9 | 3.4 | 2.2 | 3.6 | 4.5 | 3.5 | 3.0 | 3.4 | 4.0 | 2.9 |
| Bosnia and Herzegovina | ... | 0.5 | 0.3 | 3.6 | 6.1 | 1.5 | 7.4 | −0.4 | 2.1 | 5.0 | 2.5 | 2.7 | 3.1 | 5.0 | 2.5 |
| Bulgaria | 71.2 | 2.3 | 6.1 | 6.0 | 7.4 | 7.6 | 12.0 | 2.5 | 3.0 | 4.8 | 3.7 | 3.0 | 4.4 | 5.3 | 2.4 |
| Croatia | 45.9 | 1.8 | 2.0 | 3.3 | 3.2 | 2.9 | 6.1 | 2.4 | 1.0 | 3.5 | 2.4 | 3.0 | 1.9 | 3.5 | 2.4 |
| Hungary | 15.8 | 4.4 | 6.8 | 3.6 | 3.9 | 7.9 | 6.1 | 4.2 | 4.9 | 4.1 | 3.5 | 3.0 | 4.2 | 3.9 | 3.2 |
| Kosovo | ... | 0.3 | −1.1 | −1.4 | 0.6 | 4.4 | 9.4 | −2.4 | 3.5 | 8.2 | 2.1 | 1.4 | 6.6 | 5.6 | 2.0 |
| Latvia | 17.8 | 2.9 | 6.2 | 6.9 | 6.6 | 10.1 | 15.3 | 3.3 | −1.2 | 3.0 | 1.7 | 1.9 | 2.4 | 1.9 | 2.3 |
| Lithuania | ... | −1.1 | 1.2 | 2.7 | 3.7 | 5.7 | 11.0 | 4.4 | 1.2 | 3.1 | 2.9 | 2.5 | 3.6 | 3.5 | 2.5 |
| Former Yugoslav Republic of Macedonia | 30.1 | 1.2 | −0.4 | 0.5 | 3.2 | 2.3 | 8.4 | −0.8 | 1.5 | 5.2 | 2.0 | 1.9 | 3.0 | 7.5 | 2.0 |
| Montenegro | ... | 7.5 | 3.1 | 3.4 | 3.0 | 4.2 | 8.5 | 3.4 | 0.5 | 3.1 | 2.0 | 2.0 | 0.7 | 3.0 | 1.8 |
| Poland | 16.2 | 0.8 | 3.5 | 2.1 | 1.0 | 2.5 | 4.2 | 3.5 | 2.6 | 4.1 | 2.9 | 2.5 | 3.1 | 3.8 | 2.7 |
| Romania | 71.4 | 15.4 | 11.9 | 9.0 | 6.6 | 4.8 | 7.8 | 5.6 | 6.1 | 6.1 | 3.4 | 3.0 | 8.0 | 4.0 | 3.0 |
| Serbia | ... | 2.9 | 10.6 | 17.3 | 12.7 | 6.5 | 12.4 | 8.1 | 6.2 | 9.9 | 4.1 | 4.0 | 10.3 | 6.0 | 4.0 |
| Turkey | 72.0 | 25.3 | 8.6 | 8.2 | 9.6 | 8.8 | 10.4 | 6.3 | 8.6 | 5.7 | 6.0 | 4.7 | 6.4 | 7.0 | 5.4 |
| **Commonwealth of Independent States[3],[4]** | **108.2** | **12.3** | **10.4** | **12.1** | **9.5** | **9.7** | **15.6** | **11.2** | **7.2** | **9.6** | **8.1** | **6.0** | **8.9** | **9.1** | **7.5** |
| Russia | 95.3 | 13.7 | 10.9 | 12.7 | 9.7 | 9.0 | 14.1 | 11.7 | 6.9 | 9.3 | 8.0 | 6.0 | 8.8 | 8.5 | 7.5 |
| Excluding Russia | 147.1 | 8.7 | 9.1 | 10.7 | 8.9 | 11.6 | 19.5 | 10.1 | 8.0 | 10.2 | 8.4 | 5.9 | 9.2 | 10.5 | 7.6 |
| Armenia | 147.8 | 4.7 | 7.0 | 0.6 | 2.9 | 4.4 | 9.0 | 3.5 | 8.2 | 9.3 | 5.5 | 4.0 | 9.4 | 7.0 | 4.0 |
| Azerbaijan | 108.2 | 2.2 | 6.7 | 9.7 | 8.4 | 16.6 | 20.8 | 1.5 | 5.7 | 10.3 | 7.5 | 5.0 | 7.9 | 10.0 | 5.0 |
| Belarus | 247.2 | 28.4 | 18.1 | 10.3 | 7.0 | 8.4 | 14.8 | 13.0 | 7.7 | 12.9 | 9.7 | 5.5 | 9.9 | 13.0 | 9.0 |
| Georgia | ... | 4.8 | 5.7 | 8.3 | 9.2 | 9.2 | 10.0 | 1.7 | 7.1 | 12.6 | 7.9 | 5.4 | 11.2 | 9.4 | 6.5 |
| Kazakhstan | 111.7 | 6.6 | 7.1 | 7.9 | 8.7 | 10.8 | 17.1 | 7.4 | 7.4 | 9.1 | 6.4 | 6.0 | 8.0 | 8.9 | 6.3 |
| Kyrgyz Republic | 65.2 | 3.1 | 4.1 | 4.3 | 5.6 | 10.2 | 24.5 | 6.8 | 7.8 | 18.8 | 9.3 | 6.0 | 18.9 | 12.6 | 8.0 |
| Moldova | 65.7 | 11.7 | 12.4 | 11.9 | 12.7 | 12.4 | 12.7 | 0.0 | 7.4 | 7.5 | 6.3 | 5.0 | 8.1 | 7.5 | 5.0 |
| Mongolia | 40.8 | 5.1 | 7.9 | 12.5 | 4.5 | 8.2 | 26.8 | 6.3 | 10.2 | 16.4 | 16.0 | 5.0 | 14.3 | 20.0 | 12.0 |
| Tajikistan | 182.0 | 16.4 | 7.2 | 7.3 | 10.0 | 13.2 | 20.4 | 6.5 | 6.5 | 13.9 | 9.7 | 5.0 | 9.8 | 12.6 | 9.8 |
| Turkmenistan | 246.3 | 5.6 | 5.9 | 10.7 | 8.2 | 6.3 | 14.5 | −2.7 | 4.4 | 6.1 | 7.3 | 6.0 | 4.8 | 7.5 | 7.0 |
| Ukraine | 149.3 | 5.2 | 9.0 | 13.5 | 9.1 | 12.8 | 25.2 | 15.9 | 9.4 | 9.2 | 8.3 | 5.0 | 9.1 | 10.2 | 7.7 |
| Uzbekistan | 128.0 | 11.6 | 6.6 | 10.0 | 14.2 | 12.3 | 12.7 | 14.1 | 9.4 | 11.6 | 12.3 | 11.0 | 12.1 | 12.4 | 11.0 |

## Table A7. Emerging and Developing Economies: Consumer Prices[1] *(continued)*

| | Average 1993–2002 | 2003 | 2004 | 2005 | 2006 | 2007 | 2008 | 2009 | 2010 | Projections 2011 | 2012 | 2016 | End of Period[2] 2010 | Projections 2011 | 2012 |
|---|---|---|---|---|---|---|---|---|---|---|---|---|---|---|---|
| **Developing Asia** | **6.8** | **2.7** | **4.1** | **3.8** | **4.1** | **5.4** | **7.4** | **3.1** | **6.0** | **6.0** | **4.2** | **2.8** | **5.9** | **5.6** | **3.5** |
| Islamic Republic of Afghanistan | ... | 24.1 | 13.2 | 12.3 | 5.1 | 13.0 | 26.8 | −12.2 | 8.0 | 9.8 | 1.0 | 5.0 | 20.4 | −0.1 | 5.0 |
| Bangladesh | 4.9 | 5.4 | 6.1 | 7.0 | 6.8 | 9.1 | 8.9 | 5.4 | 8.2 | 7.6 | 7.3 | 5.0 | 6.9 | 8.3 | 6.3 |
| Bhutan | 7.0 | 2.1 | 4.6 | 5.3 | 5.0 | 5.2 | 8.4 | 8.6 | 7.1 | 6.5 | 6.0 | 4.5 | 9.1 | 6.3 | 5.5 |
| Brunei Darussalam | 1.5 | 0.3 | 0.9 | 1.1 | 0.2 | 1.0 | 2.1 | 1.0 | 0.5 | 1.2 | 1.2 | 1.2 | 0.5 | 1.2 | 1.2 |
| Cambodia | 13.6 | 1.0 | 3.9 | 6.3 | 6.1 | 7.7 | 25.0 | −0.7 | 4.0 | 5.1 | 5.2 | 3.0 | 3.1 | 6.5 | 4.1 |
| China | 6.2 | 1.2 | 3.9 | 1.8 | 1.5 | 4.8 | 5.9 | −0.7 | 3.3 | 5.0 | 2.5 | 2.0 | 4.7 | 4.2 | 2.0 |
| Fiji | 2.8 | 4.2 | 2.8 | 2.4 | 2.5 | 4.8 | 7.7 | 3.1 | 5.4 | 3.8 | 3.9 | 3.0 | 4.0 | 3.3 | 3.3 |
| India | 7.2 | 3.8 | 3.8 | 4.2 | 6.2 | 6.4 | 8.3 | 10.9 | 13.2 | 7.5 | 6.9 | 4.0 | 8.6 | 7.7 | 5.9 |
| Indonesia | 13.8 | 6.8 | 6.1 | 10.5 | 13.1 | 6.0 | 9.8 | 4.8 | 5.1 | 7.1 | 5.9 | 3.0 | 7.0 | 7.3 | 5.5 |
| Kiribati | 3.0 | 1.9 | −0.9 | −0.3 | −1.5 | 4.2 | 11.0 | 8.8 | −1.4 | 2.5 | 2.5 | 2.5 | −1.4 | 8.0 | 4.0 |
| Lao People's Democratic Republic | 28.5 | 15.5 | 10.5 | 7.2 | 6.8 | 4.5 | 7.6 | 0.0 | 5.4 | 5.7 | 5.2 | 3.1 | 5.5 | 5.7 | 5.2 |
| Malaysia | 3.0 | 1.1 | 1.4 | 3.0 | 3.6 | 2.0 | 5.4 | 0.6 | 1.7 | 2.8 | 2.5 | 2.3 | 2.4 | 2.8 | 2.5 |
| Maldives | 4.3 | −2.8 | 6.3 | 2.5 | 3.5 | 7.4 | 12.3 | 4.0 | 5.0 | 6.5 | 5.8 | 3.0 | 5.0 | 8.0 | 3.5 |
| Myanmar | 27.9 | 24.9 | 3.8 | 10.7 | 26.3 | 32.9 | 22.5 | 8.2 | 7.3 | 8.0 | 8.3 | 8.0 | 7.4 | 8.5 | 8.0 |
| Nepal | 6.9 | 4.7 | 4.0 | 4.5 | 8.0 | 6.4 | 7.7 | 13.0 | 9.3 | 9.9 | 8.0 | 4.2 | 8.3 | 10.0 | 6.9 |
| Pakistan | 8.0 | 3.1 | 4.6 | 9.3 | 7.9 | 7.8 | 12.0 | 20.8 | 11.7 | 15.5 | 14.0 | 7.0 | 12.7 | 16.0 | 12.0 |
| Papua New Guinea | 10.5 | 14.7 | 2.1 | 1.8 | 2.4 | 0.9 | 10.8 | 6.9 | 6.6 | 8.3 | 8.0 | 6.8 | 7.5 | 9.0 | 7.0 |
| Philippines | 6.9 | 3.5 | 6.0 | 7.6 | 6.2 | 2.8 | 9.3 | 3.2 | 3.8 | 4.9 | 4.3 | 4.0 | 3.0 | 5.1 | 4.2 |
| Samoa | 3.8 | 4.3 | 7.8 | 7.8 | 3.2 | 4.5 | 6.2 | 14.4 | −0.2 | 3.0 | 4.0 | 4.0 | −0.6 | 6.0 | 4.0 |
| Solomon Islands | 9.5 | 10.5 | 6.9 | 7.0 | 11.1 | 7.7 | 17.4 | 7.1 | 1.0 | 3.3 | 5.0 | 4.5 | 0.8 | 6.1 | 4.3 |
| Sri Lanka | 9.7 | 9.0 | 9.0 | 11.0 | 10.0 | 15.8 | 22.6 | 3.4 | 5.9 | 7.9 | 6.2 | 5.5 | 6.9 | 6.5 | 5.8 |
| Thailand | 3.8 | 1.8 | 2.8 | 4.5 | 4.6 | 2.2 | 5.5 | −0.8 | 3.3 | 4.0 | 3.4 | 2.9 | 3.0 | 5.1 | 2.4 |
| Timor-Leste | ... | 7.2 | 3.2 | 1.8 | 4.1 | 8.9 | 7.6 | 0.1 | 4.9 | 6.0 | 6.0 | 5.0 | 8.0 | 6.0 | 6.0 |
| Tonga | 4.2 | 11.5 | 10.6 | 8.3 | 6.0 | 7.5 | 7.3 | 3.4 | 4.0 | 5.9 | 4.8 | 6.0 | 6.6 | 5.8 | 3.9 |
| Tuvalu | ... | 3.3 | 2.8 | 3.2 | 3.8 | 2.2 | 10.5 | −0.3 | −1.9 | 1.2 | 1.6 | 2.2 | −1.8 | 2.4 | 1.6 |
| Vanuatu | 2.5 | 3.0 | 1.4 | 1.2 | 2.0 | 3.9 | 4.8 | 4.3 | 2.8 | 4.0 | 3.5 | 3.0 | 3.4 | 4.0 | 3.5 |
| Vietnam | 5.6 | 3.3 | 7.9 | 8.4 | 7.5 | 8.3 | 23.1 | 6.7 | 9.2 | 13.5 | 6.7 | 5.0 | 11.8 | 9.5 | 6.2 |

# Table A7. Emerging and Developing Economies: Consumer Prices[1] (continued)

| | Average 1993–2002 | 2003 | 2004 | 2005 | 2006 | 2007 | 2008 | 2009 | 2010 | Projections 2011 | Projections 2012 | Projections 2016 | End of Period[2] 2010 | End of Period[2] Projections 2011 | End of Period[2] Projections 2012 |
|---|---|---|---|---|---|---|---|---|---|---|---|---|---|---|---|
| **Latin America and the Caribbean** | **39.3** | **10.4** | **6.6** | **6.3** | **5.3** | **5.4** | **7.9** | **6.0** | **6.0** | **6.7** | **6.0** | **5.1** | **6.6** | **6.8** | **5.8** |
| Antigua and Barbuda | 2.3 | 2.0 | 2.0 | 2.1 | 1.8 | 1.4 | 5.3 | –0.6 | 3.4 | 3.7 | 2.7 | 2.2 | 2.9 | 3.0 | 3.1 |
| Argentina[5] | 4.7 | 13.4 | 4.4 | 9.6 | 10.9 | 8.8 | 8.6 | 6.3 | 10.5 | 10.2 | 11.5 | 11.0 | 10.9 | 11.0 | 11.0 |
| The Bahamas | 1.7 | 3.0 | 1.0 | 2.2 | 1.8 | 2.5 | 4.5 | 2.1 | 1.7 | 2.0 | 1.4 | 2.0 | 1.7 | 2.0 | 1.7 |
| Barbados | 1.8 | 1.6 | 1.4 | 6.1 | 7.3 | 4.0 | 8.1 | 3.7 | 5.1 | 6.1 | 4.6 | 1.9 | 5.1 | 7.0 | 2.3 |
| Belize | 1.6 | 2.6 | 3.1 | 3.7 | 4.2 | 2.3 | 6.4 | 2.0 | 0.5 | 2.9 | 3.5 | 2.5 | 1.3 | 4.4 | 2.5 |
| Bolivia | 6.0 | 3.3 | 4.4 | 5.4 | 4.3 | 8.7 | 14.0 | 3.3 | 2.5 | 10.4 | 5.4 | 4.0 | 7.2 | 7.9 | 5.0 |
| Brazil | 103.5 | 14.8 | 6.6 | 6.9 | 4.2 | 3.6 | 5.7 | 4.9 | 5.0 | 6.3 | 4.8 | 4.5 | 5.9 | 5.9 | 4.5 |
| Chile | 6.4 | 2.8 | 1.1 | 3.1 | 3.4 | 4.4 | 8.7 | 1.7 | 1.5 | 3.6 | 3.2 | 3.0 | 3.0 | 4.5 | 3.2 |
| Colombia | 15.7 | 7.1 | 5.9 | 5.0 | 4.3 | 5.5 | 7.0 | 4.2 | 2.3 | 3.6 | 2.8 | 2.8 | 3.2 | 3.2 | 3.1 |
| Costa Rica | 13.0 | 9.4 | 12.3 | 13.8 | 11.5 | 9.4 | 13.4 | 7.8 | 5.7 | 5.6 | 5.4 | 4.0 | 5.8 | 6.0 | 5.5 |
| Dominica | 1.2 | 1.6 | 2.4 | 1.6 | 2.6 | 3.2 | 6.4 | 0.0 | 2.8 | 3.6 | 1.1 | 1.5 | 2.4 | 3.5 | 1.3 |
| Dominican Republic | 7.3 | 27.4 | 51.5 | 4.2 | 7.6 | 6.1 | 10.6 | 1.4 | 6.3 | 6.1 | 5.8 | 4.0 | 6.2 | 6.0 | 5.5 |
| Ecuador | 37.0 | 7.9 | 2.7 | 2.1 | 3.3 | 2.3 | 8.4 | 5.2 | 3.6 | 3.5 | 3.2 | 3.0 | 3.3 | 3.4 | 3.1 |
| El Salvador | 6.3 | 2.1 | 4.5 | 4.7 | 4.0 | 4.6 | 7.3 | 0.4 | 1.2 | 3.5 | 3.8 | 2.8 | 2.1 | 4.8 | 2.8 |
| Grenada | 1.9 | 2.2 | 2.3 | 3.5 | 4.2 | 3.9 | 8.0 | –0.3 | 5.0 | 5.8 | 4.5 | 2.0 | 6.3 | 5.0 | 4.0 |
| Guatemala | 8.7 | 5.6 | 7.6 | 9.1 | 6.6 | 6.8 | 11.4 | 1.9 | 3.9 | 5.1 | 5.9 | 4.0 | 5.4 | 6.3 | 5.5 |
| Guyana | 6.9 | 6.0 | 4.7 | 6.9 | 6.7 | 12.2 | 8.1 | 3.0 | 3.7 | 6.2 | 6.1 | 5.4 | 4.5 | 6.9 | 5.4 |
| Haiti | 18.6 | 26.7 | 28.3 | 16.8 | 14.2 | 9.0 | 14.4 | 3.4 | 4.1 | 6.4 | 8.0 | 5.0 | 4.7 | 9.1 | 6.5 |
| Honduras | 15.4 | 7.7 | 8.0 | 8.8 | 5.6 | 6.9 | 11.5 | 8.7 | 4.7 | 7.6 | 7.1 | 6.0 | 6.5 | 8.0 | 6.5 |
| Jamaica | 14.8 | 10.1 | 13.5 | 15.1 | 8.5 | 9.3 | 22.0 | 9.6 | 12.6 | 9.0 | 6.0 | 5.5 | 11.7 | 7.4 | 5.7 |
| Mexico | 15.6 | 4.6 | 4.7 | 4.0 | 3.6 | 4.0 | 5.1 | 5.3 | 4.2 | 3.6 | 3.1 | 3.0 | 4.4 | 3.5 | 3.0 |
| Nicaragua | 9.0 | 5.3 | 8.5 | 9.6 | 9.1 | 11.1 | 19.8 | 3.7 | 5.5 | 8.7 | 8.4 | 7.0 | 9.2 | 8.6 | 7.3 |
| Panama | 1.0 | 0.6 | 0.5 | 2.9 | 2.5 | 4.2 | 8.8 | 2.4 | 3.5 | 5.0 | 3.5 | 2.5 | 4.9 | 4.4 | 3.3 |
| Paraguay | 11.3 | 14.2 | 4.3 | 6.8 | 9.6 | 8.1 | 10.2 | 2.6 | 4.7 | 9.6 | 9.0 | 4.0 | 7.2 | 10.7 | 7.5 |
| Peru | 11.2 | 2.3 | 3.7 | 1.6 | 2.0 | 1.8 | 5.8 | 2.9 | 1.5 | 2.7 | 3.2 | 2.0 | 2.1 | 3.5 | 3.0 |
| St. Kitts and Nevis | 3.0 | 2.3 | 2.2 | 3.4 | 8.5 | 4.5 | 5.4 | 1.9 | 2.5 | 3.5 | 2.9 | 2.5 | 2.2 | 3.8 | 2.9 |
| St. Lucia | 2.5 | 1.0 | 1.5 | 3.9 | 3.6 | 2.8 | 7.2 | 1.0 | 1.8 | 3.2 | 2.8 | 2.4 | –0.6 | 5.2 | 1.9 |
| St. Vincent and the Grenadines | 1.7 | 0.2 | 3.0 | 3.7 | 3.1 | 6.9 | 10.1 | 0.4 | 1.5 | 5.0 | 3.6 | 2.5 | 2.0 | 5.9 | 1.9 |
| Suriname | 73.5 | 23.0 | 9.1 | 9.9 | 11.3 | 6.4 | 14.6 | –0.1 | 6.9 | 17.9 | 10.4 | 4.0 | 10.3 | 19.9 | 7.5 |
| Trinidad and Tobago | 5.1 | 3.8 | 3.7 | 6.9 | 8.3 | 7.9 | 12.0 | 7.0 | 10.7 | 11.5 | 7.5 | 5.0 | 13.4 | 9.5 | 5.5 |
| Uruguay | 21.7 | 19.4 | 9.2 | 4.7 | 6.4 | 8.1 | 7.9 | 7.1 | 6.7 | 7.2 | 6.0 | 6.0 | 6.9 | 6.8 | 6.5 |
| Venezuela | 39.9 | 31.1 | 21.7 | 16.0 | 13.7 | 18.7 | 30.4 | 27.1 | 28.2 | 29.8 | 31.3 | 22.1 | 27.2 | 32.4 | 30.1 |
| **Middle East and North Africa** | **8.9** | **5.5** | **6.5** | **6.4** | **7.5** | **10.0** | **13.4** | **6.5** | **6.9** | **10.0** | **7.3** | **4.8** | **8.7** | **8.6** | **6.5** |
| Algeria | 11.2 | 2.6 | 3.6 | 1.6 | 2.3 | 3.6 | 4.9 | 5.7 | 4.3 | 5.0 | 4.3 | 3.7 | 4.5 | 4.5 | 4.1 |
| Bahrain | 1.0 | 1.7 | 2.2 | 2.6 | 2.0 | 3.3 | 3.5 | 2.8 | 2.0 | 3.0 | 2.7 | 2.5 | 2.0 | 2.7 | 2.5 |
| Djibouti | 2.8 | 2.0 | 3.1 | 3.1 | 3.5 | 5.0 | 12.0 | 1.7 | 4.0 | 4.6 | 2.3 | 2.5 | 2.8 | 4.0 | 2.1 |
| Egypt | 5.9 | 3.2 | 8.1 | 8.8 | 4.2 | 11.0 | 11.7 | 16.2 | 11.7 | 11.5 | 12.0 | 6.5 | 10.7 | 13.5 | 10.5 |
| Islamic Republic of Iran | 22.1 | 15.6 | 15.3 | 10.4 | 11.9 | 18.4 | 25.4 | 10.8 | 12.5 | 22.5 | 12.5 | 7.0 | 20.0 | 15.0 | 11.0 |
| Iraq | ... | ... | ... | 37.0 | 53.2 | 30.8 | 2.7 | –2.8 | 5.1 | 5.0 | 5.0 | 4.0 | 3.3 | 5.0 | 5.0 |
| Jordan | 2.7 | 1.6 | 3.4 | 3.5 | 6.3 | 4.7 | 13.9 | –0.7 | 5.0 | 6.1 | 5.6 | 2.3 | 6.1 | 5.7 | 3.6 |
| Kuwait | 1.7 | 1.0 | 1.3 | 4.1 | 3.1 | 5.5 | 10.6 | 4.0 | 4.1 | 6.1 | 2.7 | 3.2 | 4.1 | 6.1 | 2.7 |
| Lebanon | 6.3 | 1.3 | 1.7 | –0.7 | 5.6 | 4.1 | 10.8 | 1.2 | 4.5 | 6.5 | 3.0 | 2.2 | 4.5 | 5.5 | 2.6 |
| Libya[6] | 1.7 | –2.1 | 1.0 | 2.9 | 1.4 | 6.2 | 10.4 | 2.8 | 2.4 | ... | ... | ... | 2.4 | ... | ... |
| Mauritania | 5.5 | 5.3 | 10.4 | 12.1 | 6.2 | 7.3 | 7.3 | 2.2 | 6.1 | 7.3 | 6.7 | 0.0 | 6.3 | 7.5 | 6.9 |
| Morocco | 2.9 | 1.2 | 1.5 | 1.0 | 3.3 | 2.0 | 3.9 | 1.0 | 1.0 | 2.9 | 2.9 | 2.9 | 2.2 | 2.9 | 2.9 |
| Oman | –0.2 | 0.2 | 0.7 | 1.9 | 3.4 | 5.9 | 12.6 | 3.5 | 3.3 | 3.5 | 3.0 | 3.0 | 3.4 | 3.3 | 3.0 |
| Qatar | 2.2 | 2.3 | 6.8 | 8.8 | 11.8 | 13.8 | 15.0 | –4.9 | –2.4 | 4.2 | 4.1 | 4.0 | 0.4 | 4.2 | 4.1 |
| Saudi Arabia | 0.3 | 0.6 | 0.4 | 0.6 | 2.3 | 4.1 | 9.9 | 5.1 | 5.4 | 6.0 | 5.5 | 4.0 | 5.4 | 6.6 | 4.5 |
| Sudan | 45.2 | 7.7 | 8.4 | 8.5 | 7.2 | 8.0 | 14.3 | 11.3 | 13.0 | 9.0 | 7.0 | 6.0 | 15.4 | 8.0 | 6.0 |
| Syrian Arab Republic | 3.9 | 5.8 | 4.4 | 7.2 | 10.4 | 4.7 | 15.2 | 2.8 | 4.4 | 6.0 | 5.0 | 5.0 | 6.3 | 6.0 | 5.0 |
| Tunisia | 3.6 | 2.7 | 3.6 | 2.0 | 4.1 | 3.4 | 4.9 | 3.5 | 4.4 | 4.0 | 3.3 | 3.0 | 4.1 | 4.0 | 3.3 |
| United Arab Emirates | 3.2 | 3.1 | 5.0 | 6.2 | 9.3 | 11.1 | 12.3 | 1.6 | 0.9 | 4.5 | 3.0 | 2.2 | 2.7 | 3.7 | 2.7 |
| Republic of Yemen | 27.3 | 10.8 | 12.5 | 9.9 | 10.8 | 7.9 | 19.0 | 3.7 | 12.1 | 13.0 | 11.0 | 6.4 | 12.5 | 13.5 | 8.6 |

## Table A7. Emerging and Developing Economies: Consumer Prices[1] *(concluded)*

| | Average 1993–2002 | 2003 | 2004 | 2005 | 2006 | 2007 | 2008 | 2009 | 2010 | Projections 2011 | Projections 2012 | Projections 2016 | End of Period[2] 2010 | End of Period[2] Projections 2011 | End of Period[2] Projections 2012 |
|---|---|---|---|---|---|---|---|---|---|---|---|---|---|---|---|
| **Sub-Saharan Africa** | **22.9** | **10.8** | **7.6** | **8.9** | **6.9** | **6.9** | **11.7** | **10.5** | **7.5** | **7.8** | **7.3** | **5.7** | **6.9** | **8.1** | **6.6** |
| Angola | 527.9 | 98.3 | 43.6 | 23.0 | 13.3 | 12.2 | 12.5 | 13.7 | 14.5 | 14.6 | 12.4 | 5.2 | 15.3 | 13.0 | 11.2 |
| Benin | 7.4 | 1.5 | 0.9 | 5.4 | 3.8 | 1.3 | 8.0 | 2.2 | 2.1 | 4.2 | 3.0 | 3.0 | 4.0 | 4.5 | 3.0 |
| Botswana | 9.2 | 9.2 | 7.0 | 8.6 | 11.6 | 7.1 | 12.6 | 8.1 | 6.9 | 7.8 | 7.0 | 6.1 | 7.4 | 7.5 | 6.4 |
| Burkina Faso | 5.1 | 2.0 | −0.4 | 6.4 | 2.4 | −0.2 | 10.7 | 2.6 | 0.4 | 2.0 | 2.0 | 2.0 | 1.4 | 2.0 | 2.0 |
| Burundi | 14.5 | 10.7 | 8.0 | 13.5 | 2.7 | 8.3 | 24.4 | 10.7 | 6.4 | 8.4 | 13.4 | 5.0 | 4.1 | 13.9 | 12.9 |
| Cameroon[7] | 5.7 | 0.6 | 0.3 | 2.0 | 4.9 | 1.1 | 5.3 | 3.0 | 1.3 | 3.0 | 2.5 | 2.5 | 2.6 | 3.0 | 2.5 |
| Cape Verde | 4.4 | 1.2 | −1.9 | 0.4 | 4.8 | 4.4 | 6.8 | 1.0 | 2.1 | 4.4 | 5.4 | 2.0 | 3.4 | 5.7 | 4.3 |
| Central African Republic | 4.9 | 4.4 | −2.2 | 2.9 | 6.7 | 0.9 | 9.3 | 3.5 | 1.5 | 2.7 | 2.9 | 2.0 | 2.3 | 3.4 | 2.4 |
| Chad | 6.2 | −1.8 | −4.8 | 3.7 | 7.7 | −7.4 | 8.3 | 10.1 | 1.0 | 3.0 | 3.0 | 3.0 | −2.2 | −2.0 | −2.0 |
| Comoros | 4.8 | 3.7 | 4.5 | 3.0 | 3.4 | 4.5 | 4.8 | 4.8 | 2.7 | 3.9 | 3.6 | 3.0 | 3.2 | 4.3 | 2.9 |
| Democratic Republic of Congo | 546.2 | 12.8 | 4.0 | 21.4 | 13.2 | 16.7 | 18.0 | 46.2 | 23.5 | 12.0 | 11.0 | 7.7 | 9.8 | 13.0 | 9.0 |
| Republic of Congo | 7.1 | 1.7 | 3.7 | 2.5 | 4.7 | 2.6 | 6.0 | 4.3 | 5.0 | 5.9 | 5.2 | 3.1 | 5.4 | 5.0 | 4.2 |
| Côte d'Ivoire | 6.2 | 3.3 | 1.5 | 3.9 | 2.5 | 1.9 | 6.3 | 1.0 | 1.4 | 5.0 | 2.5 | 2.5 | 5.1 | 5.0 | 2.5 |
| Equatorial Guinea | 9.1 | 7.3 | 4.2 | 5.7 | 4.5 | 2.8 | 4.3 | 7.2 | 7.5 | 7.3 | 7.0 | 6.5 | 7.5 | 7.3 | 7.0 |
| Eritrea | 11.2 | 22.7 | 25.1 | 12.5 | 15.1 | 9.3 | 19.9 | 33.0 | 12.7 | 13.3 | 12.3 | 12.3 | 14.2 | 12.3 | 12.3 |
| Ethiopia | 1.9 | 15.1 | 8.6 | 6.8 | 12.3 | 15.8 | 25.3 | 36.4 | 2.8 | 12.9 | 11.2 | 9.0 | 7.3 | 16.0 | 9.0 |
| Gabon | 4.9 | 2.1 | 0.4 | 1.2 | −1.4 | 5.0 | 5.3 | 1.9 | 0.6 | 2.3 | 3.4 | 3.0 | 0.7 | 3.5 | 3.2 |
| The Gambia | 3.8 | 17.0 | 14.3 | 5.0 | 2.1 | 5.4 | 4.5 | 4.6 | 5.0 | 5.9 | 5.5 | 5.0 | 5.8 | 6.0 | 5.0 |
| Ghana | 27.6 | 26.7 | 12.6 | 15.1 | 10.2 | 10.7 | 16.5 | 19.3 | 10.7 | 8.7 | 8.7 | 6.5 | 8.6 | 9.0 | 8.5 |
| Guinea | 4.6 | 11.0 | 17.5 | 31.4 | 34.7 | 22.9 | 18.4 | 4.7 | 15.5 | 19.6 | 15.1 | 3.7 | 20.8 | 17.1 | 12.3 |
| Guinea-Bissau | 21.2 | −3.5 | 0.8 | 3.2 | 0.7 | 4.6 | 10.4 | −1.6 | 1.1 | 4.0 | 2.0 | 2.0 | 5.7 | 1.8 | 2.0 |
| Kenya | 12.0 | 9.8 | 11.8 | 9.9 | 6.0 | 4.3 | 16.2 | 9.3 | 3.9 | 7.2 | 5.0 | 5.0 | 4.5 | 6.7 | 5.5 |
| Lesotho | 9.0 | 7.3 | 5.0 | 3.4 | 6.1 | 8.0 | 10.7 | 7.2 | 3.8 | 5.4 | 5.6 | 5.6 | 3.1 | 5.6 | 5.7 |
| Liberia | ... | 10.3 | 3.6 | 6.9 | 7.2 | 13.7 | 17.5 | 7.4 | 7.3 | 9.7 | 6.0 | 5.0 | 6.6 | 9.0 | 4.7 |
| Madagascar | 16.2 | −1.1 | 14.0 | 18.4 | 10.8 | 10.4 | 9.2 | 9.0 | 9.0 | 8.8 | 7.5 | 5.0 | 9.2 | 8.5 | 6.5 |
| Malawi | 32.4 | 9.6 | 11.4 | 15.5 | 13.9 | 8.0 | 8.8 | 8.7 | 6.9 | 6.6 | 6.9 | 5.4 | 6.3 | 7.0 | 6.8 |
| Mali | 5.1 | −1.2 | −3.1 | 6.4 | 1.5 | 1.5 | 9.1 | 2.2 | 1.2 | 4.5 | 2.7 | 2.8 | 1.9 | 5.0 | 3.1 |
| Mauritius | 7.1 | 3.9 | 4.7 | 4.9 | 8.7 | 8.6 | 9.7 | 2.5 | 2.9 | 7.4 | 4.6 | 4.4 | 6.1 | 5.8 | 4.4 |
| Mozambique | 23.4 | 13.5 | 12.6 | 6.4 | 13.2 | 8.2 | 10.3 | 3.3 | 12.7 | 9.5 | 7.2 | 5.6 | 16.6 | 8.4 | 5.6 |
| Namibia | 9.1 | 7.2 | 4.1 | 2.3 | 5.1 | 6.7 | 10.4 | 8.8 | 4.5 | 5.9 | 5.6 | 4.5 | 3.1 | 5.7 | 5.5 |
| Niger | 6.2 | −1.8 | 0.4 | 7.8 | 0.1 | 0.1 | 10.5 | 1.1 | 0.9 | 3.8 | 2.0 | 2.0 | 2.7 | 3.5 | 2.0 |
| Nigeria | 26.0 | 14.0 | 15.0 | 17.9 | 8.2 | 5.4 | 11.6 | 12.5 | 13.7 | 11.1 | 9.5 | 8.5 | 11.7 | 10.5 | 8.5 |
| Rwanda | 13.8 | 7.4 | 12.0 | 9.1 | 8.8 | 9.1 | 15.4 | 10.3 | 2.3 | 3.1 | 5.5 | 5.0 | 0.2 | 6.0 | 5.0 |
| São Tomé and Príncipe | 29.3 | 9.6 | 12.8 | 17.2 | 23.1 | 18.5 | 26.0 | 17.0 | 14.4 | 10.6 | 6.7 | 3.0 | 12.9 | 8.5 | 5.0 |
| Senegal | 4.8 | −0.0 | 0.5 | 1.7 | 2.1 | 5.9 | 5.8 | −1.7 | 1.2 | 3.9 | 2.5 | 2.1 | 4.3 | 2.7 | 2.3 |
| Seychelles | 2.4 | 3.3 | 3.9 | 0.6 | −1.9 | 5.3 | 37.0 | 31.9 | −2.4 | 3.1 | 4.3 | 2.6 | 0.4 | 5.5 | 3.5 |
| Sierra Leone | 17.0 | 7.5 | 14.2 | 12.0 | 9.5 | 11.6 | 14.8 | 9.2 | 17.8 | 14.7 | 8.8 | 5.4 | 18.4 | 13.1 | 8.0 |
| South Africa | 7.6 | 5.8 | 1.4 | 3.4 | 4.7 | 7.1 | 11.5 | 7.1 | 4.3 | 4.9 | 5.8 | 4.5 | 3.5 | 5.9 | 5.6 |
| Swaziland | 9.2 | 7.3 | 3.5 | 4.8 | 5.3 | 9.7 | 13.1 | 7.5 | 4.5 | 7.9 | 6.1 | 4.5 | 4.5 | 7.3 | 5.4 |
| Tanzania | 15.3 | 4.4 | 4.1 | 4.4 | 5.6 | 6.3 | 8.4 | 11.8 | 10.5 | 6.3 | 7.0 | 5.0 | 7.2 | 7.5 | 5.5 |
| Togo | 6.6 | −0.9 | 0.4 | 6.8 | 2.2 | 0.9 | 8.7 | 1.9 | 3.2 | 6.2 | 2.0 | 1.9 | 6.9 | 6.9 | −2.1 |
| Uganda | 6.9 | 5.7 | 5.0 | 8.0 | 6.6 | 6.8 | 7.3 | 14.2 | 9.4 | 6.1 | 11.0 | 5.0 | 4.2 | 12.0 | 10.0 |
| Zambia | 41.0 | 21.4 | 18.0 | 18.3 | 9.0 | 10.7 | 12.4 | 13.4 | 8.5 | 9.0 | 6.5 | 5.0 | 7.9 | 7.0 | 6.0 |
| Zimbabwe[8] | ... | ... | ... | ... | ... | ... | ... | 6.5 | 3.0 | 4.8 | 6.1 | 5.0 | 3.2 | 7.1 | 6.5 |

[1]In accordance with standard practice in the *World Economic Outlook*, movements in consumer prices are indicated as annual averages rather than as December–December changes during the year, as is the practice in some countries. For many countries, figures for recent years are IMF staff estimates. Data for some countries are for fiscal years.

[2]December–December changes. Several countries report Q4–Q4 changes.

[3]For many countries, inflation for the earlier years is measured on the basis of a retail price index. Consumer price index (CPI) inflation data with broader and more up-to-date coverage are typically used for more recent years.

[4]Georgia and Mongolia, which are not members of the Commonwealth of Independent States, are included in this group for reasons of geography and similarities in economic structure.

[5]Private analysts estimate that consumer price inflation has been considerably higher than the official estimates from 2007 onward. The Argentine authorities have announced that they are developing a national CPI to replace the Greater Buenos Aires CPI currently in use. At the request of the authorities, the IMF is providing technical assistancce in this effort.

[6]Libya's projections are excluded due to the uncertain political situation.

[7]The percent changes in 2002 are calculated over a period of 18 months, reflecting a change in the fiscal year cycle (from July–June to January–December).

[8]The Zimbabwe dollar ceased circulating in early 2009. Data are based on staff estimates of price and exchange rate developments in U.S. dollars. Staff estimates of U.S. dollar values may differ from authorities' estimates.

## Table A8. Major Advanced Economies: General Government Fiscal Balances and Debt[1]
*(Percent of GDP unless noted otherwise)*

| | Average 1995–2004 | 2005 | 2006 | 2007 | 2008 | 2009 | 2010 | Projections 2011 | 2012 | 2016 |
|---|---|---|---|---|---|---|---|---|---|---|
| **Major Advanced Economies** | | | | | | | | | | |
| Net Lending/Borrowing | ... | −3.4 | −2.3 | −2.1 | −4.4 | −9.8 | −8.8 | −8.5 | −6.3 | −4.4 |
| Output Gap[2] | −0.1 | −0.2 | 0.4 | 0.6 | −0.9 | −5.5 | −4.0 | −3.1 | −2.2 | −0.2 |
| Structural Balance[2] | ... | −2.9 | −2.4 | −2.2 | −3.7 | −5.8 | −6.4 | −6.5 | −4.9 | −4.1 |
| **United States** | | | | | | | | | | |
| Net Lending/Borrowing | ... | −3.2 | −2.0 | −2.7 | −6.5 | −12.7 | −10.6 | −10.8 | −7.5 | −6.0 |
| Output Gap[2] | 0.1 | 0.0 | 0.3 | 0.0 | −1.8 | −6.0 | −4.8 | −3.7 | −2.7 | −0.4 |
| Structural Balance[2] | ... | −2.3 | −2.0 | −2.3 | −4.7 | −6.8 | −7.5 | −8.1 | −5.7 | −5.3 |
| Net Debt | 43.2 | 42.7 | 41.9 | 42.6 | 48.4 | 59.9 | 64.8 | 72.4 | 76.7 | 85.7 |
| Gross Debt | 62.3 | 61.7 | 61.1 | 62.2 | 71.2 | 84.6 | 91.6 | 99.5 | 102.9 | 111.9 |
| **Euro Area[3]** | | | | | | | | | | |
| Net Lending/Borrowing | −2.5 | −2.5 | −1.3 | −0.6 | −2.0 | −6.3 | −6.1 | −4.4 | −3.6 | −1.9 |
| Output Gap[2] | −0.5 | −0.4 | 1.0 | 2.1 | 1.1 | −3.5 | −2.8 | −2.3 | −1.7 | 0.0 |
| Structural Balance[2] | −2.7 | −2.8 | −2.3 | −2.1 | −2.7 | −4.3 | −4.1 | −3.2 | −2.7 | −1.7 |
| Net Debt | 54.7 | 54.7 | 53.1 | 50.7 | 52.9 | 61.0 | 64.4 | 66.9 | 68.2 | 68.1 |
| Gross Debt | 70.7 | 70.0 | 68.5 | 66.2 | 69.8 | 79.3 | 85.0 | 87.3 | 88.3 | 86.3 |
| **Germany[4]** | | | | | | | | | | |
| Net Lending/Borrowing | −3.2 | −3.4 | −1.6 | 0.3 | 0.1 | −3.0 | −3.3 | −2.3 | −1.5 | 0.0 |
| Output Gap[2] | −0.6 | −1.3 | 0.9 | 2.4 | 2.0 | −3.7 | −1.6 | −0.5 | −0.1 | 0.2 |
| Structural Balance[2,5] | −2.4 | −2.6 | −2.2 | −0.9 | −0.7 | −1.0 | −2.2 | −2.1 | −1.5 | −0.1 |
| Net Debt | 43.5 | 53.1 | 52.7 | 50.1 | 49.7 | 55.9 | 53.8 | 54.7 | 54.7 | 52.6 |
| Gross Debt | 60.4 | 68.0 | 67.6 | 64.9 | 66.3 | 73.5 | 80.0 | 80.1 | 79.4 | 71.9 |
| **France** | | | | | | | | | | |
| Net Lending/Borrowing | −3.1 | −3.0 | −2.3 | −2.7 | −3.3 | −7.6 | −7.7 | −6.0 | −5.0 | −1.5 |
| Output Gap[2] | 0.2 | 0.3 | 0.8 | 1.1 | −0.4 | −4.0 | −3.6 | −3.1 | −2.5 | 0.2 |
| Structural Balance[2,5] | −3.1 | −3.3 | −2.6 | −3.1 | −3.1 | −5.0 | −5.1 | −4.0 | −3.3 | −1.5 |
| Net Debt | 49.8 | 56.7 | 53.9 | 54.1 | 57.8 | 68.4 | 74.6 | 77.9 | 80.0 | 77.0 |
| Gross Debt | 59.2 | 66.4 | 63.7 | 63.8 | 67.5 | 78.1 | 84.3 | 87.6 | 89.7 | 86.7 |
| **Italy** | | | | | | | | | | |
| Net Lending/Borrowing | −3.6 | −4.4 | −3.3 | −1.5 | −2.7 | −5.3 | −4.6 | −4.3 | −3.5 | −2.9 |
| Output Gap[2] | 0.0 | −0.4 | 0.8 | 1.5 | −0.5 | −3.9 | −3.3 | −3.0 | −2.5 | 0.0 |
| Structural Balance[2,6] | −4.1 | −4.6 | −3.4 | −2.5 | −2.6 | −3.9 | −2.9 | −2.8 | −2.2 | −3.0 |
| Net Debt | 97.1 | 89.3 | 89.8 | 87.3 | 89.2 | 97.1 | 99.6 | 100.6 | 100.4 | 98.9 |
| Gross Debt | 112.1 | 105.9 | 106.6 | 103.6 | 106.3 | 116.1 | 119.0 | 120.3 | 120.0 | 118.0 |
| **Japan** | | | | | | | | | | |
| Net Lending/Borrowing | −6.3 | −4.8 | −4.0 | −2.4 | −4.2 | −10.3 | −9.5 | −10.0 | −8.4 | −7.4 |
| Output Gap[2] | −0.9 | −0.7 | −0.3 | 0.4 | −1.5 | −8.0 | −4.8 | −3.8 | −2.3 | 0.0 |
| Structural Balance[2] | −5.9 | −4.6 | −3.9 | −2.5 | −3.6 | −7.0 | −7.5 | −8.3 | −7.4 | −7.4 |
| Net Debt | 54.6 | 84.6 | 84.3 | 81.5 | 96.5 | 110.0 | 117.5 | 127.8 | 135.1 | 163.9 |
| Gross Debt[7] | 135.4 | 191.6 | 191.3 | 187.7 | 195.0 | 216.3 | 220.3 | 229.1 | 233.4 | 250.5 |
| **United Kingdom** | | | | | | | | | | |
| Net Lending/Borrowing | −1.8 | −3.3 | −2.6 | −2.7 | −4.9 | −10.3 | −10.4 | −8.6 | −6.9 | −1.3 |
| Output Gap[2] | −0.1 | −0.3 | 0.3 | 1.0 | 0.7 | −3.7 | −2.7 | −2.6 | −2.3 | −0.3 |
| Structural Balance[2] | −1.7 | −3.1 | −2.8 | −3.3 | −5.9 | −8.5 | −8.3 | −6.6 | −5.1 | −1.1 |
| Net Debt | 37.6 | 37.3 | 38.0 | 38.2 | 45.6 | 60.9 | 69.4 | 75.1 | 78.6 | 73.5 |
| Gross Debt | 42.8 | 42.1 | 43.1 | 43.9 | 52.0 | 68.3 | 77.2 | 83.0 | 86.5 | 81.3 |
| **Canada** | | | | | | | | | | |
| Net Lending/Borrowing | −0.2 | 1.5 | 1.6 | 1.6 | 0.1 | −5.5 | −5.5 | −4.6 | −2.8 | 0.0 |
| Output Gap[2] | 0.5 | 1.5 | 1.7 | 1.7 | 0.1 | −3.8 | −2.4 | −1.5 | −0.8 | 0.0 |
| Structural Balance[2] | −0.4 | 0.9 | 0.8 | 0.6 | 0.0 | −3.2 | −4.0 | −3.6 | −2.2 | 0.0 |
| Net Debt | 52.9 | 31.0 | 26.3 | 22.9 | 22.4 | 28.4 | 32.2 | 35.1 | 36.3 | 33.0 |
| Gross Debt | 88.1 | 71.6 | 70.3 | 66.5 | 71.3 | 83.4 | 84.0 | 84.2 | 83.1 | 72.6 |

Note: The methodology and specific assumptions for each country are discussed in Box A1 in the Statistical Appendix. The country group composites for fiscal data are calculated as the sum of the U.S dollar values for the relevant individual countries. This differs from the calculations in the October 2010 and earlier issues of the *World Economic Outlook*, for which the composites were weighted by GDP valued at purchasing power parities (PPPs) as a share of total world GDP.
[1]Debt data refer to the end of the year. Debt data are not always comparable across countries.
[2]Percent of potential GDP.
[3]Excludes Estonia.
[4]Beginning in 1995, the debt and debt-services obligations of the Treuhandanstalt (and of various other agencies) were taken over by the general government. This debt is equivalent to 8 percent of GDP, and the associated debt service to 1/2 to 1 percent of GDP.
[5]Excludes sizable one-off receipts from the sale of assets, including licenses.
[6]Excludes one-off measures based on the authorities' data and, in the absence of the latter, receipts from the sale of assets.
[7]Includes equity shares.

## Table A9. Summary of World Trade Volumes and Prices
*(Annual percent change)*

| | Averages | | 2003 | 2004 | 2005 | 2006 | 2007 | 2008 | 2009 | 2010 | Projections | |
|---|---|---|---|---|---|---|---|---|---|---|---|---|
| | 1993–2002 | 2003–12 | | | | | | | | | 2011 | 2012 |
| **Trade in Goods and Services** | | | | | | | | | | | | |
| **World Trade[1]** | | | | | | | | | | | | |
| Volume | 6.6 | 5.7 | 5.6 | 10.8 | 7.7 | 8.7 | 7.5 | 2.7 | −10.9 | 12.4 | 7.4 | 6.9 |
| Price Deflator | | | | | | | | | | | | |
| In U.S. Dollars | −1.3 | 5.3 | 10.2 | 9.5 | 5.4 | 5.8 | 8.1 | 11.3 | −10.3 | 5.8 | 8.5 | 0.8 |
| In SDRs | −0.5 | 3.4 | 1.9 | 3.6 | 5.7 | 6.3 | 3.9 | 7.8 | −8.0 | 7.0 | 5.8 | 1.0 |
| **Volume of Trade** | | | | | | | | | | | | |
| Exports | | | | | | | | | | | | |
| Advanced Economies | 6.2 | 4.7 | 3.4 | 9.2 | 6.2 | 8.7 | 6.6 | 1.9 | −12.2 | 12.0 | 6.8 | 5.9 |
| Emerging and Developing Economies | 8.3 | 8.3 | 11.5 | 14.5 | 11.2 | 9.4 | 9.6 | 4.0 | −7.5 | 14.5 | 8.8 | 8.7 |
| Imports | | | | | | | | | | | | |
| Advanced Economies | 6.5 | 4.1 | 4.2 | 9.3 | 6.5 | 7.7 | 5.1 | 0.4 | −12.6 | 11.2 | 5.8 | 5.5 |
| Emerging and Developing Economies | 7.3 | 9.4 | 10.7 | 16.1 | 11.6 | 10.3 | 13.3 | 8.8 | −8.3 | 13.5 | 10.2 | 9.4 |
| **Terms of Trade** | | | | | | | | | | | | |
| Advanced Economies | −0.1 | −0.3 | 1.0 | −0.2 | −1.4 | −1.1 | 0.4 | −2.0 | 2.7 | −1.2 | −1.1 | −0.5 |
| Emerging and Developing Economies | 0.4 | 1.5 | 0.6 | 2.9 | 5.1 | 3.2 | 0.5 | 3.7 | −5.1 | 0.2 | 4.7 | −0.3 |
| **Trade in Goods** | | | | | | | | | | | | |
| **World Trade[1]** | | | | | | | | | | | | |
| Volume | 6.5 | 5.8 | 7.0 | 11.3 | 7.4 | 8.6 | 7.1 | 2.7 | −11.7 | 13.6 | 7.7 | 6.9 |
| Price Deflator | | | | | | | | | | | | |
| In U.S. Dollars | −1.0 | 5.4 | 9.2 | 9.4 | 6.2 | 6.5 | 7.8 | 11.7 | −11.9 | 7.2 | 9.2 | 0.9 |
| In SDRs | −0.2 | 3.4 | 1.0 | 3.5 | 6.4 | 7.0 | 3.6 | 8.1 | −9.7 | 8.4 | 6.4 | 1.1 |
| **World Trade Prices in U.S. Dollars[2]** | | | | | | | | | | | | |
| Manufactures | −1.4 | 4.0 | 13.5 | 5.7 | 2.6 | 2.6 | 6.2 | 6.6 | −6.3 | 3.0 | 5.5 | 1.1 |
| Oil | 2.7 | 15.8 | 15.8 | 30.7 | 41.3 | 20.5 | 10.7 | 36.4 | −36.3 | 27.9 | 35.6 | 0.8 |
| Nonfuel Primary Commodities | −0.9 | 9.5 | 5.9 | 15.2 | 6.1 | 23.2 | 14.1 | 7.5 | −15.8 | 26.3 | 25.1 | −4.3 |
| Food | −1.5 | 7.8 | 6.3 | 14.0 | −0.9 | 10.5 | 15.2 | 23.4 | −14.7 | 11.4 | 24.1 | −4.7 |
| Beverages | 1.3 | 9.9 | 4.8 | −0.9 | 18.1 | 8.4 | 13.8 | 23.3 | 1.6 | 14.1 | 23.9 | −3.5 |
| Agricultural Raw Materials | 0.2 | 3.8 | 0.6 | 4.1 | 0.5 | 8.8 | 5.0 | −0.8 | −17.0 | 33.2 | 24.8 | −11.5 |
| Metal | −1.2 | 16.6 | 11.8 | 34.6 | 22.4 | 56.2 | 17.4 | −7.8 | −19.7 | 48.1 | 26.5 | −0.8 |
| **World Trade Prices in SDRs[2]** | | | | | | | | | | | | |
| Manufactures | −0.5 | 2.0 | 4.9 | 0.0 | 2.8 | 3.1 | 2.1 | 3.3 | −4.0 | 4.2 | 2.9 | 1.3 |
| Oil | 3.6 | 13.6 | 7.1 | 23.6 | 41.6 | 21.0 | 6.4 | 32.1 | −34.8 | 29.3 | 32.2 | 1.0 |
| Nonfuel Primary Commodities | −0.1 | 7.5 | −2.1 | 9.0 | 6.3 | 23.8 | 9.6 | 4.1 | −13.8 | 27.6 | 21.9 | −4.1 |
| Food | −0.7 | 5.8 | −1.7 | 7.8 | −0.7 | 11.0 | 10.7 | 19.5 | −12.6 | 12.6 | 21.0 | −4.5 |
| Beverages | 2.1 | 7.9 | −3.1 | −6.3 | 18.3 | 8.8 | 9.4 | 19.4 | 4.1 | 15.4 | 20.8 | −3.3 |
| Agricultural Raw Materials | 1.1 | 1.9 | −7.0 | −1.6 | 0.8 | 9.3 | 0.9 | −3.9 | −14.9 | 34.7 | 21.6 | −11.3 |
| Metal | −0.3 | 14.4 | 3.3 | 27.3 | 22.7 | 56.9 | 12.8 | −10.7 | −17.7 | 49.7 | 23.3 | −0.6 |
| **World Trade Prices in Euros[2]** | | | | | | | | | | | | |
| Manufactures | 1.8 | 0.2 | −5.2 | −3.8 | 2.4 | 1.8 | −2.7 | −0.7 | −1.0 | 8.2 | 2.3 | 1.6 |
| Oil | 6.1 | 11.6 | −3.3 | 18.9 | 41.0 | 19.5 | 1.4 | 27.1 | −32.7 | 34.3 | 31.4 | 1.3 |
| Nonfuel Primary Commodities | 2.3 | 5.6 | −11.6 | 4.8 | 5.9 | 22.3 | 4.5 | 0.1 | −11.1 | 32.5 | 21.2 | −3.8 |
| Food | 1.7 | 3.9 | −11.2 | 3.7 | −1.1 | 9.6 | 5.6 | 14.9 | −9.8 | 17.0 | 20.3 | −4.2 |
| Beverages | 4.6 | 6.0 | −12.5 | −9.9 | 17.8 | 7.5 | 4.2 | 14.8 | 7.3 | 19.8 | 20.1 | −3.0 |
| Agricultural Raw Materials | 3.5 | 0.1 | −16.0 | −5.3 | 0.3 | 8.0 | −3.8 | −7.6 | −12.3 | 39.9 | 21.0 | −11.1 |
| Metal | 2.0 | 12.4 | −6.7 | 22.4 | 22.2 | 55.0 | 7.5 | −14.2 | −15.1 | 55.5 | 22.6 | −0.3 |

## Table A9. Summary of World Trade Volumes and Prices *(concluded)*

| | Averages 1993–2002 | Averages 2003–12 | 2003 | 2004 | 2005 | 2006 | 2007 | 2008 | 2009 | 2010 | Projections 2011 | Projections 2012 |
|---|---|---|---|---|---|---|---|---|---|---|---|---|
| **Trade in Goods** | | | | | | | | | | | | |
| **Volume of Trade** | | | | | | | | | | | | |
| Exports | | | | | | | | | | | | |
|   Advanced Economies | 6.0 | 4.8 | 5.0 | 9.6 | 5.7 | 8.7 | 6.1 | 1.9 | −13.6 | 13.6 | 7.3 | 5.8 |
|   Emerging and Developing Economies | 8.2 | 8.1 | 11.5 | 14.1 | 10.9 | 8.9 | 8.7 | 4.1 | −7.8 | 15.1 | 8.9 | 8.6 |
|     Fuel Exporters | 3.6 | 3.9 | 11.8 | 9.8 | 5.8 | 2.1 | 4.1 | 2.7 | −6.9 | 2.5 | 5.1 | 3.0 |
|     Nonfuel Exporters | 9.9 | 9.7 | 11.3 | 15.6 | 12.8 | 11.8 | 10.7 | 4.7 | −8.3 | 20.1 | 10.3 | 10.6 |
| Imports | | | | | | | | | | | | |
|   Advanced Economies | 6.5 | 4.4 | 6.0 | 10.2 | 6.3 | 8.0 | 5.1 | 0.3 | −13.3 | 12.6 | 6.0 | 5.2 |
|   Emerging and Developing Economies | 7.3 | 9.2 | 11.5 | 16.2 | 11.4 | 9.8 | 12.8 | 8.2 | −9.2 | 13.8 | 10.2 | 9.6 |
|     Fuel Exporters | 3.6 | 9.2 | 10.8 | 14.8 | 16.0 | 9.8 | 21.6 | 14.5 | −12.8 | 3.4 | 9.2 | 8.2 |
|     Nonfuel Exporters | 8.4 | 9.2 | 11.6 | 16.5 | 10.5 | 9.8 | 10.9 | 6.8 | −8.3 | 16.3 | 10.4 | 9.8 |
| **Price Deflators in SDRs** | | | | | | | | | | | | |
| Exports | | | | | | | | | | | | |
|   Advanced Economies | −0.7 | 2.4 | 1.6 | 2.4 | 3.7 | 4.4 | 3.1 | 4.8 | −6.8 | 5.5 | 5.2 | 0.4 |
|   Emerging and Developing Economies | 1.9 | 6.1 | 1.2 | 7.3 | 14.0 | 12.8 | 5.6 | 13.9 | −13.9 | 12.1 | 9.8 | 1.2 |
|     Fuel Exporters | 3.6 | 11.8 | 4.5 | 16.6 | 32.3 | 20.9 | 8.1 | 26.0 | −26.6 | 24.5 | 24.6 | 0.8 |
|     Nonfuel Exporters | 1.3 | 3.8 | 0.2 | 4.1 | 7.2 | 9.4 | 4.5 | 8.7 | −7.7 | 7.2 | 4.2 | 1.4 |
| Imports | | | | | | | | | | | | |
|   Advanced Economies | −0.8 | 2.7 | 0.5 | 2.7 | 5.6 | 5.8 | 2.6 | 7.4 | −10.4 | 6.8 | 6.5 | 1.2 |
|   Emerging and Developing Economies | 1.4 | 4.6 | 0.3 | 4.5 | 7.9 | 9.1 | 5.0 | 10.2 | −8.9 | 12.7 | 4.7 | 1.7 |
|     Fuel Exporters | 0.4 | 5.3 | 1.0 | 4.5 | 8.0 | 10.7 | 5.2 | 8.9 | −5.4 | 15.3 | 6.1 | 0.5 |
|     Nonfuel Exporters | 1.6 | 4.4 | 0.2 | 4.5 | 7.8 | 8.8 | 5.0 | 10.5 | −9.8 | 12.1 | 4.4 | 1.9 |
| **Terms of Trade** | | | | | | | | | | | | |
| Advanced Economies | 0.1 | −0.4 | 1.1 | −0.4 | −1.8 | −1.3 | 0.5 | −2.4 | 4.0 | −1.2 | −1.2 | −0.8 |
| Emerging and Developing Economies | 0.5 | 1.4 | 0.9 | 2.7 | 5.7 | 3.4 | 0.5 | 3.3 | −5.4 | −0.6 | 4.8 | −0.4 |
|   Regional Groups | | | | | | | | | | | | |
|     Central and Eastern Europe | −0.3 | −0.4 | −0.5 | 1.2 | −1.6 | −1.2 | 2.0 | −2.5 | 3.8 | −2.0 | −2.2 | −0.4 |
|     Commonwealth of Independent States[3] | 1.7 | 6.1 | 8.7 | 12.4 | 15.0 | 9.4 | 2.5 | 15.1 | −20.3 | 9.9 | 13.4 | 0.2 |
|     Developing Asia | −0.3 | −1.9 | −1.0 | −2.7 | −2.2 | −1.7 | −2.1 | −2.7 | 4.3 | −10.7 | 0.3 | −0.2 |
|     Latin America and the Caribbean | 0.6 | 2.6 | 2.8 | 5.5 | 5.4 | 8.3 | 2.3 | 2.6 | −7.9 | 9.0 | 0.4 | −1.7 |
|     Middle East and North Africa | 2.4 | 5.4 | 2.0 | 8.1 | 21.9 | 6.0 | 1.9 | 13.9 | −18.3 | 7.0 | 16.8 | −0.1 |
|     Sub-Saharan Africa | 0.5 | 4.1 | −1.9 | 4.8 | 12.3 | 9.1 | 3.2 | 7.7 | −12.2 | 10.1 | 11.4 | −0.6 |
|   Analytical Groups | | | | | | | | | | | | |
|     By Source of Export Earnings | | | | | | | | | | | | |
|       Fuel Exporters | 3.2 | 6.1 | 3.5 | 11.5 | 22.5 | 9.2 | 2.8 | 15.7 | −22.3 | 8.0 | 17.5 | 0.3 |
|       Nonfuel Exporters | −0.3 | −0.6 | −0.1 | −0.4 | −0.6 | 0.5 | −0.5 | −1.6 | 2.3 | −4.3 | −0.2 | −0.5 |
| *Memorandum* | | | | | | | | | | | | |
| **World Exports in Billions of U.S. Dollars** | | | | | | | | | | | | |
| Goods and Services | 6,745 | 16,528 | 9,323 | 11,310 | 12,870 | 14,849 | 17,307 | 19,747 | 15,783 | 18,713 | 21,877 | 23,502 |
| Goods | 5,383 | 13,253 | 7,442 | 9,034 | 10,327 | 11,966 | 13,845 | 15,859 | 12,341 | 14,986 | 17,711 | 19,015 |
| Average Oil Price[4] | 2.7 | 15.8 | 15.8 | 30.7 | 41.3 | 20.5 | 10.7 | 36.4 | −36.3 | 27.9 | 35.6 | 0.8 |
|   In U.S. Dollars a Barrel | 19.82 | 70.84 | 28.89 | 37.76 | 53.35 | 64.27 | 71.13 | 97.04 | 61.78 | 79.03 | 107.16 | 108.00 |
| Export Unit Value of Manufactures[5] | −1.4 | 4.0 | 13.5 | 5.7 | 2.6 | 2.6 | 6.2 | 6.6 | −6.3 | 3.0 | 5.5 | 1.1 |

[1]Average of annual percent change for world exports and imports.

[2]As represented, respectively, by the export unit value index for manufactures of the advanced economies and accounting for 83 percent of the advanced economies' trade (export of goods) weights; the average of U.K. Brent, Dubai, and West Texas Intermediate crude oil prices; and the average of world market prices for nonfuel primary commodities weighted by their 2002–04 shares in world commodity exports.

[3]Georgia and Mongolia, which are not members of the Commonwealth of Independent States, are included in this group for reasons of geography and similarities in economic structure.

[4]Percent change in average of U.K. Brent, Dubai, and West Texas Intermediate crude oil prices.

[5]Percent change of manufactures exported by the advanced economies.

## Table A10. Summary of Balances on Current Account
*(Billions of U.S. dollars)*

| | 2003 | 2004 | 2005 | 2006 | 2007 | 2008 | 2009 | 2010 | 2011 | 2012 | 2016 |
|---|---|---|---|---|---|---|---|---|---|---|---|
| | | | | | | | | | Projections | | |
| **Advanced Economies** | **−218.9** | **−219.5** | **−411.2** | **−449.8** | **−344.2** | **−471.8** | **−101.1** | **−95.5** | **−125.6** | **−91.0** | **−302.5** |
| United States | −520.7 | −630.5 | −747.6 | −802.6 | −718.1 | −668.9 | −378.4 | −470.2 | −493.9 | −450.7 | −643.6 |
| Euro Area[1,2] | 23.4 | 76.6 | 14.6 | −12.6 | 14.7 | −196.9 | −69.4 | −77.0 | 3.8 | 6.6 | 18.3 |
| Japan | 136.2 | 172.1 | 165.7 | 170.4 | 211.0 | 157.1 | 141.8 | 194.8 | 134.1 | 138.6 | 131.5 |
| Other Advanced Economies[3] | 128.7 | 127.4 | 131.1 | 142.0 | 137.0 | 129.0 | 158.2 | 167.7 | 229.8 | 213.9 | 192.3 |
| *Memorandum* | | | | | | | | | | | |
| Newly Industrialized Asian Economies | 84.3 | 86.9 | 82.8 | 99.4 | 130.9 | 87.8 | 128.6 | 133.1 | 134.8 | 136.1 | 145.2 |
| **Emerging and Developing Economies** | **145.2** | **219.7** | **443.0** | **661.5** | **649.7** | **704.2** | **326.6** | **378.1** | **646.5** | **635.9** | **900.8** |
| **Regional Groups** | | | | | | | | | | | |
| Central and Eastern Europe | −32.5 | −52.0 | −57.7 | −85.3 | −131.7 | −151.3 | −44.3 | −76.0 | −102.0 | −116.0 | −165.6 |
| Commonwealth of Independent States[4] | 35.7 | 63.5 | 87.6 | 96.3 | 71.7 | 107.7 | 41.4 | 75.0 | 116.9 | 90.1 | 17.0 |
| Developing Asia | 85.2 | 92.9 | 167.5 | 289.2 | 418.3 | 435.9 | 328.2 | 308.1 | 348.9 | 414.7 | 843.7 |
| Latin America and the Caribbean | 9.4 | 21.5 | 36.3 | 49.5 | 14.6 | −31.2 | −25.0 | −56.9 | −79.1 | −107.0 | −179.1 |
| Middle East and North Africa | 59.8 | 101.9 | 212.7 | 281.1 | 265.8 | 343.1 | 47.9 | 152.8 | 357.1 | 349.0 | 394.5 |
| Sub-Saharan Africa | −12.4 | −8.2 | −3.4 | 30.8 | 11.0 | 0.0 | −21.6 | −24.9 | 4.7 | 5.1 | −9.7 |
| *Memorandum* | | | | | | | | | | | |
| European Union | 12.1 | 61.7 | −13.8 | −48.0 | −83.1 | −167.4 | −39.6 | −22.3 | −37.1 | −26.3 | −13.1 |
| **Analytical Groups** | | | | | | | | | | | |
| **By Source of Export Earnings** | | | | | | | | | | | |
| Fuel | 103.9 | 184.6 | 349.2 | 476.6 | 429.7 | 587.0 | 145.2 | 291.0 | 597.6 | 568.5 | 514.8 |
| Nonfuel | 41.3 | 35.1 | 93.8 | 184.9 | 220.0 | 117.2 | 181.4 | 87.0 | 48.9 | 67.4 | 386.0 |
| Of Which, Primary Products | −4.4 | −0.9 | −1.8 | 9.4 | 6.7 | −15.2 | −3.6 | −4.8 | −7.2 | −15.4 | −12.8 |
| **By External Financing Source** | | | | | | | | | | | |
| Net Debtor Economies | −31.7 | −55.9 | −95.3 | −116.8 | −212.2 | −361.6 | −180.3 | −265.4 | −360.0 | −423.2 | −519.7 |
| Of Which, Official Financing | −5.8 | −4.6 | −5.7 | −3.9 | −5.7 | −12.8 | −11.4 | −14.7 | −17.9 | −19.7 | −16.7 |
| **Net Debtor Economies by Debt-Servicing Experience** | | | | | | | | | | | |
| Economies with Arrears and/or Rescheduling during 2005–09 | 1.9 | −6.8 | −9.0 | −6.1 | −19.2 | −34.8 | −31.6 | −40.8 | −47.0 | −53.3 | −51.2 |
| **World[1]** | **−73.7** | **0.2** | **31.8** | **211.8** | **305.4** | **232.4** | **225.5** | **282.6** | **520.9** | **544.9** | **598.4** |
| *Memorandum* | | | | | | | | | | | |
| In Percent of Total World Current Account Transactions | −0.4 | 0.0 | 0.1 | 0.7 | 0.9 | 0.6 | 0.7 | 0.8 | 1.2 | 1.2 | 1.0 |
| In Percent of World GDP | −0.2 | 0.0 | 0.1 | 0.4 | 0.5 | 0.4 | 0.4 | 0.4 | 0.7 | 0.7 | 0.6 |

[1]Reflects errors, omissions, and asymmetries in balance of payments statistics on the current account, as well as the exclusion of data for international organizations and a limited number of countries. See "Classification of Countries" in the introduction to this Statistical Appendix.

[2]Calculated as the sum of the balances of individual Euro Area countries, excluding Estonia.

[3]In this table, Other Advanced Economies means advanced economies excluding the United States, Euro Area countries, and Japan but including Estonia.

[4]Georgia and Mongolia, which are not members of the Commonwealth of Independent States, are included in this group for reasons of geography and similarities in economic structure.

## Table A11. Advanced Economies: Balance on Current Account
*(Percent of GDP)*

| | 2003 | 2004 | 2005 | 2006 | 2007 | 2008 | 2009 | 2010 | Projections 2011 | 2012 | 2016 |
|---|---|---|---|---|---|---|---|---|---|---|---|
| **Advanced Economies** | **−0.7** | **−0.7** | **−1.2** | **−1.2** | **−0.9** | **−1.1** | **−0.3** | **−0.2** | **−0.3** | **−0.2** | **−0.6** |
| United States | −4.7 | −5.3 | −5.9 | −6.0 | −5.1 | −4.7 | −2.7 | −3.2 | −3.2 | −2.8 | −3.4 |
| Euro Area[1] | 0.4 | 1.2 | 0.4 | 0.4 | 0.2 | −0.6 | −0.2 | 0.1 | 0.0 | 0.0 | 0.1 |
| Germany | 1.9 | 4.7 | 5.1 | 6.5 | 7.6 | 6.7 | 5.0 | 5.3 | 5.1 | 4.6 | 3.6 |
| France | 0.7 | 0.5 | −0.5 | −0.6 | −1.0 | −1.9 | −1.9 | −2.1 | −2.8 | −2.7 | −2.2 |
| Italy | −1.3 | −0.9 | −1.7 | −2.6 | −2.4 | −2.9 | −2.1 | −3.5 | −3.4 | −3.0 | −2.4 |
| Spain | −3.5 | −5.3 | −7.4 | −9.0 | −10.0 | −9.7 | −5.5 | −4.5 | −4.8 | −4.5 | −3.5 |
| Netherlands | 5.6 | 7.6 | 7.4 | 9.3 | 6.7 | 4.3 | 4.6 | 7.1 | 7.9 | 8.2 | 6.0 |
| Belgium | 3.4 | 3.2 | 2.0 | 1.9 | 1.6 | −1.9 | 0.8 | 1.2 | 1.0 | 1.2 | 2.4 |
| Austria | 1.7 | 2.2 | 2.2 | 2.8 | 3.5 | 4.9 | 2.9 | 3.2 | 3.1 | 3.1 | 3.2 |
| Greece | −6.6 | −5.9 | −7.4 | −11.2 | −14.4 | −14.7 | −11.0 | −10.4 | −8.2 | −7.1 | −3.8 |
| Portugal | −6.5 | −8.4 | −10.4 | −10.7 | −10.1 | −12.6 | −10.9 | −9.9 | −8.7 | −8.5 | −5.7 |
| Finland | 4.8 | 6.2 | 3.4 | 4.2 | 4.3 | 2.9 | 2.3 | 3.1 | 2.8 | 2.6 | 2.8 |
| Ireland | −0.0 | −0.6 | −3.5 | −3.6 | −5.3 | −5.6 | −3.0 | −0.7 | 0.2 | 0.6 | 0.1 |
| Slovak Republic | −5.9 | −7.8 | −8.5 | −7.8 | −5.3 | −6.6 | −3.6 | −3.4 | −2.8 | −2.7 | −3.1 |
| Slovenia | −0.8 | −2.7 | −1.7 | −2.5 | −4.8 | −6.7 | −1.5 | −1.2 | −2.0 | −2.1 | −2.6 |
| Luxembourg | 8.1 | 11.9 | 11.5 | 10.4 | 10.1 | 5.3 | 6.7 | 7.7 | 8.5 | 8.7 | 9.3 |
| Estonia | −11.3 | −11.3 | −10.0 | −15.3 | −17.2 | −9.7 | 4.5 | 3.6 | 3.3 | 3.1 | −3.7 |
| Cyprus | −2.3 | −5.0 | −5.9 | −7.0 | −11.7 | −17.2 | −7.5 | −7.0 | −8.9 | −8.7 | −8.0 |
| Malta | −3.1 | −6.0 | −8.7 | −9.3 | −5.6 | −5.6 | −6.9 | −0.6 | −1.1 | −2.3 | −3.3 |
| Japan | 3.2 | 3.7 | 3.6 | 3.9 | 4.8 | 3.2 | 2.8 | 3.6 | 2.3 | 2.3 | 2.0 |
| United Kingdom | −1.6 | −2.1 | −2.6 | −3.4 | −2.6 | −1.6 | −1.7 | −2.5 | −2.4 | −1.9 | −1.0 |
| Canada | 1.2 | 2.3 | 1.9 | 1.4 | 0.8 | 0.4 | −2.8 | −3.1 | −2.8 | −2.6 | −1.3 |
| Korea | 2.4 | 4.5 | 2.2 | 1.5 | 2.1 | 0.3 | 3.9 | 2.8 | 1.1 | 1.0 | 0.6 |
| Australia | −5.2 | −6.0 | −5.7 | −5.3 | −6.2 | −4.5 | −4.2 | −2.6 | −0.4 | −2.1 | −6.2 |
| Taiwan Province of China | 9.8 | 5.8 | 4.8 | 7.0 | 8.9 | 6.9 | 11.4 | 9.4 | 11.6 | 10.9 | 8.0 |
| Sweden | 7.0 | 6.6 | 6.8 | 8.4 | 9.2 | 8.7 | 7.2 | 6.5 | 6.1 | 5.8 | 5.6 |
| Switzerland | 13.3 | 13.4 | 14.0 | 14.8 | 8.9 | 2.3 | 11.5 | 14.2 | 13.2 | 12.8 | 12.0 |
| Hong Kong SAR | 10.4 | 9.5 | 11.4 | 12.1 | 12.3 | 13.7 | 8.6 | 6.6 | 5.2 | 5.5 | 7.9 |
| Singapore | 22.7 | 17.0 | 21.1 | 24.8 | 27.3 | 14.6 | 19.0 | 22.2 | 20.4 | 19.0 | 14.9 |
| Czech Republic | −6.3 | −5.3 | −1.3 | −2.5 | −3.3 | −0.6 | −1.1 | −2.4 | −1.8 | −1.2 | −0.7 |
| Norway | 12.3 | 12.7 | 16.3 | 17.2 | 14.1 | 17.9 | 13.1 | 12.9 | 16.3 | 16.0 | 14.8 |
| Israel | 0.6 | 1.8 | 3.2 | 5.1 | 2.9 | 0.8 | 3.6 | 3.1 | 3.3 | 3.1 | 3.4 |
| Denmark | 3.7 | 3.3 | 4.1 | 3.1 | 1.4 | 2.4 | 3.8 | 5.0 | 4.8 | 4.8 | 4.9 |
| New Zealand | −3.9 | −5.7 | −7.9 | −8.2 | −8.0 | −8.7 | −2.9 | −2.2 | −0.2 | −4.4 | −7.0 |
| Iceland | −4.8 | −9.8 | −16.1 | −25.7 | −15.7 | −28.3 | −10.4 | −8.0 | 1.1 | 2.1 | −0.6 |
| *Memorandum* | | | | | | | | | | | |
| Major Advanced Economies | −1.5 | −1.4 | −1.9 | −2.0 | −1.3 | −1.3 | −0.8 | −1.0 | −1.3 | −1.1 | −1.4 |
| Euro Area[2] | 0.3 | 0.8 | 0.1 | −0.1 | 0.1 | −1.4 | −0.6 | −0.6 | 0.0 | 0.0 | 0.1 |
| Newly Industrialized Asian Economies | 7.0 | 6.5 | 5.5 | 6.0 | 7.2 | 5.1 | 8.0 | 7.1 | 6.3 | 6.0 | 4.8 |

[1]Calculated as the sum of the balances of individual Euro Area countries excluding Estonia.
[2]Corrected for reporting discrepancies in intra-area transactions, excluding Estonia.

## Table A12. Emerging and Developing Economies: Balance on Current Account
*(Percent of GDP)*

| | 2003 | 2004 | 2005 | 2006 | 2007 | 2008 | 2009 | 2010 | Projections 2011 | 2012 | 2016 |
|---|---|---|---|---|---|---|---|---|---|---|---|
| **Central and Eastern Europe** | **–4.1** | **–5.3** | **–4.9** | **–6.5** | **–8.1** | **–7.9** | **–2.8** | **–4.3** | **–5.4** | **–5.7** | **–6.2** |
| Albania | –5.0 | –4.0 | –6.1 | –5.6 | –10.4 | –15.2 | –14.0 | –10.1 | –11.2 | –9.8 | –5.0 |
| Bosnia and Herzegovina | –19.4 | –16.4 | –17.2 | –8.0 | –10.7 | –14.5 | –6.9 | –6.0 | –6.0 | –5.7 | –4.6 |
| Bulgaria | –5.3 | –6.4 | –11.7 | –17.6 | –30.2 | –23.3 | –10.0 | –0.8 | –1.5 | –2.0 | –4.0 |
| Croatia | –6.3 | –4.4 | –5.5 | –7.0 | –7.6 | –9.2 | –5.5 | –1.9 | –3.6 | –3.6 | –5.7 |
| Hungary | –8.0 | –8.4 | –7.6 | –7.6 | –6.9 | –7.3 | –0.5 | 1.6 | 1.5 | 0.9 | –3.7 |
| Kosovo | –8.1 | –8.3 | –7.4 | –6.7 | –8.3 | –15.2 | –16.8 | –17.3 | –23.1 | –25.6 | –16.7 |
| Latvia | –8.1 | –12.9 | –12.5 | –22.5 | –22.3 | –13.1 | 8.6 | 3.6 | 2.6 | 1.5 | –2.6 |
| Lithuania | –6.9 | –7.6 | –7.1 | –10.7 | –14.6 | –13.4 | 4.5 | 1.8 | –0.9 | –2.9 | –3.3 |
| Former Yugoslav Republic of Macedonia | –3.8 | –7.6 | –2.6 | –0.8 | –6.5 | –13.9 | –6.4 | –2.8 | –4.2 | –4.8 | –4.5 |
| Montenegro | –6.7 | –7.2 | –8.5 | –24.1 | –39.5 | –50.6 | –30.3 | –25.6 | –24.5 | –22.1 | –8.9 |
| Poland | –2.5 | –4.0 | –1.2 | –2.7 | –4.8 | –4.8 | –2.2 | –3.3 | –3.9 | –4.2 | –4.3 |
| Romania | –5.8 | –8.4 | –8.6 | –10.4 | –13.4 | –11.6 | –4.2 | –4.2 | –5.0 | –5.2 | –5.0 |
| Serbia | –7.2 | –12.1 | –8.7 | –10.2 | –16.0 | –21.1 | –6.9 | –7.1 | –7.4 | –6.6 | –5.1 |
| Turkey | –2.5 | –3.7 | –4.6 | –6.1 | –5.9 | –5.7 | –2.3 | –6.5 | –8.0 | –8.2 | –8.4 |
| **Commonwealth of Independent States[1]** | **6.2** | **8.2** | **8.7** | **7.4** | **4.2** | **4.9** | **2.5** | **3.8** | **4.7** | **3.2** | **0.4** |
| Russia | 8.2 | 10.1 | 11.1 | 9.5 | 5.9 | 6.2 | 4.1 | 4.9 | 5.6 | 3.9 | 0.3 |
| Excluding Russia | 0.2 | 2.2 | 1.3 | 0.6 | –1.3 | 0.8 | –2.0 | 0.7 | 2.0 | 0.7 | 0.8 |
| Armenia | –6.8 | –0.5 | –1.0 | –1.8 | –6.4 | –11.8 | –16.0 | –13.7 | –12.4 | –11.3 | –8.5 |
| Azerbaijan | –27.8 | –29.8 | 1.3 | 17.6 | 27.3 | 35.5 | 23.6 | 27.7 | 28.4 | 24.2 | 17.2 |
| Belarus | –2.4 | –5.3 | 1.4 | –3.9 | –6.7 | –8.6 | –13.0 | –15.5 | –15.7 | –15.2 | –12.0 |
| Georgia | –9.6 | –6.9 | –11.1 | –15.1 | –19.7 | –22.6 | –11.2 | –9.8 | –13.0 | –12.0 | –6.1 |
| Kazakhstan | –0.9 | 0.8 | –1.8 | –2.5 | –8.1 | 4.6 | –3.7 | 2.5 | 5.8 | 4.2 | 1.5 |
| Kyrgyz Republic | 1.7 | 4.9 | 2.8 | –3.1 | –0.2 | –8.1 | 2.0 | –7.4 | –6.7 | –7.8 | –3.9 |
| Moldova | –6.6 | –1.8 | –7.6 | –11.4 | –15.3 | –16.3 | –8.5 | –10.9 | –11.1 | –11.2 | –9.3 |
| Mongolia | –7.1 | 1.3 | 1.3 | 6.5 | 6.3 | –12.9 | –9.0 | –15.2 | –13.3 | –14.0 | 13.2 |
| Tajikistan | –1.3 | –3.9 | –1.7 | –2.8 | –8.6 | –7.6 | –5.9 | 2.2 | –4.1 | –7.2 | –4.3 |
| Turkmenistan | 2.7 | 0.6 | 5.1 | 15.7 | 15.5 | 16.5 | –16.1 | –11.4 | –4.7 | –3.9 | 6.1 |
| Ukraine | 5.8 | 10.6 | 2.9 | –1.5 | –3.7 | –7.1 | –1.5 | –1.9 | –3.6 | –3.8 | –2.9 |
| Uzbekistan | 5.8 | 7.2 | 7.7 | 9.1 | 7.3 | 8.7 | 2.2 | 6.7 | 10.0 | 6.7 | 2.7 |

## Table A12. Emerging and Developing Economies: Balance on Current Account *(continued)*

| | 2003 | 2004 | 2005 | 2006 | 2007 | 2008 | 2009 | 2010 | Projections 2011 | 2012 | 2016 |
|---|---|---|---|---|---|---|---|---|---|---|---|
| **Developing Asia** | **2.8** | **2.6** | **4.1** | **6.0** | **6.9** | **5.9** | **4.1** | **3.3** | **3.3** | **3.6** | **4.8** |
| Islamic Republic of Afghanistan | −16.5 | −4.7 | −2.7 | −5.7 | 0.9 | −1.6 | −2.6 | 2.0 | −0.7 | −3.6 | −7.4 |
| Bangladesh | 0.3 | −0.3 | 0.0 | 1.2 | 1.1 | 1.9 | 3.3 | 1.4 | −1.0 | −1.2 | −0.2 |
| Bhutan | −22.5 | −17.6 | −28.7 | −4.2 | 12.1 | −2.2 | −9.2 | −5.2 | −12.0 | −18.1 | −19.0 |
| Brunei Darussalam | 50.6 | 48.3 | 52.7 | 56.4 | 51.1 | 54.3 | 40.2 | 42.8 | 44.6 | 44.5 | 50.9 |
| Cambodia | −3.6 | −2.2 | −3.8 | −0.6 | −2.5 | −6.2 | −5.2 | −4.3 | −11.4 | −10.0 | −4.7 |
| China | 2.8 | 3.6 | 7.1 | 9.3 | 10.6 | 9.6 | 6.0 | 5.2 | 5.7 | 6.3 | 7.8 |
| Fiji | −6.4 | −12.6 | −9.9 | −18.7 | −13.6 | −17.9 | −7.9 | −7.1 | −8.9 | −8.5 | −6.4 |
| India | 1.5 | 0.1 | −1.3 | −1.0 | −0.7 | −2.0 | −2.8 | −3.2 | −3.7 | −3.8 | −1.6 |
| Indonesia | 3.5 | 0.6 | 0.1 | 3.0 | 2.4 | 0.0 | 2.6 | 0.9 | 0.9 | 0.4 | −1.0 |
| Kiribati | −15.0 | −21.8 | −41.7 | −24.2 | −29.4 | −34.7 | −29.8 | −23.1 | −28.9 | −23.7 | −21.3 |
| Lao People's Democratic Republic | −13.1 | −17.8 | −18.1 | −11.2 | −15.9 | −18.5 | −17.6 | −10.2 | −13.6 | −15.4 | −16.3 |
| Malaysia | 12.0 | 12.1 | 15.0 | 16.4 | 15.9 | 17.5 | 16.5 | 11.8 | 11.4 | 10.8 | 8.6 |
| Maldives | −3.4 | −11.6 | −27.6 | −23.4 | −29.3 | −36.9 | −23.5 | −26.9 | −30.4 | −28.0 | −30.9 |
| Myanmar | −1.0 | 2.4 | 3.7 | 7.1 | 0.6 | −2.2 | −1.3 | −2.0 | −3.5 | −4.5 | 5.1 |
| Nepal | 2.4 | 2.7 | 2.0 | 2.1 | −0.1 | 2.7 | 4.2 | −2.7 | −1.0 | −1.0 | −0.3 |
| Pakistan | 4.9 | 1.8 | −1.4 | −3.9 | −4.8 | −8.5 | −5.7 | −2.3 | −1.5 | −2.4 | −4.4 |
| Papua New Guinea | 4.3 | 2.1 | 6.1 | 9.2 | 3.3 | 10.1 | −7.6 | −23.7 | −24.2 | −17.6 | 10.3 |
| Philippines | 0.4 | 1.9 | 2.0 | 4.5 | 4.9 | 2.2 | 5.8 | 4.5 | 2.9 | 2.8 | 0.9 |
| Samoa | −8.3 | −8.4 | −9.6 | −11.1 | −15.9 | −6.2 | −2.0 | −8.0 | −13.1 | −8.9 | −2.4 |
| Solomon Islands | 6.3 | 16.3 | −7.0 | −9.3 | −13.8 | −19.3 | −17.9 | −25.6 | −16.8 | −15.2 | −39.4 |
| Sri Lanka | −0.4 | −3.1 | −2.5 | −5.3 | −4.3 | −9.8 | −0.5 | −3.5 | −4.1 | −4.5 | −5.0 |
| Thailand | 3.4 | 1.7 | −4.3 | 1.1 | 6.3 | 0.8 | 8.3 | 4.6 | 2.7 | 1.9 | 2.0 |
| Timor-Leste | −15.1 | 21.1 | 78.8 | 165.5 | 329.0 | 455.6 | 245.4 | 227.1 | 196.9 | 167.6 | 63.7 |
| Tonga | 0.7 | 0.4 | −5.2 | −8.1 | −8.6 | −11.7 | −11.1 | −9.4 | −11.3 | −11.2 | −6.9 |
| Tuvalu | −34.5 | −4.5 | 21.7 | −1.5 | −1.9 | −10.2 | −5.2 | −24.1 | 6.3 | −3.4 | 5.1 |
| Vanuatu | −5.9 | −4.5 | −8.7 | −6.5 | −7.0 | −11.1 | −8.2 | −5.9 | −5.7 | −6.0 | −6.0 |
| Vietnam | −4.9 | −3.5 | −1.1 | −0.3 | −9.8 | −11.9 | −6.6 | −3.8 | −4.0 | −3.9 | −3.5 |

**Table A12. Emerging and Developing Economies: Balance on Current Account** *(continued)*

| | 2003 | 2004 | 2005 | 2006 | 2007 | 2008 | 2009 | 2010 | Projections 2011 | 2012 | 2016 |
|---|---|---|---|---|---|---|---|---|---|---|---|
| **Latin America and the Caribbean** | **0.5** | **1.0** | **1.4** | **1.6** | **0.4** | **−0.7** | **−0.6** | **−1.2** | **−1.4** | **−1.8** | **−2.4** |
| Antigua and Barbuda | −12.9 | −14.5 | −21.7 | −31.4 | −34.3 | −30.5 | −22.5 | −13.9 | −18.6 | −18.2 | −24.3 |
| Argentina | 6.3 | 1.7 | 2.6 | 3.2 | 2.3 | 1.3 | 1.8 | 0.9 | 0.1 | −0.5 | −0.9 |
| The Bahamas | −5.4 | −2.8 | −9.9 | −19.6 | −17.8 | −15.9 | −11.7 | −12.4 | −15.0 | −14.3 | −12.0 |
| Barbados | −5.6 | −10.6 | −10.7 | −6.9 | −4.5 | −9.6 | −5.5 | −7.4 | −6.7 | −6.0 | −4.7 |
| Belize | −18.2 | −14.7 | −13.6 | −2.1 | −4.1 | −9.8 | −8.4 | −2.7 | −8.1 | −6.7 | −7.3 |
| Bolivia | 1.0 | 3.8 | 6.5 | 11.3 | 12.0 | 12.1 | 4.7 | 4.8 | 3.8 | 4.4 | 2.9 |
| Brazil | 0.8 | 1.8 | 1.6 | 1.2 | 0.1 | −1.7 | −1.5 | −2.3 | −2.6 | −3.0 | −3.6 |
| Chile | −1.1 | 2.2 | 1.2 | 4.9 | 4.5 | −1.9 | 1.6 | 1.9 | 0.5 | −1.3 | −2.5 |
| Colombia | −0.9 | −0.6 | −1.1 | −1.9 | −2.9 | −3.0 | −2.2 | −3.1 | −2.1 | −2.2 | −1.8 |
| Costa Rica | −5.0 | −4.3 | −4.9 | −4.5 | −6.3 | −9.3 | −2.0 | −3.6 | −4.5 | −4.7 | −5.1 |
| Dominica | −20.0 | −20.4 | −26.0 | −15.7 | −25.0 | −31.8 | −28.1 | −28.0 | −29.2 | −27.5 | −22.5 |
| Dominican Republic | 5.1 | 4.8 | −1.4 | −3.6 | −5.3 | −9.9 | −5.0 | −8.6 | −8.3 | −5.4 | −4.0 |
| Ecuador | −1.4 | −1.6 | 1.0 | 3.9 | 3.6 | 2.2 | −0.7 | −4.4 | −4.0 | −4.0 | −4.0 |
| El Salvador | −4.7 | −4.1 | −3.5 | −4.2 | −6.0 | −7.6 | −1.8 | −2.1 | −3.8 | −3.6 | −3.5 |
| Grenada | −25.3 | −9.0 | −31.3 | −33.2 | −43.2 | −38.7 | −33.2 | −27.1 | −25.3 | −27.1 | −26.2 |
| Guatemala | −4.7 | −4.9 | −4.6 | −5.0 | −5.2 | −4.3 | −0.0 | −2.1 | −3.3 | −4.0 | −5.4 |
| Guyana | −5.8 | −6.7 | −10.1 | −13.1 | −11.1 | −13.1 | −9.2 | −9.8 | −11.9 | −22.9 | −10.1 |
| Haiti | −1.6 | −1.6 | 2.6 | −1.4 | −1.5 | −4.4 | −3.4 | −2.3 | −4.0 | −4.6 | −2.9 |
| Honduras | −6.8 | −7.7 | −3.0 | −3.7 | −9.0 | −15.4 | −3.7 | −6.2 | −7.3 | −7.1 | −6.1 |
| Jamaica | −7.6 | −6.4 | −9.5 | −10.0 | −16.5 | −17.8 | −10.9 | −8.1 | −8.3 | −7.7 | −4.3 |
| Mexico | −1.0 | −0.7 | −0.6 | −0.5 | −0.9 | −1.5 | −0.7 | −0.5 | −0.9 | −1.1 | −1.5 |
| Nicaragua | −16.0 | −14.4 | −14.9 | −13.4 | −16.6 | −23.3 | −11.9 | −14.1 | −17.6 | −16.5 | −12.1 |
| Panama | −4.5 | −7.5 | −4.9 | −3.1 | −7.2 | −11.9 | −0.2 | −11.2 | −12.5 | −12.6 | −6.8 |
| Paraguay | 2.3 | 2.1 | 0.2 | 1.4 | 1.5 | −1.8 | 0.6 | −3.2 | −4.1 | −3.7 | −2.8 |
| Peru | −1.5 | 0.0 | 1.4 | 3.1 | 1.4 | −4.2 | 0.2 | −1.5 | −2.1 | −2.8 | −1.4 |
| St. Kitts and Nevis | −34.8 | −20.1 | −18.3 | −20.4 | −24.3 | −33.2 | −34.0 | −27.5 | −30.5 | −28.9 | −24.5 |
| St. Lucia | −14.7 | −10.9 | −17.1 | −30.2 | −31.3 | −27.8 | −14.4 | −16.7 | −29.1 | −20.8 | −16.9 |
| St. Vincent and the Grenadines | −20.5 | −24.4 | −22.3 | −23.7 | −34.6 | −35.2 | −35.0 | −33.6 | −37.5 | −34.3 | −25.2 |
| Suriname | −18.0 | −10.3 | −13.0 | 7.8 | 10.7 | 9.6 | −1.1 | 1.0 | 0.4 | −0.2 | 0.1 |
| Trinidad and Tobago | 8.7 | 12.4 | 22.5 | 39.6 | 24.8 | 31.3 | 9.0 | 17.6 | 18.7 | 19.2 | 17.9 |
| Uruguay | −0.7 | 0.0 | 0.2 | −2.0 | −0.9 | −4.7 | 0.6 | 0.5 | −1.0 | −1.6 | −1.9 |
| Venezuela | 14.1 | 13.8 | 17.7 | 14.8 | 8.8 | 12.0 | 2.6 | 4.9 | 7.0 | 6.3 | 2.0 |
| **Middle East and North Africa** | **6.6** | **9.5** | **16.1** | **17.9** | **14.4** | **14.9** | **2.4** | **6.5** | **12.7** | **11.2** | **9.3** |
| Algeria | 13.0 | 13.0 | 20.5 | 24.7 | 22.8 | 20.2 | 0.3 | 9.4 | 17.8 | 17.4 | 14.6 |
| Bahrain | 2.0 | 4.2 | 11.0 | 13.8 | 15.7 | 10.2 | 2.9 | 4.6 | 13.0 | 13.4 | 10.3 |
| Djibouti | 3.4 | −1.3 | −3.2 | −11.5 | −21.4 | −24.3 | −9.1 | −6.7 | −15.4 | −18.8 | −17.4 |
| Egypt | 2.4 | 4.3 | 3.2 | 1.6 | 2.1 | 0.5 | −2.3 | −2.0 | −2.7 | −2.3 | −1.4 |
| Islamic Republic of Iran | 0.6 | 0.6 | 8.8 | 9.2 | 11.9 | 7.3 | 4.2 | 6.0 | 11.7 | 10.4 | 6.8 |
| Iraq | ... | ... | 6.2 | 19.0 | 12.5 | 12.8 | −26.6 | −6.2 | −3.2 | −0.7 | 15.8 |
| Jordan | 11.5 | 0.1 | −18.0 | −11.0 | −16.9 | −9.0 | −6.3 | −5.4 | −8.5 | −8.7 | −4.6 |
| Kuwait | 19.7 | 26.2 | 37.2 | 44.6 | 36.8 | 40.5 | 26.1 | 31.8 | 39.4 | 39.4 | 41.8 |
| Lebanon | −13.0 | −15.3 | −13.4 | −5.3 | −6.8 | −9.2 | −9.4 | −10.2 | −12.9 | −12.8 | −9.8 |
| Libya[2] | 8.4 | 20.3 | 39.6 | 49.7 | 41.7 | 41.7 | 15.6 | 16.0 | ... | ... | ... |
| Mauritania | −13.6 | −34.6 | −47.2 | −1.3 | −18.3 | −15.8 | −12.3 | −4.9 | −6.9 | −5.0 | −7.3 |
| Morocco | 3.2 | 1.7 | 1.8 | 2.2 | −0.1 | −5.2 | −4.9 | −4.2 | −5.7 | −4.1 | −1.8 |
| Oman | 2.4 | 4.5 | 16.8 | 15.4 | 5.9 | 8.3 | −0.6 | 11.6 | 14.9 | 14.7 | 12.3 |
| Qatar | 25.3 | 22.4 | 30.9 | 25.3 | 25.0 | 29.2 | 10.2 | 18.7 | 36.1 | 34.0 | 26.2 |
| Saudi Arabia | 13.1 | 20.8 | 28.5 | 27.8 | 24.3 | 27.8 | 6.1 | 8.7 | 19.8 | 13.8 | 6.2 |
| Sudan | −7.9 | −6.5 | −11.1 | −15.2 | −12.5 | −9.0 | −12.4 | −8.5 | −5.5 | −6.6 | −6.5 |
| Syrian Arab Republic | −12.5 | −1.6 | −2.3 | −2.3 | −3.6 | −2.8 | −5.7 | −4.4 | −4.6 | −4.8 | −5.0 |
| Tunisia | −2.7 | −2.4 | −0.9 | −1.8 | −2.4 | −3.8 | −2.8 | −4.8 | −7.8 | −5.8 | −1.6 |
| United Arab Emirates | 5.2 | 5.6 | 11.6 | 15.4 | 6.0 | 7.4 | 3.0 | 7.7 | 10.4 | 10.5 | 11.2 |
| Republic of Yemen | 1.5 | 1.6 | 3.8 | 1.1 | −7.0 | −4.6 | −10.2 | −4.4 | −4.0 | −4.0 | −4.4 |

## Table A12. Emerging and Developing Economies: Balance on Current Account  (concluded)

| | 2003 | 2004 | 2005 | 2006 | 2007 | 2008 | 2009 | 2010 | Projections 2011 | Projections 2012 | Projections 2016 |
|---|---|---|---|---|---|---|---|---|---|---|---|
| **Sub-Saharan Africa** | **−2.8** | **−1.4** | **−0.5** | **4.3** | **1.3** | **0.0** | **−2.4** | **−2.4** | **0.4** | **0.4** | **−0.6** |
| Angola | −5.6 | 3.8 | 18.2 | 27.5 | 15.7 | 8.6 | −10.0 | −1.8 | 6.2 | 9.5 | 4.4 |
| Benin | −9.4 | −7.0 | −6.3 | −5.3 | −10.1 | −8.0 | −8.9 | −6.3 | −5.3 | −6.8 | −5.2 |
| Botswana | 5.7 | 3.5 | 15.2 | 17.2 | 15.0 | 7.5 | −5.5 | −2.5 | −2.4 | 0.0 | 4.0 |
| Burkina Faso | −9.0 | −11.0 | −11.6 | −9.1 | −8.2 | −11.5 | −4.9 | −4.2 | −4.1 | −7.6 | −5.6 |
| Burundi | −4.6 | −8.4 | −1.2 | −14.5 | −24.6 | −15.0 | −16.1 | −12.0 | −15.8 | −14.9 | −17.2 |
| Cameroon | −1.8 | −3.4 | −3.4 | 1.6 | 1.4 | −0.8 | −3.7 | −3.9 | −3.1 | −3.0 | −2.9 |
| Cape Verde | −11.1 | −14.3 | −3.5 | −5.4 | −14.7 | −15.7 | −15.3 | −11.8 | −18.0 | −15.7 | −7.9 |
| Central African Republic | −2.2 | −1.8 | −6.5 | −3.0 | −6.2 | −10.4 | −7.9 | −8.7 | −9.1 | −8.5 | −6.6 |
| Chad | −49.0 | −17.1 | 2.4 | −9.0 | 1.1 | −0.1 | −22.1 | −21.3 | −8.0 | −6.1 | −4.3 |
| Comoros | −3.2 | −4.6 | −7.4 | −6.7 | −6.3 | −11.1 | −9.0 | −6.8 | −12.1 | −10.1 | −6.8 |
| Democratic Republic of Congo | 0.9 | −3.0 | −13.3 | −2.7 | −1.1 | −17.5 | −10.5 | −6.8 | −2.8 | −0.7 | 1.1 |
| Republic of Congo | 2.5 | −7.6 | 2.0 | 2.0 | −8.0 | 1.2 | −8.9 | 2.7 | 12.5 | 16.0 | 6.1 |
| Côte d'Ivoire[3] | 2.1 | 1.6 | 0.2 | 2.8 | −0.7 | 1.9 | 7.4 | 3.9 | . . . | . . . | . . . |
| Equatorial Guinea | −33.3 | −21.6 | −6.2 | 7.1 | 4.3 | 9.1 | −17.1 | −23.8 | −10.2 | −9.0 | −5.6 |
| Eritrea | 9.7 | −0.7 | 0.3 | −3.6 | −6.1 | −5.5 | −7.6 | −5.8 | −0.9 | 0.2 | −1.3 |
| Ethiopia | −1.3 | −1.4 | −6.3 | −9.1 | −4.5 | −5.6 | −5.0 | −4.3 | −8.1 | −8.1 | −4.2 |
| Gabon | 9.5 | 11.2 | 22.9 | 15.6 | 17.3 | 23.7 | 7.9 | 11.8 | 17.0 | 15.3 | 5.9 |
| The Gambia | −7.3 | −7.0 | −13.4 | −10.2 | −9.6 | −12.7 | −9.9 | −12.0 | −12.0 | −12.8 | −13.8 |
| Ghana | −1.1 | −2.5 | −5.1 | −6.2 | −8.0 | −10.8 | −4.0 | −7.2 | −6.8 | −5.2 | −2.3 |
| Guinea | −0.8 | −2.8 | −0.4 | 7.0 | −10.3 | −7.5 | −10.8 | −12.7 | −11.4 | −12.1 | −14.4 |
| Guinea-Bissau | −0.5 | 1.4 | −2.1 | −5.6 | −4.4 | −4.9 | −6.0 | −6.2 | −5.7 | −4.3 | −1.5 |
| Kenya | −0.2 | 0.1 | −1.5 | −2.3 | −4.0 | −6.7 | −5.6 | −7.9 | −9.3 | −7.9 | −4.0 |
| Lesotho | −13.9 | −5.5 | −7.6 | 4.7 | 13.9 | 7.9 | −0.5 | −16.2 | −23.4 | −17.8 | −11.8 |
| Liberia | −24.4 | −20.2 | −37.4 | −13.9 | −31.4 | −57.3 | −38.3 | −44.1 | −37.6 | −65.5 | −7.0 |
| Madagascar | −6.0 | −9.2 | −10.6 | −8.8 | −12.7 | −20.6 | −20.7 | −13.4 | −7.1 | −6.4 | 0.3 |
| Malawi | −11.7 | −11.2 | −14.7 | −12.5 | 1.0 | −10.2 | −5.8 | −1.3 | −3.8 | −3.7 | −2.0 |
| Mali | −7.0 | −7.9 | −8.5 | −4.1 | −6.9 | −12.7 | −7.5 | −8.5 | −6.8 | −8.0 | −7.8 |
| Mauritius | 1.6 | −1.8 | −5.0 | −9.1 | −5.4 | −10.1 | −7.4 | −9.5 | −11.6 | −9.6 | −3.5 |
| Mozambique | −17.5 | −10.7 | −11.6 | −10.7 | −9.7 | −11.9 | −10.5 | −12.7 | −12.0 | −12.1 | −12.2 |
| Namibia | 6.1 | 7.0 | 4.7 | 13.9 | 9.1 | 2.7 | −0.7 | −1.1 | −0.9 | −3.3 | 0.7 |
| Niger | −7.5 | −7.3 | −8.9 | −8.6 | −8.2 | −13.0 | −28.7 | −30.7 | −22.7 | −14.1 | −4.0 |
| Nigeria | −5.9 | 5.7 | 6.5 | 26.5 | 18.7 | 15.4 | 13.0 | 6.4 | 14.6 | 13.3 | 9.0 |
| Rwanda | −2.5 | 1.8 | 1.0 | −4.3 | −2.2 | −4.9 | −8.5 | −6.8 | −9.2 | −6.2 | −3.3 |
| São Tomé and Príncipe | −14.1 | −16.2 | −9.5 | −27.5 | −37.6 | −37.8 | −28.0 | −32.0 | −44.7 | −42.5 | −24.9 |
| Senegal | −6.4 | −6.9 | −9.0 | −9.5 | −11.8 | −14.3 | −7.7 | −8.3 | −11.5 | −10.8 | −8.2 |
| Seychelles | 0.2 | −5.8 | −18.8 | −13.2 | −20.5 | −48.9 | −40.0 | −50.7 | −32.7 | −18.6 | −2.1 |
| Sierra Leone | −4.8 | −5.8 | −7.1 | −5.6 | −5.5 | −11.5 | −8.4 | −9.7 | −11.9 | −11.4 | −9.2 |
| South Africa | −1.0 | −3.0 | −3.5 | −5.3 | −7.0 | −7.1 | −4.1 | −2.8 | −4.4 | −5.1 | −6.0 |
| Swaziland | 1.4 | −0.3 | −7.6 | −10.3 | −5.2 | −11.1 | −16.8 | −20.6 | −16.0 | −12.9 | −7.5 |
| Tanzania | −0.2 | −2.5 | −3.8 | −7.6 | −10.0 | −11.1 | −10.2 | −8.6 | −9.5 | −10.7 | −7.2 |
| Togo | −10.8 | −10.0 | −9.9 | −8.4 | −8.7 | −9.6 | −6.9 | −7.9 | −8.4 | −7.4 | −6.1 |
| Uganda | −4.7 | 0.1 | −1.4 | −3.4 | −3.1 | −3.1 | −6.8 | −9.9 | −10.6 | −9.2 | −4.1 |
| Zambia | −14.3 | −10.4 | −8.5 | −0.4 | −6.5 | −7.2 | 4.2 | 3.8 | 5.9 | 3.3 | 0.0 |
| Zimbabwe[4] | . . . | . . . | −10.9 | −8.6 | −7.2 | −23.2 | −24.4 | −18.3 | −17.5 | −17.5 | −12.9 |

[1]Georgia and Mongolia, which are not members of the Commonwealth of Independent States, are included in this group for reasons of geography and similarities in economic structure.

[2]Libya's projections are excluded due to the uncertain political situation.

[3]Côte d'Ivoire's projections are not shown due to the uncertain political situation.

[4]The Zimbabwe dollar ceased circulating in early 2009. Data are based on staff estimates of price and exchange rate developments in U.S. dollars. IMF staff estimates of U.S. dollar values may differ from the authorities' estimates.

## Table A13. Emerging and Developing Economies: Net Financial Flows[1]

*(Billions of U.S. dollars)*

| | Average 2000–02 | 2003 | 2004 | 2005 | 2006 | 2007 | 2008 | 2009 | 2010 | Projections 2011 | Projections 2012 |
|---|---|---|---|---|---|---|---|---|---|---|---|
| **Emerging and Developing Economies** | | | | | | | | | | | |
| Private Financial Flows, Net | 76.6 | 172.9 | 226.4 | 291.2 | 252.1 | 694.7 | 230.3 | 236.6 | 470.1 | 388.1 | 411.5 |
| Private Direct Investment, Net | 155.5 | 146.0 | 187.7 | 252.7 | 258.1 | 418.3 | 439.6 | 247.7 | 371.1 | 357.7 | 378.7 |
| Private Portfolio Flows, Net | −33.9 | 0.0 | 16.2 | 35.1 | −40.5 | 89.2 | −57.9 | 120.2 | 162.2 | 69.0 | 93.2 |
| Other Private Financial Flows, Net | −45.0 | 26.9 | 22.5 | 3.4 | 34.5 | 187.2 | −151.4 | −131.4 | −63.2 | −38.5 | −60.4 |
| Official Financial Flows, Net[2] | −17.0 | −47.6 | −51.3 | −104.0 | −167.5 | −100.9 | −102.2 | 125.4 | 87.5 | −41.0 | −91.0 |
| Change in Reserves[3] | −109.4 | −321.5 | −410.9 | −587.9 | −749.8 | −1,214.6 | −735.9 | −503.8 | −885.4 | −969.8 | −938.1 |
| *Memorandum* | | | | | | | | | | | |
| Current Account[4] | 75.0 | 145.2 | 219.7 | 443.0 | 661.5 | 649.7 | 704.2 | 326.6 | 378.1 | 646.5 | 635.9 |
| **Central and Eastern Europe** | | | | | | | | | | | |
| Private Financial Flows, Net | 21.0 | 38.5 | 50.0 | 101.9 | 117.3 | 183.4 | 153.4 | 29.0 | 75.4 | 119.5 | 139.7 |
| Private Direct Investment, Net | 14.8 | 14.6 | 30.6 | 37.8 | 64.1 | 74.8 | 66.4 | 31.2 | 22.3 | 39.4 | 43.4 |
| Private Portfolio Flows, Net | 1.4 | 5.1 | 15.4 | 20.8 | 0.6 | −3.3 | −9.8 | 10.0 | 28.9 | 34.5 | 27.8 |
| Other Private Financial Flows, Net | 4.8 | 18.8 | 4.0 | 43.3 | 52.6 | 112.0 | 96.8 | −12.2 | 24.2 | 45.7 | 68.4 |
| Official Flows, Net[2] | 4.9 | 5.0 | 9.7 | 3.5 | 4.8 | −6.7 | 21.9 | 52.2 | 38.5 | 23.0 | 8.4 |
| Change in Reserves[3] | −4.6 | −10.9 | −12.8 | −43.6 | −32.4 | −36.8 | −4.1 | −29.0 | −35.1 | −40.0 | −30.8 |
| **Commonwealth of Independent States[5]** | | | | | | | | | | | |
| Private Financial Flows, Net | −4.6 | 20.9 | 5.6 | 29.1 | 51.6 | 129.2 | −96.2 | −62.0 | −23.7 | 6.2 | 10.7 |
| Private Direct Investment, Net | 4.1 | 5.4 | 13.2 | 11.7 | 21.3 | 28.3 | 52.2 | 16.6 | 19.0 | 29.0 | 32.8 |
| Private Portfolio Flows, Net | 1.3 | 2.0 | 4.7 | 3.9 | 4.9 | 19.5 | −31.4 | −9.5 | 5.5 | 6.8 | 5.1 |
| Other Private Financial Flows, Net | −10.0 | 13.4 | −12.3 | 13.5 | 25.4 | 81.4 | −117.0 | −69.1 | −48.2 | −29.6 | −27.2 |
| Official Flows, Net[2] | −4.3 | −11.2 | −10.1 | −18.3 | −25.4 | −6.0 | −19.0 | 42.5 | 1.2 | 3.6 | 0.0 |
| Change in Reserves[3] | −16.7 | −32.7 | −54.9 | −77.1 | −127.8 | −168.0 | 27.0 | −7.9 | −54.5 | −114.8 | −90.4 |
| **Developing Asia** | | | | | | | | | | | |
| Private Financial Flows, Net | 25.4 | 81.7 | 144.0 | 90.0 | 50.2 | 190.0 | 49.4 | 162.6 | 280.7 | 169.7 | 125.2 |
| Private Direct Investment, Net | 50.8 | 58.5 | 68.3 | 93.9 | 85.7 | 153.7 | 134.5 | 66.8 | 175.3 | 110.1 | 108.1 |
| Private Portfolio Flows, Net | −13.6 | 22.1 | 39.2 | 16.7 | −44.5 | 68.7 | 21.2 | 58.2 | 82.6 | 66.3 | 68.6 |
| Other Private Financial Flows, Net | −11.9 | 1.1 | 36.5 | −20.5 | 8.9 | −32.4 | −106.3 | 37.7 | 22.9 | −6.7 | −51.6 |
| Official Flows, Net[2] | −5.4 | −18.3 | −0.6 | −2.9 | 1.3 | 0.4 | −5.4 | 17.2 | 16.6 | 13.2 | 11.8 |
| Change in Reserves[3] | −63.0 | −188.6 | −243.0 | −277.8 | −355.3 | −616.3 | −505.0 | −453.0 | −581.7 | −541.4 | −567.4 |
| **Latin America and the Caribbean** | | | | | | | | | | | |
| Private Financial Flows, Net | 38.8 | 17.0 | 16.7 | 46.8 | 39.5 | 110.0 | 66.3 | 33.1 | 104.3 | 131.1 | 137.8 |
| Private Direct Investment, Net | 64.4 | 37.3 | 50.8 | 56.7 | 33.0 | 91.5 | 97.4 | 68.8 | 75.3 | 112.3 | 123.4 |
| Private Portfolio Flows, Net | −9.9 | −12.5 | −23.1 | 3.1 | 16.5 | 39.5 | −12.8 | 34.7 | 71.5 | 39.0 | 42.8 |
| Other Private Financial Flows, Net | −15.7 | −7.8 | −11.0 | −13.1 | −10.0 | −21.0 | −18.3 | −70.3 | −42.5 | −20.1 | −28.4 |
| Official Flows, Net[2] | 11.1 | 5.1 | −10.7 | −39.6 | −55.1 | −6.6 | 1.8 | 44.1 | 48.5 | 37.1 | 38.2 |
| Change in Reserves[3] | −1.1 | −32.5 | −23.3 | −36.1 | −52.5 | −133.9 | −50.7 | −49.3 | −103.7 | −85.8 | −64.8 |
| **Middle East and North Africa** | | | | | | | | | | | |
| Private Financial Flows, Net | −7.5 | 11.0 | −3.6 | 2.5 | −19.7 | 54.0 | 33.0 | 49.5 | 11.6 | −75.3 | −40.2 |
| Private Direct Investment, Net | 9.9 | 17.7 | 13.1 | 35.3 | 44.9 | 47.1 | 57.2 | 36.4 | 52.7 | 34.8 | 39.6 |
| Private Portfolio Flows, Net | −10.2 | −15.6 | −23.6 | −12.8 | −29.9 | −43.2 | −3.4 | 22.9 | −28.4 | −82.2 | −63.4 |
| Other Private Financial Flows, Net | −7.1 | 8.9 | 6.9 | −20.0 | −34.8 | 50.2 | −20.8 | −9.8 | −12.8 | −27.9 | −16.4 |
| Official Flows, Net[2] | −21.9 | −27.0 | −36.4 | −38.9 | −58.5 | −75.7 | −101.7 | −41.3 | −37.5 | −124.9 | −157.5 |
| Change in Reserves[3] | −21.3 | −57.0 | −58.1 | −129.7 | −151.5 | −230.8 | −185.2 | 26.0 | −106.3 | −158.6 | −152.8 |
| **Sub-Saharan Africa** | | | | | | | | | | | |
| Private Financial Flows, Net | 3.4 | 3.7 | 13.7 | 20.9 | 13.3 | 28.1 | 24.5 | 24.4 | 21.7 | 36.9 | 38.2 |
| Private Direct Investment, Net | 11.5 | 12.5 | 11.6 | 17.3 | 8.9 | 23.0 | 31.9 | 28.0 | 26.4 | 32.2 | 31.4 |
| Private Portfolio Flows, Net | −2.9 | −1.2 | 3.6 | 3.3 | 11.9 | 8.0 | −21.6 | 4.0 | 2.0 | 4.5 | 12.2 |
| Other Private Financial Flows, Net | −5.1 | −7.5 | −1.6 | 0.2 | −7.5 | −3.0 | 14.2 | −7.6 | −6.7 | 0.2 | −5.3 |
| Official Flows, Net[2] | −1.4 | −1.3 | −3.2 | −7.8 | −34.5 | −6.2 | 0.3 | 10.7 | 20.2 | 6.9 | 8.0 |
| Change in Reserves[3] | −2.7 | 0.2 | −18.7 | −23.6 | −30.3 | −28.8 | −17.9 | 9.4 | −4.1 | −29.2 | −32.0 |
| *Memorandum* | | | | | | | | | | | |
| **Fuel Exporting Countries** | | | | | | | | | | | |
| Private Financial Flows, Net | −20.6 | 19.3 | −6.0 | 6.3 | −2.2 | 117.2 | −132.1 | −58.4 | −62.0 | −115.3 | −100.9 |
| **Other Countries** | | | | | | | | | | | |
| Private Financial Flows, Net | 97.2 | 153.6 | 232.3 | 284.9 | 254.4 | 577.5 | 362.4 | 295.0 | 532.1 | 503.4 | 512.3 |

[1]Net financial flows comprise net direct investment, net portfolio investment, other net official and private financial flows, and changes in reserves.
[2]Excludes grants and includes transactions in external assets and liabilities of official agencies.
[3]A minus sign indicates an increase.
[4]The sum of the current account balance, net private financial flows, net official flows, and the change in reserves equals, with the opposite sign, the sum of the capital account and errors and omissions.
[5]Georgia and Mongolia, which are not members of the Commonwealth of Independent States, are included in this group for reasons of geography and similarities in economic structure.

## Table A14. Emerging and Developing Economies: Private Financial Flows[1]

*(Billions of U.S. dollars)*

| | Average 2000–02 | 2003 | 2004 | 2005 | 2006 | 2007 | 2008 | 2009 | 2010 | Projections 2011 | Projections 2012 |
|---|---|---|---|---|---|---|---|---|---|---|---|
| **Emerging and Developing Economies** | | | | | | | | | | | |
| Private Financial Flows, Net | 76.6 | 172.9 | 226.4 | 291.2 | 252.1 | 694.7 | 230.3 | 236.6 | 470.1 | 388.1 | 411.5 |
| Assets | −111.7 | −124.3 | −263.4 | −373.9 | −743.6 | −949.2 | −576.7 | −247.0 | −433.2 | −425.0 | −498.4 |
| Liabilities | 187.9 | 295.6 | 489.3 | 664.2 | 994.1 | 1,642.6 | 803.7 | 484.3 | 902.7 | 812.6 | 908.1 |
| **Central and Eastern Europe** | | | | | | | | | | | |
| Private Financial Flows, Net | 21.0 | 38.5 | 50.0 | 101.9 | 117.3 | 183.4 | 153.4 | 29.0 | 75.4 | 119.5 | 139.7 |
| Assets | −6.7 | −10.2 | −30.0 | −17.8 | −56.3 | −44.3 | −28.8 | −10.7 | −7.5 | 7.6 | −2.0 |
| Liabilities | 27.8 | 48.6 | 80.0 | 119.6 | 173.4 | 226.9 | 181.3 | 39.8 | 82.7 | 111.8 | 141.7 |
| **Commonwealth of Independent States[2]** | | | | | | | | | | | |
| Private Financial Flows, Net | −4.6 | 20.9 | 5.6 | 29.1 | 51.6 | 129.2 | −96.2 | −62.0 | −23.7 | 6.2 | 10.7 |
| Assets | −19.5 | −24.4 | −53.1 | −80.5 | −100.4 | −160.7 | −265.0 | −73.3 | −91.5 | −78.8 | −85.5 |
| Liabilities | 14.9 | 45.3 | 58.6 | 109.6 | 151.9 | 289.9 | 168.8 | 11.3 | 67.8 | 84.9 | 96.2 |
| **Developing Asia** | | | | | | | | | | | |
| Private Financial Flows, Net | 25.4 | 81.7 | 144.0 | 90.0 | 50.2 | 190.0 | 49.4 | 162.6 | 280.7 | 169.7 | 125.2 |
| Assets | −34.8 | −23.5 | −53.2 | −114.5 | −226.3 | −245.9 | −167.0 | −82.7 | −112.9 | −132.7 | −195.1 |
| Liabilities | 59.8 | 104.8 | 197.0 | 204.5 | 275.5 | 435.7 | 215.5 | 245.6 | 394.1 | 303.6 | 320.5 |
| **Latin America and the Caribbean** | | | | | | | | | | | |
| Private Financial Flows, Net | 38.8 | 17.0 | 16.7 | 46.8 | 39.5 | 110.0 | 66.3 | 33.1 | 104.3 | 131.1 | 137.8 |
| Assets | −30.8 | −33.6 | −45.5 | −49.8 | −90.6 | −114.1 | −76.0 | −92.7 | −161.7 | −90.6 | −92.3 |
| Liabilities | 69.3 | 49.4 | 61.8 | 95.9 | 129.9 | 223.9 | 141.0 | 126.4 | 265.5 | 221.1 | 229.1 |
| **Middle East and North Africa** | | | | | | | | | | | |
| Private Financial Flows, Net | −7.5 | 11.0 | −3.6 | 2.5 | −19.7 | 54.0 | 33.0 | 49.5 | 11.6 | −75.3 | −40.2 |
| Assets | −12.7 | −22.5 | −71.3 | −93.6 | −237.3 | −356.0 | −20.9 | 24.7 | −39.2 | −115.6 | −96.5 |
| Liabilities | 5.2 | 33.5 | 67.7 | 96.1 | 217.6 | 410.0 | 53.9 | 24.7 | 50.8 | 40.3 | 56.4 |
| **Sub-Saharan Africa** | | | | | | | | | | | |
| Private Financial Flows, Net | 3.4 | 3.7 | 13.7 | 20.9 | 13.3 | 28.1 | 24.5 | 24.4 | 21.7 | 36.9 | 38.2 |
| Assets | −7.3 | −10.1 | −10.4 | −17.7 | −32.7 | −28.2 | −18.9 | −12.3 | −20.4 | −14.9 | −26.9 |
| Liabilities | 10.9 | 13.8 | 24.2 | 38.5 | 45.7 | 56.2 | 43.2 | 36.5 | 41.7 | 50.9 | 64.1 |

[1]Private financial flows comprise direct investment, portfolio investment, and other long- and short-term investment flows.
[2]Georgia and Mongolia, which are not members of the Commonwealth of Independent States, are included in this group for reasons of geography and similarities in economic structure.

## Table A15. Emerging and Developing Economies: Reserves[1]

| | 2003 | 2004 | 2005 | 2006 | 2007 | 2008 | 2009 | 2010 | Projections 2011 | Projections 2012 |
|---|---|---|---|---|---|---|---|---|---|---|
| | | | | | *Billions of U.S. Dollars* | | | | | |
| **Emerging and Developing Economies** | **1,341.4** | **1,792.0** | **2,304.4** | **3,073.3** | **4,368.6** | **4,950.4** | **5,596.9** | **6,481.2** | **7,450.8** | **8,388.4** |
| **Regional Groups** | | | | | | | | | | |
| Central and Eastern Europe | 114.5 | 134.0 | 164.3 | 208.9 | 264.8 | 261.5 | 300.4 | 335.5 | 375.6 | 406.4 |
| Commonwealth of Independent States[2] | 91.8 | 148.2 | 213.8 | 355.2 | 547.8 | 502.1 | 512.2 | 566.8 | 681.5 | 771.9 |
| Russia | 73.8 | 121.5 | 176.5 | 296.2 | 467.6 | 412.7 | 417.8 | 456.2 | 544.2 | 614.2 |
| Excluding Russia | 18.0 | 26.7 | 37.3 | 59.0 | 80.3 | 89.4 | 94.5 | 110.5 | 137.3 | 157.7 |
| Developing Asia | 670.3 | 934.6 | 1,156.1 | 1,489.4 | 2,128.7 | 2,533.9 | 3,077.7 | 3,658.4 | 4,199.5 | 4,766.4 |
| China | 409.2 | 615.5 | 822.5 | 1,069.5 | 1,531.3 | 1,950.3 | 2,417.9 | 2,889.6 | 3,353.4 | 3,841.6 |
| India | 99.5 | 127.2 | 132.5 | 171.3 | 267.6 | 248.0 | 266.2 | 292.3 | 301.2 | 305.8 |
| Excluding China and India | 161.6 | 191.8 | 201.1 | 248.5 | 329.8 | 335.6 | 393.7 | 476.5 | 544.9 | 619.0 |
| Latin America and the Caribbean | 195.4 | 220.6 | 255.3 | 310.3 | 445.1 | 497.3 | 547.8 | 651.4 | 737.3 | 802.0 |
| Brazil | 48.9 | 52.5 | 53.3 | 85.2 | 179.5 | 192.9 | 237.4 | 287.5 | 340.1 | 387.9 |
| Mexico | 59.0 | 64.1 | 74.1 | 76.3 | 87.1 | 95.1 | 99.6 | 120.3 | 130.3 | 140.3 |
| Middle East and North Africa | 230.3 | 293.8 | 434.1 | 595.5 | 836.9 | 999.5 | 1,001.2 | 1,107.5 | 1,266.1 | 1,418.9 |
| Sub-Saharan Africa | 39.1 | 60.7 | 80.9 | 114.0 | 145.2 | 156.2 | 157.5 | 161.6 | 190.8 | 222.8 |
| Excluding Nigeria and South Africa | 25.3 | 30.4 | 33.8 | 48.4 | 64.0 | 72.4 | 77.3 | 85.7 | 99.2 | 117.3 |
| **Analytical Groups** | | | | | | | | | | |
| **By Source of Export Earnings** | | | | | | | | | | |
| Fuel | 291.7 | 419.1 | 612.9 | 927.2 | 1,343.1 | 1,473.5 | 1,442.6 | 1,592.5 | 1,890.9 | 2,145.5 |
| Nonfuel | 1,049.6 | 1,372.9 | 1,691.5 | 2,146.1 | 3,025.5 | 3,477.0 | 4,154.3 | 4,888.8 | 5,559.9 | 6,242.9 |
| Of Which, Primary Products | 31.8 | 35.4 | 38.7 | 46.8 | 58.4 | 71.3 | 82.3 | 99.8 | 124.9 | 135.3 |
| **By External Financing Source** | | | | | | | | | | |
| Net Debtor Economies | 564.5 | 664.8 | 773.6 | 971.5 | 1,350.7 | 1,399.1 | 1,585.5 | 1,820.1 | 2,003.7 | 2,168.9 |
| Of Which, Official Financing | 11.7 | 14.3 | 31.9 | 34.8 | 41.5 | 44.3 | 54.8 | 58.8 | 65.7 | 72.1 |
| **Net Debtor Economies by Debt- Servicing Experience** | | | | | | | | | | |
| Economies with Arrears and/or Rescheduling during 2005–09 | 35.9 | 46.4 | 60.1 | 73.2 | 101.5 | 105.2 | 119.6 | 129.7 | 141.9 | 154.8 |
| **Other Groups** | | | | | | | | | | |
| Heavily Indebted Poor Countries | 18.6 | 23.3 | 24.3 | 31.4 | 41.5 | 45.1 | 54.5 | 61.1 | 70.1 | 81.3 |

## Table A15. Emerging and Developing Economies: Reserves[1] *(concluded)*

| | 2003 | 2004 | 2005 | 2006 | 2007 | 2008 | 2009 | 2010 | Projections 2011 | Projections 2012 |
|---|---|---|---|---|---|---|---|---|---|---|
| *Ratio of Reserves to Imports of Goods and Services[3]* | | | | | | | | | | |
| **Emerging and Developing Economies** | **59.6** | **62.6** | **67.2** | **75.5** | **87.0** | **80.0** | **109.3** | **102.0** | **100.2** | **101.9** |
| **Regional Groups** | | | | | | | | | | |
| Central and Eastern Europe | 38.4 | 34.3 | 36.1 | 37.8 | 37.6 | 30.7 | 49.8 | 48.0 | 45.8 | 45.5 |
| Commonwealth of Independent States[2] | 52.2 | 65.1 | 76.6 | 100.9 | 115.4 | 81.1 | 118.1 | 103.7 | 99.5 | 101.2 |
| Russia | 71.5 | 93.0 | 107.4 | 141.7 | 165.5 | 112.3 | 164.8 | 136.5 | 129.4 | 130.9 |
| Excluding Russia | 24.7 | 27.5 | 32.5 | 41.3 | 41.8 | 35.5 | 52.4 | 52.1 | 51.9 | 53.8 |
| Developing Asia | 74.4 | 79.4 | 81.7 | 89.5 | 107.1 | 106.2 | 144.7 | 131.0 | 129.4 | 129.4 |
| China | 91.1 | 101.5 | 115.5 | 125.4 | 148.0 | 158.2 | 217.2 | 189.3 | 189.8 | 187.4 |
| India | 107.1 | 97.0 | 72.8 | 75.5 | 95.1 | 71.3 | 73.8 | 68.4 | 60.6 | 54.4 |
| Excluding China and India | 44.9 | 43.6 | 38.6 | 42.5 | 49.0 | 41.7 | 60.2 | 56.8 | 55.5 | 57.8 |
| Latin America and the Caribbean | 47.2 | 44.4 | 43.4 | 44.8 | 53.9 | 49.7 | 70.4 | 65.3 | 61.8 | 62.5 |
| Brazil | 76.8 | 65.6 | 54.4 | 70.7 | 113.8 | 87.6 | 135.9 | 117.6 | 113.0 | 121.5 |
| Mexico | 31.4 | 29.8 | 30.5 | 27.4 | 28.5 | 28.5 | 38.7 | 36.8 | 33.0 | 32.7 |
| Middle East and North Africa | 72.9 | 74.7 | 89.9 | 103.7 | 113.6 | 104.5 | 117.2 | 118.5 | 119.9 | 123.4 |
| Sub-Saharan Africa | 27.4 | 34.8 | 38.4 | 48.1 | 49.3 | 42.0 | 48.8 | 42.3 | 43.6 | 48.0 |
| Excluding Nigeria and South Africa | 34.9 | 34.0 | 31.4 | 40.0 | 41.7 | 35.3 | 39.8 | 39.3 | 39.3 | 43.6 |
| **Analytical Groups** | | | | | | | | | | |
| **By Source of Export Earnings** | | | | | | | | | | |
| Fuel | 66.7 | 76.8 | 89.6 | 112.7 | 123.7 | 104.9 | 123.1 | 118.2 | 120.1 | 124.7 |
| Nonfuel | 58.0 | 59.3 | 61.6 | 66.0 | 76.8 | 72.7 | 105.2 | 97.7 | 94.8 | 95.8 |
| Of Which, Primary Products | 56.7 | 51.7 | 45.6 | 47.9 | 47.0 | 43.6 | 63.6 | 59.6 | 60.6 | 61.0 |
| **By External Financing Source** | | | | | | | | | | |
| Net Debtor Economies | 45.8 | 42.9 | 41.7 | 44.0 | 50.1 | 42.4 | 60.1 | 56.8 | 53.0 | 52.7 |
| Of Which, Official Financing | 21.8 | 22.1 | 40.8 | 38.4 | 37.3 | 31.9 | 42.9 | 37.4 | 34.7 | 35.4 |
| **Net Debtor Economies by Debt-Servicing Experience** | | | | | | | | | | |
| Economies with Arrears and/or Rescheduling during 2005–09 | 31.1 | 31.3 | 33.4 | 34.4 | 38.5 | 31.5 | 43.8 | 39.0 | 35.5 | 35.6 |
| **Other Groups** | | | | | | | | | | |
| Heavily Indebted Poor Countries | 32.0 | 32.1 | 27.3 | 30.2 | 32.7 | 28.1 | 38.0 | 37.1 | 36.9 | 40.3 |

[1]In this table, official holdings of gold are valued at SDR 35 an ounce. This convention results in a marked underestimation of reserves for countries that have substantial gold holdings.
[2]Georgia and Mongolia, which are not members of the Commonwealth of Independent States, are included in this group for reasons of geography and similarities in economic structure.
[3]Reserves at year-end in percent of imports of goods and services for the year indicated.

## Table A16. Summary of Sources and Uses of World Savings
(Percent of GDP)

| | Averages | | 2005 | 2006 | 2007 | 2008 | 2009 | 2010 | Projections | | |
| --- | --- | --- | --- | --- | --- | --- | --- | --- | --- | --- | --- |
| | 1989–96 | 1997–2004 | | | | | | | 2011 | 2012 | 2013–16 |
| **World** | | | | | | | | | | | |
| Savings | 22.1 | 21.8 | 22.7 | 24.0 | 24.1 | 23.9 | 21.6 | 23.0 | 24.0 | 24.7 | 25.7 |
| Investment | 23.1 | 22.0 | 22.5 | 23.2 | 23.7 | 23.7 | 21.7 | 22.9 | 23.4 | 24.1 | 25.2 |
| **Advanced Economies** | | | | | | | | | | | |
| Savings | 21.9 | 20.8 | 20.1 | 20.8 | 20.6 | 19.4 | 16.9 | 17.8 | 18.4 | 19.2 | 19.9 |
| Investment | 22.5 | 21.2 | 21.2 | 21.6 | 21.6 | 20.9 | 17.8 | 18.6 | 19.0 | 19.6 | 20.5 |
| Net Lending | –0.6 | –0.4 | –1.1 | –0.8 | –1.0 | –1.5 | –0.9 | –0.8 | –0.6 | –0.4 | –0.6 |
| Current Transfers | –0.4 | –0.6 | –0.7 | –0.7 | –0.8 | –0.8 | –0.8 | –0.8 | –0.8 | –0.8 | –0.7 |
| Factor Income | –0.5 | 0.3 | 0.7 | 1.0 | 0.4 | 0.2 | –0.1 | 0.2 | 0.4 | 0.6 | 0.6 |
| Resource Balance | 0.4 | –0.1 | –0.9 | –1.0 | –0.5 | –0.7 | 0.1 | 0.0 | –0.1 | –0.1 | –0.3 |
| **United States** | | | | | | | | | | | |
| Savings | 15.8 | 16.6 | 15.1 | 16.2 | 14.3 | 12.4 | 10.9 | 11.6 | 12.4 | 14.3 | 15.4 |
| Investment | 18.3 | 19.7 | 20.3 | 20.5 | 19.6 | 18.0 | 14.8 | 15.9 | 16.2 | 17.2 | 18.5 |
| Net Lending | –2.4 | –3.1 | –5.2 | –4.3 | –5.2 | –5.6 | –4.0 | –4.3 | –3.8 | –2.9 | –3.1 |
| Current Transfers | –0.4 | –0.6 | –0.8 | –0.7 | –0.8 | –0.8 | –0.9 | –0.9 | –0.9 | –0.8 | –0.7 |
| Factor Income | –0.8 | 0.9 | 1.3 | 2.0 | 0.6 | 0.1 | –0.4 | 0.0 | 0.6 | 1.3 | 1.2 |
| Resource Balance | –1.2 | –3.4 | –5.7 | –5.7 | –5.0 | –4.9 | –2.7 | –3.4 | –3.5 | –3.4 | –3.6 |
| **Euro Area[1]** | | | | | | | | | | | |
| Savings | ... | 21.4 | 21.2 | 22.0 | 22.5 | 21.3 | 18.7 | 19.3 | 19.1 | 19.4 | 19.9 |
| Investment | ... | 20.8 | 20.8 | 21.7 | 22.3 | 21.8 | 18.9 | 19.0 | 19.1 | 19.4 | 19.8 |
| Net Lending | ... | 0.5 | 0.4 | 0.4 | 0.3 | –0.6 | –0.2 | 0.2 | –0.1 | 0.0 | 0.1 |
| Current Transfers[2] | –0.6 | –0.7 | –0.9 | –0.9 | –1.0 | –1.1 | –1.1 | –1.1 | –1.1 | –1.1 | –1.1 |
| Factor Income[2] | –0.7 | –0.5 | –0.2 | 0.1 | –0.4 | –0.7 | –0.6 | –0.4 | –0.5 | –0.4 | –0.4 |
| Resource Balance[2] | 1.0 | 1.8 | 1.6 | 1.3 | 1.6 | 1.1 | 1.5 | 1.6 | 1.6 | 1.6 | 1.7 |
| **Germany** | | | | | | | | | | | |
| Savings | 22.5 | 20.2 | 22.0 | 24.1 | 25.9 | 25.2 | 21.5 | 22.8 | 22.2 | 22.1 | 22.1 |
| Investment | 23.2 | 19.7 | 16.9 | 17.6 | 18.3 | 18.5 | 16.5 | 17.5 | 17.1 | 17.5 | 18.1 |
| Net Lending | –0.7 | 0.5 | 5.1 | 6.5 | 7.6 | 6.7 | 5.0 | 5.3 | 5.1 | 4.6 | 4.1 |
| Current Transfers | –1.6 | –1.3 | –1.3 | –1.2 | –1.3 | –1.4 | –1.4 | –1.5 | –1.5 | –1.5 | –1.5 |
| Factor Income | –0.3 | –0.3 | 1.1 | 1.9 | 1.8 | 1.2 | 1.0 | 1.0 | 1.3 | 1.5 | 1.8 |
| Resource Balance | 1.1 | 2.2 | 5.3 | 5.7 | 7.2 | 6.9 | 5.4 | 5.8 | 5.3 | 4.5 | 3.7 |
| **France** | | | | | | | | | | | |
| Savings | 20.0 | 21.0 | 19.8 | 20.6 | 21.2 | 20.1 | 17.1 | 17.3 | 17.3 | 17.7 | 18.5 |
| Investment | 19.9 | 19.2 | 20.3 | 21.1 | 22.2 | 22.0 | 19.0 | 19.3 | 20.1 | 20.4 | 20.8 |
| Net Lending | 0.2 | 1.8 | –0.5 | –0.6 | –1.0 | –1.9 | –1.9 | –2.1 | –2.8 | –2.7 | –2.3 |
| Current Transfers | –0.6 | –1.0 | –1.3 | –1.2 | –1.2 | –1.2 | –1.4 | –1.3 | –1.3 | –1.3 | –1.3 |
| Factor Income | –0.4 | 1.1 | 1.4 | 1.6 | 1.6 | 1.5 | 1.2 | 1.5 | 1.4 | 1.4 | 1.4 |
| Resource Balance | 1.2 | 1.7 | –0.6 | –1.0 | –1.4 | –2.2 | –1.7 | –2.2 | –3.0 | –2.9 | –2.4 |
| **Italy** | | | | | | | | | | | |
| Savings | 20.5 | 20.6 | 19.0 | 19.0 | 19.4 | 18.3 | 16.8 | 16.7 | 16.5 | 17.1 | 18.1 |
| Investment | 20.6 | 20.4 | 20.7 | 21.6 | 21.9 | 21.2 | 18.9 | 20.2 | 19.9 | 20.1 | 20.8 |
| Net Lending | –0.1 | 0.2 | –1.7 | –2.6 | –2.4 | –2.9 | –2.1 | –3.5 | –3.4 | –3.0 | –2.8 |
| Current Transfers | –0.5 | –0.5 | –0.7 | –0.9 | –0.9 | –1.0 | –0.8 | –0.8 | –0.8 | –0.8 | –0.8 |
| Factor Income | –1.5 | –1.1 | –1.0 | –0.9 | –1.3 | –1.2 | –0.7 | –0.9 | –1.7 | –1.6 | –1.4 |
| Resource Balance | 1.9 | 1.7 | 0.0 | –0.8 | –0.3 | –0.7 | –0.6 | –1.8 | –0.9 | –0.6 | –0.6 |
| **Japan** | | | | | | | | | | | |
| Savings | 32.5 | 27.6 | 27.2 | 27.7 | 28.5 | 26.7 | 22.9 | 23.8 | 24.3 | 24.8 | 25.2 |
| Investment | 30.4 | 24.8 | 23.6 | 23.8 | 23.7 | 23.6 | 20.2 | 20.2 | 21.9 | 22.5 | 23.0 |
| Net Lending | 2.2 | 2.8 | 3.6 | 3.9 | 4.8 | 3.2 | 2.7 | 3.6 | 2.4 | 2.3 | 2.2 |
| Current Transfers | –0.2 | –0.2 | –0.2 | –0.2 | –0.3 | –0.3 | –0.2 | –0.2 | –0.2 | –0.2 | –0.1 |
| Factor Income | 0.8 | 1.5 | 2.3 | 2.7 | 3.1 | 3.1 | 2.5 | 2.4 | 2.4 | 2.5 | 2.8 |
| Resource Balance | 1.5 | 1.5 | 1.5 | 1.4 | 1.9 | 0.4 | 0.5 | 1.4 | 0.1 | 0.0 | –0.5 |
| **United Kingdom** | | | | | | | | | | | |
| Savings | 15.6 | 15.8 | 14.5 | 14.1 | 15.6 | 15.0 | 11.8 | 12.4 | 13.2 | 14.5 | 17.3 |
| Investment | 17.8 | 17.4 | 17.1 | 17.5 | 18.2 | 16.6 | 13.5 | 14.8 | 15.6 | 16.4 | 18.5 |
| Net Lending | –2.2 | –1.6 | –2.6 | –3.4 | –2.6 | –1.6 | –1.7 | –2.5 | –2.4 | –1.9 | –1.2 |
| Current Transfers | –0.7 | –0.8 | –0.9 | –0.9 | –1.0 | –1.0 | –1.1 | –1.4 | –1.1 | –1.1 | –1.1 |
| Factor Income | –0.4 | 0.9 | 1.7 | 0.6 | 1.4 | 1.9 | 1.5 | 2.2 | 1.7 | 1.5 | 1.3 |
| Resource Balance | –1.1 | –1.7 | –3.4 | –3.1 | –3.1 | –2.6 | –2.1 | –3.3 | –3.1 | –2.4 | –1.4 |

## Table A16. Summary of Sources and Uses of World Savings *(continued)*

| | Averages | | 2005 | 2006 | 2007 | 2008 | 2009 | 2010 | Projections | | |
| | 1989–96 | 1997–2004 | | | | | | | 2011 | 2012 | 2013–16 |
|---|---|---|---|---|---|---|---|---|---|---|---|
| **Canada** | | | | | | | | | | | |
| Savings | 16.5 | 21.3 | 24.0 | 24.4 | 24.1 | 23.6 | 18.1 | 19.0 | 18.9 | 19.2 | 20.0 |
| Investment | 19.3 | 20.1 | 22.1 | 23.0 | 23.2 | 23.1 | 21.0 | 22.1 | 21.7 | 21.9 | 21.7 |
| Net Lending | −2.8 | 1.2 | 1.9 | 1.4 | 0.8 | 0.4 | −2.9 | −3.1 | −2.8 | −2.6 | −1.8 |
| Current Transfers | −0.1 | 0.1 | −0.1 | −0.1 | −0.1 | 0.0 | −0.1 | −0.2 | −0.1 | −0.1 | −0.1 |
| Factor Income | −3.6 | −2.7 | −1.7 | −0.9 | −0.9 | −1.0 | −0.9 | −1.0 | −1.3 | −1.5 | −1.3 |
| Resource Balance | 0.9 | 3.9 | 3.7 | 2.4 | 1.9 | 1.5 | −1.8 | −2.0 | −1.4 | −1.1 | −0.3 |
| **Newly Industrialized Asian Economies** | | | | | | | | | | | |
| Savings | 35.0 | 32.3 | 31.8 | 32.5 | 33.4 | 32.8 | 31.4 | 33.3 | 33.0 | 32.8 | 32.0 |
| Investment | 32.5 | 27.3 | 26.1 | 26.4 | 26.1 | 27.7 | 23.4 | 26.2 | 26.7 | 26.8 | 26.7 |
| Net Lending | 2.5 | 5.1 | 5.7 | 6.1 | 7.3 | 5.0 | 8.0 | 7.1 | 6.3 | 6.0 | 5.3 |
| Current Transfers | −0.1 | −0.5 | −0.7 | −0.7 | −0.7 | −0.6 | −0.6 | −0.7 | −0.7 | −0.7 | −0.7 |
| Factor Income | 0.9 | 0.4 | 0.1 | 0.6 | 0.7 | 0.9 | 1.0 | 0.6 | 0.7 | 0.7 | 0.8 |
| Resource Balance | 1.7 | 5.2 | 6.3 | 6.2 | 7.3 | 4.7 | 7.7 | 7.2 | 6.3 | 6.0 | 5.2 |
| **Emerging and Developing Economies** | | | | | | | | | | | |
| Savings | 23.4 | 25.5 | 31.0 | 32.9 | 33.1 | 33.7 | 32.1 | 33.0 | 34.2 | 34.2 | 34.7 |
| Investment | 25.9 | 25.0 | 26.8 | 27.8 | 29.1 | 30.1 | 30.3 | 31.3 | 31.6 | 31.9 | 32.5 |
| Net Lending | −1.9 | 0.5 | 4.1 | 5.1 | 4.0 | 3.6 | 1.9 | 1.8 | 2.6 | 2.3 | 2.2 |
| Current Transfers | 0.6 | 1.2 | 1.7 | 1.8 | 1.6 | 1.5 | 1.4 | 1.3 | 1.2 | 1.1 | 1.1 |
| Factor Income | −1.6 | −1.9 | −1.8 | −1.6 | −1.6 | −1.5 | −1.3 | −1.5 | −1.5 | −1.5 | −1.0 |
| Resource Balance | −0.9 | 1.2 | 4.3 | 5.1 | 4.0 | 3.7 | 1.7 | 2.0 | 3.0 | 2.6 | 2.2 |
| *Memorandum* | | | | | | | | | | | |
| Acquisition of Foreign Assets | 1.5 | 4.1 | 9.1 | 11.2 | 13.5 | 6.8 | 4.5 | 5.8 | 5.6 | 5.2 | 5.0 |
| Change in Reserves | 1.0 | 1.9 | 5.4 | 5.8 | 7.7 | 3.9 | 2.8 | 4.1 | 4.0 | 3.5 | 3.6 |
| **Regional Groups** | | | | | | | | | | | |
| **Central and Eastern Europe** | | | | | | | | | | | |
| Savings | 20.7 | 17.8 | 16.5 | 16.8 | 16.6 | 17.1 | 16.5 | 16.8 | 16.9 | 16.8 | 16.8 |
| Investment | 22.4 | 21.3 | 21.4 | 23.3 | 24.7 | 24.9 | 19.1 | 21.0 | 22.3 | 22.4 | 22.8 |
| Net Lending | −1.5 | −3.5 | −4.9 | −6.6 | −8.1 | −7.8 | −2.7 | −4.3 | −5.4 | −5.6 | −6.0 |
| Current Transfers | 1.7 | 2.1 | 1.9 | 2.0 | 1.8 | 1.7 | 1.9 | 1.6 | 1.5 | 1.4 | 1.3 |
| Factor Income | −1.6 | −1.3 | −2.0 | −2.4 | −2.9 | −2.4 | −2.4 | −2.3 | −2.2 | −2.1 | −2.0 |
| Resource Balance | −1.7 | −4.3 | −5.0 | −6.3 | −7.1 | −7.3 | −2.4 | −3.7 | −4.8 | −5.1 | −5.5 |
| *Memorandum* | | | | | | | | | | | |
| Acquisition of Foreign Assets | 0.7 | 2.4 | 5.3 | 6.3 | 5.1 | 2.2 | 2.5 | 2.9 | 2.5 | 2.4 | 3.4 |
| Change in Reserves | 0.2 | 1.1 | 3.7 | 2.5 | 2.3 | 0.2 | 1.8 | 2.0 | 2.1 | 1.5 | 2.4 |
| **Commonwealth of Independent States[3]** | | | | | | | | | | | |
| Savings | ... | 25.9 | 30.0 | 30.2 | 30.7 | 30.1 | 21.8 | 25.7 | 29.7 | 29.2 | 28.0 |
| Investment | ... | 20.3 | 21.2 | 23.0 | 26.7 | 25.2 | 19.0 | 21.7 | 24.9 | 25.9 | 26.9 |
| Net Lending | ... | 5.6 | 8.8 | 7.3 | 4.0 | 4.8 | 2.7 | 4.0 | 4.8 | 3.2 | 1.1 |
| Current Transfers | ... | 0.5 | 0.5 | 0.4 | 0.3 | 0.4 | 0.4 | 0.3 | 0.1 | 0.1 | 0.1 |
| Factor Income | ... | −2.9 | −2.7 | −3.3 | −2.9 | −3.4 | −3.6 | −3.6 | −3.0 | −2.6 | −1.4 |
| Resource Balance | ... | 7.8 | 11.0 | 10.3 | 6.8 | 8.0 | 5.8 | 7.1 | 7.7 | 5.8 | 2.5 |
| *Memorandum* | | | | | | | | | | | |
| Acquisition of Foreign Assets | ... | 7.7 | 15.4 | 14.8 | 17.4 | 10.0 | 1.5 | 5.6 | 7.3 | 5.6 | 3.4 |
| Change in Reserves | ... | 3.1 | 7.7 | 9.8 | 9.8 | −1.2 | 0.5 | 2.8 | 4.6 | 3.2 | 1.1 |
| **Developing Asia** | | | | | | | | | | | |
| Savings | 31.1 | 33.5 | 40.2 | 42.9 | 43.8 | 44.3 | 45.6 | 45.5 | 45.8 | 46.2 | 46.7 |
| Investment | 33.4 | 31.6 | 36.1 | 36.9 | 36.9 | 38.3 | 41.4 | 42.2 | 42.5 | 42.6 | 42.2 |
| Net Lending | −2.3 | 1.9 | 4.1 | 6.0 | 6.9 | 6.0 | 4.1 | 3.2 | 3.3 | 3.6 | 4.5 |
| Current Transfers | 1.0 | 1.7 | 2.2 | 2.2 | 2.2 | 2.0 | 1.9 | 1.8 | 1.8 | 1.7 | 1.6 |
| Factor Income | −1.7 | −1.5 | −0.7 | −0.4 | −0.2 | 0.1 | 0.1 | −0.2 | −0.2 | −0.2 | −0.1 |
| Resource Balance | −1.6 | 1.8 | 2.6 | 4.2 | 4.9 | 3.9 | 2.2 | 1.7 | 1.8 | 2.1 | 2.9 |
| *Memorandum* | | | | | | | | | | | |
| Acquisition of Foreign Assets | 2.7 | 5.0 | 8.8 | 10.7 | 13.4 | 7.5 | 6.6 | 6.8 | 5.6 | 5.7 | 6.4 |
| Change in Reserves | 1.8 | 3.0 | 6.8 | 7.4 | 10.2 | 6.8 | 5.7 | 6.2 | 5.2 | 4.9 | 5.7 |

## Table A16. Summary of Sources and Uses of World Savings *(continued)*

| | Averages | | 2005 | 2006 | 2007 | 2008 | 2009 | 2010 | Projections | | |
|---|---|---|---|---|---|---|---|---|---|---|---|
| | 1989–96 | 1997–2004 | | | | | | | 2011 | 2012 | 2013–16 |
| **Latin America and the Caribbean** | | | | | | | | | | | |
| Savings | 18.7 | 18.7 | 22.0 | 23.3 | 22.5 | 22.6 | 19.3 | 20.4 | 20.8 | 20.9 | 21.0 |
| Investment | 20.1 | 20.7 | 20.5 | 21.7 | 22.5 | 23.8 | 20.1 | 21.8 | 22.4 | 22.9 | 23.5 |
| Net Lending | −1.4 | −1.9 | 1.5 | 1.6 | 0.0 | −1.2 | −0.7 | −1.4 | −1.6 | −2.0 | −2.5 |
| Current Transfers | 0.8 | 1.3 | 2.0 | 2.1 | 1.8 | 1.6 | 1.5 | 1.3 | 1.2 | 1.2 | 1.2 |
| Factor Income | −2.2 | −2.9 | −2.9 | −3.1 | −3.1 | −3.1 | −2.7 | −2.7 | −2.7 | −2.7 | −2.8 |
| Resource Balance | 0.0 | −0.4 | 2.4 | 2.6 | 1.3 | 0.3 | 0.5 | 0.0 | −0.1 | −0.5 | −0.9 |
| *Memorandum* | | | | | | | | | | | |
| Acquisition of Foreign Assets | 1.0 | 2.0 | 3.4 | 3.2 | 6.2 | 2.2 | 3.6 | 4.8 | 2.6 | 2.0 | 1.4 |
| Change in Reserves | 0.8 | 0.4 | 1.4 | 1.7 | 3.6 | 1.2 | 1.2 | 2.1 | 1.6 | 1.1 | 0.9 |
| **Middle East and North Africa** | | | | | | | | | | | |
| Savings | 21.5 | 27.9 | 39.9 | 41.2 | 40.4 | 41.8 | 30.6 | 32.9 | 37.5 | 36.3 | 35.1 |
| Investment | 24.5 | 23.4 | 23.5 | 23.3 | 26.3 | 26.8 | 28.3 | 26.5 | 24.6 | 25.0 | 22.8 |
| Net Lending | −3.0 | 4.7 | 16.5 | 18.1 | 14.4 | 14.9 | 3.3 | 6.9 | 13.3 | 11.7 | −6.0 |
| Current Transfers | −2.2 | −1.1 | 0.0 | −0.4 | −0.9 | −1.0 | −1.5 | −1.3 | −1.3 | −1.4 | 1.3 |
| Factor Income | 1.0 | 0.6 | −0.3 | 0.8 | 0.9 | 0.5 | 0.1 | −0.6 | −0.9 | −0.7 | −2.0 |
| Resource Balance | −1.9 | 5.2 | 16.9 | 17.9 | 14.5 | 15.5 | 3.9 | 8.5 | 15.0 | 13.4 | −5.5 |
| *Memorandum* | | | | | | | | | | | |
| Acquisition of Foreign Assets | 1.0 | 6.7 | 21.8 | 30.8 | 34.7 | 15.0 | 2.6 | 7.2 | 12.2 | 11.0 | 3.4 |
| Change in Reserves | 0.7 | 2.4 | 9.8 | 9.6 | 12.5 | 8.0 | −1.3 | 4.5 | 6.0 | 5.0 | 2.4 |
| **Sub-Saharan Africa** | | | | | | | | | | | |
| Savings | 15.8 | 16.2 | 18.8 | 24.6 | 22.6 | 22.5 | 19.9 | 20.4 | 22.5 | 22.6 | 21.3 |
| Investment | 16.9 | 18.6 | 19.4 | 20.3 | 21.2 | 22.4 | 22.1 | 22.3 | 21.8 | 21.9 | 21.3 |
| Net Lending | −1.1 | −2.3 | −0.6 | 4.3 | 1.4 | 0.1 | −2.2 | −1.9 | 0.7 | 0.8 | 0.1 |
| Current Transfers | 2.0 | 2.3 | 2.6 | 4.6 | 4.6 | 4.5 | 4.7 | 3.9 | 3.7 | 3.5 | 3.3 |
| Factor Income | −3.1 | −4.4 | −5.8 | −4.6 | −5.8 | −5.8 | −3.8 | −4.5 | −5.2 | −5.1 | −4.5 |
| Resource Balance | 0.3 | −0.1 | 2.6 | 4.4 | 2.7 | 1.4 | −3.0 | −1.2 | 2.2 | 2.4 | 1.3 |
| *Memorandum* | | | | | | | | | | | |
| Acquisition of Foreign Assets | 0.6 | 2.2 | 4.4 | 9.2 | 7.5 | 3.6 | 2.8 | 3.2 | 5.3 | 5.9 | 5.4 |
| Change in Reserves | 0.8 | 1.0 | 3.8 | 4.2 | 3.5 | 1.9 | −1.1 | 0.4 | 2.4 | 2.5 | 2.4 |
| **Analytical Groups** | | | | | | | | | | | |
| **By Source of Export Earnings** | | | | | | | | | | | |
| **Fuel Exporters** | | | | | | | | | | | |
| Savings | 21.8 | 28.6 | 37.5 | 39.2 | 37.6 | 37.8 | 28.0 | 30.4 | 35.3 | 34.3 | 32.3 |
| Investment | 25.5 | 22.8 | 22.2 | 22.9 | 26.0 | 25.2 | 24.1 | 23.6 | 24.0 | 24.7 | 25.5 |
| Net Lending | −1.9 | 5.9 | 15.3 | 16.4 | 11.7 | 12.6 | 4.4 | 7.0 | 11.5 | 9.7 | 6.6 |
| Current Transfers | −3.3 | −1.7 | −0.6 | −0.3 | −0.7 | −0.7 | −1.0 | −1.0 | −1.0 | −1.0 | −1.1 |
| Factor Income | 0.2 | −1.3 | −2.5 | −2.0 | −2.1 | −2.5 | −2.2 | −2.8 | −2.8 | −2.4 | −0.9 |
| Resource Balance | 1.5 | 9.0 | 18.5 | 18.9 | 14.6 | 16.0 | 7.2 | 10.6 | 15.0 | 13.0 | 8.9 |
| *Memorandum* | | | | | | | | | | | |
| Acquisition of Foreign Assets | 1.4 | 7.7 | 20.7 | 24.6 | 26.7 | 13.7 | 2.8 | 7.0 | 11.3 | 9.5 | 6.7 |
| Change in Reserves | 0.2 | 2.5 | 9.1 | 10.1 | 10.8 | 3.6 | −1.6 | 3.5 | 5.8 | 4.3 | 2.6 |
| **Nonfuel Exporters** | | | | | | | | | | | |
| Savings | 23.7 | 24.8 | 29.2 | 31.1 | 31.8 | 32.4 | 33.1 | 33.7 | 33.9 | 34.2 | 35.3 |
| Investment | 25.6 | 25.5 | 28.1 | 29.2 | 30.0 | 31.5 | 31.8 | 33.2 | 33.6 | 33.9 | 34.3 |
| Net Lending | −1.9 | −0.6 | 1.2 | 1.9 | 1.8 | 0.9 | 1.3 | 0.5 | 0.3 | 0.3 | 1.0 |
| Current Transfers | 1.4 | 1.8 | 2.3 | 2.4 | 2.3 | 2.2 | 2.0 | 1.9 | 1.8 | 1.7 | 1.7 |
| Factor Income | −1.9 | −2.0 | −1.6 | −1.6 | −1.5 | −1.2 | −1.1 | −1.2 | −1.2 | −1.2 | −1.1 |
| Resource Balance | −1.4 | −0.5 | 0.4 | 1.1 | 1.0 | −0.1 | 0.3 | −0.2 | −0.3 | −0.2 | 0.4 |
| *Memorandum* | | | | | | | | | | | |
| Acquisition of Foreign Assets | 1.6 | 3.3 | 5.9 | 7.3 | 9.6 | 4.6 | 4.9 | 5.5 | 4.0 | 4.0 | 4.5 |
| Change in Reserves | 1.2 | 1.8 | 4.4 | 4.6 | 6.8 | 3.9 | 3.9 | 4.3 | 3.5 | 3.3 | 3.9 |

## Table A16. Summary of Sources and Uses of World Savings *(concluded)*

| | Averages | | 2005 | 2006 | 2007 | 2008 | 2009 | 2010 | Projections | | |
|---|---|---|---|---|---|---|---|---|---|---|---|
| | 1989–96 | 1997–2004 | | | | | | | 2011 | 2012 | 2013–16 |
| **By External Financing Source** | | | | | | | | | | | |
| **Net Debtor Economies** | | | | | | | | | | | |
| Savings | 19.7 | 19.2 | 21.5 | 22.5 | 22.9 | 22.1 | 20.9 | 22.1 | 22.3 | 22.6 | 23.8 |
| Investment | 21.8 | 21.3 | 23.1 | 24.2 | 25.5 | 25.9 | 22.9 | 24.6 | 25.4 | 25.9 | 27.0 |
| Net Lending | –2.1 | –2.1 | –1.5 | –1.6 | –2.6 | –3.8 | –2.0 | –2.6 | –3.1 | –3.3 | –3.2 |
| Current Transfers | 1.7 | 2.4 | 3.0 | 3.0 | 2.9 | 2.8 | 2.9 | 2.7 | 2.5 | 2.5 | 2.4 |
| Factor Income | –1.8 | –2.3 | –2.5 | –2.6 | –2.7 | –2.6 | –2.4 | –2.3 | –2.4 | –2.4 | –2.4 |
| Resource Balance | –1.9 | –2.2 | –2.0 | –2.1 | –2.9 | –4.1 | –2.6 | –2.9 | –3.2 | –3.4 | –3.2 |
| *Memorandum* | | | | | | | | | | | |
| Acquisition of Foreign Assets | 1.0 | 2.1 | 3.1 | 4.6 | 6.3 | 1.5 | 2.4 | 3.7 | 2.0 | 1.8 | 2.2 |
| Change in Reserves | 0.9 | 0.9 | 2.1 | 2.5 | 4.1 | 1.0 | 1.6 | 2.2 | 1.6 | 1.3 | 1.6 |
| **Official Financing** | | | | | | | | | | | |
| Savings | 16.7 | 19.0 | 21.6 | 22.9 | 23.2 | 22.2 | 22.0 | 21.8 | 22.1 | 22.7 | 23.9 |
| Investment | 19.3 | 20.9 | 23.2 | 23.5 | 23.6 | 24.5 | 24.0 | 24.9 | 25.6 | 26.2 | 26.6 |
| Net Lending | –2.6 | –1.9 | –1.5 | –0.6 | –0.4 | –2.3 | –2.1 | –3.0 | –3.5 | –3.5 | –2.8 |
| Current Transfers | 4.6 | 6.8 | 10.2 | 10.3 | 10.8 | 10.5 | 10.7 | 10.6 | 9.5 | 9.1 | 8.5 |
| Factor Income | –2.6 | –2.7 | –2.2 | –1.9 | –0.8 | –1.4 | –1.7 | –2.3 | –3.4 | –3.2 | –2.9 |
| Resource Balance | –4.7 | –6.0 | –9.7 | –9.1 | –10.4 | –11.6 | –11.3 | –11.6 | –9.9 | –9.6 | –8.3 |
| *Memorandum* | | | | | | | | | | | |
| Acquisition of Foreign Assets | 1.6 | 2.2 | –4.4 | 1.9 | 2.5 | 0.7 | 0.9 | 0.8 | 0.9 | 0.9 | 1.3 |
| Change in Reserves | 1.5 | 1.2 | 0.7 | 1.3 | 2.4 | 1.2 | 1.8 | 1.2 | 1.5 | 1.3 | 1.4 |
| **Net Debtor Economies by Debt-Servicing Experience** | | | | | | | | | | | |
| **Economies with Arrears and/or Rescheduling during 2005–09** | | | | | | | | | | | |
| Savings | 14.6 | 15.8 | 20.9 | 22.6 | 21.9 | 20.3 | 18.4 | 19.0 | 19.6 | 19.5 | 19.2 |
| Investment | 18.2 | 19.0 | 22.2 | 23.3 | 24.3 | 25.0 | 22.3 | 24.2 | 24.5 | 24.3 | 23.3 |
| Net Lending | –3.5 | –3.1 | –1.3 | –0.7 | –2.4 | –4.6 | –3.9 | –5.2 | –4.8 | –4.8 | –4.1 |
| Current Transfers | 1.9 | 3.5 | 5.6 | 5.5 | 5.0 | 4.5 | 4.5 | 4.3 | 3.5 | 3.2 | 3.0 |
| Factor Income | –3.5 | –4.5 | –4.3 | –3.9 | –4.1 | –5.0 | –4.2 | –4.9 | –4.8 | –4.7 | –5.1 |
| Resource Balance | –1.9 | –2.2 | –2.6 | –2.3 | –3.4 | –4.3 | –4.4 | –4.6 | –3.7 | –3.4 | –2.0 |
| *Memorandum* | | | | | | | | | | | |
| Acquisition of Foreign Assets | 2.4 | 2.7 | 2.6 | 3.7 | 5.6 | 1.0 | 0.8 | 1.0 | 1.4 | 1.2 | 1.2 |
| Change in Reserves | 0.4 | 0.4 | 3.2 | 2.2 | 3.7 | 0.6 | 1.5 | 1.1 | 1.1 | 1.1 | 0.9 |

Note: The estimates in this table are based on individual countries' national accounts and balance of payments statistics. Country group composites are calculated as the sum of the U.S. dollar values for the relevant individual countries. This differs from the calculations in the April 2005 and earlier issues of the *World Economic Outlook*, where the composites were weighted by GDP valued at purchasing power parities as a share of total world GDP. For many countries, the estimates of national savings are built up from national accounts data on gross domestic investment and from balance-of-payments-based data on net foreign investment. The latter, which is equivalent to the current account balance, comprises three components: current transfers, net factor income, and the resource balance. The mixing of data sources, which is dictated by availability, implies that the estimates for national savings that are derived incorporate the statistical discrepancies. Furthermore, errors, omissions, and asymmetries in balance of payments statistics affect the estimates for net lending; at the global level, net lending, which in theory would be zero, equals the world current account discrepancy. Despite these statistical shortcomings, flow of funds estimates, such as those presented in these tables, provide a useful framework for analyzing developments in savings and investment, both over time and across regions and countries.

[1]Excludes Estonia.

[2]Calculated from the data of individual Euro Area countries excluding Estonia.

[3]Georgia and Mongolia, which are not members of the Commonwealth of Independent States, are included in this group for reasons of geography and similarities in economic structure.

## Table A17. Summary of World Medium-Term Baseline Scenario

| | Averages | | | | Projections | | | |
|---|---|---|---|---|---|---|---|---|
| | 1993–2000 | 2001–08 | 2009 | 2010 | 2011 | 2012 | 2009–12 | 2013–16 |
| | *Annual Percent Change Unless Noted Otherwise* | | | | | | | |
| **World Real GDP** | **3.5** | **4.0** | **−0.5** | **5.0** | **4.4** | **4.5** | **3.3** | **4.6** |
| Advanced Economies | 3.1 | 2.1 | −3.4 | 3.0 | 2.4 | 2.6 | 1.1 | 2.4 |
| Emerging and Developing Economies | 4.1 | 6.6 | 2.7 | 7.3 | 6.5 | 6.5 | 5.7 | 6.7 |
| *Memorandum* | | | | | | | | |
| Potential Output | | | | | | | | |
| Major Advanced Economies | 2.5 | 2.1 | 1.0 | 1.1 | 1.3 | 1.5 | 1.2 | 1.7 |
| **World Trade, Volume[1]** | **7.9** | **5.8** | **−10.9** | **12.4** | **7.4** | **6.9** | **3.8** | **7.1** |
| Imports | | | | | | | | |
| Advanced Economies | 7.8 | 4.4 | −12.6 | 11.2 | 5.8 | 5.5 | 2.1 | 5.7 |
| Emerging and Developing Economies | 7.9 | 10.0 | −8.3 | 13.5 | 10.2 | 9.4 | 5.8 | 9.8 |
| Exports | | | | | | | | |
| Advanced Economies | 7.6 | 4.7 | −12.2 | 12.0 | 6.8 | 5.9 | 2.7 | 5.6 |
| Emerging and Developing Economies | 9.2 | 8.6 | −7.5 | 14.5 | 8.8 | 8.7 | 5.8 | 9.5 |
| Terms of Trade | | | | | | | | |
| Advanced Economies | −0.2 | −0.3 | 2.7 | −1.2 | −1.1 | −0.5 | 0.0 | −0.2 |
| Emerging and Developing Economies | 0.8 | 1.7 | −5.1 | 0.2 | 4.7 | −0.3 | −0.2 | −0.3 |
| **World Prices in U.S. Dollars** | | | | | | | | |
| Manufactures | −1.1 | 4.0 | −6.3 | 3.0 | 5.5 | 1.1 | 0.7 | 1.0 |
| Oil | 5.1 | 16.7 | −36.3 | 27.9 | 35.6 | 0.8 | 2.7 | −0.5 |
| Nonfuel Primary Commodities | −0.8 | 8.3 | −15.8 | 26.3 | 25.1 | −4.3 | 6.2 | −4.6 |
| **Consumer Prices** | | | | | | | | |
| Advanced Economies | 2.3 | 2.2 | 0.1 | 1.6 | 2.2 | 1.7 | 1.4 | 1.8 |
| Emerging and Developing Economies | 34.6 | 6.8 | 5.2 | 6.2 | 6.9 | 5.3 | 5.9 | 4.0 |
| **Interest Rates (in percent)** | | | | | | | | |
| Real Six-Month LIBOR[2] | 3.6 | 0.7 | 0.2 | −0.4 | −0.6 | −0.5 | −0.3 | 1.2 |
| World Real Long-Term Interest Rate[3] | 3.6 | 1.8 | 3.2 | 1.6 | 1.3 | 2.5 | 2.1 | 3.3 |
| | *Percent of GDP* | | | | | | | |
| **Balances on Current Account** | | | | | | | | |
| Advanced Economies | −0.1 | −0.9 | −0.3 | −0.2 | −0.3 | −0.2 | −0.2 | −0.4 |
| Emerging and Developing Economies | −1.1 | 2.9 | 1.8 | 1.8 | 2.6 | 2.3 | 2.1 | 2.2 |
| **Total External Debt** | | | | | | | | |
| Emerging and Developing Economies | 37.0 | 31.0 | 27.0 | 24.6 | 23.2 | 22.8 | 24.4 | 21.9 |
| **Debt Service** | | | | | | | | |
| Emerging and Developing Economies | 8.2 | 10.0 | 9.6 | 8.2 | 7.5 | 7.6 | 8.2 | 7.4 |

[1]Data refer to trade in goods and services.
[2]London interbank offered rate on U.S. dollar deposits minus percent change in U.S. GDP deflator.
[3]GDP-weighted average of 10-year (or nearest maturity) government bond rates for Canada, France, Germany, Italy, Japan, United Kingdom, and United States.

## World Economic Outlook Archives

## I. Methodology—Aggregation, Modeling, and Forecasting

## IV. Inflation and Deflation, and Commodity Markets

## V.  Fiscal Policy

## VI. Monetary Policy, Financial Markets, and Flow of Funds

## VII. Labor Markets, Poverty, and Inequality

## VIII. Exchange Rate Issues

## IX.  External Payments, Trade, Capital Movements, and Foreign Debt

## X. Regional Issues

## XI. Country-Specific Analyses

## XII. Special Topics

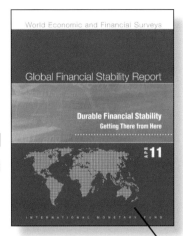
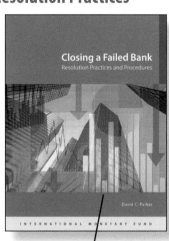
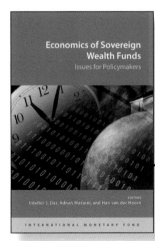